VASCO DA GAMA AND HIS
SUCCESSORS: 1460-1580

VASCO DA GAMA

" Grande sobre as ondas, em lucta com os temporaes,
é a imagem da nação, cuja grandeza está na coragem e
na teima com que soube vencer o Mar Tenebroso."

VASCO DA GAMA

AND HIS SUCCESSORS

1460-1580

BY

K. G. JAYNE

WITH TWENTY-ONE ILLUSTRATIONS AND MAP

BARNES & NOBLE, Inc.
New York
METHUEN & CO. Ltd
London

Sept 6'77

74-13736

First published, 1910

This edition reprinted, 1970
by Barnes & Noble, Inc.
and Methuen & Co. Ltd.

Barnes & Noble SBN 389 03965 9
Methuen SBN 416 17370 5/33

PREFACE

MY intention, in this book, has been to outline the biographies of certain representative Portuguese of the fifteenth and sixteenth centuries, giving some account of the society in which they lived and the history which they made.

The most momentous incident in that history is Vasco da Gama's first voyage to India in 1497-1499 ; not only because it closed the main period of the Portuguese discoveries and ushered in a period of conquest and empire ; but also because it made an epoch in the history of civilization by establishing direct and permanent contact between Europe and the Far East. Vasco da Gama was the instrument by which Portugal rendered her chief service to humanity. But he was also a true type of the national character at its best and worst. He had what a seventeenth-century writer calls its " mortal staidness "—courage, loyalty, endurance ; he had its ignorant ferocity. His achievement and personality single him out as the most representative Portuguese of his time, and as such Camões has made him the hero of *The Lusiads*.

Chief among the other illustrious Portuguese whose portraits I have attempted to draw are Prince Henry the Navigator, Diogo Cão and Bartholomeu Dias, the principal forerunners of Vasco da Gama ; Albuquerque, a genius too many-sided to be dismissed in a phrase ; King Manoel, the cynical autocrat who played one of the greatest games of diplomacy ever lost ; D. João de Castro, the fine flower of Portuguese chivalry and culture ; King Sebastian, the last of the crusaders, gallant and futile ; Camões, the singer who crowned them all with imperishable bays. To these must be added the names of the Humanist George Buchanan and of Francis Xavier, the " Apostle of the Indies." A Scotsman and a Basque may seem out of place among the heroes of Portugal. But the records of Buchanan's university career and trial throw light upon the educational system of the country, and upon certain vital points at issue between its Humanists and Churchmen ; while Xavier fulfilled his apostolic mission under the Portuguese flag.

The lives of all these men are but episodes in one great drama, of which the whole Portuguese nation is the protagonist.

In 1460 Portugal was one among several petty Iberian principalities : by 1521 it had become an empire of world-wide fame, with dominions extending eastward from Brazil to the Pacific. Then followed a period of decline, caused partly by certain defects of national character, but more by the pressure of inevitable misfortune, which ended in the loss not only of greatness but even of independence. In 1580 Portugal entered upon what is known as the " Spanish Captivity," and became for sixty years—in fact, though never in constitutional theory—a subject province of Spain.

I have tried to keep in view the main course of these dramatic changes of fortune, from the death of Prince Henry in 1460 to the beginning of the " Spanish Captivity " in 1580. But I have not been able to follow a strict chronological sequence in narrating the lives of men some of whom were contemporaries. Nor have I devoted so much space to purely political history as to those tendencies and ideas which better express the character of a nation—its religion, its social, educational and economic ideals, its attitude towards alien civilizations, its art and literature. My excuse for venturing to touch, however unskilfully and superficially, upon these large subjects, is that some acquaintance with the beliefs and aspirations of sixteenth-century Portugal is necessary for those who would envisage the characters of Gama and Albuquerque, Xavier and Camões. No other background will show them in the right historical perspective.

As a critical bibliography is given in Appendix A, and as, if every controversial point were fully annotated, the commentary would occupy more space than the text, I have used footnotes very sparingly, except when it seemed desirable to give some further bibliographical reference or to express my indebtedness to the work of a living or recent writer. I hope that I have sufficiently acknowledged what I owe to the researches of Dr E. G. Ravenstein, Dr Theophilo Braga, Senhor Luciano Cordeiro, and Mr R. S. Whiteway, whose work in the domain of Portuguese geographical and literary history it were an impertinence for me to praise.

Readers are asked to observe that wherever a book is mentioned in the text or footnotes under an abbreviated title or the name of its author, without further particulars, full details will be found in Appendix A under that title or name.

As Portuguese is not yet the "universal language," and this book is not primarily intended for those who are already acquainted with the sources of Portuguese history, I have systematically referred to such translations as are available ; but there are no adequate English versions of many of the most important authorities, notably the chronicles of Barros, Castanheda, Corrêa and Couto. For similar reasons I have excluded from Appendix A many manuscripts which nobody can consult without paying a visit to Portugal.

My thanks are due to those friends in Lisbon who have aided me with advice ; to Messrs Sampson Low & Co., for kindly allowing me to reproduce the portrait of Prince Henry the Navigator which forms the frontispiece to R. H. Major's classic *Life* ; to the Lisbon Geographical Society and the managers of the Casa Pia at Belem, whose courtesy has permitted me to reproduce various pictures, etc., in their collections ; and to Senhor J. M. da Silva, of 21 Rua Poço dos Negros, Lisbon, in whose photographs of faded sixteenth-century manuscripts and paintings many technical difficulties have been skilfully surmounted.

CONTENTS

PAGE

LIST OF ILLUSTRATIONS xi

CHRONOLOGICAL TABLES. xiii

THE EARLY DISCOVERERS, *c.* 1415-1497

CHAP.

I. THE MAKING OF PORTUGAL 1

II. PRINCE HENRY THE NAVIGATOR . . . 7

III. SEAMEN AND SLAVES 15

IV. CÃO, DIAS AND COLUMBUS 24

VASCO DA GAMA, 1497-1524

V. BY SEA TO INDIA: THE START . . . 33

VI. BY SEA TO INDIA: ROUNDING THE CAPE . . 39

VII. BY SEA TO INDIA: CIVILIZED AFRICA . . 45

VIII. BY SEA TO INDIA: CALICUT 52

IX. VASCO DA GAMA'S SECOND VOYAGE . . . 60

X. VASCO DA GAMA IN RETIREMENT . . . 67

FROM SEA-POWER TO EMPIRE, 1505-1548

XI. D. FRANCISCO DE ALMEIDA 71

XII. ALBUQUERQUE THE CONQUEROR: GOA AND MALACCA 78

XIII. ALBUQUERQUE THE CONQUEROR: ADEN AND ORMUZ 91

XIV. ALBUQUERQUE: THE STATESMAN . . . 99

XV. KING MANOEL THE FORTUNATE: 1495-1521 . . 115

XVI. D. VASCO DA GAMA, VICEROY. . . . 123

XVII. D. JOÃO DE CASTRO 130

XVIII. A RED SEA RAID 135

XIX. THE EPOS OF DIU 143

XX. THE LAST OF THE HEROES 150

JUDAISM, HUMANISM AND THE CHURCH

CHAP. PAGE

XXI. THE JEWS IN PORTUGAL 156
XXII. AT THE UNIVERSITY OF PARIS . . . 162
XXIII. THE TRIAL OF GEORGE BUCHANAN . . 168
XXIV. AN ACT OF FAITH 176
XXV. THE CHURCH IN THE EAST . . . 182
XXVI. FRANCIS XAVIER IN GOA 188
XXVII. XAVIER AMONG THE PEARL-FISHERS . . 195
XXVIII. XAVIER IN THE MALAY ISLES . . . 202
XXIX. A PIOUS PIRATE 210
XXX. THE FIRST MISSION TO JAPAN . . . 218
XXXI. THE PORTUGUESE IN CHINA . . . 227
XXXII. XAVIER : THE END 232

ART AND LITERATURE

XXXIII. THE ART AND LITERATURE OF DISCOVERY . 241
XXXIV. CAMÕES AT COIMBRA 250
XXXV. CAMÕES AT COURT 256
XXXVI. CAMÕES IN THE EAST 263
XXXVII. CAMÕES : LAST YEARS 273

THE DECLINE OF PORTUGAL, 1548-1580

XXXVIII. THE LAST CRUSADE 279
XXXIX. THE DECADENCE AND ITS CAUSES . . 285
XL. THE FIDALGUIA 295

APPENDIXES

A. LIST OF AUTHORITIES 299
B. COINAGE 311
INDEX 313

LIST OF ILLUSTRATIONS

VASCO DA GAMA . . . . . . *Frontispiece*
From a Flemish Portrait painted during his life and preserved
in the Museu Nacional das Bellas Artes, Lisbon.

PAGE

PRINCE HENRY THE NAVIGATOR 10
From a Fifteenth Century French Manuscript.

VASCO DA GAMA 34
From a Statue in the Casa Pia, Belem.

DOCUMENT WRITTEN AND SIGNED BY VASCO DA GAMA, AS
COUNT OF VIDIGUEIRA AND ADMIRAL OF INDIA . 70
From the Museum of the Lisbon Geographical Society.

MALACCA, EARLY IN THE SIXTEENTH CENTURY . . 86
From the "Lendas da India" of Gaspar Corrêa.

ADEN IN THE YEAR 1512 92
From the "Lendas da India" of Gaspar Corrêa.

CONCLUDING PARAGRAPH OF ALBUQUERQUE'S LAST LETTER
TO KING MANOEL 97
From the Museum of the Lisbon Geographical Society.

AFFONSO DE ALBUQUERQUE 100
From the Drawing by Gaspar Corrêa in the Museum of the
Lisbon Geographical Society.

KING MANOEL THE FORTUNATE 116
From a Sixteenth Century Painting in the Casa Pia, Belem.

THE TOWER OF ST VINCENT, BELEM 121
From a Photograph by J. M. da Silva.

RECEIPT WRITTEN AND SIGNED BY VASCO DA GAMA . . 126
From the Museum of the Lisbon Geographical Society.

THE FORTRESS OF DIU IN 1539 134
From Dom João de Castro's "Roteiro de Goa à Dio."

MASSAWA IN 1541 138
From Dom João de Castro's "Roteiro de viagem . . . ao Mar Roxo.

PAGE

DOM JOÃO DE CASTRO 150
From Gaspar Corrêa's "Lendas da India."

GEORGE BUCHANAN 174
From a Picture in the National Portrait Gallery, London, painted
in 1581 by an unknown Artist.

A FIDALGO TAKING THE AIR IN GOA 190
From Jan Huyghen van Linschoten's "Itinerario" (1595).

FRANCIS XAVIER 238
From the "Vida" of Orazio Torsellino, S.J. (1596).

CLOISTER OF THE CONVENTO DOS JERONYMOS . . 244
From a Photograph by J. M. da Silva.

LUIZ DE CAMÕES 262
From a Bust in the Museu Nacional das Bellas Artes, Lisbon.

LUIZ DE CAMÕES 278
From a Statue by Victor Bastos, in the Largo de Camões,
Lisbon.

KING SEBASTIAN 284
From a Sixteenth Century Painting in the Casa Pia, Belem.

MAP SHOWING VASCO DA GAMA'S VOYAGES . . . 38

CHRONOLOGICAL TABLES

I. CONTEMPORARY EVENTS: 1460-1580

PORTUGUESE HISTORY | GENERAL HISTORY

1460. Death of Prince Henry the Navigator.

1469. Marriage of Ferdinand and Isabella.

1470. Birth of the dramatist Gil Vicente, and of Garcia de Resende, poet and compiler of the *Cancioneiro Geral*.

1471. Portuguese ships cross the equator. Capture of Tangier.

1471. Sixtus IV. elected Pope.

1477. Caxton's printing-press set up in Westminster. Birth of Titian.

1478. Birth of Thomas More.

1479. Union of Castile and Aragon.

1481. Death of King Affonso V. John II. becomes king.

1482. Diogo Cão reaches the mouth of the Congo. Birth of the pastoral poet Bernardim Ribeiro.

1483. Birth of Raphael, Luther and Rabelais.

1484. Foundation of São Jorge da Mina. John II. crushes the feudal nobility.

1484. Birth of Julius Cæsar Scaliger.

1485. Diogo Cão reaches Cape Cross. Birth of the poet Francisco de Sá de Miranda.

1485. Death of Richard III. of England and succession of Henry VII.

1486. Birth of Andrea del Sarto.

1487. Bartholomeu Dias rounds the Cape of Good Hope. Affonso de Paiva and João Pires sent overland in quest of Prester John. Printing-press established in Faro by Jews.

1490. Birth of the botanist Garcia de Orta (?) and of the architect João de Castilho.

1490. Birth of Paracelsus (?).

PORTUGUESE HISTORY	GENERAL HISTORY
	1492 Columbus reaches the West Indies. Alexander VI. elected Pope. The Spaniards conquer Granada, the last Moorish state in the Peninsula.
1493. Bull of Demarcation issued by Alexander VI.	
1494. Treaty of Tordesillas.	1494. Death of Politian.
1495. Death of John II. Accession of Manoel.	
1497. Forcible baptism of 20,000 Jews. Vasco da Gama sails for India. Marriage of King Manoel to Isabella, daughter of the " Catholic Kings."	1497. John Cabot sights Cape Breton. Birth of Holbein and Melanchthon.
1498. Vasco da Gama reaches India, Isabella dies in giving birth to Prince Miguel, who is recognized as heir to the thrones of both Spain and Portugal.	1498. Columbus discovers South America. Death of Savonarola. Erasmus visits England.
1499. Return of Vasco da Gama. Foundation of the Convento dos Jeronymos.	1499. Leonardo da Vinci's " Last Supper" painted. Birth of Prince Charles, afterwards the Emperor Charles V.
1500. Pedro Alvares Cabral rediscovers Brazil and claims it for Portugal. Death of Prince Miguel. King Manoel marries his sister-in-law, Mary of Castile. Birth of the chronicler and Humanist Damião de Goes. Birth of D. João de Castro.	
1502. Vasco da Gama's second voyage to India. Birth of Prince John, afterwards King John III.	1502. Columbus lands for the first time on the mainland of North America.
1504. Defence of Cochin by Duarte Pacheco.	1503. Death of Pope Alexander VI. 1504. Sannazaro's *Arcadia* published. Death of Isabella the Catholic.
1505. D. Francisco de Almeida sails to India as first viceroy. Capture of Kilwa and Mombasa. Fort built at Sofala.	
1506. Birth of Francis Xavier and Jeronymo Osorio. Massacre of converted Jews in Lisbon. Occupation of Mozambique and destruction of Brava.	1506. Death of Columbus.
	1508. Michael Angelo decorates the Sistine Chapel.

PORTUGUESE HISTORY

1509. Almeida defeats the Egyptian fleet off Diu ; he is succeeded in office by Albuquerque. Birth of Fernão Mendes Pinto.

1510. Almeida killed by Hottentots. Albuquerque captures Goa.

1511. Albuquerque captures Malacca. First expedition to the Moluccas. Duarte Fernandes sent as ambassador to Siam.

1512. Magellan enters the service of Spain. Birth of Prince Henry, afterwards Cardinal and King of Portugal.

1513. Albuquerque attacks Aden.

1514. Embassy from King Manoel to Leo X.

1515. Capture of Ormuz. Death of Albuquerque. Capture of Azamor in Morocco.

1516. Fernão Pires de Andrade visits China. Death of Mary Queen of Portugal. Publication of the Cancioneiro Geral.

1517. João de Castilho appointed architect of the Convento dos Jeronymos. Franciscan mission to India.

1518. King Manoel marries Eleanor, niece of his second wife and sister of Charles V.

1520. Probable date of birth of the novelist and poet Jorge de Montemôr (Montemayor).

1521. Death of Manoel. Accession of John III.

GENERAL HISTORY

1509. Death of Henry VII. of England and succession of Henry VIII. Birth of Calvin. Erasmus' Encomium Moriæ published. Raphael decorates the Vatican.

1510. Death of Botticelli. Titian's " Sacred and Profane Love " painted. Ariosto's Orlando Furioso published.

1512. Death of Amerigo Vespucci.

1513. Leo X. elected Pope. Machiavelli's Principe composed.

1515. Francis I. succeeds Louis XII. as King of France. Raphael's Madonna di San Sisto painted.

1516. Death of Ferdinand of Aragon. Accession of Charles I. as King of Spain. More's Utopia published. Concordat of Bologna.

1517. Luther challenges the Pope at Wittenberg. Capture of Cairo by the Turkish Sultan, Selim I. Egypt, Syria and the Hejaz annexed to Turkey. Osmanli sultans become caliphs of Islam.

1518. Birth of Tintoretto.

1519. Death of Leonardo da Vinci. Charles I., King of Spain, elected Emperor as Charles V.

1520. Death of Raphael. Magellan crosses the Pacific from east to west.

1521. Death of Magellan. Death of Leo X. Luther translates the Scriptures into German. Death of Josquin des Près.

PORTUGUESE HISTORY	GENERAL HISTORY
	1522. Surrender of Rhodes to the Turks.
1523. The Order of Christ changed from a military to a monastic fraternity.	
1524. Viceroyalty and death of Vasco da Gama. Birth of Luiz de Camões. Marriage of John III. to Catherine, sister of Charles V. and of his own stepmother.	1524. Birth of Ronsard.
	1525. Tyndale's *New Testament* in English. Death of Ismail Shah of Persia.
	1526. Battle of Mohács and conquest of Hungary by the Turks.
	1527. Death of Machiavelli. Birth of Prince Philip (afterwards Philip II. of Spain).
1528. Birth of the poet and dramatist Antonio Ferreira.	1528. Birth of Albrecht Dürer & Paolo Veronese.
1529. Partition of the Malay Archipelago between Spain and Portugal.	
1530. First Portuguese colonies planted in Brazil.	1530. Copernicus completes his account of the solar system in the *De Revolutionibus*.
	1532. *Il Principe* and *Gargantua and Pantagruel* published.
1533. Death of Duarte Pacheco. Birth of Jeronymo Corte-Real.	1533. Independence of the English Church established. Capture of Tunis by Khair ed-Din Barbarossa. Death of Ariosto. Birth of Montaigne.
1535. Bahadur Shah, Sultan of Gujarat, grants the Portuguese a site for a fortress at Diu.	1535. Execution of Sir Thomas More. Coverdale's translation of the Bible.
1536. Establishment of the Holy Office in Lisbon. Death of Garcia de Resende. Galvão becomes governor of the Moluccas.	1536. Death of Erasmus. Calvin's *Christianæ Religionis Institutio* published.
1538. A Turkish fleet threatens India. First siege of Diu.	
1539. Bishopric of Goa created.	
1540. Death of Gil Vicente. Persecution of the Hindus in Goa.	1540. Formation of the Society of Jesus.
1541. D. João de Castro's Red Sea voyage.	
1542. Discovery of Japan by the Portuguese. Francis Xavier arrives in India. First Jesuit college founded at Coimbra.	1542. Inquisition established in Rome.
1543. Princess Mary of Portugal marries Philip of Spain.	1543. Death of Copernicus and Holbein.

PORTUGUESE HISTORY

1545. D. João de Castro becomes Governor of India.

1546. Second siege of Diu.

1547. George Buchanan at Coimbra. Failure of the Portuguese at Aden.

1548. Death of D. João de Castro.

1549. Francis Xavier lands in Japan.

1551. Grand Mastership of the Orders of Santiago, Aviz, Crato and Christ permanently vested in the Crown. Trial and imprisonment of George Buchanan by the Lisbon Inquisition.

1552. Francis Xavier's voyage to China and death. Death of Bernardim Ribeiro. First volumes of Barros' *Decades* and Castanheda's *History* published.

1553. Camões sails for India.

1554. First edition of Ribeiro's romance *Menina e Moça*. Death of the heir-apparent, Prince John.

1555. Jesuits gain control of Portuguese education.

1557. Death of John III. Accession of Sebastian. Death of the poet Christovão Falcão.

1558. Return of Fernão Mendes Pinto from the Far East. Death of Sá de Miranda.

1560. First mission to the Bantu. Establishment of the Inquisition in Goa.

1561. Death of Montemôr.

1563. Publication of Orta's *Colloquies*.

GENERAL HISTORY

1544. Birth of Tasso.

1545. First session of the Council of Trent.

1546. Death of Luther. Birth of Tycho Brahe.

1547. Henry VIII. of England succeeded by Edward VI. Battle of Mühlberg.

1549. English *Book of Common Prayer* issued.

1550. Inauguration of the *Pléiade*.

1551. More's *Utopia* translated into English.

1552. Birth of Edmund Spenser and Walter Raleigh.

1553. Death of Edward VI. of England ; coronation and imprisonment of Lady Jane Grey ; accession of Queen Mary. Death of Rabelais.

1554. Execution of Lady Jane Grey. Marriage of Philip of Spain to Queen Mary. Birth of Philip Sidney.

1555. Persecution of English Protestants.

1556. Execution of Cranmer. Death of Ignatius de Loyola. Abdication of Charles V. and succession of Philip II.

1558. Death of Queen Mary and succession of Elizabeth. Death of Charles V.

1560. Publication of the Geneva ("Breeches") Bible. First edition of the collected works of Ronsard. Death of Du Bellay and Melanchthon.

1561. Birth of Francis Bacon.

1563. The Thirty-Nine Articles accepted as an essential part of English Church doctrine.

PORTUGUESE HISTORY	GENERAL HISTORY
1564. Osorio created Bishop of Silves.	1564. Birth of Shakspere, Marlowe and Galileo. Death of Michael Angelo and Calvin. Last session of the Council of Trent.
1565. Overthrow of Vijayanagar at Talikot.	
	1566. Death of Suleiman the Magnificent.
1568. Sebastian declared of age by the Cortes.	
1569. Plague and famine in Portugal. Death of Ferreira.	
1570. Camões returns to Portugal.	
1571. Goes imprisoned by the Inquisition.	1571. Bull of Deposition issued by Pius V. against Queen Elizabeth. Destruction of Turkish naval supremacy at Lepanto.
1572. Publication of *The Lusiads*.	1572. Massacre of St Bartholomew.
1573. Death of the archæologist André de Resende and of Goes.	
1574. Sebastian's first expedition to Morocco.	
	1576. Death of Titian.
	1577. Birth of Rubens.
1578. Destruction of the Portuguese army at El-Kasr el-Kebir.	
1580. Portugal united to Spain. Death of Camões. Death of Osorio.	1580. Circumnavigation of the world by Sir Francis Drake.

II. KINGS OF PORTUGAL, 1385–1580

JOHN I.	April 6th, 1385-1433.
EDWARD	August 11th, 1433-1438.
AFFONSO V.	September 9th, 1438-1481.
JOHN II.	August 8th, 1481-1495.
MANOEL	October 25th, 1495-1521.
JOHN III.	December 13th, 1521-1557.
SEBASTIAN	June 1st, 1557-1578.
HENRY	August 4th, 1578-January 31st, 1580.

III. VICEROYS AND GOVERNORS OF INDIA, 1505–1580

D. Francisco de Almeida [1] . .	September 1505-1509.
Affonso de Albuquerque . . .	December 1509-1515.
Lopo Soares de Albergaria . .	December 1515-1518.
Diogo Lopes de Sequeira . . .	September 1518-1522.
D. Duarte de Menezes . . .	January 1522-1524.
D. Vasco da Gama [1]	September-December 1524.
D. Henrique de Menezes . . .	January 1525-1526.
Lopo Vaz de Sampayo . . .	February 1526-1529.
Nuno da Cunha	November 1529-1538.
D. Garcia de Noronha [1] . . .	September 1538-1540.
D. Estevão da Gama	April 1540-1542.
Martim Affonso de Sousa . . .	May 1542-1545.
D. João de Castro [1]	September 1545-1548.
Garcia de Sá	June 1548-1549.
Jorge Cabral	July 1549-1550.
D. Affonso de Noronha [1] . . .	November 1550-1554.
D. Pedro Mascarenhas [1] . . .	September 1554-1555.
Francisco Barreto	June 1555-1558.
D. Constantino de Bragança [1] . .	September 1558-1561.
D. Francisco Coutinho [1] . . .	September 1561-1564.
João de Mendonça	February-September 1564.
D. Antão de Noronha [1] . . .	September 1564-1568.
D. Luiz de Athayde [1] . . .	September 1568-1571.
D. Antonio de Noronha [1] . . .	September 1571-1573.
Antonio Moniz Barreto . . .	December 1573-1576.
D. Diogo de Menezes . . .	September 1576-1578.
D. Luiz de Athayde [1] . . .	August 1578-1581.

[1] Viceroy.

VASCO DA GAMA AND HIS SUCCESSORS: 1460-1580

THE EARLY DISCOVERERS, *c.* 1415-1497

CHAPTER I

THE MAKING OF PORTUGAL

IN the opening years of the twelfth century Portugal was
an obscure county, tributary to the petty Iberian kingdom of Leon. Its territories consisted in large measure
of barren mountains, forests, and heaths. Its ruler, Count
Henry, was a Burgundian free-lance, who earned his title
by the services he rendered to his feudal lord, the King of
Leon, as warden of the Galician marches and husband of
the King's illegitimate daughter, Theresa. The dominions
of Count Henry stretched southwards from Galicia to the
river Mondego, beyond which the Moors were still supreme.
His chief city was Oporto, built on the north bank of the
Douro estuary, over against the site of Portus Cale, an
ancient seaport which ultimately gave its name to the
whole region known as Portucalia, or the Terra Portucalensis.

In all the chronicles of the Middle Ages there are few
episodes more dramatic than the change of fortune which
transformed a half-civilized border fief of Leon into the
foremost maritime power in Europe. Within four centuries
the Portuguese had wrested their freedom from Moors and
Christians alike, had founded an independent kingdom and
extended its frontiers to their present continental limits.
Other peoples had accomplished as much. But Portugal
at the beginning of the sixteenth century had also become
the pioneer of intercourse between Europe and the Far

East. Her flag was supreme in half the known seas of the world ; every year her royal fleets brought home a vast treasure in gold and ivory, spices and slaves ; her chain of trading-posts extended from Brazil to the Malay Archipelago.

To understand how so much power came to be concentrated in the hands of so small a community, it is necessary to glance first at the situation, and afterwards at the history of the kingdom. As the south-westernmost of the free States of Europe, Portugal was a natural outpost of the civilization of Christendom, almost in touch with Muhammadan Africa. She had a coast-line more than three hundred miles long, and an abundance of deep and sheltered harbours. All her main rivers flowed west or south to the Atlantic, and the chief cities of the realm had grown up on their estuaries. Inland lay the rival kingdoms of Leon and Castile, which interposed an impassable barrier between Portugal and the markets of Europe beyond the Pyrenees. Thus the currents of Portuguese commercial and industrial life set strongly outwards, away from the Spanish frontier and towards the Atlantic littoral, where the great seaports were crowded with shipping, and offered a hundred chances of glory or gain to all who dared risk the hazard of the seas.

The Portuguese of the later Middle Ages were not men to " fear their fate too much." In their character, as in their deeds, they were the true forerunners of the greathearted West Country seamen, Drake, Hawkins and Raleigh. Even in the fourteenth century their caravels were well known on the coasts of England and Flanders, and in the Hanse towns. *The Libelle of English Polycye* gives a catalogue of their wares—

> " Here londe hatt oyle, wine, osey, wax and grayne
> Fygues, reysyns, honey, and cordewayne ;
> Dates and salt, hydes and such marchandy." [1]

From an even earlier period there had been potential explorers and conquerors among the Portuguese sea-fishermen,

---

[1] Printed in Wright's *Political Songs*, Rolls Series, vol. ii.; written about 1435.

who had learned to handle their boats with consummate hardihood and skill, off a shore exposed to the whole strength of the Atlantic.

If the geographical and economic situation of Portugal encouraged the nation to seek fortune across the sea, its history pointed in the same direction. The blood of four conquering races, Romans, Suevi, Visigoths and Moors, ran in the veins of the Portuguese. Their independence had been won by the sword. It was not until the middle of the thirteenth century that the Algarve, the southernmost province of the kingdom, was finally occupied by the Christians, and its Moorish rulers driven eastward into Andaluçia, or over the sea to Morocco. It was not until 1385 that the rout of the Castilians at Aljubarrota finally delivered Portugal from the fear of Spanish supremacy. Meanwhile, there had been a protracted struggle—varied at intervals by the interference of the Papacy—between the Crown, the military Orders and the commercial classes on one side, and the feudal nobility and the clergy on the other. A contest very similar in its main features took place in Plantagenet England ; and the resemblance is heightened by the action of the Portuguese Parliament or Cortes. The representatives of the nation showed that the monarchy could only maintain its power as a national institution ; at the Cortes of Leiria in 1385 the Crown was actually declared to be elective, and the Grand Master of the Knights of Aviz was chosen as King.

One distinctive feature of this internal struggle was the part played by the great military orders, foreign and native. As early as 1147 a contingent of crusaders halted in Portugal on their way to the Holy Land, and joined the Portuguese armies encamped before Moorish Lisbon. Most of them were Englishmen, says Henry of Huntingdon ; but a Flemish annalist claims the chief credit for his compatriots, while the Portuguese historian Herculano sagely observes that his own nation would have received its due share of honour if a detailed native narrative had survived.

Lisbon was captured, and thenceforward knights and pilgrims flocked to Portugal in increasing bands, eager

to win forgiveness of their sins by striking a blow at the
" infidel hordes of Mahound." The King of Portugal
induced many to remain by conferring knighthood and
citizenship upon those who would serve in his armies or
commercial marine, and by granting to settlers a liberal
share of the lands which had been depopulated by war,
or never reclaimed from their indigenous tenants, the wolves
and wild boars. The influence of these foreign knights and
their descendants in moulding the character of the Portuguese can hardly be overrated. It gave permanence to that
union between military and religious enthusiasm of which
the Portuguese empire was the direct outcome.

Four native Orders were also founded to carry on the
campaign against the Moors. In spirit and organization
they were akin to the monastic fraternities of knights from
whom the ranks of the crusaders had been so largely re-
cruited—to the Templars, Hospitallers, Teutonic Knights.
The Orders of Crato, of St Benedict of Aviz, and of Santiago
of the Sword were established in the twelfth century, the
traditional dates of their incorporation being 1113, 1162 and
1170. The Portuguese branch of the Knights of Santiago
(São Thiago da Espada) began its separate existence about
1290. These three fraternities were known by the names
of their headquarters, Crato and Aviz in Alemtejo, Santiago
de Compostela in the Spanish province of Galicia. Each
played a heroic part in the wars which ended in the conquest
of the Algarve. But the fourth and last Order was the
most celebrated of all. Its origin was due to the suppression
of the Templars by the Papal Bull *Ad Providam*, which was
issued by Clement V. on the 2nd of May 1312. For fifty
years at least it had been whispered that the vast and
powerful community of the Templars was tainted with
heresy, and that its most sacred ceremonies had been
perverted into orgies of unspeakable vice. Philip IV. of
France, an implacable enemy of the Templars, urged the
Pope to destroy the Order root and branch, but in Portugal,
where it owned large estates and wielded a corresponding
weight of influence, the ecclesiastical commissioners of
inquiry found in its favour ; and while the reigning King,

Diniz the Farmer, still hesitated, the two arch-enemies of the Order were silenced by death. There is a legend that the Burgundian Grand Master of the Templars, Jacques de Molay, who was burned at the stake in Paris, had in his dying words summoned the Pope and the King of France to meet him within six months before the tribunal of God. Their death within this period probably gave rise to the legend ; it also confirmed Diniz in his resolve to maintain the Order under a new name. As the " Order of Chivalry of Our Lord Jesus Christ " it was refounded " for the defence of the faith, the discomfiture of the Moors, and the extension of the Portuguese monarchy," and it received the blessing of the Vatican in 1319. Under the Grand Mastership of Prince Henry the Navigator it was closely associated with the progress of maritime discovery, as a means of transferring the crusade against Islam from Iberian to African soil. Prince Henry bestowed upon its members the tithes of St Michael's in the Azores, one-half of the revenues derived from the sugar trade of that island, the ecclesiastical dues of Madeira, the tithe of all Guinea merchandise, and other gifts. Pope Eugenius IV. granted absolution to all repentant Knights of Christ who might perish in the service of the Church. Affonso V. promised in 1454 that they should have spiritual jurisdiction in all lands which they might discover, and Pope Alexander VI.—somewhat superfluously —absolved them from their vows of chastity and poverty.

For a right comprehension of the Portuguese character in the sixteenth century, it is necessary to appreciate the vitality of the ideal which the military Orders embodied. This mediæval ideal of chivalry, of a life consecrated to knightly and religious service, continued to survive when all the energies of the race appared to be focussed upon the most practical and material schemes of exploration, conquest and trade. In other respects the Portuguese were at least as progressive as the most advanced peoples of the West ; the art of printing, for example, was introduced into their country only ten years after Caxton had set up his press in Westminster. But all the forces of modernity—the Revival of Learning, the new religious influences liberated by Erasmus and Luther and Ignatius de Loyola, the discoveries of Columbus and Vasco da Gama, the new scheme of the universe outlined by Copernicus—all these forces were powerless to dislodge the old crusading zeal which centuries of war against the Muslim had fixed in the nature of the Portuguese, and made an essential part of their patriotism. Portugal was to them the armed apostle of Christianity. This ideal supplied the spiritual motive-power for the whole task of discovery and conquest. It was perverted to justify the slave-trade and the excesses of Jew-baiters and Inquisitors ; sometimes it vanished altogether in the morasses of corruption which threatened to overwhelm the Portuguese dominion in Africa and India. But throughout the sixteenth century it always re-emerged—personified in Galvão and Xavier, transfigured in the epic of Camões, caricatured in a hundred lesser men. Its last manifestation was the crusade against the Moors, which ended with the defeat and death of King Sebastian at El-Kasr el-Kebir on the 4th of August 1578.

CHAPTER II

APART from the feats of individual travellers such as William of Rubrouck and Marco Polo, the exploration of unknown shores had for centuries past been achieved almost entirely by two races. First, the Scandinavian sea-rovers had voyaged far and wide in quest of plunder. Ashore they had founded the mediæval state of Russia ; afloat, they had penetrated through fog and storm to Greenland and America—" Wineland the Good " as it is called in the Saga of Red Eric.[1] Next the Arabs, schooled to travel by the Mecca pilgrimage, and free to journey from Cordova to Delhi without setting foot in any land save those which owed allegiance to the faith of Allah and Muhammad, had carried on the work of exploration with the zest of an imperial race, and in a more scientific spirit than their precursors. Arabian doctors had pored over Aristotle and Ptolemy. They had inherited an acquaintance with the immemorial eastern lore of stars and planets. They were skilled in mathematics and shipbuilding. Hence it was that geographers like Edrisi and travellers like Ibn Batuta did more than the hardiest viking of them all to enlarge the bounds of the world. And it is not irrational to suppose that the Portuguese had learned from the Arabs something of their ardour for exploration and their nautical science.

However this may be, they began where the Arabs left off, by setting sail into the " Green Sea of Darkness," that vast uncharted ocean which classical and mediæval fancy had filled with monsters and marvels. Greek myth, Norse, Arab and Celtic legend died hard among the seafaring folk

[1] Details will be found in *The Finding of Wineland the Good*, by A. M. Reeves, Oxford, 1890.

7

of western Europe, whose frail craft rarely ventured far
from the friendly shore, and so rarely enabled the crews to
test their superstitions by experience. It was well established that too arrogant a trust in the winds and waves
meant the risk of an encounter with the sirens, whose beauty
and sweet singing lured mariners to their doom. The
dreadful Bishop of the Seas, with his phosphorescent mitre,
had been descried in mid-Atlantic, vast and menacing.
Those who eluded his grip might still fall victims to the sea-
unicorn, whose horn could transfix three caravels at a blow.
Did not the tide ebb as often as the Kraken rose like some
giant cuttle-fish, to breathe and play on the surface—flow,
when the hairy black hand thrust him down again ? Such
phantoms haunted the seas on the way to that ideal common-
wealth, set in an enchanted island, of which men dreamed
in the Middle Ages, until they so far mistook the dream for
reality that cartographers marked the island in their maps.

Many names were used to express the idea of an earthly
paradise hidden somewhere in the western seas. It was
the Atlantis of which Plato had written ; Bimini, wherein
rose the fountain of perpetual youth ; the Isle of Seven
Cities, founded by the seven Portuguese Bishops who had
fled thither from the fury of the Moors ; Avalon, where
King Arthur slept ; the Fortunate Isles, the Isles of St
Brendan, of Antillia or of Brazil. Some of these traditions
outlived the Middle Ages. In 1474 the Toscanelli letters
(if these be authentic) advised Columbus to take Antillia
as a landmark in measuring the distance between Lisbon
and the undiscovered island of Cipangu (Japan or Java).
Portuguese and Breton fishermen still hear the sirens
singing ; and it was not until 1721 that the last expedition
set sail from the Canaries in search of St Brendan's Isle.
Even in 1759 the abode of the saint was sighted, but the
crass materialism of the age explained it as an effect of
mirage. Long before this, however, the Atlantic had been
robbed of its most sacred mysteries ; learned triflers
identified the Fortunate Isles with Madeira and the Canaries,
the Isle of the Seven Cities with St Michael's in the Azores ;
Ponce de Leon discovered Bimini and its fountain in the

West Indies ; Avalon became the ridge that culminates in Glastonbury Tor.

To Portugal belongs the credit of having dispelled the fog of terror which overhung the Atlantic. No doubt a few daring pioneers—Italians, Catalan, English, Norman—had to some extent anticipated the Portuguese. Such were Lancelot Malocello, who reached the Canaries in 1278, or the Genoese adventurers who sailed as far as Cape Nun before 1300. A Lisbon armada visited the Canaries in 1341, and five years afterwards a Catalan expedition left Mallorca for the " River of Gold " and was heard of no more. Madeira, sighted before 1351 and then forgotten, was refound some twenty years later through a romantic accident. An Englishman, Robert Machin or Macham, had eloped with Anna d'Arfet, a Bristol heiress, and was driven to Madeira by stress of weather. There Anna died of terror and fatigue, and five days afterwards her lover was laid in the same grave. Their crew, seeking to return, was wrecked on the Barbary Coast and enslaved, but in 1416 the pilot Pedro Morales of Seville and some of his shipmates were ransomed. On the voyage home Morales fell into the hands of a Portuguese captain named João Gonçalves Zarco, who learned from his prisoner how Madeira had been discovered.

The attempted conquest of the Canaries by two gentlemen of Normandy, Jean de Béthencourt and Gadifer de la Salle was begun in 1402, but the Guanchi islanders offered so fierce a resistance that parts of the archipelago remained unsubdued when Béthencourt died in 1425. Little else was accomplished before the era of Prince Henry the Navigator ; for it is impossible to admit the claim that Rouen and Dieppe merchants had opened a trade in gold, ivory, and pepper with the Guinea Coast, and, between 1364 and 1410, had established factories there at " Petit Paris," " Petit Dieppe," and " La Mine."

It was no mere hermit or cloistered scholar that propelled the Portuguese along the road to empire. Prince Henry was also an alert man of affairs, whose titles, as Grand Master of the Order of Christ, Duke of Vizeu, Lord of Covilhã, and Governor of the Algarve, had been earned.

His learning had been acquired in the intervals of war and administration ; from the day in 1415 when he had won his spurs at the siege of Ceuta, his activities had been manifold. Ceuta, called the African Gibraltar, had been the first stronghold wrested from the Moors in their own land ; its capture was the first dimly-realized movement towards the foundation of a Portuguese empire ; probably it also gave to the mind of Prince Henry its first definite impulse towards the work of his life. Thenceforward he devoted himself to the cause of maritime exploration. From his head-quarters at Sagres, overlooking the " Infant's Town " which he had founded as a base, he financed and organized expedition after expedition down the coast of Africa ; he planted colonies, established the Madeiran sugar-trade, promoted missions, secured the favour of Rome, and supervised every detail down to the designing of a caravel or the drawing of a map.[1]

His character is something of a paradox. At heart a dreamer, a scholar and a monk, he had the brain of a consummate man of business, the initiative and dynamic will which enabled him to transmute his dreams into facts. One can picture him, an austere student, busied among his charts and nautical instruments, in that upper room where he could overlook the Atlantic and feel the south-west wind. There would be no glass to hinder its passage through the fantastic Moorish window-traceries, as it blew straight in from the far coasts whence the mariners of the Order of Christ would presently return with new tales of peril and

[1] Quite apart from this exploration of the African coast, it has been suggested that Brazil was accidentally discovered by a Portuguese ship during the lifetime of Prince Henry (in 1447 or 1448). This theory involves too many debateable questions to be discussed here : most of the evidence is reviewed in *The Geographical Journal*, vol. v. p. 221 *seq.*, vol. v. p. 239 *seq.*, and especially vol. ix. pp.185-210, with which may be compared Azurara, vol. ii. p. ciii., *note*. But the most important part of the evidence has not yet been examined in relation to the theory ; and I hope to deal with it in a separate monograph. On the assumption that the supposed pre-Columban discovery of Brazil can be proved, there is reason to believe that the later " discovery " of Brazil by Pedro Alvares Cabral in 1500 (see chap. xi.) was not fortuitous—as most of the chroniclers assert—but prearranged.

PRINCE HENRY THE NAVIGATOR

FROM A FIFTEENTH CENTURY FRENCH MANUSCRIPT

achievement. The chamber would be furnished as barely as a convent cell ; the walls inlaid with painted tiles representing, in all likelihood, scenes of Biblical life, or adventures afloat. One can picture Prince Henry amid such surroundings, wearing the odd monkish garb in which he is shown in a fifteenth-century medallion—a stark ascetic figure, with the deep-set eyes and multitude of crowsfeet that stamp all those, seamen or scholars, who spend much of their lives in facing wind and tropical sun, or in poring over some crabbed archaic script. Such a man, doubtless, must Prince Henry have seemed as he sat listening to his pilot's discourse of strange lands, or watching while some tarry forefinger traced out a course over a parchment Ocean, among the dolphins and tritons beloved of cartographers in the Middle Ages.

The headland of Sagres forms part of the group of promontories which terminate, at the south-western limit of Europe, in Cape St Vincent. It is a rugged ness, overgrown with tamarisk and other shrubs coarse enough to thrive in the strong salt winds. The Celtiberian priests who built their rude stone altars on its summit, must have regarded it as the end of the world, washed by the surges of an illimitable sea. Theirs were not the only minds to which this remote and barren rock—the Promontorium Sacrum of the Romans—has seemed almost to be consecrated ground. To Prince Henry the Navigator, watching the horizon for the sails of his homeward-bound caravels, there must often have come such " home-thoughts from the sea," as moved Robert Browning to write his lyric, five centuries later. It is certain that the master motive which animated the Navigator was neither scientific, nor commercial, nor political, although it involved the extension of knowledge, of trade, and of the Portuguese kingdom. It was essentially religious. Before all else, Prince Henry was a crusader ; the rest was a side issue of his crusading enterprises. In all likelihood the idea of a sea-way to India never entered his mind ; he was absorbed in the desire to emulate his patron St Louis by breaking the power of heathendom and securing the triumph of the Cross.

The means by which he hoped to achieve his purpose

illustrate the limitations of geographical knowledge in the fifteenth century. It was commonly held that there was a branch of the Nile which flowed westward across Africa and issued into the Atlantic. Somewhere at the sources of this great river—in Ethiopia, or it might be in India— lay the half fabulous realm of Prester John, whose name, ever since the twelfth century, had stirred Christendom with the hope of a champion who should stay the instant advance of Islam. A day would surely come when this mighty potentate, whose dominions extended from Babylon to the confines of the dawn, would hear the appeal of Europe. Already Constantinople was threatened, and soon the litanies chanted in every church of south-eastern Europe would contain a prayer for deliverance from the fury of the Turks.

Little by little the shadowy outlines of Prester John and his empire gained substance and definition. It was rumoured that he had chosen the plain title of Prester, Presbyter, or Priest, as the Roman Pontiff had chosen that of Servus Servorum, not only as a token of humility, but because every other style, however magnificent, would appear too mean for the expression of his temporal and spiritual power. He is first mentioned in the chronicle of Otho, Bishop of Freisingen, who had learned of his existence in 1145 from the Bishop of Jibal in Syria. According to this authority Prester John was a descendant of the Magi, and had undertaken a crusade to rescue the Holy Places from the Saracens. After routing the Persians he had encamped for some years on the banks of the Tigris, awaiting a frost which might enable him to cross; disappointed, he had marched back again. Lesser men might have built a bridge, but it was no common brain that conceived the vision of a frost-bound Mesopotamia. About 1165 a letter was widely circulated, which purported to come from Prester John himself, and was addressed to the Emperor Manuel Comnenus at Constantinople. Prester John claimed to be the greatest king upon earth, and the most orthodox of Christians. His sceptre was of solid emerald, his robe woven of the incombustible tissue which the salamanders fashioned in their fiery habitation. Seventy-two kings were his vassals;

he was waited upon by seven kings, sixty dukes, and a fresh count for every day in the year. The fauna of his territories included all the dragons and monsters of mediæval bestiaries, fish which yielded purple, giant ants which excavated gold. In that kingdom crime and vice were unknown ; but for fear of accidents Prester John had set in front of his palace a magic mirror, in which he could scrutinize the uttermost corners of his realm, and detect conspiracies.

Such was the tale to which a hundred legends and some half-understood truths—memories of great Oriental Kings and conquerors, rumours of the Nestorians in the Far East, and of the Abyssinians—had contributed their several shares until all Europe came to believe in Prester John. It was not until the fourteenth century that he was definitely located in Abyssinia, and even in the fifteenth the belief in his power and splendour was unabated.

With the image of Prester John to inspire invention, Prince Henry devised a plan for the salvation of Christendom, as brilliant in its audacity and, considering the state of geographical knowledge at the time, fully as reasonable, as the projects of Dias or Columbus must have appeared to the unlettered majority of their contemporaries. The Western Nile should be sought out ; the knights of Portugal should sail up stream to the empire of the Prester, and enrol him as the protagonist of Christianity. Then the allied hosts of Portugal and Ethiopia should outflank Islam, rescue the Holy Places, crush the Turks and avert the disaster which had already cast its shadows over the Byzantine Empire.

Azurara has recorded how the supposed Western Nile or Nile of the Negroes came to be discovered by Lançarote and his fleet of six caravels in 1445. They were coasting down the seaboard of Guinea, keeping close inshore, and watching for two tall palms which an earlier voyager, Diniz Dias, had noted as a landmark of much importance.

"Some of those who were present said afterwards that it was clear from the smell that came off that land how good must be the fruits of that country, for it was so delicious that from the point they reached, though they were on the sea, it seemed to them that they stood in some gracious fruit garden ordained for the sole end of their delight. . . . And when the men in the caravels saw the first palms and lofty trees as we have related, they understood right well that they were close to the river of the Nile, at the point where it floweth into the western sea, the which river is there called the Senegal. . . . And so, as they were going along scanning the coast to see if they could discern the river, they perceived before them, as it might be about two leagues of land measure, a certain colour in the water of the sea which was different from the rest, for this was of the colour of mud. . . . And it happened that one of those who were throwing in the sounding lead, by chance and without any certain knowledge, put his hand to his mouth and found the water sweet. . . . ' Of a surety,' said they, ' we are near the river of Nile, for it seemeth that this water belongeth to the same, and by its great might the water doth cut through the sea and so entereth into it.' Thereat they made signs to the other caravels, and all of them began to coast in and look for the river, and they were not very long in arriving at the estuary." [1]

It has been shown that the Portuguese were a hardy people, seamen by nature, conquerors by descent, and crusaders by tradition and creed. But without a leader they might have halted for another century on the brink of their destiny. It was the genius of Prince Henry the Navigator that brought into play all the latent forces tending towards expansion.

[1] Azurara, vol. ii. p. 178.

CHAPTER III

EVER since 1317, when King Diniz had appointed a Genoese, Emmanuele Pezagna or Pessanha, as the first admiral of his newly-founded navy, some of the ablest foreign seamen had from time to time enlisted under the Portuguese flag. At the beginning of the fifteenth century, although the native fishermen and traders were probably unsurpassed in practical skill, the science of navigation was better understood in the seaports of Italy, while the Jews were supreme in their knowledge of astronomy. Barros relates how Prince Henry secured cartographers and designers of nautical instruments to teach his own mariners the deeper mysteries of their calling ; and on the register of those who actually commanded ships or served before the mast were many alien surnames—Vallarte the Dane, Balthasar the German, the Genoese Antonio Uso di Mare, and Luigi or Alvise da Ca' da Mosto, or Cadamosto as he is commonly styled. Cadamosto, the discoverer of the Cape Verde Islands (1456), left an account of some of his own voyages, which was first printed in 1507. He states that the Portuguese caravels, the most important of the four classes of ships used by the earlier navigators, were in their day the fastest sailing vessels afloat.[1]

These caravels were rakish, three-masted craft, very similar in build and rig to the Mediterranean felucca and the Arab dhow ; fishing-boats of kindred type may be seen to-day in any Portuguese harbour. They measured about 65 to 100 feet from stem to stern, and 20 to 25 feet in beam. Each stumpy mast carried a huge, triangular lateen-sail,

[1] See the plans in *Esmeraldo* and the *Revista portuguez colonial* for May 1898, pp. 32-52. For Cadamosto, see Appendix A. Special Bibliography : " Prince Henry the Navigator."

slung to a pole with tapering ends, the higher of which stretched far above and behind the mast-head, while the lower hardly swung clear of the gunwale. No ordnance was carried by the pioneers of African exploration, though room may have been found for a few horses, to be employed in hunting down slaves. The navigating officers would possess charts of the nearer and more familiar waters, a compass and a cross-staff, or rude quadrant used in taking the altitude of sun and stars. They steered, as a rule, close inshore, noting, as they passed, every landmark, such as a headland, an estuary, or a grove of trees which might help to identify their position. At frequent intervals they disembarked to take observations, being unable otherwise to correct the errors to which their primitive instruments were liable, owing to the motion of the waves. They had no chronometer except sun and moon, and no log-line by which to measure the length of their daily run, or the speed of their ship. For this they were compelled to rely upon dead reckoning, an art which can be practised in many ways. One of the simplest, though possible only in a dead calm, is to spit overboard, and then to calculate the ship's rate of progress by the time taken in passing the more or less fixed point thus formed.

In navigation, the great problem of the age was the determination of longitude. It has been suggested that the usual practice was based upon the variation of the compass-needle, a phenomenon observed at least as long ago as the year 1269. Such variation is due to the difference in position between the magnetic and geographical poles, and occurs when the needle, instead of pointing due north, takes a slight dip or trend towards the north-east or north-west. The pilots of the fifteenth and sixteenth centuries believed in the existence of a true meridian, where the direction of the compass-needle always coincided exactly with the straight line north and south ; they held that this meridian passed through Hierro, or Ferro, one of the Canary Islands. Taking this standard for the measurement of longitudes, as we take Greenwich, they aimed at the discovery of isogonic lines, *i.e.*, lines at every point of which the angles formed by the needle in its deviation from the true north were found to be identical. It has been supposed that they regarded isogonic lines and meridians as one and the same, and marked out their longitudes in accordance with this theory. Thus if the angles formed by the variation of the compass-needle were shown to be identical in Lisbon and Cape Verde, these two places would be regarded as having the same longitude east of Hierro, and as equidistant from the true meridian. Such a method of calculating distances east and west would naturally be fruitful in error, for while the meridians run straight from geographical Pole to Pole, the isogonic lines pursue a sinuous course, and are deflected from time to time by the almost imperceptible degrees of movement which together make up the great secular changes in their direction. Thus an estimate of longitude based on the discovery of isogonic lines could only be correct by accident.[1]

Of the men who turned their faulty theories and rude appliances to such splendid account, we know all too little. The official chroniclers wrote for the pride and pleasure of princes, forgetting the humbler folk who slung their hammocks in the forecastle, and did the hard work. For any insight into the daily lives of the crew one must look elsewhere, and especially into the codes of maritime law.

Foremost among these is the *Consolat del Mar*, or " Consulate of the Sea," a worthy monument of that genius for seafaring which the Catalans displayed in the later Middle Ages. The first extant edition bears the date 1494, and was published at Barcelona in the Catalan dialect of Spanish ; but long ere this its rulings were regarded as precedents in the tribunals of many a maritime power. No detail is too small for its compilers, who even enlarge upon the duty of a shipmaster to provide cats " where he can find them for sale, or as a gift, or get them on board in any manner,"

[1] In view of the accurate results obtained by cartographers as well as navigators in the period under consideration, I am inclined to reject the theory just described. A good statement of it will be found in the article *Des lignes isogoniques au seizième siècle*, by J. de Andrade Corvo, in the *Jornal das Sciencias Mathematicas, Physicas e Naturaes*, vol. xxxi., Lisbon, Academia Real, 1881.

2

so as to check the ravages of rats and mice in the hold and store-room.

The diet of the crew is carefully prescribed, meat and wine on Sundays, Tuesdays and Thursdays, porridge during the rest of the week, being the staple dishes. Every evening bread and more wine must be served out, with some relish (*companatge*), such as cheese, onions, or sardines. If ever wine became too dear, prunes or figs were to be substituted, and festivals were to be celebrated by an issue of double rations. No doubt the mariners of Portugal did not fare so well as the *Consolat* requires when they were cruising in the tropics, but as the earlier voyagers sailed close along the shore, they were more readily able to obtain fruit and game. According to Castanheda, the daily rations of Vasco da Gama's crews, in the voyage of 1497-9, comprised $1\frac{1}{2}$ pounds of biscuit, 1 pound of beef or half a pound of pork, $2\frac{1}{2}$ pints of water, $1\frac{1}{4}$ pints of wine, and smaller quantities of oil and vinegar. On fast days, half a pound of rice, dried stockfish or cheese was served out instead of meat; and the stores, which were calculated to last three years, also included flour, lentils, sardines, plums, almonds, garlic, mustard, salt, sugar and honey. This expedition, however, was equipped on an exceptionally lavish scale.

In some respects the rules of the *Consolat* are as humane as could be desired; sick seamen were to be landed and placed under the care of a nurse, while the immunity of a sailor from inconsiderate assault was safeguarded by some of the oddest provisions ever devised. The mariner was exhorted to bear with any abuse the master might please to shower upon him, but if words passed to blows, he was to run away into the bows and firmly take his stand beside the anchor-chain. Should an infuriated master, armed with a belaying-pin or other death-dealing weapon, chase him to this stronghold, the mariner was to slip discreetly round to the farther side of the chain. Here he was sacrosanct. Should he be still pursued, he was to call his messmates to witness that the master had broken the rules by circumventing the chain. Then, at last, he was to defend himself. So elaborate an etiquette of brawling could only have been devised for a people in whom the love of law and order had taken deep root. It was the more necessary because every mariner was required to equip himself with arms and armour.

Discipline was severe enough in these early days, though afterwards it relaxed, especially in the case of high-born officers. The ship's clerk (*escriva*, Portuguese *escrivão*), a privileged person who acted as book-keeper, purser and cargo-master, was liable to be branded in the forehead, to lose his right hand, and to forfeit all his property, if he made a wrong entry in the ship's book, or connived at such an entry. Curiously enough, a seaman who fell asleep on his watch was only put on a diet of bread and water, unless the offence were committed in hostile waters. In that case he must also be stripped naked, flogged by his messmates, and ducked thrice in the sea ; if he were an officer, however, he would only " lose all his food except his bread," and have a pail of water flung over him " from the head downwards." Water appears to have been unpopular, for no common sailor was permitted to undress himself " except he be in a port for the winter."

The presence of a gang of slaves under hatches would hardly add to the amenities of life on shipboard, yet it was this cargo which reconciled the home-keeping critics of Prince Henry to his undertakings. At first men had scoffed at him as a visionary, whose enterprises resulted only in a vast expenditure of treasure and human lives. According to Azurara the critics changed their tune when Antão Gonçalves and Nuno Tristão brought home the first ship-loads of slaves.

The Portuguese are still commonly regarded as the modern originators of this traffic, but slavery was no new thing in Europe, nor did it evoke general horror. In the Middle Ages, the unlettered poor might well judge the lot of a slave to be little, if at all, worse than their own ; while the educated classes could quote from the *Ethics* of Aristotle, their supreme arbiter in mundane matters, the comfortable doctrine that nature intended some men to be slaves.

Throughout the fourteenth century, to go back no further, the Italian settlements on the lower Danube and the Black Sea conducted a brisk trade in Slavs and Rumans, Circassians and Armenians. In 1317 Pope John XXII. formally denounced the Genoese merchants who made a business of consigning Christian girls to the harems of Eastern princes. In 1386 the multitude and turbulence of the slaves in Venice caused a panic among the citizens. The Barbary Corsairs provoked reprisals in kind by selling into bondage every Christian who would not fetch a ransom, and Spanish and Portuguese law recognized a distinction between the free Moors, descended from the conquerors of the Peninsula, and their servile co-religionists, taken at sea or in Africa. In the Canaries, the Guanchi prisoners were enslaved as a matter of course by the Norman invaders. Even in England, an Act [1] passed in 1547 by the first Parliament of Edward VI. made it lawful for any citizen to hale a confirmed vagabond before two justices ; and they, on finding the prisoner guilty, were ordered to have him branded on the chest with a V, and to adjudge " the said parsoune thus living so idelye to such presentour, to be his slave " for two years. Should he run away, he was to be branded with an S on forehead or cheek, and sentenced to servitude for life ; while a repetition of the offence was felony, punishable with death.

Slavery was thus a recognized institution. The new thing which the Portuguese did was to systematize the importation of blacks, who were almost universally regarded as lower in the scale of humanity than the vilest of Europeans, Arabs, Berbers, or Indians. It will be remembered that even the saintly historian Bartolomé de las Casas, Bishop of Chiapas in Mexico, conceded the validity of this tenet, when he sought to lighten the miseries of the native Americans by inducing his Government to import African slaves instead. Las Casas lived to repent of his error ; smaller men repeated it with no pangs of conscience, or stifled any remorse they may have felt by reminding themselves that, if the niggers lost their freedom, they gained Christianity. So Barros maintains that black men, as heathen, are outside the law

[1] 1 Edw. VI., chap. iii.

of Christ, and at the disposition, so far as their bodies are concerned, of any Christian nation. Azurara alludes, more piously than accurately, to " the curse which Noah laid upon Cain after the Deluge, cursing him thus, that his race should be subject to all the other races of men." The same chronicler, moved to tears by the agony of the slaves in Lagos market, actually prayed to be forgiven for his unorthodox emotion, which missed being heresy because he was thinking of the captives not as heathen but as men. Divines and jurists shared his view. Peter Martyr advanced the argument a stage, when he affirmed that slavery was needful to restrain those whom the Church had once converted, from a relapse into their former idolatry and error. To describe this doctrine as sheer hypocrisy would be grossly to misinterpret the spirit of the age. It cannot, however, be maintained that the Portuguese acted up to their devout theories; Prince Luiz, a pattern of orthodoxy, left several unbaptized slaves at his death, two of whom were called Ali, while two others bore the still more shocking name of Muhammad.

It seems probable that the first slaves brought into Portugal were mercifully handled, and that the worst evils of the trade only manifested themselves later. Azurara describes the fortunes of one cargo of black ivory, which was landed at Lagos in the Algarve, in 1441, and the picture is not wholly unpleasant ; although it is prudent to remember that the chronicler was the professional eulogist of Prince Henry.

" Very early in the morning, by reason of the heat, the seamen began to make ready their boats, and to take out those captives, and carry them on shore, as they were commanded. And these, placed all together in that field, were a marvellous sight ; for amongst them were some white enough, fair to look upon, and well proportioned ; others again were as black as Ethiops, and so ugly, both in features and in body, as almost to appear (to those who saw them) the images of a lower hemisphere. But what heart could be so hard as not to be pierced with piteous feeling to see that company ? . . . And though we could not understand the words of their language, the sound of it right well accorded with the measure of their sadness. But to increase their sufferings still more, there now arrived those who had charge of the division of the captives, and who began to separate one from another, in order to make an equal partition of the fifths ; and then was it needful to part fathers from sons, husbands from wives, brothers from brothers. . . .

" As our people did not find them hardened in the belief of the other Moors, and saw how they came in unto the law of Christ with a good will, they made no difference between them and their free servants, born in our own country ; but those whom they took while still young, they caused to be instructed in mechanical arts, and those whom they saw fitted for managing property they set free and married to women who were natives of the land. . . . Yea, and some widows of good family who bought some of these female slaves, either adopted them or left them a portion of their estate by will ; so that in future they married right well ; treating them as entirely free. Suffice it that I never saw one of these slaves put in irons like other captives, and scarcely any one who did not turn Christian and was not very gently treated." [1]

The Portuguese, judged by the standards of their own time, have ever been a kindly race ; cruelty to helpless things, to children and animals, is rarer with them than with us ; even in their bullfights all the brutalities of the Spanish arena have been refined away, and there is no killing, except of too venturesome sportsmen. From a phrase used by Azurara it may be inferred that the scene at Lagos provoked something like a riot among the countrymen who had flocked to town at the tidings of so novel a spectacle. So, too, in later days, there were many who braved the wrath of King and Church by sheltering persecuted Jews.

But the sons and grandsons of Azurara's contemporaries became hardened by the sight of heretics burned at the stake, by their own power to do as they pleased with their human cattle. Things were worst in India, where men shook off even the restraints which bound them at home ; and to understand what slavery meant under Portuguese rule it is necessary to turn from the picture drawn by Azurara to another, sketched more than a century and a half later by Jean Mocquet.[2]

" As for the slaves, it is pitiful what cruel chastisements they give them, making them suffer a thousand kinds of torment. For they

[1] Azurara, vol. i. pp. 81-5.
[2] See Appendix A : General Bibliography, *s.v.* Mocquet.

put them in double sets of irons, and then beat them, not with twenty or thirty blows of a staff, but with as many as five hundred. . . . The master, a Portuguese or half-caste, standing by, and counting the strokes on his rosary.

" While I was lodging at Goa, I heard nothing but blows all night long, and some weak voice which could hardly sigh ; for they stuff their mouths with a linen cloth, to keep them from crying aloud, and scarce allow them to breathe. After they have well beaten them in this sort, they slash their bodies with a razor, then rub them with salt and vinegar, lest they should mortify.

" One woman had a slave who was not alert enough, nor prompt to rise when summoned ; her half-caste mistress caused a horse-shoe to be nailed to her back, so that the poor creature died some time after. . . . Another, for not being wide enough awake, had her eyelids sewn to her brows. . . . Another there was, who was hanged up in a room by the hands, for two or three days together, and that for a very small matter, to wit for having let spill about a pint (*quelque chopine*) of milk. . . . The master of the lodging, having one day bought a Japanese slave girl, chanced, while conversing with his wife, to remark that the girl had very white teeth. The woman said nothing then, but biding her time until her husband was out of doors, she caused this poor slave to be seized and bound, and all her teeth to be torn out, without compassion. . . ."[1]

There is no need to continue the shameful catalogue. The worst charges brought by Mocquet are too vile for print, but they are authenticated by the testimony of other travellers.

[1] Mocquet, pp. 213 *seq.*

CHAPTER IV

CÃO, DIAS AND COLUMBUS

PRINCE HENRY the Navigator died in 1460 and his mantle fell upon King Affonso V., who was surnamed the " African " because—in the picturesque words of Barros—he " raged round Africa as a hungry lion roars around some guarded fold." Affonso leased the Guinea trade for five years to one Fernão Gomes, exacting an annual rent of 500 cruzados (£223),[1] and requiring that 100 leagues of coast should be explored in each year, or 500 in the whole term, which expired in 1475. The caravels chartered by Gomes were the first to round Cape Palmas, whence they pressed on eastward to the Ivory Coast and the Gold Coast ; and before the King's death in 1481, his subjects had passed the delta of the Niger, and reached Cape Catherine, 2° S. of the equator, thus traversing the entire Gulf of Guinea.

The accession of King John II. wrought a change in Portuguese policy. Not content with the revenues he had already—even as Crown Prince—derived from annual trading voyages, the King determined to establish a Christian empire on the mainland of West Africa ; and in 1481 he imposed upon Diogo d' Azambuja,[2] one of his most trusted navigators, the duty of forming the first permanent settlement. Azambuja was accompanied by two young officers who were in time to win fame far surpassing his own— Bartholomeu Dias and Christopher Columbus. He founded the fortress of São Jorge da Mina, " St George of the Mine," so called because it was the central mart for the precious ores of the Gold Coast. The fortress soon received the title and privileges of a city ; it had a church in which masses were sung daily for the soul of Prince Henry the Navigator ;

[1] See Appendix B : Coinage.
[2] See Luciano Cordeiro, *Diogo d' Azambuja*, in the *Boletim* for 1892.

and its harbour enabled those explorers who were gradually opening up the African coast to refit and revictual their fleets before proceeding south into unknown latitudes. An esquire of the King's household, Diogo Cão by name, was in the same year commissioned to undertake a voyage of discovery beyond Cape Catherine, the most southerly point yet reached, and about the midsummer of 1482 he set sail from Lisbon.[1] Aboard his ships were certain granite pillars (*padrões*), each surmounted by a cross, which were to be set up in sign that the newly discovered territories belonged to Christendom and to Portugal.[2] On every pillar the royal arms were sculptured, and Cão was ordered to add duplicate inscriptions in Latin and Portuguese, stating by whom the expedition was sent forth, with the captain's name and the date.

It was probably in April 1482 that Diogo Cão rounded the headland now known as Shark Point and there set up the first of his pillars beside the estuary of a mighty river, which rolled down to the Atlantic in such tremendous volume that, according to Barros, the water ran sweet for twenty leagues off shore. Cão, who named his new discovery the " São Jorge," steered up stream through the archipelago of low alluvial islands which rise from its bed, and turning aside into the mouth of a tributary [3] which enters the main river from the south, anchored in a quiet backwater overshadowed by a wall of sheer cliff. There, on the smooth face of the cliff, his men carved a cross, the shield of Aviz, and the still legible inscription—" Hither came the ships of the illustrious King Dom John II. of Portugal : Diogo Cão, Pedro Anes, Pedro da Costa." [4]

---

[1] Barros, *Dec.* I. Bk. III. chap. iii. p. 171 incorrectly gives the date as 1484.

[2] Similar *padrões* were afterwards used by Dias and Gama, and much importance was attached to them, as symbols of Portuguese sovereignty. The four erected by Cão (1482-6) have been recovered, though more or less damaged. One, from Cape Cross, is in Kiel museum, the others in the collection of the Royal Geographical Society of Lisbon.

[3] The Mpozo.

[4] Reading *Aqy chegaram os navios do esclaricydo Rei Dom Joam ho sego de Portugall : Do Cãao Po Anes Po da Costa.* See the photograph in *The Old Kingdom of Kongo*, by the Rev. Thomas Lewis, in *The Geographical Journal*, vol. xxxi. p. 590, and compare *Id.* vol. xxxii. p. 185 for the later names and the reading *esclaricydo*.

Other names and emblems have been added, probably by a later hand.

From the " black men with frizzled hair " who came aboard to barter ivory for cloth, Diogo Cão learned that the river was called the Zaire, and that it watered the rich and populous kingdom of Kongo.[1] He sent some Christian negroes inland to visit the Lord of Kongo, taking hostages for their safety, and continued his voyage as far as Cape St Mary—his Monte Negro or Cabo do Lobo—in 13° 28′ S. There he erected another *padrão*, returning to Lisbon in April 1484.

He was rewarded with promotion to the rank of a cavalier in the royal household, with an annuity of 18 milreis (£20, 2s.), a patent of nobility, and a coat-of-arms charged with two padrões. In the following summer he revisited the Congo and sent rich presents to the King, exhorting him to abjure idolatry and embrace the true religion, while the hostages were also permitted to return home and spread among their friends the fame of Portuguese hospitality and power. The subsequent history of the kingdom of Kongo is a fascinating study. Missionaries, lawyers and the slave-trade were rapidly introduced, churches were built, and dusky potentates hurried to invest themselves with the more showy trappings of civilization, styling themselves Dom Affonso or Dom Alvaro, decorating their kraals with heraldic devices, and conferring dukedoms and knighthoods broadcast upon a host of more or less naked aristocrats.[2]

Cão coasted southward from the Congo estuary until he reached Cape Cross, where in 21° 50′ S. he erected the last of his pillars. He had followed the African seaboard for almost the entire distance between the equator and Walvisch Bay, an achievement which, even apart from his discovery of the Congo, would entitle him to a sure place in the annals of exploration. His ships returned home before August 1487 ; for some of the negroes he had kidnapped were taken as interpreters by Bartholomeu Dias, who sailed from Lisbon

[1] It is usual to write *Kongo* for the ancient kingdom, and *Congo* for the river and later political divisions.

[2] For a full account of Kongo see *Andrew Battell in Guinea*, edited for the Hakluyt Society by E. G. Ravenstein, London, 1901.

in that month. According to a legend on the map of Henricus Martellus Germanus (1489), Cão died at sea off Cape Cross, in 1486 ; but both Barros and Ruy de Pina give an elaborate account of his return to the Congo and to Lisbon.[1]

Bartholomeu Dias de Novaes came last in the succession of great Portuguese seamen who opened the way for Vasco da Gama. Little is known for certain of his early life, but probably he was kinsman to Diniz Dias, the discoverer of Cape Verde. He had commanded a caravel in the royal fleet of which Diogo d' Azambuja was admiral, and King John II. had granted him an annuity of six milreis (£6, 14s.), for services to come. In August 1487—a year later than the traditional date—he set sail from the Tagus to resume the work left unfinished by Cão.

His three ships arrived at Cape Cross without misadventure, and then coasted south to the headland now called Dias Point. Here the captain set up a stone pillar, of which certain weather-beaten fragments have been recovered ; these are preserved partly in the collection of the Royal Geographical Society of Lisbon, partly in the Cape Town museum. From Dias Point the explorers drove southwards before a favouring wind which soon freshened to a gale. For thirteen days it blew hard from the north, carrying the ships far beyond the Cape and into the high latitudes of the South Atlantic, whither no European had ever before penetrated. At last the wind sank, and Dias steered east and north until he found land again at Mossel Bay. He named this inlet Bahia dos Vaqueiros or Bay of the Herdsmen, from the Hottentot drovers who were descried pasturing their cattle on shore. In the storm his ships had rounded the Cape ; but unaware of this triumph, Dias continued his voyage past Algoa Bay, which he named the Bahia da Roca, and made the Great Fish River, which he called the Rio de Infante, after João Infante who

---

[1] On Cão and Dias generally, see *The Voyages of Diogo Cão and Bartholomeu Dias, 1482-8*, by E. G. Ravenstein, in *The Geographical Journal*, vol. xvi. pp. 625-55 (1900), and Luciano Cordeiro's *Diogo Cão* in the *Boletim* for 1892.

commanded one of his three ships.[1]   Here the trend of the coast-line changes from east to north-east, and it became clear that the southernmost point of the continent had been passed.

Dias therefore yielded to the earnest demand of his crew, and put about for home.   To Table Mountain and the highlands and promontories by which it is buttressed he gave the name of Cabo Tormentoso, Cape Tempestuous ; but this was soon changed, either by Dias himself or by his royal master, into Cabo da Boa Esperança, Cape of the Good Hope.   In December 1488, Dias once more dropped anchor in the Tagus, after exploring more than 1250 miles of a seaboard previously unknown.   The annals of his voyage are meagre and arid, a bare record of facts and dates, but in modern times that voyage has been recognized as one of the main landmarks in geographical history, for it ended all doubt as to the possibility of reaching India by sea.

As the fame of the Portuguese discoveries spread abroad, Lisbon became the resort of adventurers from all parts of Europe, and especially from Italy, Flanders and England. A motley crowd of shipwrights and slave-dealers, gold-smiths and spice-merchants, tanned and tarry sailors and wide-eyed yokels, would crowd down to the waterside whenever the royal fleets, with the great red cross of the Order of Christ emblazoned on their main-sails, hove in sight outside the bar of the Tagus.   To all daring spirits who might feel, like John Cabot, " a great flame of desire to attempt some notable thing," Lisbon afforded the chance of sudden fortune and fame ; in Lisbon the inventor of a new astrolabe, the designer of an improved anchor, the draughtsman who could accurately transcribe a map or chart, was sure of a market for his knowledge.

Among such men there was one, the son of a poor Genoese wool-comber, who was destined for immortality.   He was tall, with large powerful limbs, and eyes of the light blue or grey common in North Italy.   His forehead was lofty

[1] Or, if the name should be read Rio *do* Infante, after the *Infante*, or Prince, *i.e.* Henry the Navigator.

and furrowed with the long brooding over one master-idea which had turned his hair and beard white, though as yet he was not middle-aged. He was something of a mystic, for he trusted in dreams and omens, and heard the voice of Isaiah in a vision ; something of an ascetic, for he restricted himself as far as possible to a vegetarian diet, preferred water to wine and often wore the habit of an associate of the Franciscan Order. Passers-by, casually noting his gown and his preoccupied air, might have mistaken him for some foreign monk or student, out of place amid the bustle and activity of the quays. In truth he was both scholar and seer ; but he was also a man of action, gifted with an iron perseverance and a capacity for leadership and seamanship which in no way fell short of genius.

Still dreaming of a western sea-way from Europe to Cipangu and India, Christopher Columbus had joined his brother Bartholomeu, a clever pilot and cartographer who resided in Lisbon. Christopher also worked at map-making and the illumination of manuscripts, but in his leisure hours he pored over the two volumes which had fired his ardour for discovery, the *Book* of Messer Marco Polo and the *Imago Mundi* of Pierre d'Ailly. Some of his time was also spent at sea, for it was in 1477, the year after he had made Lisbon his headquarters, that he visited Great Britain and perhaps extended his itinerary to " Ultima Thule " or Iceland.

His marriage in no way mended his fortunes. The bride was Felippa Moniz, daughter of Bartolommeo Perestrello, who had served under Prince Henry the Navigator. His services had been rewarded by the grant of Porto Santo, an island in the Madeira group, which he was empowered to govern and colonize. There is an old story of an accident which brought about his ruin. Some rabbits imported by the first settlers are said to have multiplied until they overran the island and destroyed every hope of harvest. It was thus a fitting union. The bride's dowry was a reversion to a desert island ; the bridegroom's chief asset was the vision of an undiscovered continent.

Felippa was fatherless, and for a time the newly-wedded pair made their home in the Madeiras with the widowed

Isabella Moniz Perestrello. Though few authentic details of their life have been preserved, it is certain that Columbus resided in Porto Santo during part of the year 1479, and probable that his plans for a western passage to Asia came to maturity at this period. There is a well-founded tradition that Isabella placed in his hands a mass of charts, logs and other documents bequeathed by her husband. These records of many voyages in the remote Atlantic would no doubt be eagerly studied by Columbus, who can hardly have failed to profit by the teaching of so experienced a pilot. In Madeira he received definite information which tended to confirm the vague rumours current concerning land in the Far West. Pedro Corrêa, a Portuguese pilot who had married an elder daughter of Perestrello by his first wife, had found on the beaches of Madeira huge hollow canes, capable of holding four quarts of liquid between one joint and another. He had heard of certain men washed ashore at Flores in the Azores " very broad of face, and unlike Christians in aspect." Another Portuguese mariner, Martim Vicente by name, had picked up a piece of driftwood, carved by some instrument not of iron and borne eastward by wind and waves. At the time he was sailing more than four hundred leagues west of Cape St Vincent.

In 1484, soon after his return from São Jorge da Mina, Columbus went boldly to the King of Portugal and propounded his scheme for the western voyage. John referred it to the Bishop of Ceuta, a Jewish mathematician named Moses, and the Rabbi Joseph Vecinho. Martin Behaim, the famous cosmographer, and Rodrigo, the Court physician, may also have been consulted. It was to " the Jew Joseph " that Columbus primarily attributed his failure. Vecinho had studied mathematics under the great astronomer Abraham Zacuto ben Samuel, and had been sent by the King to Guinea, to take the altitude of the sun. His arguments formed the basis of an address made by D. Pedro de Menezes to the Council of State, which resulted in the final rejection of Columbus' project. Meanwhile a caravel was secretly despatched to test the value of Columbus' theory, but its crew lost courage and returned with nothing to report.

Finding his ideas discredited or pirated, Columbus turned his back on Portugal. Felippa his wife was dead, his prospects of advancément were slender and he was probably in danger of arrest for debt ; so, taking his only son Diego, he set forth in search of another patron. In 1488 he returned to Lisbon at the request of the King, who had perhaps reconsidered his verdict and had certainly guaranteed him against any annoyance from his numerous creditors. There Columbus witnessed the triumphant home-coming of Dias, and learned that the sea-way to Asia had already been opened, though some part of the distance still remained to be traversed.[1] Now all the resources of Portugal were to be concentrated for the completion of this mighty adventure. There was nothing to be gained in Lisbon, and once more Columbus departed, resolute as ever in the face of disappointment, to lay his case before the Kings of England, France and Castile.

Thus ended his association with Portugal. It would be irrelevant to trace any further the events which culminated on the 12th of October 1492 in the discovery of a New World, or to follow the after career of Columbus to its lamentable close. It is worth while, however, to emphasize the fact that Columbus' voyage to America was an integral part of the process of Atlantic exploration initiated by Prince Henry the Navigator. Columbus' knowledge of Atlantic winds and tides had been mostly acquired on Portuguese ships ; his inference that a westerly course would bring him to Cipangu was to a great extent founded on data furnished by Portuguese pilots. To recognize that he, like Dias and Gama, had built upon the foundations laid by Prince Henry is in no way to belittle the splendour of his achievement.

One result of the discovery of America was the famous partition of the unexplored world between Spain and Portugal. Two Bulls were promulgated by Pope Alexander VI. on the 4th of May 1493, the first of which granted to

[1] From a manuscript note by Columbus in his own copy of the *Imago Mundi* (now in the Columbine Library, Seville) it is clear that he was present when Dias described his adventures to John II.

Castile all regions discovered, or to be discovered, in the west of the Atlantic Ocean ; while the second gave instructions for the tracing of a straight boundary-line from the Arctic pole to the Antarctic, so as to divide the Spanish and Portuguese hemispheres. " This line," said the Bull, " is to be distant from any one of the islands commonly called de los Azores and Cabo Verde, by one hundred leagues towards the west and south." [1] His Holiness did not condescend to explain how a line drawn straight from Pole to Pole could run " to the west *and south* " of either archipelago ; and the Bull was otherwise so cryptic that Spanish and Portuguese plenipotentiaries were appointed to reconsider the whole matter. On the 7th of June 1494, they signed the treaty of Tordesillas, which was confirmed by Pope Julius II. in a Bull dated the 24th of January 1506. According to this covenant the boundary-line was to be drawn due north and south of a point 370 leagues west of Cape Verde—doubtless an excellent solution if it could have been carried into effect. But as there was no known method of determining longitude with precision, the line of demarcation could not be delimited, nor could the 370 leagues be measured ; and it was a matter of opinion where the Portuguese hemisphere ended and the Spanish began. The treaty was invoked by King Manoel to justify the Portuguese annexation of Brazil, and by the Emperor Charles V. when he claimed the Malay Archipelago ; but in general it remained a pious aspiration, which both parties ignored or respected to suit their own convenience.

---

[1] *Quae linea distet a qualibet insularum, quae vulgariter nuncupantur de los Azores et Cabo Verde, centum leucis versus occidentem et Meridiem.*

VASCO DA GAMA, 1497-1524

CHAPTER V

BY SEA TO INDIA : THE START

BARTHOLOMEU DIAS had found the sea-gates of the Orient ; it remained for some mariner of equal daring to force them open. Wars with Castile and the death of King John II. had delayed this venture for a decade, but Manoel, who succeeded to the throne in 1495, did not long hesitate to resume the historic mission bequeathed to his country by Prince Henry the Navigator. This had now come to mean the search for a sea-route to India.

The twofold purpose of the quest was explained with admirable brevity by the first Portuguese sailor who disembarked on Indian soil. "Christians and spices," he replied, when asked what had brought him and his comrades so far.

All those who still cherished the crusading ideals of a bygone age dreamed of an alliance with Prester John's empire and with the other Catholic powers which were believed to exist on the other side of the world. This accomplished, the chivalry of Portugal would lead the united hosts of European and Asiatic Christendom in a campaign for the destruction of Muhammadanism. Others hoped to divert for their own profit the trade in Indian wares, and especially in spices, which had hitherto filled the treasuries of Genoa, Venice and Ragusa.

Shortly after his accession King Manoel summoned to his court at Estremoz the son of a certain Estevão da Gama, who had been chosen to lead the way to India but had died while the preparations for the voyage were still incomplete. His third son Vasco was appointed in his stead to the office

33

3

of Captain-Major (*Capitão-Mór*) or Commander-in-chief. Castanheda states that the honour was first offered to Vasco's eldest brother, Paulo da Gama, who declined it on the ground of ill-health.

Vasco da Gama was born about 1460 in the town of Sines, of which his father was Alcaide-Mór or Civil Governor. Sines, one of the few seaports on the Alemtejo coast, consisted of little more than a cluster of whitewashed, red-tiled cottages, tenanted chiefly by fisherfolk. Its inhabitants could hardly fail to be men of the sea, for a waste of barren sand, inhospitable as the unreclaimed Landes of Southern France, stretched for leagues behind the town and made all agriculture unprofitable. But westward lay the endless Atlantic, where the men of Sines could reap a surer harvest than any they could wring from the dunes, and on the north a little haven sheltered by granite cliffs gave a secure berth to their fishing-fleet. Born and bred in such an environment, Vasco da Gama was also fated to follow the sea. When he was chosen for the Indian voyage, he was already an expert navigator, about thirty-six years of age and unmarried. Courage, ambition, pride and unwavering steadfastness of purpose were the bedrock of his character. Although on occasion he might unbend so far as to join his sailors in a hornpipe, he allowed no relaxation of discipline ; and although he made promotion depend exclusively on merit, never on the fortune of birth—" preferring," as Corrêa puts it, " a low man who had won honour with his right arm to a gentleman Jew "—he was at heart an aristocrat.

Early in the summer of 1497 he was granted an audience of King Manoel at Montemór-o-Novo, near Evora, where he took the oath of fealty, and was presented with a silken banner emblazoned with the Cross of the Order of Christ. He then journeyed to Lisbon to assume command of four ships which already lay moored in the Tagus estuary.

Two sister ships of about 100 or 120 tons,[1] the *São Raphael*

---

[1] The Portuguese ton was of greater capacity than the English ; on this subject, and all matters connected with the preparations for the voyage, see Dr Ravenstein's *Roteiro*, Appendices C, D and E.

VASCO DA GAMA
FROM A STATUE IN THE CASA PIA, BELEM

and *São Gabriel*, had been built expressly for this voyage. Their architect was Bartholomeu Dias, who had set himself to design a vessel better adapted than the caravel type for a long cruise in stormy latitudes. He was compelled to sacrifice some good qualities of the older vessel—its speed, its handiness in working to windward, its finer lines. But the new ships were strong and seaworthy enough to hold their own among the greybeards of the South Atlantic, and roomy enough to accommodate men and officers without overmuch discomfort. Low amidships, with high castles towering fore and aft, they rode the water like ducks— square-sterned, bluff-bowed, their length about thrice their beam. Each had three masts, the fore and main carrying two square sails apiece, while the mizzen bore a single lateen sail. The bowsprit was tilted upwards at so high an angle that it resembled a fourth mast, fitted with one square-sail.

Vasco da Gama had chosen the *São Gabriel* as his flagship, while Paulo da Gama commanded the *São Raphael*. The flotilla was completed by the *Berrio*, a caravel of 50 tons, commanded by Nicolau Coelho ; and a storeship of 200 tons, under a retainer of Vasco da Gama named Gonçalo Nunes. Castanheda gives the total number of men aboard the fleet as 148, Barros as 170, including a few convicts who were to be employed in dangerous tasks on land. Diogo Dias, a brother of Bartholomeu, served as clerk on the *São Gabriel* ; the chief pilot was Pedro de Alemquer, who had already steered Bartholomeu's flagship round " Cape Tempestuous."

Gama, Dias and their advisers had done their utmost to organize success by giving a technical training to the crews, providing stores for three years,[1] and securing the best scientific outfit available. According to Corrêa,

" Vasco da Gama spoke to the sailors who were told off for the voyage, and strongly recommended them, until the time of their departure, to endeavour to learn to be carpenters, rope-makers, caulkers, blacksmiths, and plank-makers ; and for this purpose he gave them an increase of two cruzados (19s. 3½d.) a month beyond

---

[1] See above, p. 18.

the sailors' pay which they had, which was of five cruzados (48s. 2¾d.) a month ; so that all rejoiced at learning, so as to draw more pay. And Vasco da Gama bought for them all the tools which befitted their crafts." [1]

Tables showing the declination of the sun were provided by the astronomer-royal, Abraham Zacuto ben Samuel. These, which enabled navigators to determine their latitude by calculating the altitude of the sun when the pole-star was invisible, had been translated from Hebrew into Latin in the previous year, and printed at Leiria under the title of *Almanach perpetuum Celestium motuum cujus radix est 1473*. Other books, maps, and charts were supplied by D. Diogo Ortiz de Vilhegas, titular Bishop of Tangier and (as Bishop of Ceuta) one of the three royal commissioners who had discredited Columbus' plans for a voyage to Cipangu under the Portuguese flag. Among these documents were, almost certainly, the Geography of Ptolemy, the *Book* of Marco Polo, and copies of the reports sent home by the Jew Pedro de Covilhã and other Portuguese explorers who had been sent overland to Asia, besides a transcript of the information furnished by Lucas Marcos, an Abyssinian priest who visited Lisbon in 1490. The log and charts of Dias were of course available, conceivably also the map of Henricus Martellus Germanus.

Gama's instruments included a large wooden astrolabe, smaller astrolabes of brass and iron invented by Zacuto, " Genoese needles " or mariner's compasses, hour-glasses and sounding-leads. Dr Ravenstein suggests [2] that he may also have possessed quadrants, a *catena a poppa*, or rope towed astern to determine the ship's leeway, somewhat after the manner of a log-line, and a *toleta de marteloia*, which served the purpose of traverse tables, both of them being " contrivances long since in use among the Italians " ; possibly also an equinoctial compass for determining the hour of high-tide when in port, and a variation compass.

When all was ready, Vasco da Gama and his three captains

---

[1] Stanley's *Correa*, p. 34.　　　　[2] *Roteiro*, Appendix D.

went down to the chapel of Our Lady of Bethlehem (Belem), which Prince Henry the Navigator had built for his mariners, on the right bank of the Tagus. There they all kept vigil during the night of Friday the 7th of July. On the morrow they started in solemn procession for the place of embarcation, Vasco and his officers leading the way, with lighted candles in their hands, while a body of priests and friars followed, chanting a Litany. A vast concourse had assembled on the mud-flats which then lined the estuary; they stood bare-headed in the blazing July sunshine, murmuring the responses to the Litany, and moving with the procession as it wound slowly across the foreshore, down to that landing-place which Barros calls " a beach of tears for those who depart, a land of delight for those who arrive."

As the procession halted beside the margin of the river, the whole multitude fell on their knees in silence, while the vicar of the chapel received a general confession and granted absolution to all who might lose their lives on the voyage. Then Gama and his comrades took leave of the weeping crowd and were rowed out to their ships. The royal standard was hoisted at the maintop of the *São Gabriel*, the Captain's scarlet pennant fluttered above her crow's-nest; eager and excited sailors ran to weigh anchor and unfurl the sails, on each of which was painted the great red cross of the Order of Christ. Friends and kinsmen said their last farewells; the attendant flotilla of small boats sheered off, and, with a stern wind filling their canvas, the four ships dropped down the Tagus, outward bound upon the longest and, with one exception, the most momentous voyage which had ever been undertaken. With them went a caravel commanded by Bartholomeu Dias, whose destination was São Jorge da Mina. He had been made captain of the mine, as a reward for his many services.

Off the Canaries the flotilla lay-to awhile, and fished. Wind and weather had hitherto kept fair, but soon afterwards a fog descended, so dense that the *São Raphael* parted from her consorts. It had been arranged that the flotilla should in such a case meet at São Thiago in the Cape Verde archipelago. Off the neighbouring island of Sal the *São Raphael* fell in with the *Berrio*, the storeship, and Dias' caravel. Before long the flagship was also sighted some leagues ahead, and the whole fleet arrived safely at São Thiago on the 27th of July. There they took in wood, provisions and water, and bade farewell to Dias.

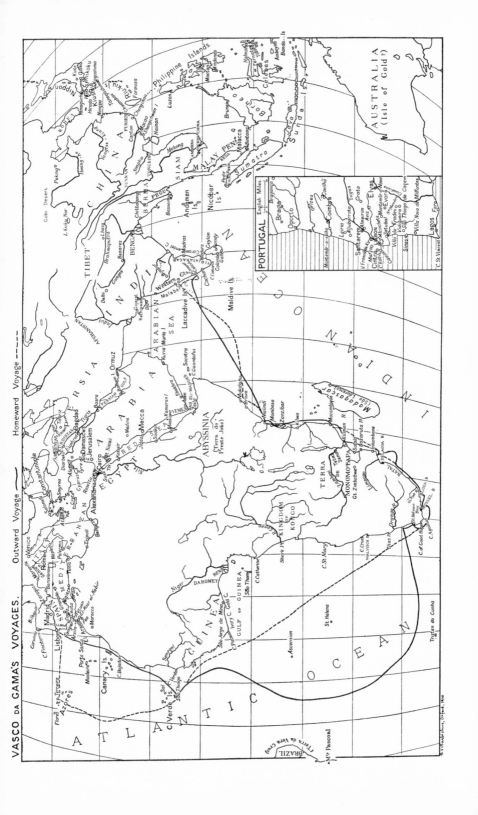

VASCO DA GAMA'S VOYAGES.   Outward Voyage ——   Homeward Voyage ------

CHAPTER VI

BY SEA TO INDIA : ROUNDING THE CAPE

LEAVING the Cape Verdes on the 3rd of August, Gama stood south-east and parallel to the African coast until, in about 10° N., he reached the region of calms and encountered evil weather. When the wind blew at all its direction was contrary, and sudden squalls arose from time to time and rushed down upon the fleet with tropical fury. To escape at once from the doldrums and from the baffling winds and currents of the Gulf of Guinea, Vasco da Gama conceived the bold and original idea of fetching a wide compass through the South Atlantic, so that, if possible, he might reach the Cape of Good Hope after circling round the tract in which the experience of Cão and Dias had shown that unfavourable weather might be expected. He crossed the equator in about 19° W. and steered south-westward into an unknown Ocean—*por mares nunca d'antes navegados*.

Few incidents of this adventure have been recorded. In September the fleet reached its westernmost limit, within 600 miles of South America, and then headed round for the Cape, beating slowly back against the south-east trades until, in higher latitudes, a west wind arose and carried the explorers on their way. In the last week of October a flock of seafowl " resembling herons " came in view, flying strongly to the S.S.E. " as though towards the land." The author of the *Roteiro* notes how a whale was sighted one day, and after that seals [1] and ' sea-wolves ' —possibly porpoises. In each case he is precise about the date and circumstances ; as though any sign of life which broke the monotony of long weeks at sea

---

[1] Reading *phocas* for the unintelligible *quoquas* of the *Roteiro*.

were a memorable event, to be recorded with scrupulous care.

At last, on All Saints' Day, the 1st of November, the weary mariners perceived some drifting strands of the gulf-weed which grows along the South African coast. Three days later the leadsmen found bottom in 110 fathoms, and at nine in the morning the look-out in the crow's-nest signalled land in sight. Then the ships drew together and ran up all their bunting ; the crews turned out on deck, in holiday attire, and fired a salute from their artillery.

On the 7th of November they dropped anchor in an inlet to which the commander-in-chief gave its present name of St Helena Bay. Since leaving the Cape Verdes his fleet had spent ninety-six days in the South Atlantic and had sailed fully 4500 miles. No navigator of whom there is any authentic record had ever completed so long a voyage without sight of land. Columbus himself had only traversed 2600 miles between his departure from the Canaries and his first landfall at Guanahani.

At St Helena Bay Gama went ashore to take the altitude of the sun ; on board it was impossible to obtain an accurate reading from his primitive astrolabes, owing to the motion of the waves. Here the ships were careened[1] and fresh supplies of wood and water taken in ; here, too, the Portuguese made the acquaintance of some beachranger Hottentots from a neighbouring kraal. The *Roteiro* describes them as a tawny folk, clad in skin karosses and wearing seashells or bits of copper as earrings. Their arms were wooden fish-spears, tipped with antelope-horns, and their dogs, according to the same observant author, " barked like those of Portugal "—no doubt a friendly sound, as reminiscent of home as the notes of the crested

---

[1] This could only be done in a dead calm, unless the vessels were beached. The usual method was to shift the ballast and cargo so as to give the ship a heavy list. When she was canted over as far as might be safe, a rough scaffolding was fastened to the exposed side, all weed, barnacles and other growth were scraped off, and the seams were recaulked. She was then righted and heeled over on the opposite side, which was similarly treated.

larks and turtledoves which flitted among the alien trees. The first Hottentot they saw was gathering honey among the sandhills which edged the beach ; he was captured, given a good meal and a suit of clothes, and sent to summon his tribe. Some days of friendly intercourse followed, but to the disappointment of the Portuguese, the natives showed no interest in samples of gold or cinnamon, though they grasped eagerly at such baubles as tin rings and bells. A soldier named Fernão Velloso received permission to accompany them to their kraal. On the way he was regaled with a banquet of roots and roasted seal ; but some misunderstanding arose, and presently his comrades noticed him hurrying back with shouts and excited gestures. They had been fishing in the Bay, and had obtained a very mixed catch, including some lobsters and a whale, which had dived when it felt the harpoon, and had nearly capsized a boat with Paulo da Gama aboard. According to Barros they were in no hurry to aid Velloso, who " was for ever boasting of his prowess." Camões tells, with a touch of humour, how one of Velloso's shipmates called to him as he ran down to the beach : " That hillside seems better to descend than to climb." " It is," the soldier shouted back, " but when these black dogs came thronging round me, I hastened a little, remembering that you were there—without my protection." The *Roteiro*, however, states that Velloso's cries were heard on board the ships and a rescue-party set off at once ; a scuffle ensued, in which the Hottentots bombarded the Portuguese with stones and arrows, and a fish-spear struck Vasco da Gama in the leg.

No lives were lost in the skirmish and the voyage was resumed on Thursday, November the 16th. Pedro de Alemquer reckoned the distance to the Cape at about thirty leagues, an excellent guess.[1] On Saturday the dreaded promontory came in sight ; legend had already surrounded it with fantastic perils similar to those which had made

---

[1] Dr Ravenstein states that the actual distance is thirty-three leagues (*Roteiro*, p. 9).

the whole Atlantic so formidable to mediæval mariners. But among Vasco da Gama's crews were seasoned men, who had served with Dias, and it is unlikely that they believed the rumours current on shore. During four days the wind was dead ahead, and it was not until noon on Wednesday, the 22nd of November 1497, that the Cape was finally doubled.[1]

A few days later, the fleet cast anchor in the Angra de São Braz—the Bahia dos Vaqueiros of Dias, the Mossel Bay of modern maps. Here, during a stay of thirteen days, the storeship was broken up and burned, and her contents transferred to the other vessels. Dias had found the natives hostile at this point ; they had stoned him when he came ashore to fetch water, and he had killed a native with a bolt from his crossbow. But Gama was surprised, on landing with an armed bodyguard, to find himself welcome. He bartered some red caps and small round bells for ivory armlets and bought a fat black ox " as toothsome as the beef of Portugal " ; for the Hottentots kept large herds of hornless bullocks, docile beasts, which were saddled and ridden by their masters. The Portuguese and their hosts vied with each other to display their accomplishments : first the natives " began to play on four or five flutes,[2] some producing high notes and others low ones, thus making a pretty harmony for negroes, who are not expected to be musicians ; and they danced in the style of negroes " ; then the sailors, and among them Vasco himself, proceeded also to dance—in their boats, and accompanied by trumpets. Later on, however, a quarrel arose ; the artillery was fired, though only as a ' demonstration,' and the Hottentots took refuge in the bush. The *Roteiro* has some curious notes on the ' seals ' of the Bay, which were " as big as bears, with large tusks," and on the Cape penguins (*fotylicayros*, the *sotylicayros* of Castanheda, Goes and Osorio), birds " as large as ducks, which had featherless wings and brayed like asses."

On Friday the 8th of December Gama set sail once more,

[1] On this date, see *Roteiro, l.c.*
[2] The *gora*, a kind of panpipes, made of reeds.

and by the 16th he had passed the Rio de Infante, the farthest landmark discovered by Dias. Northerly winds, and the race of the Agulhas current, which here sets strongly inshore, flowing in a south-westerly direction, now carried the flotilla back, and at one point the pilots found themselves no less than sixty leagues abaft their dead reckoning. For a time it was feared that no further progress could be achieved, but a brisk wind sprang up astern, and presently the fleet came abreast of a land to which, as it was Christmas Day, Vasco da Gama gave the name of Natal.

Soon afterwards, they stood away from the land, either hoping to escape the force of the Agulhas current and to make northing in calmer seas, or fearing to be driven on a lee shore by the strong easterly wind. But the mainmast of Paulo da Gama's ship was broken and an anchor lost through the parting of a cable ; finally the supply of drinking water ran short, so that it became necessary to cook with brine. The fleet was compelled to turn eastward again, and put in at the estuary of the Limpopo.

A crowd of Bantu, both men and women, had gathered on shore, and an interpreter named Martim Affonso, who had lived long in Kongo and had learned some of the Bantu dialects of the west coast, was sent ashore with one of his comrades. They were hospitably received, and in consequence Vasco da Gama sent the chief of the blacks a jacket, a pair of red pantaloons, a bracelet and a Moorish cap. These garments the chief donned while escorting his two guests inland to the straw-built huts of his capital, where they were fed on porridge of millet and " a fowl just like those of Portugal." All night long, crowds of men and women came to stare at the oddly-coloured strangers.

The *Roteiro* notes that weapons of the Bantu were long bows and arrows, iron-bladed assegais, and daggers which had ivory sheaths and hilts decorated with tin. The people wore copper ornaments, and for this reason Vasco da Gama named the Limpopo *Rio do Cobre*, ' River of the Copper.' The country he called *Terra da Boa Gente*, ' Land of the Good People,' because the Bantu made his men welcome, and supplied them with fowls and fresh water. On the 16th of January 1498, he continued his voyage and soon afterwards rounded the headland known, from the force with which the Agulhas current sweeps past it, as Cape Correntes. By so doing, he had unawares re-entered the civilized world.

CHAPTER VII

BY SEA TO INDIA : CIVILIZED AFRICA

VASCO DA GAMA'S journey brought him face to face with three different stages of civilization. The first had been that of the Hottentots and Bantu, who had never risen far above the level of savagery on which their neighbours the Bushmen still halted. The second was the Musalman culture of certain hybrid states, half Arab half African, which had arisen along the seaboard north of Cape Correntes. The third was the civilization of India itself.

With the second of these Vasco da Gama was now to come in contact. Its southern limit was fixed by climatic conditions at the Cape he had just doubled. Between the Arabian Sea and the Bay of Bengal, the main currents of the Indian Ocean sweep round from east to west in an immense coil, impelled by the south-east trades and the Pacific tides which pour through the barrier of the East Indies. As the outer rim of the coil breaks against the north coast of Madagascar, a vast volume of water is deflected, and rushes south along the shores of Africa. It is known first as the Mozambique current, and where it nears the southern limit of the Continent, as the Agulhas current. Its stream, charged with the warmth of the equatorial zone, meets a cold Antarctic current at the confluence of the Indian and Atlantic Oceans. A region of swift atmospheric change is thus created, so that these latitudes have an evil fame as a breeding-ground of hurricanes.

It was small wonder that the Arab navigators did not venture their frail dhows on the " jinn-haunted waters " south of Cape Correntes. But farther north the gold and ivory of East Africa had for centuries lured adventurous merchants from Arabia and Persia, first to trade and then to build cities along the littoral. These Muhammadan colonists soon acquired harems of native beauties, whose half-caste children acted as intermediaries between the Asiatics and the tribes of the interior, travelling freely among races who would have resented the presence of an Arab or European. In time, the half-castes outnumbered their fellow-citizens of pure blood. They controlled the local traffic, while the maritime commerce remained in the hands of the Asiatics, whose dhows—heavy sea-going vessels, constructed of rough-hewn planks bolted together with wooden tree nails, and made fast with coir rope—could cross the ocean to India, Persia and Arabia.[1]

The southernmost of the Muslim settlements was Inhambane ; among the most important were the Bazaruta Islands, headquarters of a thriving pearl-fishery ; Sofala, in the Mozambique Channel, and Kilwa, the principal trading-station between Zanzibar and Cape Guardafui. Sofala was the most famous of all, being the port of shipment for much ivory and for all the gold collected at the mines of Great Zimbabwe, in what is now Rhodesia. An ancient and improbable tradition, accepted by the first Portuguese explorers, identified this region with the Ophir to which King Solomon sent " ships of Tarshish " in quest of " ivory and gold, apes, peacocks and almug trees." [2]

Passing Sofala, as he had already passed Delagoa Bay, without sighting it, Vasco da Gama anchored in the estuary of the Kiliman or Quilimane River on the 24th of January. He called it the *Rio dos Bons Signaes,* or River of Good Tokens, because here at last he found signs of civilization. Among the Bantu inhabitants were two " gentlemen," one of whom wore a head-dress with a silk-embroidered fringe and the other a cap of green satin.

---

[1] A detailed account of Muhammadan civilization in East Africa will be found in vol. i. of Dr G. M. Theal's *History and Ethnography of South Africa before 1795,* London, 1907.

[2] On this theory, see Carl Peters, *The Eldorado of the Ancients,* London, 1902 ; D. Randall MacIver, *Mediæval Rhodesia,* London, 1906 ; R. N. Hall, *Prehistoric Rhodesia,* London, 1909. Malacca has also a good claim to be regarded as Ophir.

" They were very haughty," says the *Roteiro*, " and valued nothing which we gave them. . . . A young man in their company—so we understood from their signs—had come from a distant country, and had already seen big ships like ours." [1]

Thirty-two days (Jan. 24th to Feb. 24th inclusive) were spent in taking in water, cleaning the ships again, and repairing the broken mast. Just as all seemed to promise well, an epidemic of scurvy broke out among the sailors ; men's hands and feet swelled, and their gums grew over their teeth so that they could not eat. According to Castanheda, Paulo da Gama, who was of a more humane character than his brother, busied himself night and day in visiting and cheering the sick, among whom he distributed the contents of his private medicine-chest.

Mozambique, the next halting-place, was reached on the 2nd of March. It was a low-lying coral island, in the mouth of an inlet which afforded good anchorage ; its houses were of white stone, and along the mainland gardens and palm groves had been planted. Four ocean-going Arab ships lay in the roadstead, and although the native inhabitants were of mixed race, Arabic was freely spoken. Through his interpreter, Fernão Martins, who had been for some time a prisoner in Morocco, Gama learned that the vessels of the " white Moors," or Arabs, were laden with gold, silver, cloves, pepper, ginger, and quantities of rubies, pearls, and other gems, all of which, except their gold, had been brought overseas. Farther on, so Martins was told, precious stones and spices were so plentiful that there was no need to buy them ; they could be collected in baskets. Equally welcome was the tidings that there were Christian settlements along the coast, and that Prester John lived on the mainland, though far away and only to be reached on camel-back. Two supposed Christians had been brought from India as captives ; Barros describes them as Abyssinians, and adds that they bowed down and adored the figurehead of the Portuguese flagship—a wooden statuette of the Angel Gabriel. As this is not in accordance with Abyssinian usage, the men were probably Hindus, and mistook the angel for

[1] *Roteiro*, p. 20.

one of their own deities. The information gained at Mozambique, says the *Roteiro*, " made us so happy that we wept for joy, and prayed God to grant us health that we might see what we so desired." [1]

The Shaikh [2] who governed Mozambique for his suzerain, the Sultan of Kilwa, exchanged courtesies with Nicolau Coelho and Vasco da Gama, and promised to furnish two pilots. But on Saturday, March the 10th, the flotilla changed its quarters, taking up a berth off the adjacent island of São Jorge, where mass was said on Sunday. The Muhammadans now learned that their guests were Christians. So shocked were the pilots at this discovery, that one of them could only be retained on board by force, and when the Portuguese attempted to seize the other, they were ordered off by a crowd of armed men in boats.

Leaving Mozambique on the 13th of March, the fleet lay becalmed for two days, and after drifting some leagues to the southward, was compelled to return to its moorings. The Shaikh sent a conciliatory message, but when the Portuguese attempted to disembark on the mainland for water, their landing was challenged, and during the night the Muslims erected a palisade for the defence of their springs. Vasco da Gama ordered the ships' boats to be launched, and artillery to be placed in the bows ; his men kept up a cannonade for three hours and succeeded in killing two of the defenders, after which they rowed back in triumph to dinner. Sufficient water was ultimately obtained, but as the wind remained light it was not until the 29th of March that the fleet was able to leave the neighbourhood of Mozambique, having secured two Arab pilots—skilled men, accustomed to the use of compass, quadrant, and navigating chart.

Mombasa was reached on the eve of Palm Sunday, April 7th. The Portuguese were eager to go ashore and join the supposed Christian community in the celebration of mass. After the usual exchange of presents between Gama and the local ruler, two men were sent ashore and taken round the

---

[1] *Roteiro*, p. 24.
[2] Barros calls him Zacoeja—possibly a corruption of Shah Khwaja.

city. " They stopped on their way," says the *Roteiro*, " at the house of two Christian merchants, who showed them a paper, an object of their adoration, on which was a sketch of the Holy Ghost." [1] Meanwhile the orthodox folk of Mombasa were, in their turn, scandalized to learn from the Mozambique pilots and some half-castes [2] captured by Paulo da Gama that the new-comers were dogs of Christians. Vasco da Gama's suspicions were soon aroused, especially when his pilots leapt overboard and escaped to a native dhow. By a judicious application of boiling oil, he induced two of the half-caste prisoners to divulge the details of a scheme by which his fleet was to be boarded and seized.

A daring attack was made at midnight by armed swimmers who strove to cut the anchor-cables of the *Berrio* and *São Raphael*. The watch aboard the *Berrio* at first mistook the splashing and movement for a shoal of tunny, but soon discovered their mistake and raised an alarm. Some of the Muhammadans had contrived to secure a footing in the mizzen-chains of the *São Raphael*, and were beginning to clamber up the shrouds ; but on finding themselves detected they slid silently back into the water and vanished.

Despite these alarms, Vasco da Gama remained two more days off Mombasa, either, as Castanheda suggests, in the hope of securing a pilot, or because all the sick on board had benefited by the climate. He left on the 13th of April, still steering in a northerly direction, and at sunset on the following day cast anchor off Malindi.

Malindi, with its lofty whitewashed houses lining the curve of a broad bay, and its background of coco-palms, maize-fields and herb-gardens, reminded the Portuguese of Alco-chete on the Tagus : nor did their welome belie this friendly aspect. An old " Moor " who with some companions had been captured in a dug-out (*almadia*) during the brief run

---

[1] *Roteiro*, p. 36. Burton, *Camoens*, vol. ii. p. 420, has the following note : " It might have been a figure of Kapot-eshwar or Kapotesi, the Hindú pigeon-god and goddess ; incarnations of Shiva and his wife, the third person of the Hindú Triad noticed in my ' Pilgrimage,' iii. 218."

[2] The *Roteiro* calls them indifferently ' negroes ' or ' Moors.'

from Mombasa, was sent ashore to greet the Raja and assure him of Vasco da Gama's goodwill. The answer, accompanied by a gift of three sheep, was that the strangers might enter the port ; they were free of all it contained, including the pilots. Not to be outdone in munificence, Vasco sent the Raja a return present consisting of a cassock, two strings of coral, three wash-hand basins, a hat, some little bells and two lengths of striped cotton cloth. This did not end the competition : the Raja doubled his gift of sheep and added a really valuable consignment of spices, while Vasco released all his Muhammadan captives. But he had learned caution from experience, and on being invited to the royal palace, he answered with more discretion than accuracy that the King of Portugal had forbidden him to go ashore. He dared not disobey, so would the Raja honour him with a visit on board ?

To this the Raja replied, " What would my own subjects have to say if I ventured ? " But curiosity overcame fear, and he was rowed out to the ships, royally attired in a damask robe trimmed with green satin, and an embroidered turban. His dignity required the support of two cushioned chairs of bronze ; a crimson satin umbrella protected him from the sun, and a band discoursed more or less sweet music on various kinds of trumpets, including two which were fashioned of ivory and were as large as the musicians who performed on them. In this state the Raja made a circuit of the Portuguese ships, while the artillery fired off salvos in his honour.

Four vessels in the harbour were said to belong to " Indian Christians "—who avowed a curious distaste for beef. Some of these " Christians," tawny, bearded men, with long braided hair, boarded the *São Raphael*, and prostrated themselves before " an altar-piece representing Our Lady at the foot of the Cross, with Jesus Christ in her arms and the apostles around her." [1] This they probably regarded as a crude and barbaric representation of their own Hindu divinities. When Vasco da Gama passed in a boat, " they raised their hands and shouted lustily ' Christ ! ' Christ ! ' "

[1] *Roteiro*, p. 44.

So says the author of the *Roteiro* : Burton suggests that the word was Krishna.[1]

Nine days, from the 15th to the 23rd of April 1498, were spent in festivals, music and sham fights. On the 24th the Portuguese weighed anchor and set sail, under the guidance of a Gujarati pilot named Cana, steering east-north-east across the Arabian Sea so as to fetch up at Calicut on the Malabar Coast of India.

[1] Burton, *Camoens, l.c.*

CHAPTER VIII

FOR twenty-three days the ships held on a straight course, favoured by a steady breeze from the south-west, the herald of the winter rains. During three weeks no land was visible ; but on Friday the 18th of May, after skirting the northern islets of the Laccadive group, the pilot gave orders to turn eastward, and presently the lookout signalled land ahead. It may be supposed—though the *Roteiro* and the chronicles are almost silent on the emotions aroused in this moment of supreme triumph—that all hands rushed on deck for a first glimpse of unknown Asia. They could discern, far away, the outline of mountain peaks rising above the horizon, dark under gathering clouds. On the morrow a thunderstorm broke, and a downpour of tropical rain blotted out the Malabar Coast before the pilot had time to take his bearings ; but the heights which had first come into view may almost certainly be identified not as the main rampart of the Western Ghats, but as the outlying promontories of Mount Dely.

On the 21st of May, after a voyage lasting ten months and two weeks, the Captain-Major brought his ships to anchor off Calicut. One of the convicts, a converted Jew named João Nunes, who was acquainted with Hebrew and Arabic, was ordered to seek information on shore. By some fortunate chance he was led to the house of two " Moors " from Oran, who accosted him in Castilian with the words " The devil take you ! What has brought you hither ? " To this unexpected greeting he answered that he had come with a Portuguese armada, seeking Christians and spices. The Muhammadans, undisturbed by the reference to a rival creed, inquired why the King of France, the King of Castile, or the Seignory of Venice did not send ships to India, and were told that the King of Portugal would not allow such an infringement of his rights. Tactfully agreeing that the King of Portugal was wise, they took their guest home to a dinner of bread and honey; and one of them, whom the Portuguese called Monçaide, afterwards accompanied him back to the flagship. On coming aboard, this Moor exclaimed, " A lucky venture, a lucky venture ! Plenty of rubies, plenty of emeralds ! You should thank God for having brought you to so rich a country." Calicut was indeed a city well worth sacking. Its resources are truthfully set forth on a map which the Genoese Nicholas de Canerio drew in 1501-2.

" This is Caliqut," Canerio's legend runs. " It is a most noble city discovered by the most renowned prince D. Manoel, King of Portugal. Here are much benjamin of fine quality, and pepper and numerous other commodities from many regions, with cinnamon, ginger, cloves, incense, sandalwood, and all sorts of spices ; stones of great value, pearls of great value, and seed-pearls."

The ruler of the city was called by the Portuguese the Çamorij, which is usually anglicized as Samuri or Zamorin. The origin of this term is doubtful ; it may be a corruption of the Malayalam *Tamūri* (Sanskrit *Sāmundri*) *Raja* meaning " lord of the sea," and either a title or a family name. The Samuri was a Hindu who lived in a stone palace outside the city, surrounded by his aristocracy—priestly Brahmans, and polyandrous Nairs or members of the fighting caste. Within the city Hindu mechanics and retail traders dwelt in wooden houses thatched with palm-leaves ; a few stone buildings, including at least two mosques, had also been built by the rich Mopla merchants, descendants of Arab fathers and native women, who enjoyed a monopoly of maritime commerce. The rule of the Samuri was singularly tolerant towards these Muhammadans, as the Muslim author of the *Tahafut* points out. Friday was kept sacred, no Muhammadan criminal was executed without the consent of his co-religionists, and converts to Islam went unmolested. The Persian Abd ur-Razzak, describing Calicut as he saw it in 1442, says—

" Security and justice are so firmly established in this city that the most wealthy merchants bring thither from maritime countries considerable cargoes, which they unload, and unhesitatingly send to the markets and bazaars, without thinking in the meantime of any necessity of checking the accounts or keeping watch over the goods." [1]

Ludovico di Varthema, writing for Portuguese patrons of his own visit in 1505, similarly praises the uprightness of judges and merchants. It is clear that the advent of Europeans to this well-ordered state was not an unmixed blessing.

Calicut was a free port, its ruler a Hindu bound by immemorial custom, which he could only disregard at his peril. He was probably not over eager for friendship with a crew of piratical adventurers whose exploits on the African coast may already have been denounced by the Moplas. His European guests told him of a mighty kingdom, so far away that its existence could not easily be verified ; they sought an alliance and commercial privileges, but their only visible resources were three battered ships, their gifts were unworthy of acceptance, their very touch meant ceremonial defilement. Nevertheless, the Samuri was prepared to receive them with courtesy, at the risk of offending his best customers, the Moplas. As the monsoon was now at its height, and Gama would not venture his ships inside the harbour for fear of treachery, the Samuri sent one of his own pilots to take them to a safe berth near Pandarani Kollam, some fifteen miles farther north. He also acceded to the request for an audience, and on the 28th of May Vasco da Gama landed with thirteen companions and started for Calicut in a palanquin carried by relays of bearers.

On the way he was taken by his native guides to a large stone pagoda, roofed with tiles, at the entrance of which rose a bronze pillar, tall as a mast and surmounted by the

[1] R. H. Major, *India in the Fifteenth Century*, London, Hakluyt Society, 1857, p. 14 of Abd ur-Razzak's narrative.

figure of a cock. Within was a sanctuary or chapel, containing a small image, which the guides were supposed to identify as a figure of the Virgin Mary. The Portuguese felt that their hopes were at last near fulfilment, and that the great discovery of a new Christendom in Asia had been achieved. They all knelt in prayer, while the Hindus prostrated themselves and, if Damião de Goes can be believed, pointed to the image, crying " Maria, Maria ! "[1] The author of the *Roteiro* observes, without a trace of surprise, that " many other saints were painted on the walls, wearing crowns. They were painted variously with teeth protruding an inch from the mouth and four or five arms." The unorthodox aspect of these frescoes may have caused some misgiving, for Castanheda relates that one João de Sá, clerk aboard the *São Raphael*, exclaimed as he fell on his knees, " If these be devils, I worship the true God." The *Roteiro* adds that the *quafees* who ministered in the church wore certain threads, " in the same manner as our deacons wear the stole "—an obvious allusion to the *janeo* or sacred cord worn by Brahman priests. " They asperged us with holy water," it continues, " and gave us some white earth which the Christians of this country are wont to sprinkle on the forehead and chest, round the neck and on the forearm." The Captain-Major, on receiving a supply of " white earth " for his private use, handed it to somebody else, giving the priests to understand that he would " put it on later." He may have discerned the fact that the principal ingredients of the sacred mixture were dust and cow-dung.

Arrived at Calicut, Gama and his men were met by a native magnate, whose attendants escorted them through the town, marching to the lively strains of drums, trumpets and bagpipes, while every roof and window was thronged with spectators. After a scuffle at the palace gates, in which knives were unsheathed and several men injured—

[1] Upon this Dr Ravenstein has an illuminating note : " The Rev. J. Jacob Jaus, of the Basel Mission at Calicut, informs me that there is a local deity called *Mari* or *Mariamma*, much dreaded as the goddess of small-pox, and highly venerated. *Amma*, in Malayalam, means mother." *Roteiro*, p. 54.

possibly owing to the pressure of the crowd—the Portuguese were ushered into the royal presence. They saw the Samuri reclining on a green velvet couch under a gilt canopy, and holding a massive golden spittoon in his left hand, while a cupbearer served him with betel from a golden bowl, so large that a man could hardly encircle it with both arms. After listening graciously to Gama's recital of the virtues and resources of King Manoel, the Samuri replied that the ambassadors were welcome, and that he would regard their sovereign as a brother.

Custom required that all gifts should be forwarded to the Samuri through his factor and *wali*, who were summoned on the following day to inspect King Manoel's present. To the astonishment of these officials it comprised such articles as washing-basins, casks of oil and strings of coral— goods which might be acceptable to the headman of a savage African tribe, but seemed hardly an appropriate gift to the ruler of the greatest commercial port on the west coast of India. The factor and the *wali* were unable to conceal their amusement, and although Gama sought an escape from his embarrassment by protesting that the gift came from himself, not from his sovereign, they advised him to send gold or nothing. As, however, gold was none too plentiful aboard his ships, the second audience proved final. The Samuri pertinently inquired what they had come to discover, stones or men. If men, why had they brought no gift ? But Gama was allowed to present the letters he had brought from King Manoel, which were read aloud by Arab interpreters ; and he was granted liberty to land his goods and to sell them if he could find a purchaser.

On the 31st of May the Portuguese started back to Pandarani. The sun had already set, and as it was a windy night the native boatmen refused to undertake the long row out to the ships, which had been moored far from the shore. It was not until the 2nd of June that Gama and his men were able to return on board ; meanwhile their suspicion had magnified the delay into an imprisonment. This was perhaps natural, as they were watched at night

by armed guards—a precaution almost certainly intended
to secure them from molestation by the Muhammadan
traders, who spat ostentatiously whenever they met a
Portuguese. Once he was safe on board, the Captain Major
seems to have discarded his fears. He unloaded some of
his merchandise and endeavoured to sell it, but the Muslim
traders came only to scoff. Gama then despatched a letter
of protest to the Samuri, who replied courteously, sent an
agent to assist in selling the goods, and finally had them
conveyed at his own expense to Calicut.

From the last week of June until the middle of August
the fleet remained off Pandarani. Meanwhile small parties
of sailors went ashore and busied themselves in hawking
shirts, bracelets and other articles. Their object was to raise
enough money to buy samples of spices and precious stones.
Their own goods, however, could not be sold except at a
heavy loss, and at last Vasco da Gama sent Diogo Dias
with a gift of " amber, corals and many other things "
—to inform the Samuri that his ships were about to leave
for Portugal, and to ask for a consignment of spices on
behalf of King Manoel.

The Samuri's factor then explained that before the
Portuguese departed they must pay the usual customs-
dues on the merchandise they had landed, amounting to
600 xerafins (£223). The goods had been warehoused in
Calicut, and left there in charge of a Portuguese factor,
a clerk and a party of sailors. A guard was set over these
men, who were evidently to be held as hostages until the
duty was paid. Vasco da Gama retaliated by seizing
eighteen Hindus who had come to visit his ships. Among
them were six Nairs whom it was necessary to exchange
every day for other hostages ; they would have starved to
death rather than taste the " unclean " food provided by
their captors.

On the 25th the ships stood off and anchored outside
Calicut. They were presently joined by Diogo Dias, who
brought a letter from the Samuri to King Manoel, written
with an iron pen on a palm leaf. Its tenor, says the *Roteiro*,
was as follows :—

" Vasco da Gama, a gentleman of your household, came to my country, whereat I was much pleased. My country is rich in cinnamon, cloves, ginger, pepper, and precious stones. That which I ask of you in exchange is gold, silver, corals, and scarlet cloth."

Soon afterwards an exchange of hostages was effected : all the Portuguese and a portion of their merchandise were restored, the residue being probably withheld in lieu of duty. Gama yielded up all his captives except five, whom he may have kept to compensate himself for the partial loss of his goods, though the *Rotciro* asserts that his object was to use these men " for the establishment of friendly relations " when he should return to India on a second voyage.

On Wednesday, the 29th of August, the Portuguese captains unanimously agreed that as they had discovered Christian India, with its spices and precious stones, it would be well to depart, especially as the Christians did not appear anxious for friendly intercourse. That same day the ships set sail for Portugal.

There is no need to describe the homeward voyage in any detail. The passage of the Arabian Sea was delayed by calms and contrary winds, while a terrible outbreak of scurvy caused the loss of thirty lives. So many of the crews fell ill that only six or seven men were left to work each vessel. The African coast was at last sighted in the neighbourhood of Mukdishu, and on the 7th of January 1499 the fleet anchored once more in the friendly harbour of Malindi. But here also many of the crew died, and after five days the voyage was resumed. The *São Raphael* was abandoned and set on fire near Mozambique, because there were insufficient hands to work her, and the two surviving ships rounded the Cape of Good Hope on the 20th of March. About a month later they parted company, Nicolau Coelho taking the *Berrio* on to Lisbon, where he arrived on the 10th of July, while Gama steered for the Azores in his flagship. There, in the island of Terceira, his brother Paulo died of consumption.

The date of Vasco da Gama's return to Lisbon is not certain, but it seems probable that he landed at Belem on the 8th or 9th of September 1499, and made his triumphal entry into the capital on the 18th, the interval being spent in mourning and memorial masses for his brother. The whole voyage had lasted some two years, and only fifty-five men returned out of the 170 who had sailed from Belem ; but the quest for Christians and spices had been accomplished, and Portugal was mistress of the sea-route to India.

CHAPTER IX

VASCO DA GAMA'S SECOND VOYAGE

IT is a truism that the discovery of an ocean route to India modified the whole course of human history by bringing about new and far closer relations between East and West. Its other consequences were hardly less momentous.

Vasco da Gama completed what the Hanseatic League, the slave-trade, the finding of America, and the Turkish and Barbary corsairs had begun. The Mediterranean had been the principal arena of maritime commerce ever since the galleys of Tyre and Carthage had set sail in quest of tin and amber, slaves and sea-purple. But in the later Middle Ages the experience of shipping and exchange acquired by the Hansards was studied in the counting-houses of a hundred seaports between Cadiz and the Baltic ; and when African slaves and American gold began to arrive, the middlemen of these ports were well equipped for handling the new commodities. Meanwhile the Ottoman navy and the swarm of Muslim pirates or privateers that hovered round the littoral of North Africa had been preying upon Christian vessels in the Mediterranean and making every trade-route perilous. Last of all the traffic in spices, drugs and the other priceless wares of the Orient, was diverted from its old channels and carried by the Portuguese round the Cape to the Atlantic seaboard of Europe.

Such a change, albeit ruinous to the cities that had grown rich on the proceeds of the Eastern trade, brought new life to Cadiz, Corunna, Lisbon, Antwerp, Dieppe and Bristol. In less than a century, the headquarters of trade and finance were transferred from Southern to Western Europe, and the

Atlantic superseded the Mediterranean as the focus of European commerce.

This change involved another, of even greater importance. In every country of Europe, the men who cared for ideas looked especially to the artists and poets and thinkers of Italy for guidance and illumination. No other state could vie with Venice and Genoa, Rome and Florence, in brilliancy or depth of culture. The Italy of Leo X. was the supreme arbiter of taste and science. It set the tone of western civilization.

But the origin of this supremacy was in large measure economic. The society described by Benvenuto Cellini in his inimitable diary was one in which luxury and splendour ranked among the necessaries of life. Without vast revenues, the patrons of Cellini and Michael Angelo could never have gratified their passion for beauty and learning. But the raw material of this opulence came, in the last resort, from the East, and came chiefly in the merchant ships of Venice. When Portugal took command of the sea-borne traffic of India and Persia, the intellectual hegemony of the Italian cities was doomed to pass gradually away with the passing of their maritime and commercial greatness ; and in the seventeenth and eighteenth centuries their place was taken by France, England and the Low Countries. The headquarters of civilization, as of commerce, were shifted from the coasts of the Mediterranean to the coasts of the Atlantic.

But the growth of Portuguese sea-power compensated the peoples of central and south-eastern Europe for the loss of trade it inflicted, by helping to avert the peril of Muslim preponderance in those regions. In 1500, the tide of the Ottoman invasion was nearing the full : two centuries later it had hardly begun to recede. As late as 1683 the Turkish armies were encamped before Vienna, and long ere this they might have been the unchallenged masters not only of the Balkan Peninsula, Hungary, Austria, Moldo-Wallachia, East Poland and South Russia, but perhaps of Italy itself, had they but succeeded in their endeavour to win control of the Indian Ocean and to utilize the resources of the East for the subjugation of the West. The Portuguese arrived opportunely to cut off the Turks from this reserve of military and financial strength, and in so doing almost accomplished what Prince Henry the Navigator had hoped to achieve with the aid of Prester John.

But men had hardly begun to dream of these far-reaching changes when Vasco da Gama came home in 1499. King Manoel's first care was to determine how he might use his good fortune to the best advantage ; and ere many days elapsed he had thought out a policy. Its nature is indicated in a letter he wrote to Ferdinand and Isabella within a month of Gama's return.

" The Christian people whom these explorers reached are not as yet strong in the faith, nor thoroughly conversant with it. . . . But when they shall have been fortified in the faith, there will be an opportunity to destroy the Moors of those regions. Moreover we hope, with the help of God, that the great trade which now enriches those Moors . . . shall be diverted to the natives and ships of our own realm." [1]

Friendship with the ' Christians,' war with the ' Moors ' : these were to be the watchwards of Portuguese policy in the East.

On the 9th of March 1500, thirteen powerfully-armed ships sailed from Lisbon under the command of Pedro Alvares Cabral. On board were skilled gunners, Franciscan friars, and merchants under orders to buy and sell in the King's name. Cabral himself went forth not as an explorer but as a conqueror ; as the envoy of a monarch who had already assumed the grandiose title—" King, by the Grace of God, of Portugal and of the Algarves, both on this side the sea and beyond it in Africa, Lord of Guinea and of the Conquest, Navigation, and Commerce of Ethiopia, Arabia, Persia, and India." [2] Cabral was accompanied by the veteran Bartholomeu Dias, who was charged with the foundation of a factory in Sofala. Sailing far to the west, so as to shun the stormier middle reaches of the Atlantic,

---

[1] *Roteiro*, p. 114, for a full history and translation of this letter.

[2] The title was first used by the King in a letter dated August 28th, 1499. It was confirmed by Pope Alexander VI. in 1502. *Roteiro, l.c.*

the voyagers came, on the 22nd of April, to a new land which they called the Terra da Santa Cruz, though that name was soon discarded in favour of Brazil. And thus, by chance or by design,[1] Cabral secured for Portugal an empire destined to be richer and greater than all her dominions in Asia.

In the last week of May, his ships were lying becalmed not far from the Cape, with canvas set ready to catch the first faint stir of air. There was no time to shorten sail when a sudden tornado swooped down on the fleet, bringing darkness and a mountainous sea. Four ships foundered with all hands, and in one of them Bartholomeu Dias went down, finding a grave in those waters of the *Mar Tenebroso* whose secret he had been the first to fathom.[2]

Many weeks passed before Cabral could reunite his scattered armada, and it was only on the 13th of September 1500 that he at last anchored before Calicut. The Samuri vouchsafed him an audience, and permitted him to found the first Portuguese factory ever opened in India ; but disputes soon arose between the Muslim traders and their competitors, who sought to monopolize the first choice of cargo. The result was a riot, in which an infuriated mob of the faithful stormed the factory and put all its occupants to the sword. Cabral retaliated by bombarding the city until its wooden houses caught fire. He then sailed away to the neighbouring Malabar port of Cochin, where the Hindu Raja permitted the establishment of a second factory. This was the beginning of a durable friendship ; for Cochin remained the headquarters of the Portuguese in India until they secured a capital of their own. Cabral next visited Cananor, at the invitation of the Hindu Rani, and loaded his ships with pepper for the homeward voyage. He was back in Lisbon by the 31st of July 1501.

His experience enlightened King Manoel on the distinction between Christianity and Hinduism ; it also proved that Indian merchandise well repaid the cost of transportation

---

[1] See above, p. 10, *note.*

[2] Duarte Pacheco's fine coloured drawing of the armada overtaken by this storm is reproduced in *Esmeraldo de Situ Orbis* ; as the work of an eye-witness, it has much historical interest.

by sea, despite the length and manifold hazards of the voyage.

Four ships of burden had already been despatched to Malabar under the command of João da Nova ; but their adventures are not memorable except for the discovery of Ascension (originally named Conception) on the outward run, and of St Helena on the return. The equipment of a larger fleet was decreed as soon as Cabral returned, and after some delay the supreme command was entrusted to D. Vasco da Gama, who set sail from the Tagus on the 10th of February 1502.[1]

A Portuguese squadron, left behind by Cabral to cruise along the coast of East Africa and prospect for trade, had already visited Sofala, where its commodore, Sancho de Toar, had made a friend of the local Shaikh Isuf. Gama touched at the same port, but the " gold of Ophir "[2] was not forthcoming in such quantities as to detain him long, and after calling at Mozambique he made north to Kilwa. Cabral had put in here on his homeward passage, and had met with a rebuff from Ibrahim, the Emir, who showed a not unnatural reluctance either to accept Christianity or to forgo his share in the Sofala gold trade at the dictation of an entire stranger. This behaviour was interpreted as arrogance and malice ; Gama accordingly threatened to burn the town if Ibrahim would not own himself a vassal of King Manoel and pay tribute. The Emir consented to acknowledge Portuguese suzerainty, and gave as security for the tribute a rich and unpopular citizen named Muhammad Ankoni. As Muhammad knew that the money would be withheld and his own life forfeited, he handed over 2,000 mithkals[3] (£1041) out of his private fortune—an arrangement

[1] D. Vasco—for he was now entitled to use the prefix *Dom*—had fifteen ships : the Flemish author of *Calcoen*, who was on board, says seventy, but this must be a clerical error. Five more ships, under the Admiral's cousin Estevão da Gama, followed on the 1st of April, and joined the main body near Kilwa. Thomé Lopes, author of the chief extant account of the voyage, sailed with this second squadron. See Appendix A. Special Bibliography : " Vasco da Gama," for these narratives.

[2] Lopes, p. 134.

[3] Goes and Castanheda agree in making 2000 mithkals the amount. Barros puts it at 500. *Calcoen* is silent and Lopes had not yet joined the

readily accepted by D. Vasco who did not trouble to enquire whence the money came so long as it was paid.

Near the Malabar Coast, the fleet overhauled a large dhow named the *Meri*, which was bringing a crowd of Muhammadan pilgrims home from Mecca. Lopes [1] declares that the wealth on board would have sufficed to ransom every Christian slave in " the kingdom of Fez," and even then to leave a handsome balance. But the owners refused to yield up more than a tithe of their riches, and so incurred the wrath of D. Vasco. In a vivid and moving passage, Lopes describes how the Portuguese fired the *Meri* and then stood by to watch her burn, heedless of the women who thronged the blazing decks, holding up their babies in a vain appeal for pity.[2] The narrative in *Calcoen* is even more eloquent in its naked callousness :—

" We took a Mecca ship on board of which were 380 men and many women and children, and we took from it fully 12,000 ducats, with goods worth at least another 10,000. And we burned the ship and all the people on board with gunpowder, on the first day of October."

D. Vasco proceeded on his way, doubtless well pleased with this exploit, and anchored off Calicut on the 30th of October 1502. The Samuri, now thoroughly alarmed, sent envoys to make overtures of peace and alliance, but D. Vasco treated them with scorn, declaring that his royal master could fashion a king as good as the Samuri out of a palm-tree, and demanding nothing less than the banishment of every Musalman in Calicut. To emphasize this mandate, he seized and hanged a number of helpless traders and fishermen, whose vessels were then in harbour. The heads, hands and feet of these unfortunates were then cut off and flung into a boat, which was allowed to drift ashore, bearing an appropriate message written in Arabic. Corrêa

main fleet. The mithkal was a certain weight of pure uncoined metal, used as a standard of exchange. In East Africa it was worth 467 *reis* in 1554, or 1 mithkal = 10s. 5d. (taking the *real* at ·268d.).

[1] Lopes, pp. 136-137.

[2] " Alcune donne pigliauano iloro piccoli figluoli, e alzauangli con le mani, faccendo segno, secondo il nostro giudicio che si hauesse pietà di quelli innocenti."

5

says that the missive recommended the Samuri to make curry of the severed members.[1]

Calicut was bombarded once more, and D. Vasco sailed away to load spices at Cochin, Cananor and other ports which were either friendly or afraid to be hostile. He then headed for home, leaving behind him the trail of blood and ashes which was so often to advertise the movements of a Portuguese armada.

The main body of the fleet arrived in Lisbon on the 1st of September 1503 : " and so," concludes the devout author of *Calcoen*, " we reached Portugal safe and sound—*Deo gratias*." There can be little doubt that the burning of the *Meri* and similar achievements were regarded in Europe as laudable manifestations of zeal for religion. D. Vasco, had his conduct been challenged, would assuredly have answered, with honest and indignant surprise, that he was only doing his duty as a Christian in exterminating the vile brood of Muhammad ; that his acts of piracy and pillage were authorized by " letters of marque from God." [2]

D. Vasco had left in Indian waters five ships commanded by his mother's brother, Vicente Sodré, who was commissioned to guard the Cochin and Cananor factories, and to watch the Strait of Bab el-Mandeb in summer, so as to intercept Muhammadan merchantmen and pilgrim transports. These five ships, with Sancho de Toar's squadron, were the first permanent naval force stationed by Europeans in the Orient ; and their presence, in contrast with the earlier trading-voyages and plundering raids, indicates that King Manoel was determined to render effective his command of the Indian and Arabian Seas.

[1] Corrêa's narrative is far more horrible than those of the two eye-witnesses. It has been suggested that he exaggerated to enhance the glory of his hero—a curious point of view.

[2] The phrase coined or made famous by the ' abolitionist ' John Brown exactly expresses the point of view of these ' crusaders.'

CHAPTER X

VASCO DA GAMA IN RETIREMENT

AFTER his second voyage to India, Vasco da Gama ceased for twenty-one years to take any prominent part in public affairs. His retirement has been ascribed to pique at the meagreness of his reward, and to the King's jealousy of able and strong-willed servants. Neither view is quite consistent with the few documents which illuminate this part of Gama's career, nor is there any real difficulty to be solved. The great navigator had so many inducements to a life ashore that nothing but a strong sense of duty or an insatiable thirst for adventure could have lured him to sea again.

He had married D. Catherina de Athayde, a lady of rank, and doubtless he felt that desire for land and a home which is not rare among those who follow the sea. Moreover, the King had given him the means to gratify such an ambition. In January 1500 [1] Gama and his heirs had been granted a pension of 300,000 *reis* (£362). In February 1501 a pension of 1000 *cruzados* (£483), and in February 1504 a hereditary annuity of 1000 *cruzados* had been added. These revenues, which appear to have been paid partly in kind, were secured by a multiplicity of charges—on the fisheries of Sines and Villa Nova de Milfontes, neighbouring ports ; on the gold brought home from São Jorge da Mina ; on the excise levied at Sines and the adjacent village of São Thiago de Caçem ; on the Lisbon salt tax and timber octroi. Gama also received a hereditary interest in the royal commerce with India. So rich had he become by 1507 that the Venetian ambassador Leonardo Masser

---

[1] *i.e.* within six months of his return. The date is commonly given as 1502, but see *Ar. Hist. Port.*, I. ii. 25 *seq.* (1903).

estimated his income at £1929 : in the whole of Portugal only six noblemen and seven princes of the Church could boast of larger revenues.[1] According to the ambassador, Gama had a fitful temper, and showed no gratitude for the favours lavished on him. The great man's wrath may, however, have been patriotism in disguise. He probably chafed under the conviction that his country and service were going to the dogs ; and when he foregathered with his retired shipmates—stout, florid and peppery old gentlemen like himself—that conviction would be expressed in pretty vigorous terms.

Vasco da Gama's personal ambition by no means stopped short at vast wealth. It is quite clear that he sought a place among the feudal nobility, a title and a manorial domain. He had been given, almost certainly in 1499, the coveted hereditary style of *Dom* ; this was confirmed in 1502 not only to him, but to his brother Ayres and, in its feminine form of *Dona*, to his sister Tareyja (Theresa). In January 1500, a new office, the Admiralty of India, was created for his benefit by a royal rescript which is still extant. In language which strives to be worthy of the occasion, it names D. Vasco da Gama, Gentleman of the King's Household, as

" Admiral of the aforesaid India, with all the pre-eminences, liberties, power, jurisdiction, revenues, privileges and rights which, as appertaining to the aforesaid Admiralty, our Admiral of those our realms ought by right to possess, and does hereby possess." [2]

That the honour was no empty form is shown by a document dated the 30th of March 1522, which affirms D. Vasco's right, as Admiral of India, to the anchorage-dues of Goa, Malacca and Ormuz.[3]

There remained the problem of a territorial title and an estate. On Christmas Eve 1499 Gama had been promised the manor of Sines, his birthplace ; but it was first necessary to obtain the consent of its owners, the Order of São Thiago, together with a dispensation from the Pope. The Order

---

[1] *Roteiro*, p. 227.   [2] *Ar. Hist. Port.*, *l.c.*
[3] L. Cordeiro, *O Premio da Descoberta*, Lisbon, 1897, pp. 46-47.

had also to be compensated by the grant of another town, which was no easy matter to arrange. Tired of waiting, the Admiral took the law into his own hands, began to build a manor-house, and generally behaved as though Sines already belonged to him. A church which he founded there still stands, grey and weather-beaten, on a headland overlooking the Atlantic.

The Grand Master of São Thiago, incensed by these highhanded proceedings, complained to King Manoel, and in March 1507 Gama was warned that he must leave Sines within a month or take the consequences.[1] The fact that the royal pleasure was made known through João da Gama, uncle of the Admiral and Bursar of the Order of São Thiago, probably did not tend to lighten the blow. D. Vasco withdrew to Evora, a quiet cathedral city in the heart of the Alemtejo, where he lived in a house decorated with painted figures of Indians and Indian beasts and plants : the gilded scrollwork on the walls was said to have been made of gold brought home from the East.[2]

Gama had six sons and one daughter, Isabella de Athayde by name. Francisco, the eldest son, succeeded to his fortune and rank ; Estevão, the second, became Governor of India in 1540 and died in Venice, whither he had emigrated to avoid marrying a wife selected by his sovereign ; Paulo, the third, was killed in a naval action off Malacca, in 1534 ; Christovão, the fourth, died the hero of a forlorn hope in Abyssinia, in 1542 ; Pedro da Silva, the fifth, became Captain of Malacca in 1541 ; Alvaro de Athayde, the youngest, succeeded to the same office.

Despite the Sines imbroglio, Gama was not in disgrace. It is possible that he acted as informal adviser to the Crown on matters of Indian and maritime policy ; if Corrêa can be trusted, he certainly did so until 1505.[3] King Manoel sought in 1508 to bestow on him the town of Villafranca de Xira, in the Tagus valley, but the transfer was never com-

---

[1] Teixeira de Aragão, *Vasco da Gama e a Vidigueira*, pp. 250-52.

[2] The street in which it stands is still known as the Rua das Casas Pintadas ; but Gama's house has been modernized and its decorations have disappeared.

[3] Corrêa, vol. i. pp. 525 and 529.

pleted. Ten years passed and still the Admiral remained without his title and his manor. At last, in August 1518, he protested that if nothing were done he would leave the kingdom.[1] One famous navigator, Fernão Magalhães, better known as Magellan, had already deserted Portugal for Castile, because he considered himself insufficiently paid, and the King was not disposed to lose another servant so valuable.

He bade the Admiral wait until December and try to realise the error of his ways. Meanwhile the Duke of Bragança came forward and offered to surrender the town of Vidigueira and the title of Count, in exchange for a hereditary pension of 1000 cruzados and 4000 cruzados (£1932) paid down. These conditions were duly fulfilled, and in December 1519 King Manoel formally conferred on D. Vasco da Gama the title Count of Vidigueira, with civil and criminal jurisdiction, ecclesiastical patronage, and all other privileges and revenues which had been enjoyed by the Duke of Bragança as lord of the manor of Vidigueira and Villa de Frades.[2] These two villages lie close to one another among the southern foothills of the Serra Mendro, commanding a wide prospect over the undulating plains of southern Alemtejo. There is no evidence to show that the Count Admiral ever resided on his new estates ; except, indeed, for the documents relating to his honours and rewards, his life during the twenty-one years of his retirement is completely unrecorded. It is not until after the death of King Manoel in 1521, that he emerges once more into the half-light of history.

---

[1] Aragão, pp. 257-58.
[2] Aragão, pp. 258-59, and Cordeiro in *Boletim* for 1892, p. 289.

DOCUMENT WRITTEN AND SIGNED BY D. VASCO DA GAMA, AS COUNT
OF VIDIGUEIRA AND GOVERNOR OF INDIA

FROM SEA-POWER TO EMPIRE, 1505-1548

CHAPTER XI

D. FRANCISCO DE ALMEIDA

WHILE D. Vasco remained at home amassing wealth and honour, his countrymen were winning fresh laurels in the East. Their artillery gave them an immense advantage in maritime warfare ; while on land their fighting power was demonstrated in 1504, when a handful of Portuguese and some natives under Duarte Pacheco Pereira [1] held Cochin for months against an overwhelming host, sent for their destruction by the Samuri of Calicut. As a reward for this exploit, the Raja of Cochin granted Pacheco a coat of arms—an escutcheon gules " in token of the blood he had shed," charged with five crowns emblematic of the five princes he had ovrethrown in battle : so runs the original patent,[2] dated 1504, which gives the Raja's name as Itiramamarnetim Qulluniramá Coul Trimumpate. On his return to Portugal, in July 1505, Pacheco received further rewards from King Manoel [3] ; when he married, the Treasury was commanded to pay a dowry of 120 milreis (£223) to his wife, D. Antonia ; pensions were bestowed upon his children and grandchildren, and he was immortalized by Camões as the *Achilles Lusitano.*

But although the defence of Cochin cast a reflected lustre upon King Manoel, it revealed certain weaknesses. Isolated factories were in jeopardy whenever the seasonal winds

---

[1] See Appendix A : General Bibliography, *s.v. Esmeraldo.*

[2] Printed in *Esmeraldo*, p. xix.

[3] This is certain, despite the suggestions—they cannot be called statements—to the contrary of Goes, Camões and others. The documentary evidence will be found in the introduction to *Esmeraldo*. In 1509 Pacheco was employed to hunt down the French corsair Mondragon ; in 1522 he was made Governor of São Jorge da Mina ; in 1524 he was pensioned.

prevented navigation, and the growth of commerce required that the old haphazard methods of piracy and pillage should give place to order and system. Accordingly, a new office, the Viceroyalty of India, was created in 1505, and the first Viceroy, a soldier of tried wisdom named D. Francisco de Almeida, sailed from Lisbon in March of the same year, invested with full power to wage war, conclude treaties and regulate commerce. East of the Cape his word was to be law wherever the Portuguese flag flew.[1]

The Viceroy was more than a mere conqueror : in a letter to King Manoel he formulated a system of government based on definite strategic and commercial principles.[2] Its fundamental idea is the importance of sea-power ; for the " blue water-school " of naval strategy never had a more convinced champion than Almeida. " Avoid the annexation of territory," he writes, " build no more fortresses than may be absolutely necessary to protect your factories from a sudden raid : we can spare no men from the navy."

The dearth of trained men was, indeed, already manifest and ominous. Even in Almeida's fleet one caravel was manned by sons of the soil so raw that they could hardly distinguish between their right and left hands. As the ships wore to sea, these bold mariners found themselves confronted by a problem still more recondite—the subtle difference between starboard and larboard. They faced the problem without prejudice and steered accordingly, until their captain, João Homem, lit upon the happy notion of tying a bundle of garlic over one side of the ship and a handful of onions over the other, and bidding the pilot give his orders to the helmsmen thus—" Onion your helm ! " " Garlic your helm ! "

[1] Since 1505 the Viceroy or Governor has always been the highest legislative and executive authority in Portuguese India. The normal tenure of office in the sixteenth century was for three years. The distinction between a Viceroyalty and a Governorship was purely titular—a matter of rank and precedence, not of power.

[2] Reproduced by Corrêa, and transcribed from the original by H. Lopes de Mendonça in the *Annaes das Sciencias e Lettras* of the Academia Real, Lisbon, 1857.

Almeida regarded maritime power solely as a means to commercial supremacy in the East. Missionary and crusading ideals were for the moment in abeyance : the whole purpose of his policy was to secure for King Manoel a monopoly in the exportation of Indian and East African products to Europe. This merchandise, of which the letter gives a somewhat miscellaneous catalogue—including pepper, slavegirls, silk—had hitherto reached Europe through the Persian Gulf and the Red Sea, whence it passed by caravan to the Italian and Levantine ships awaiting it in various Mediterranean ports. In Indian waters, the carrying trade was exercised almost exclusively by Muhammadans—Arab and Persian, Turk and Egyptian. Almeida's plan was to drive these infidels from the seas, to put Portuguese traders in their place, and to divert the Indian export-trade to the Cape route.

As for the King's interests on land, they would be secured by alliances with the Hindu Rajas, who would supply cargo and guard the factories in return for the protection of the Portuguese navy. Thus the original policy of friendship with the " Christians " and war against the Muhammadans was brought up to date. And here Almeida found a sage counsellor in a Hindu corsair named Timoja, who, as Albuquerque's *Commentaries* affirm, " had risen by piracy to high honour." Timoja commanded a squadron of the swift, undecked, single-masted galleys known as foists, with which he was wont to sally forth and harry Muhammadan traders, partly in the interest of his sovereign, the Raja of Honawar (tributary to Vijayanagar). In an encounter with D. Vasco da Gama he had learned to respect the strength of the Portuguese, whose favour he thenceforward courted.

Acting on Timoja's counsel, the Viceroy sought to conciliate the Hindu empire of Vijayanagar, which embraced nearly the whole of the Indian Peninsula south of the rivers Kistna and Tungabhadra. Since the fourteenth cenutry, when the Muslim conquerors had swept down over Northern India, Vijayanagar had been the stronghold of fighting Hinduism. Its warriors were reckoned by hundreds of thousands : its material resources were boundless, as Firishta and the Portuguese annalists alike testify. During the critical years in which the Portuguese empire was being founded and stablished, Vijayanagar drew the fire of Islam. It occupied the forces which might otherwise have united to hurl the Christian intruders back into their sea. Its downfall, in 1565, did at last permit the formation of such a coalition, but by that time the Portuguese dominion had acquired strength to weather the storm unaided. Meanwhile, Almeida was the first to comprehend how vital it was to the interests of his country that Vijayanagar should be friendly or neutral.[1]

His ability to maintain command of the sea was soon tested. Two Oriental powers—Egypt,[2] which was still supreme in the Red Sea, and the Ottoman empire, which had access to the Persian Gulf at Basra—possessed naval forces quite strong enough to cope with any European rival. Their fleets were equipped with powerful artillery and were partly manned by mercenaries who had learned the arts of war and seamanship in the Mediterranean. Neither power was willing tamely to acquiesce in the ruin of its Indian trade, but the first challenge came from the Memluk Sultan of Egypt. In 1508 an Egyptian fleet left Suez for India, commanded by Mir Hussain, whom the Portuguese chroniclers call " Admiral of the Grand Soldan of Cairo and Babylonia." Mir Hussain surprised and defeated a small Portuguese squadron off Chaul ; and the Viceroy's only son, D. Lourenço de Almeida, was killed in the action. A cannon-ball shattered both his legs, but he sat by the mainmast and continued calmly to direct the fighting and navigation of his ship until a second shot ended his life.

The Viceroy, whose whole being centred in his devotion

---

[1] Two detailed descriptions of Vijayanagar, by Portuguese travellers who visited the country during the sixteenth century, will be found (translated) in *A Forgotten Empire : Vijayanagar*, by R. Sewell, London, 1900. See also *A History of Vijayanagar*, by B. S. Row, London, 1906.

[2] Egypt was independent until 1517, when it was conquered by the Ottoman Sultan Selim I.

to his son, received the tidings with outward stoicism,[1] telling his captains that regrets were for women, and that " those who had eaten the cockerel must eat the cock or pay the price." Having mustered a force of 19 ships and 1300 men, he hurried north to take vengeance.

Mir Hussain had selected as a base the island seaport of Diu, lying south of the Kathiawar Peninsula (in Gujarat). The fame of his first success had brought him reinforcements—300 foists from the Samuri of Calicut and some local auxiliaries commanded by the Governor of Diu, a Russian renegade who had adopted the creed of Islam and the name of Malik Aiyaz.

The two opposing fleets met on the 3rd of February 1509. Mir Hussain had berthed his ships at the mouth of the narrow channel which flows between Diu and the mainland of Gujarat : it was his purpose, as soon as the Portuguese boarders grappled them, to run close inshore where he would have the support of Malik Aiyaz's batteries, while the enemy's ships would be entangled with his own, and their crews too hotly engaged in a hand-to-hand combat to repel by gunfire the swarm of foists from Calicut. Almeida, however, had foreseen this manœuvre, and was prepared to frustrate it by anchoring his ships from the stern.

The sea-fight which was to decide whether Egypt and Portugal should rule in Indian waters began about noon, and was long and stubbornly contested. On either side the towering fore and after castles of the galleons and other great fighting-craft broke into flame from a multitude of guns—sakers and culverins, hopes and cradles, serpents and camels, falcons and black eagles : every piece had its generic title, and many were also baptized as the fancy of each gun-crew might dictate, often with the name of the master-gunner's patron saint or sweetheart.

The long-range artillery-duel was only the prelude to more deadly work at close quarters. Favoured by a stern-wind the Portuguese ships bore rapidly down on the

---

[1] Corrêa describes the scene in a passage of singular dramatic power, vol. i. p. 775.

Egyptians, until they were near enough for the Malabar longbowmen stationed amidships and in the fighting tops to open fire : few matchlocks had yet been imported from Europe. As the hostile vessels came to grips, each manœuvred for an opportunity to ram her adversary ; and where these tactics failed, grappling irons were flung and boarding-parties, armed with half-pikes and axes, leaped down from the bows and charged, some calling on Allah to smite the dogs of Christians, others shouting their invocation to St Vincent of Lisbon or St Blaise, the guardian of mariners, whose festival it was. At intervals, above the din of prayers, oaths and shrieks—of volleying guns, splintered oars and shattered hulls—the commands of the officers rang out sharply, to be repeated word for word by subordinates hidden somewhere amid clouds of sulphurous smoke or dimly revealed by the glimmer of the battle-lanterns. Down below, the surgeon and his assistants were overworked ; in the magazine-room, where tarpaulins dripping with sea-water served as fenders against flying sparks, the fire-captain dealt out gunpowder, hand-grenades and cannon-balls of cast-iron, bronze or granite. In every galley the overseer paced to and fro, distributing blows and curses among the half-naked slaves who groaned and sweated over the long sweeps to which they were manacled in pairs.

When it became evident that Mir Hussain's plan had miscarried, the foists ventured forth from the channel in the desperate hope of effecting a diversion. They were manned by warrior Nairs, who had donned all their caste-ornaments and dedicated themselves to death : but courage availed nothing against artillery, and their fragile craft were sunk in batches. Before night the carnage came to an end ; and Almeida, as Corrêa says, could bid his captains rejoice over "the good vengeance Our Lord has been pleased, of His mercy, to grant us."

Meanwhile his term as Viceroy was already ended, and his successor, Affonso de Albuquerque, was waiting in Cochin to take over the administration. Albuquerque had previously attempted to render Ormuz tributary to

King Manoel, but had been baffled by the insubordination of his officers, whose ringleader was João da Nova, the discoverer of St Helena and Ascension. In India, the mutineers formed a hostile faction against the new Governor, and urged Almeida not to yield up his authority. There ensued an elaborate wrangle, illustrating, even at this early period, the saying of Faria y Sousa that " Portuguese officials and their places were like soul and body—not to be severed without agony." At last, in November 1509, a fleet arrived from Lisbon under D. Fernando do Coutinho, the Marshal of Portugal, a kinsman and representative of King Manoel, whose word could not be gainsaid. The Marshal installed Albuquerque in office, and on the 1st of December D. Francisco de Almeida sailed for Europe.

On the voyage home, he put in at Table Bay (then known as the Agoada de Saldanha) for fresh water ; and there some of his men were injured in a skirmish with the native Hottentots. The affair seems to have been due to a mis-understanding, but the ever bellicose fidalgos vowed that it was an insult to Portuguese honour, and that the savages must be chastised. They prevailed upon Almeida to lead a punitive expedition, although he appears to have felt some misgivings : " Whither are you carrying sixty years ? " he enquired, as they helped him to disembark.

A strong force was landed, but its swords and pikes were useless against the assegais of fire-hardened wood which could kill at long range. Having decoyed the white men inland, the Hottentots prevented a retreat by whistling their cattle to rush in between the boats and those who vainly attempted to fly. Sixty-five Portuguese were slaughtered in this inglorious affray, and among them was D. Francisco de Almeida.

CHAPTER XII

A FFONSO DE ALBUQUERQUE could claim kinship with the royal houses of Portugal and Castile. His surname and ancestral estates were originally acquired through the marriage of D. Theresa Martins, a granddaughter of Sancho III. of Castile, to D. Affonso Sanches, natural son of the Portuguese King Diniz the Farmer and of his Spanish mistress, D. Aldonsa de Sousa. Theresa had brought large estates to her husband, among them being the castle and manor of Albuquerque—or more correctly Alboquerque [1]—near Badajoz. Her descendants on both sides of the frontier had distinguished themselves in war and statecraft ; one had been Grand Master of the Knights of Santiago, another Lord High Admiral of Portugal, a third Lord High Steward of Castile.

Believers in heredity will not find it hard to account for the military and administrative talents of Albuquerque. His skill in finance may similarly be an inheritance from his maternal grandmother, D. Guiomar de Castro. This lady solaced her widowhood by keeping a kind of aristocratic pawnshop, in which even King Affonso V. was not ashamed to pledge the royal plate (*baixella*), when he needed funds for his African enterprises.

Albuquerque's early training is described in sonorous language by Diogo Barbosa Machado :—

" D. Affonso de Albuquerque, surnamed the Great, by reason of the heroic deeds wherewith he filled Europe with admiration, and Asia with fear and trembling, was born in the year 1453, in the Estate called, for the loveliness of its situation, the Paradise of the Town of Alhandra, six leagues distant from Lisbon. He was the second son

---

[1] This was the spelling invariably adopted by Albuquerque himself.

of Gonçalo de Albuquerque, Lord of Villaverde, and of D. Lenor de Menezes, daughter of D. Alvaro Gonçalves de Athayde, Count of Atouguia, and of his wife D. Guiomar de Castro, and corrected this injustice of nature [1] by climbing to the summit of every virtue, both political and moral. He was educated in the Palace of the King D. Affonso V., in whose palæstra he strove emulously to become the rival of that African Mars." [2]

It cannot be said that his efforts brought him early fame. He was page to Affonso V. and equerry to John II. ; he fought against the Moors in Africa and the Turks in the Mediterranean ; after 1503 he saw much service in the East. But his most ambitious venture, at Ormuz, was frustrated by the disloyalty of his captains, and he had as yet given no clear proof of his genius when he became Governor of India in December 1509.

Nor was he at once invested with sovereign power. The Marshal of Portugal ranked above him in India proper ; Duarte de Lemos had been sent to cruise off Arabia, with an independent roving commission ; Diogo Lopes de Sequeira was in supreme command at Malacca. But fortune removed these competitors one by one.

The Marshal insisted on obeying King Manoel's orders to assail Calicut, though his forces were absurdly inadequate and Albuquerque besought him to await a better opportunity. He vowed that he was ashamed to cross swords with a rabble of half-naked niggers, and that he would take the Samuri's palace with no weapon but a cane in his hand. The boast was so far fulfilled that the Portuguese were allowed to reach the palace, which they stormed and sacked. Then the Samuri's Nair soldiers closed in on the disorganized looters ; the Marshal and many of his men were shot down in a narrow passage through which they strove to escape. Albuquerque, whose foresight in leaving a strong rearguard to hold the landing-place alone enabled the survivors to reach their ships, was himself carried out of action, severely wounded. But he was now supreme

[1] *i.e.* the fact that he was only a younger son.
[2] *Bibliotheca Lusitana*, vol. i. p. 22, quoted in *Commentaries*, vol. i. pp. xxxvii-xxxviii.

in India proper, and could add the Marshal's fleet to his own.

The defeat at Calicut took place on the 3rd of January 1510. Before the month ended Sequeira had sailed for Europe, after a narrow escape from disaster. The inhabitants of Malacca, being mostly Muhammadans, and so having cause to hate the Portuguese, conspired to rise at a given signal and to massacre their unwelcome guests. According to one version of the affair, a native woman swam out to the ships to warn her Portuguese lover of the plot. According to another, Sequeira was seated on deck, busy with a game of chess, when his pilot, the famous Magellan (Fernão Magalhães) called his attention to a picturesque group of Malays who were watching the players. One of them had already unsheathed his kris ; another was explaining in dumb show that the hour of vengeance had not yet come.

Sequeira thus learned that the climate of Malacca was unwholesome for Portuguese admirals. Having completed the lading of his ships he steered for India, where he learned that Almeida had been succeeded by Albuquerque. This decided him to return to Europe. He had left behind in Malacca an agent named Ruy de Araujo and a staff of clerks, whose subsequent adventures were exciting but uncomfortable.

Later in the year, Duarte de Lemos grew weary of the Arabian coast, where the weather was sultry and prize-money scarce. He too shaped a course for Europe, leaving the chief part of his squadron to Albuquerque, who was now rid of all his rivals.

The details of Albuquerque's policy will be discussed later. In this chapter and the next, which will deal mainly with his military achievements, it is only necessary to point out the strategic and commercial motives underlying his fourfold scheme for the conquest of Goa, Malacca, Aden, and Ormuz. He desired to occupy Goa as a naval base and a colony ; Malacca, because it was the head-quarters of maritime commerce between the Far and Middle East ; Aden and Ormuz, because they commanded the entrance to the Red Sea and the Persian Gulf.   The possession of Goa meant for Portugal the final step from mere command of the sea to territorial empire in the Orient. The control of Malacca, Aden and Ormuz meant complete commercial ascendancy in the Indian Ocean and the Arabian Sea, so long as Portugal also maintained her naval supremacy in those waters and her monopoly of the Cape route to Europe.

These were the objects which Albuquerque set himself to achieve, and his first undertaking was the seizure of Goa.

Originally a Hindu seaport, Goa had been conquered by the Musalmans in 1469, and had become, after Calicut, their principal seaport in Western India.   It was built upon the island of Tisvadi, a triangular territory sundered from the mainland by two navigable rivers—the Juari on the south and the Mandavi on the north.   These are connected by a narrow creek and discharge their waters into the Arabian Sea.   In 1510 they afforded firm anchor-hold in fifteen fathoms, at all tides and seasons.   They also constituted a formidable line of defence, for although the connecting creek could be forded at low tide, it had been stocked with crocodiles for the benefit of foemen and runaway slaves ;   and under Hindu rule these guardians of the fort had been educated on a diet of criminals and militant missionaries of Islam.

The ruler of Goa was Yusuf Adil Shah, King of Bijapur, whose career is one of the romances of Oriental history. According to Firishta, he was a son of the Ottoman Sultan Murad or Amurath II., famous as the antagonist of Scanderbeg and Hunyadi János.   When Murad died in 1451, an elder son succeeded, and hastened to secure his tenure by ordering his servants to strangle those of his kinsmen who stood too near the throne.   Yusuf, however, was smuggled over the frontier into Persia, and there educated in the Shia creed.   In his eighteenth year, impelled, as Firishta states, by a vision, he took ship for India, where he began his life of adventure as a warrior slave and ended it as a king.

Early in 1510 Albuquerque sailed from Cochin, with twenty ships of the line and some smaller craft, ostensibly

6

bound for Ormuz. At Honawar he was reinforced by a
flotilla of foists under Timoja, from whom he learned that
the internal state of the city was favourable to his attempt.
The Adil Shah was absent, and had entrusted Goa to a
garrison of 200 Turks, whose violence and insolence had
shaken the loyalty even of the Musalman townsfolk.

About the middle of February the Portuguese fleet
entered the Mandavi. The Hindus in Goa conveniently
remembered that the conquest of the city by alien sea-
rovers had been foretold by an inspired *yogi*. They remained passive, and the Muhammadans, having neither
time nor heart to concert measures of defence, surrendered
almost before an arrow had been fired. Seated on a gaily
caparisoned charger, Albuquerque gave audience to eight
of the leading citizens, who knelt before him and handed
over the keys of Goa. Then, preceded by his chaplains
bearing a gilt cross, he marched to the Adil Shah's palace,
while the fickle Hindus acclaimed him as their deliverer
from the yoke of Islam, and strewed filigree flowers of gold
and silver in his path.

Albuquerque's triumph was short lived. The Musalmans
soon sighed for an orthodox tyrant, and bitterly resented
the fate of a zealous *kazi*, who, having assassinated one of
his flock to save him from a lapse into Christianity, had
therefore, as Firishta expresses it, been compelled to " quaff
the sherbet of martyrdom."

In May the Adil Shah came to their rescue, with 60,000
men. On a starless night of tropical rain, his troops forced
the passage of the creek, and rushed the batteries which
had been posted to command the ford. They were at once
joined by the Musalman malcontents within the walls,
and thus Albuquerque's position became untenable. After
a week of desperate resistance, he gave orders for a massacre.
The richest ' Moors ' were seized as hostages, the fairest
women as wives for the soldiers ; a few children were
reserved for baptism and slavery. The remainder were
slaughtered without mercy to age or sex. Then, on the
23rd of May, the Portuguese struggled back to their ships.

The monsoon prevented Albuquerque from putting to

sea, and he could do little but anchor his ships in the Mandavi, return the fire of the Adil Shah's batteries, in which his own lost guns had been mounted, and await a change of weather. As week followed week, his stores began to run short or to turn sour in the damp and brooding heat; and his men, worn by fasting, fighting, and watching, were glad to eke out their meagre daily ration of four ounces of biscuit with rats and offal. The Adil Shah sent over a boatload of victuals under a flag of truce, declaring that he wished to conquer by force rather than famine, but Albuquerque suspected that his real aim was to discover how the Portuguese fared; and when the Musalman envoys came aboard, they were shown a mock banquet at which all the wine and other delicacies reserved for the sick were displayed, while hungry sailors and soldiers crowded eagerly round the dishes they were forbidden to taste.

If this anecdote is true, it must have been later, and in even direr straits, that Albuquerque bartered some of his hostages for food.

He may well have rejoiced to be rid of an encumbrance which had nearly caused a mutiny. The captive women had been quartered in the flagship, to be beyond reach of enterprising gallants. There one Ruy Dias, who had swum over from his own vessel by night, was detected in an intrigue and sentenced to be hanged. So severe a verdict on a man of good family created an uproar. Excited captains rowed from ship to ship, shouting " murder," and one bold warrior gave Dias a reprieve by cutting through the hangman's rope. But Albuquerque was bound to maintain discipline, at a time when the banks of the river were lined with Portuguese renegades, who openly incited their former messmates to desert. " Here is my authority," he exclaimed, touching his scabbard, when the mutineers clamoured to know by what warrant he had acted. The ringleaders were put in irons and Dias duly hanged.

At last, early in August, the turn of the monsoon enabled Albuquerque to steer seaward once more. Beaten but undiscouraged, he had already made up his mind to return as soon as he could organize a sufficient force. Near

Anjadiva he sighted the advance guard of a fleet of fourteen vessels newly arrived from Portugal. Some were merchant-men, commissioned to load spices for the King, who would not allow them to be used for other business.[1] The remainder, two squadrons bound respectively for Malacca and the Red Sea, were taken over by Albuquerque, despite the protests of their commanders, Diogo Mendes de Vasconcellos and João Serrão. By the 3rd of October, Albuquerque had mustered 28 ships and 1700 Portuguese soldiers, and at Honawar he was reinforced by a large body of Hindu troops provided by Timoja. This formidable expedition reached Goa on the 24th of November 1510.

The King of Bijapur had just died,[2] bequeathing his crown to an infant son, Ismail Adil Shah, whose army had been withdrawn from the coast ; and the island of Tisvadi was garrisoned by 8000 Persian and Ottoman mercenaries, under Ras ul-Khan.

On St Catherine's Day, the 25th of November, Albuquerque disembarked his soldiers and led them against the arsenal —a stockaded enclosure between the Mandavi and the city walls, approached from Goa by a gate so narrow that a routed force could hardly escape in time to avoid destruction. After overcoming a stubborn resistance and breaking through the stockade, the besiegers penned up a large number of Ras ul-Khan's men in the enclosure, and cut them to pieces. Then, scaling the city walls, they planted their standards on the battlements, and charged down into the streets, shouting for Portugal and St Catherine. Hundreds of the Muhammadans were killed in battle or drowned in attempting to cross to the mainland, where Hindus and marauding hillmen from the Ghats rounded up the remaining fugitives.[3]

Albuquerque had watched the fight from a neighbouring hillock. He now descended to take part in a solemn service

---

[1] *Cartas*, p. 189.

[2] The Portuguese historians give an earlier date for his death ; but on this point the authority of Firishta seems decisive.

[3] Firishta (vol. iii. p. 34) and the *Tahafut* (p. 135) attribute the Portuguese success to an act of treachery by Ras ul-Khan, but this is very mprobable.

of thanksgiving; after which he commanded his men to sack the city and to complete the former massacre by slaying every Muhammadan left in it, sparing neither women nor children. Corrêa has described the three days of rapine and torture which followed.[1] When the soldiers had sated their lust for vengeance, Albuquerque could rest assured that the Muhammadan citizens of Goa were no longer formidable.

He determined to forestall any further attempt at recapture by strengthening the battered ramparts of the city, adding towers to the gateways and rebuilding the citadel. He gave orders that a stone should be set conspicuously in the wall, inscribed with his own name and those of all the captains who had helped to take Goa. But as each hero clamoured for the first place on the list, Albuquerque bade the masons fix the stone face inwards, and engrave on it the text *Lapidem quem reprobaverunt ædificantes*, " The stone which the builders rejected." [2]

Meanwhile Diogo Mendes de Vasconcellos had grown restive. He had lent his ships for the reconquest of Goa on the understanding that his own expedition to Malacca should be undertaken immediately afterwards, with assistance from the Indian navy. But as Albuquerque evidently intended to keep the borrowed vessels, Diogo Mendes absconded, purposing to return to Lisbon and lay his grievances before King Manoel. Albuquerque promptly gave chase and overhauled the fugitives, using his artillery to force a surrender. After two pilots had been hanged for desertion, Mendes and his runaway officers were shipped off home under arrest, although, as the commanders of an independent fleet, they were not legally subject to Albuquerque's jurisdiction. The Governor excused himself to the King by claiming that the retention of Mendes' ships could not safely be avoided.[3]

As Goa was now considered secure, Albuquerque made

[1] Corrêa, vol. ii. pp. 154-155.
[2] The *Commentaries* (vol. iii. p. 137) differ from Barros (*Dec*. II. Bk V., chap. xi. p. 558) and Corrêa (vol. ii. p. 157) in stating that this incident took place at Malacca.
[3] *Cartas*, pp. 59-63.

ready for a voyage to Malacca, and set sail on the 20th of April 1511. Touching at Pedir and Pasai in Sumatra, he picked up some of the men left behind by Diogo Lopes de Sequeira. They and their chief Ruy de Araujo had been imprisoned by the Muhammadan Sultan of Malacca, who vainly endeavoured to convert them by torture to his own faith. Some of the survivors had been befriended by a Hindu named Ninachetty, through whose good offices they had escaped to Sumatra ; but the rest, with Araujo himself, remained in captivity. Albuquerque anchored off Malacca on the first of July and at once demanded their release, threatening reprisals if it were denied. He was encouraged in this attitude by a brave letter from Araujo, who warned him not to hesitate for fear of what might befall the Christian prisoners, but to act forthwith.

The most vulnerable part of Malacca was its water-frontage. A tract of malarial swamp and tiger-haunted jungle stretched far inland behind the town, which lay outspread along the low sea-shore. Its houses, timber-built and thatched with palm-fronds, were encircled by roomy compounds and set widely apart in streets as broad as the squares of a European city, so as to minimize the danger from fire. Goats and cattle browsed in the inter-spaces, often under the shade of date or coco-nut groves, which gave Malacca a rural appearance in odd contrast with the mercantile activity of its quays and bazaars. It resembled a vast village given up to a perennial fair.

The vessels in port came from many nations : there were foists, galleys and almadias, Malay praus, Chinese junks, Mopla dhows from Malabar ; and among the business quarters this diversity of rig and build had its counterpart in a like diversity of race and language. The bulk of the native inhabitants were Muhammadan Malays, but large foreign colonies had also been established—Chinese, Javanese, Gujaratis, Bengalis—each domiciled in a separate purlieu under its own headman. Other aliens were the Burmans from Pegu and Chittagong, the Ceylon cinnamon-dealers and the Japanese from the Riu-Kiu archipelago. A seaport

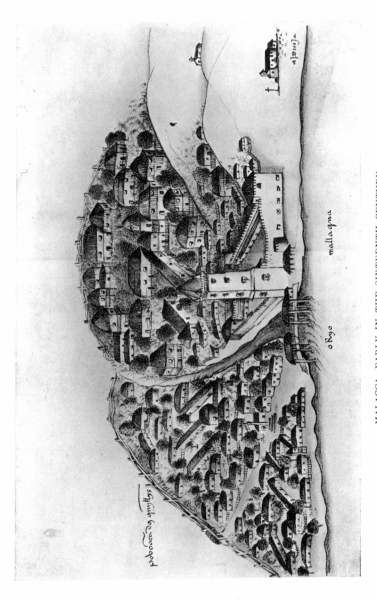

MALACCA, EARLY IN THE SIXTEENTH CENTURY

AFTER CORRÊA

so frequented could not but possess a trade of immense volume and variety. Was not Malacca the central market of Ptolemy's Aurea Chersonesus, perhaps even the more ancient Ophir of Hiram and Solomon ? [1]

As the Sultan refused to surrender his captives unless a treaty of peace were previously signed, Albuquerque sent boats to fire the waterside houses and the Muhammadan vessels in port. This vigorous action so far succeeded that Araujo and his comrades were at once liberated, and Albuquerque was emboldened to press for a grant of land, on which he might build a fortified factory. The Sultan, however, was naturally unwilling to see a Portuguese stronghold established in his own capital, and contrived to prolong the negotiations for three weeks. Albuquerque then resolved to force an immediate issue.

A navigable waterway bisected the town and carried the drainage from the marshes away to sea. It was spanned by a single bridge, upon which Albuquerque was advised by Ruy de Araujo to concentrate his attack. He had only 600 Portuguese troops, with a small reserve of native auxiliaries and slaves, while Malacca was strongly held by 30,000 fighting-men who possessed some artillery. Nevertheless, on the 25th of July 1511 the Portuguese stormed the bridge, and held it for some hours, until they were compelled to retreat by volleys of poisoned darts and arrows. During the next few days Albuquerque secured the cooperation of some Chinese traders, and entered into negotiations with Utemuta Raja, the headman of the Javanese settlers, who thenceforward took no part in the struggle until the end, when they joined the invaders. This was an important gain, for the Javanese were noted warriors, expert in handling kris and blowpipe.

On the 8th of August the bridge was retaken, but on this occasion the Portuguese had brought, in a hired junk, the materials for rigging up a temporary shelter against the hail of poisoned missiles. This was formed by stretching

---

[1] For the identification of Malacca with Ophir and of Galle in Ceylon with Tarshish, see *Ceylon*, vol. ii. pp. 100-103. The case here made out seems a strong one. For a rival theory, see above, p. 46.

sheets of canvas across a framework of scaffolding fixed upright in barrels of earth. It proved quite effective, enabling the Portuguese to establish themselves on the bridge, where they could move on interior lines without fear of having their communications cut, so long as their boats kept the waterway open. Step by step they forced their way inward, until, after nine nights of bombardment and as many days of street fighting—in which the sultan's elephant-corps played a part more conspicuous than useful —Malacca had fallen and its ruler had fled.

Albuquerque had at once set to work to build a fort and a factory. He expelled all the Malay inhabitants, appointed Ninachetty headman of the Hindus, and arranged for all the other communities to live as before, except that a Portuguese Captain took the place of the Malay Sultan as representative of sovereignty. Utemuta Raja desired to rule over the Javanese ; and as his aid had been of the utmost value, his request might have been granted, had not Ruy de Araujo and the other liberated captives accused him of having instigated the plot against Sequeira in 1509, and of intending to grasp the supreme authority in Malacca after Albuquerque's departure. How far these charges were proven it is impossible to ascertain ; but when Utemuta Raja, his son, son-in-law, and grandson were arrested and tried before the Auditor (*Ouvidor*) of Portuguese India, all were found guilty and executed.

Having arranged for the government of his new dependency, Albuquerque returned to India, reaching Cochin in February 1512. Here he learned that the armies of Ismail Adil Shah were encamped before the walls of Goa. After the outbreak of hostilities, the Shah's Turkish general, Fulad Khan, had been ordered to resign his command in favour of Albuquerque's former antagonist, Ras ul-Khan, but had shown no eagerness to obey. Thereupon Ras ul-Khan calmly appealed to the Portuguese Captain of Goa for assistance in enforcing his claims, and the brilliant audacity of this request was justified in the issue ; for with the aid of that power which he was commissioned to destroy, Ras ul-Khan made himself master of the Bijapur forces.

He then turned upon the allies he had duped, and demanded the surrender of Goa in Ismail's name.[1]

The siege was far advanced when Albuquerque's fleet arrived, on the 8th of November 1512. A strong fort had been built by the Muhammadans at Benasterim, to protect the ford across the connecting creek, and piles had been driven into the mud on each side of the crossing, so as to form submerged stockades, serving much the same purpose as the booms used in modern harbour-defence. Seeing that the Benasterim fort guarded the only line of retreat which his superior naval strength left open to the enemy, Albuquerque determined to seize it at all hazards. Leaving in Goa every man except those required to navigate his ships and serve the guns, he sailed up the river and anchored just within range of the fort. As his men grew seasoned to working under an incessant cannonade, he gradually manœuvred his ships closer and closer to the walls. One vessel caught fire and was abandoned until Albuquerque boarded her and, standing alone on deck, shamed the crew back to duty. After eight days of bombardment, the ships bristled with arrows from maintop to waterline, and were so riddled with stone shot that it was necessary to shore them up with timber staddles lest they should sink. But the guns of the fort were now silent, and the pile-stockades had been grappled and wrenched away. Meanwhile a sortie by the reinforced garrison of Goa drove the besiegers back into the fort, and although an attempt to carry the walls by escalade was repulsed with heavy loss, the Musalmans were now entrapped between Albuquerque's land and sea forces.[2]

As it would have been dangerous to weaken the Portuguese army by a fight to a finish, the beaten remnant of Ras ul-Khan's men was permitted to escape across the ford. But Albuquerque first required the surrender of certain Portuguese deserters, promising to spare their lives. The letter of this promise was not violated, but

---

[1] Some comments by Albuquerque will be found in *Cartas*, pp. 42-43.

[2] Albuquerque's detailed account of the operations at Benasterim is of great interest: *Cartas*, pp. 100-116.

the noses, ears, right hands, and left thumbs of the renegades were cut off, and all their hair plucked out, in order,
as Albuquerque wrote to King Manoel, that others might
" take warning when they remembered the treason and
evil wrought by these men." [1]

[1] *Cartas*, p. 116.

CHAPTER XIII

ALBUQUERQUE'S work was half done, now that Portugal was supreme in Goa and Malacca. It remained for him to extend that supremacy to the Straits of Bab el-Mandeb and the Persian Gulf. He sailed for Aden in February 1513, taking 1700 Portuguese and 1000 native troops in 24 ships.

On the 25th of March, the lofty crag of Aden came in view—a mass of sunburnt lava, connected with the mainland only by a narrow strip of sand. The eastern face of the crag was cloven from top to bottom by a deep fissure, probably the crater of an extinct volcano, which enclosed the city and its haven. For a fortress the site was nearly perfect ; its only natural disadvantages, the torrid climate, barren soil and scarcity of water, had been mitigated by the construction of a splendid system of reservoirs. As the Portuguese came nearer, they saw the city girt by a high wall, which abutted on the beach. In the background, the rim of the crater rose in a series of jagged peaks, each surmounted by a tower.

A brief parley showed that Mir Amrjan, the Governor, was unprepared to surrender, and Albuquerque determined to attack on the following day. His men passed the night in making their wills, and at sunrise, after they had confessed and received absolution, they launched their boats, taking a supply of scaling-ladders which had been specially constructed to bear four, and in some cases six men abreast. The harbour proved so shallow that it was necessary to wade ashore, and on landing, the matchlock-men found their powder soaked. As their comrades had left their spears behind, dreading the encumbrance of

91

weapons so unwieldy in an escalade, the whole force was dangerously underarmed.

Albuquerque's nephew D. Garcia de Noronha was directed to assail a gateway on the right, while two other storming-parties, under João Fidalgo and Albuquerque himself, tried at different points to scale the wall which fronted the beach. It had been prophesied by a Musalman *wali* that Aden would be captured through the gateway on the right, which had therefore been bricked up. Here, however, Noronha's men planted their scaling-ladders. A soldier named Garcia de Sousa and his mulatto servant were the first to set foot on the battlements, shouting " Victory, victory ! Portugal ! Portugal ! " João Fidalgo's detachment also reached the top of the wall, and Albuquerque's men, finding their own ladders too short, rushed over to join them. This led to disaster, for the ladders gave way beneath masses of men in armour, all struggling to be in front. By Albuquerque's orders, an attempt was made to prop the ladders up with halberds, but this device only caused further casualties, as the men who fell either were impaled, or crushed the halberdiers standing at the foot of the wall.

D. Garcia de Noronha forced open an embrasure, and a body of soldiers rushed in headlong ; but all were repulsed or killed by masses of flaming straw. Even to retreat was now hazardous, but many were glad to jump from the wall at the cost of broken bones, while others slid down an improvised rope-ladder. Garcia de Sousa and his mulatto comrade were left alone in a turret, where no reinforcement could reach them. Albuquerque appealed to them to seek safety as he and his fidalgos had done, but Garcia de Sousa merely turned to the mulatto and said " Save yourself. I shall die here. God would never have it that I should go down except by the same way I came up. Take this buckler to the King, to show how I met my end here in his service." Then he turned to finish his last fight, still seconded by the mulatto, who refused to save himself until his master had fallen with an arrow through his brain.

The Portuguese dropped back in disorder to their boats ;

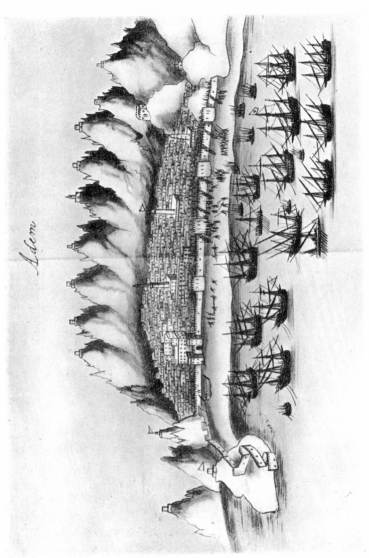

ADEN IN THE YEAR 1512

AFTER CORRÉA

and although an outlying fort was taken while a council of war was discussing whether it should be attacked, they had no reason for lingering at Aden. The fleet made Kamaran Island without misadventure, and proceeded towards Jidda ; but calms and unfavourable winds compelled it to put back again. To reach India so late in the season was impossible ; so the ships were careened and overhauled. There was nothing on Kamaran Island except a few farms and fishermen's huts ; and as the Portuguese stayed from mid-May to mid-July, they were overtaken by famine. Even the roots of palm-trees were grubbed up for food, and a diet consisting mainly of shellfish, combined with want of fresh water and hard work in the full fervour of a Red Sea summer, soon thinned the ranks. When the ships headed for India once more, on the 15th of July, 500 Portuguese and nearly all the native auxiliaries had succumbed. Though valuable information had been acquired, and many captured fishermen had been mutilated for the greater glory of Christendom in general and Portugal in particular, Aden was still inviolate, Jidda unapproached, the Red Sea open.

From September 1513 to February 1515 Albuquerque remained in India, remodelling the administration and setting in order the various forts and factories on the Malabar coast.[1] But at the end of this period lack of funds sent him forth on an enterprise which he had long wished to undertake, the capture of Ormuz. He sailed on the 21st of February 1515, with 27 ships and 3000 men, of whom 1500 were Portuguese and 600 Malabar archers.

Ormuz, which commanded the entrance to the Persian Gulf, was built on a triangular plain, forming the northern half of the island of Jerun. To the south rose a tumultuous range of hills, composed partly of rock-salt and sulphur, fantastic in outline, vivid in colour, and topped by white peaks which glittered like snow mountains in the sun.

The opulence of the city was renowned in all the East.

---

[1] It was during this time that the Samuri permitted the Portuguese to build a fort in Calicut : a striking testimony to the fear inspired by Albuquerque.

Abd ur-Razzak,[1] envoy from Shah Rukh to the Sultan of Vijayanagar, declares that even the distant states of China, Pegu and Siam sent their wares to Ormuz for distribution ; and the Russian traveller Athanasius Nikitin [2] calls the city " a vast emporium of all the world." In Albuquerque's day an Arabic proverb said : " The earth is a ring, and Ormuz the jewel set in it." Swarthy Egyptians and Persians haggled in its bazaars with fur-dealers from the steppes of Muscovy, with Arab horse-copers, silk-vendors from Bagdad and slant-eyed Mongols from Central Asia. The export trade in horses alone brought in an almost fabulous sum, as the Indian demand for cavalry-mounts could never be met in full.[3]

Albuquerque reached Ormuz in March 1515 and found it a hotbed of dynastic intrigue. Saif ud-Din, the former King, had been poisoned by a powerful Wazir, Rais Nur ud-Din, who followed up this diplomatic triumph by giving the royal title to Saif ud-Din's brother Turan [4] Shah. Nur ud-Din had been the actual ruler of Ormuz until, growing old and gouty, he invited his own nephew Rais Ahmad to share in the toils and profits of government. Rais Ahmad showed his gratitude by promptly dismissing his uncle from office and placing him under arrest. He enjoyed the confidence of Ismail Shah of Persia, one of the strongest of Oriental sovereigns, whose ambassador, Ibrahim Beg, was in Ormuz when Albuquerque arrived. To secure Persian support, the King had been persuaded to accept what the *Commentaries* call Ismail's " cap and prayer," *i.e.* Persian suzerainty and the Shia creed.

The only other personages with whom it might have been necessary for Albuquerque to reckon were the " fifteen blind kings," princes of the blood-royal, who had paid the

---

[1] R. H. Major, *India in the Fifteenth Century*, London, Hakluyt Society, 1857, pp. 5-6 (of Abd ur-Razzak's narrative).

[2] *Op. cit.* p. 19 (of Nikitin's narrative).

[3] *Cartas*, pp. 374-375.

[4] This appears to be the correct transliteration of the name given by Corrêa (vol. ii. p. 420) as Turuxa, by the *Commentaries* (vol. iv. p. 109) as Terunxa, and by Couto (*Dec.* V. Bk. IX. chap. x.) as Torunxá. Corrêa gives his age as twenty-two, *Commentaries* as eighteen.

penalty for their too exalted birth. Lest they should one day aspire to the throne, a bronze bowl had been made red-hot and held before their eyes until all power of sight was shrivelled away.

On learning that a Portuguese fleet was near, Rais Ahmad had released his uncle the Wazir. Nur ud-Din had everything to gain and Turan Shah little to lose by a change of masters. Each saw in Albuquerque a possible deliverer, and Albuquerque was quite ready to listen to their grievances

The one man to be feared in Ormuz was Rais Ahmad. It was even hinted that he intended to organize a revolt and to murder Albuquerque ; but this rumour may have been coined to justify the Portuguese for a breach of faith. At all events, Albuquerque invited Rais Ahmad to be present, on the 18th of April, at a conference to which the King and the Wazir were also bidden. When the day came every Portuguese wore a dagger under his doublet, although it had been prearranged that they should go unarmed. At the appointed hour, Rais Ahmad strode in —a tall, black-bearded Persian of soldierly bearing, magnificent in his uniform and armed with mace and sword. The youthful King and his decrepit minister followed, cringing and afraid. Hardly had Rais Ahmad crossed the threshold, when the interpreter, Alexandre de Athayde, gripped him by the elbow, and hurried him forward into the audience-chamber, where Albuquerque at once began to reproach him for wearing weapons. Rais Ahmad was returning a dignified answer, when he suddenly perceived his danger and grasped at the velvet tag of Albuquerque's coat, intending either to sell his own life dear or to appeal for mercy. But before the doomed man had time to speak, the Governor turned to his own cousin Pedro de Albuquerque, with the laconic order, " Kill him " ; and immediately the bystanders, among whom was the historian Corrêa, leapt upon their victim and hacked him to death, slashing one another's hands in their zeal. A moment later they were stripping the rags of blood-stained finery from the corpse : Corrêa's share was a scarf embroidered with gold, for which he afterwards obtained twenty *xerafins* (£6, 19s. 2d.). Turan Shah, who had witnessed the assassination, screamed out that they were all being murdered ; but Athayde barred the street-door to prevent Rais Ahmad's partisans from essaying a rescue, and Albuquerque came blandly forward to congratulate the terrified monarch on the death of a traitor.

Organized resistance was no longer possible, and although the King was permitted to retain all the outward pomp of royalty, the murder of Rais Ahmad had riveted Portuguese supremacy upon Ormuz. Turan Shah could only obey the Turkish maxim, " Kiss the hand which you dare not cut off " ; and whenever he met Albuquerque on business of state the pair did actually kiss one another, with an edifying show of affection.

On the 3rd of May 1515, Albuquerque laid the foundation-stone of a Portuguese fort ; and until November all hands were kept busy, fidalgos and galley-slaves toiling shoulder to shoulder with hod and trowel. Many died of fever and hard labour under the blinding summer sky,[1] and at last Albuquerque himself was laid low by dysentery. Always a strong man, he had never taken a week's rest during the six years of his governorship ; but the strain had at last broken his health. Believing himself to be doomed, he bade his comrades farewell, and on the 8th of November set sail, hoping to reach India before he died. His ambition was still unfulfilled, for he had intended to capture Aden and afterwards, returning home to Portugal, to " lean awhile on the handle of the hoe." [2]

In the Arabian Sea, his ship overhauled a dhow bearing dispatches from India. When these were opened, Albuquerque learned that he was to be superseded by one Lopo Soares de Albergaria, and that his old rival Diogo

---

[1] So impressed was Abd ur-Razzak by the terrific heat of this region that he improvised a poem on the subject : the concluding lines are—

" In the plains the chase became a matter of perfect ease,
For the desert was filled with roasted gazelles."
                              —*India in the Fifteenth Century*, p. 10.

[2] *Commentaries*, vol. iv. p. 208.

CONCLUDING PARAGRAPH OF ALBUQUERQUE'S LAST LETTER TO D. MANOEL

FROM THE MUSEUM OF THE LISBON GEOGRAPHICAL SOCIETY

Mendes had been appointed Captain of Cochin. At this tidings,

" He lifted up his hands, and gave thanks to Our Lord, and cried : ' In bad repute with men because of the King, and in bad repute with the King because of the men. It were well that I were gone.' " [1]

Soon afterwards he dictated a last letter to King Manoel :—

" Sire, I do not write to your Highness with my own hand, because when I do so I tremble greatly, which presages death. Here, Sire, I leave this son of mine [2] to perpetuate my memory ; and to him I bequeath all my estate, which is little enough ; but I also bequeath him the obligation due to me for all my services, which is very great. As for the affairs of India, they will speak for me and for him. I leave India with the principal heads fallen into your power ; everything is settled except that it were well to lock the door of the Straits. And so I have done what your Highness charged me. Sire, I advise you always, if you would have India secure, to continue making it pay its own expenses.[3] I pray your Highness, as my reward, that you will remember all this, and make my son a nobleman, and pay him in full for my services. I put all my trust in the hands of your Highness and of your lady the Queen, to whom I commend myself, in the hope that you will prosper my affairs ; since I die serving you, and for this deserve to be recompensed. As for my pensions, which I have almost finished earning, as your Highness knows, I kiss your hands for them on my son's behalf. Written at sea on the sixth day of December 1515. " (*In Albuquerque's handwriting*) Done by your Highness' servant,
" A. D'ALBOQUERQUE."

Throughout the voyage from Ormuz, Albuquerque had longed to see Goa once more, and as his ship crossed the bar of the Mandavi he rose with a great effort, and stood propped against the doorway of his cabin, to gaze for the last time on the city. By his own desire, he was robed as a commander of the Order of Santiago, with a velvet cap and stole, spurs on his boots and a sword in his girdle. About an hour before daybreak, on Sunday the 16th of December, he died while the ship was coming to anchor.

As the sun rose over the Western Ghats, a multitude of

[1] *Commentaries*, vol. iv. p. 195.
[2] Braz, afterwards D. Affonso de Albuquerque. See Appendix A, Special Bibliography, " Albuquerque."
[3] This is the sense of the original *irdes uos tirando de despesas.*

7

boats put off to welcome him, and when the people learned that he was dead, " so great was the crying and weeping that it seemed as though the very river of Goa were being poured out." [1] The body was placed on a bier covered with a pall and a cushion of black velvet, and was borne to the church of Nossa Senhora da Serra, which Albuquerque himself had founded. Even the Musalmans shared in the common grief, and as for the Hindus—

" When they beheld his body stretched upon the bier, his long beard reaching down to his waist, and his eyes half open, they declared, after their heathen notions, that it could not be that he was dead, but that God had need of him for some war, and had therefore sent for him." [1]

He was buried in the church ; and thither, for many years afterwards, the poor and oppressed came to pray at his tomb, bringing sweet-scented flowers and oil for his lamp. Even King Manoel, who had slighted him in life, honoured him in death, and would never permit his bones to be removed to Portugal, averring that India was safe while Albuquerque was there.

[1] *Commentaries*, vol. iv. p. 198.

CHAPTER XIV

ALBUQUERQUE : THE STATESMAN

ALBUQUERQUE is described as a man of medium stature, lean but ruddy, with a massive nose and a high forehead. His left arm was partly crippled by a wound, received at Calicut in 1510. When Goa was retaken by the Musalmans he vowed never to trim his beard until he had won the city back ; and it is possible that he kept his vow beyond the stipulated hour, as at his death his snow-white beard brushed his girdle.

He was a visionary with a talent for finance ; a martinet, whose followers either hated or adored him ; a loyal Churchman, who refused to make Muhammadanism a crime ; a Portuguese Governor, who died poor. His temper was uncertain ; his laughter might in a moment blaze into anger ; but he was as ready to forgive an injury as to take vengeance. When his bitter opponent João da Nova died forsaken and a pauper, the *Commentaries* declare that

> " Affonso de Albuquerque forgot all the wrong that he had done towards himself, and only remembered that this man had been his comrade, and had aided him like a gallant knight in all the troubles connected with the conquest of the kingdom of Ormuz. And he ordered him to be buried at his own expense, with the usual display of torches, and himself accompanied the body to the grave, clad all in mourning." [1]

Braz de Albuquerque, the Governor's natural son and biographer, is an unilluminating guide to his father's character. In the *Commentaries* he tones down the irritable genius into a fidalgo cast in the conventional mould, half courtier, half crusader. He puts orations which are obviously unhistorical into his father's mouth, and bowdlerizes

[1] *Commentaries*, vol. ii. p. 49.

his correspondence. Amid the carnage at Goa he makes the Governor address Manoel de Lacerda, whose armour ran blood, in these terms : " Sir Manoel de Lacerda, I declare to you that I am greatly envious of you, and so would Alexander the Great be, were he here ; for you look more gallant for an evening's rendezvous than the Emperor Aurelian."

The *Commentaries* laud Albuquerque for the correctness of his Latinity and the elegance of his speech, declaring that he never used an oath more profane than " I abhor the life I live." But the *Cartas*—Albuquerque's own words—give a truer picture of the fiery old autocrat, whose verdicts upon men and things were homely, lucid, pungent as proverbs. Such are his portraits of the panic-stricken crew, " for ever with the pumps in their hands and the Virgin Mary in their mouths " ; or of the aggressive Malik Aiyaz, " with his leg always lifted for a kick."

He understood the uses of pageantry as a means of impressing native minds with the might of Portugal, but his own habits were simple. All the chroniclers have described him as one who lived and worked among his men, taking his full share of toil and danger. They have portrayed him at Goa, helping with his own hands to plaster up the fortifications, or splashed to the helmet with the blood of a wounded comrade ; at Calicut, leading in the thickest of a hot rearguard action, until he was borne from the field with a broken head and an arrow through the left arm ; at Ormuz, leaning on his spear to eat his dinner of curry among his men. When he was at home in Goa, he kept no porter, but left his door wide open all day, except during his short afternoon siesta. Every morning he took his stick, put on a straw hat, and rode off attended by four clerks with inkhorns and paper. As each item of business arose, it was noted by the clerks, who took down the Governor's orders and handed over the manuscript to be checked and signed. In this way lawsuits which might have dragged on for weeks, reports and memoranda which might have been pigeon-holed and forgotten, were disposed of without cost or delay.

AFFONSO DE ALBUQUERQUE

The simplicity of his daily life throws into relief the magnitude of his schemes for conquest and commerce. His projects were conceived on a Napoleonic scale, and like Napoleon he dreamed of achievements never to be compassed with the forces at his disposal.

Such was his plan to shatter the power of Islam by ranging the Shia empire of Ismail Shah against the Suni Ottomans. He hoped to induce Prester John to divert the Nile into the Red Sea, and so to starve Egypt. To King Manoel he sketched the course of a campaign designed to ruin Turkey and redeem the Holy Sepulchre. Using Massawa as a base, and reinforced by a contingent of Abyssinian cavalry, he proposed to seize Alexandria and Suez, closing the main channel by which the Turks could still approach India. From Massawa, again, he would raid Jidda, dash inland across the desert and burn Mecca to the ground.

" It is but a day's journey," he wrote to the King in 1513, " and what resistance can be offered by the Memluk garrison of twenty troopers in Jidda, perhaps twenty-five in Mecca ? The rest of the inhabitants are peaceful hermits, of whom five hundred Portuguese, or at most a thousand, could make short work. It seems to me, Sire, so trifling an affair to carry through that I look on it as already done."

Then, leaving Mecca a heap of smouldering ashes, they could press forward over the arid waste which stretched away northward—to Sinai, to Suez, to Jerusalem itself. There was nothing to bar their progress except naked, unarmed camel-drivers [1]—so it seemed to Albuquerque, ever wont to make light of difficulties and to underrate his adversary.

But in his dreams he never forgot the necessities of the hour. He was a master of laborious detail, whose interests ranged from world-policy down to the cost of fowls in Cochin. His letters deal with the instruction of clerks, the best method of polishing arms or packing goods for a voyage, the right length for oars, the most suitable material

[1] *Cartas* p. 282. *Cf.* 325 *seq.* and 395 *seq.*

for clothing and sails, the grades and prices of pepper, the devices by which cargoes of wine were tapped aboard ship, the advantages of leather cuirasses in a tropical climate, and the demerits of steel armour. His presents to the King illustrate the same versatility of interest : they included an elephant and a rhinoceros ; specimens of the coinage struck in the Malacca mint ; a chart drawn by a clever Javanese pilot ; two Abyssinians, captured on the pilgrimage to Jerusalem, and sent to Lisbon with an Arab interpreter ; a ruby from the Red Sea ; a Goanese gunsmith, who could fashion " as good matchlocks as any made in Bohemia," a Musalman from Aden, learned in the compounding of opium. King Manoel was advised to make his fortune by cultivating poppies at home and in the Azores, and exporting the product to the East ; " for," said Albuquerque, " the people of India are lost without opium to eat." [1]

This many-sided activity of mind was reflected in Albuquerque's career as a statesman. He must be studied not merely as conqueror and empire-builder, but as financier, diplomatist, administrator.

Colonial Policy.—Before he assumed office, the Portuguese had not annexed a foot of Indian soil. Albuquerque definitely committed them to a policy of territorial expansion in the East. The merchant princes of many a maritime state, from Tyre to Venice, had been led, in pursuit of sea-power and commerce, first to the establishment of factories for the exchange of goods ashore, and afterwards to the occupation of seaports and the foundation of colonies. In following these examples, Albuquerque did not reverse the aims of Almeida, but enlarged and fulfilled them. No man better understood that sea-power and commerce were the chief interests of Portugal in the East ; but he was the first to realise that an armada sent out from Lisbon could not hope to maintain those interests, nor to control the trade-routes of the Indian Ocean from a base 3000 miles away.

The Portuguese were encompassed by enemies, actual or

[1] *Cartas,* p. 174.

potential. Every orthodox Hindu was bound to regard them as unclean freebooters of no caste : every Muhammadan, as infidels and—worse still—as rival traders. But no Indian foe was so greatly to be dreaded as Turkey.

" The Turks are powerful," Albuquerque wrote, " they have much artillery, and know how to build ships like our own. They hate us, and long to destroy all we possess. They are well furnished with arquebusiers and bombardiers, with master-gunners as skilful as ours, naval architects who can rival our best work—smiths, carpenters, caulkers, as good as any we have." [1]

Before meeting an antagonist so formidable it was necessary to secure a port where ships could be built, repaired and manned ; where the sick and wounded could be tended ; where stores of every kind could be replenished. For such services the fleets could not rely on the factories, because the very existence of the factories depended on the fleets. Security of trade was impossible as long as every European on Indian soil was a foreigner, subject to the caprice of some local ruler and in peril of torture or death from the moment when the sails of King Manoel's fleet vanished below the horizon. It was quite as impossible for Portuguese diplomatists in India to command the respect which was accorded to the representatives of such states as Bijapur, Gujarat, Vijayanagar, kingdoms renowned from Java to the Red Sea for their opulence and armed strength. Portugal was far away ; the monarchs of India had heard rumours of its power, but they perceived no visible symbol of greatness save a squadron of weather-beaten ships ; and they might be pardoned if, even after the sea-fight at Diu, they mistook these for the cruisers of some pirate community, terrible in its daring and maritime science, but not overmuch to be dreaded on dry land, nor worthy the deference due to an equal. Albuquerque solved the whole problem, strategic, commercial and political, so far as it could be solved, by the seizure of Goa, which gave to Portugal a naval base, an

---

[1] *Cartas*, p. 412. The power of Egypt was already paralysed by internal dissensions.

emporium famous throughout India, and the nucleus of a colonial empire. In the hands of a wise ruler well served, Goa meant security, commerce, an assured status for Portugal among the nations of the Orient. The difference between this colony and one of the fortified factories elsewhere was akin to the difference between Hong-Kong and a British settlement in any of the Chinese treaty-ports.

" In Cochin," Albuquerque told the King, " you cannot cut a stick without asking leave of the Raja. If one of our men refuses to pay full market price in the bazaar, or touches a Musalman woman, the fort is besieged. In Cochin 500 extra men mean famine. There is no fish, no flesh, and fowls are dear. In Goa, beef, fish, bread and vegetables are plentiful, and an additional 2000 men are scarcely noticed ; in Goa there are gunsmiths, armourers, carpenters, shipwrights, everything we require." [1]

The clique of slanderers who strove to belittle every act of the Governor, and to thwart him at every turn, persuaded King Manoel that Goa was not worth the cost of occupation, and that Albuquerque only retained it to enhance his own reputation. The King wrote commanding him to submit the question of its abandonment to his council of captains, and Albuquerque obeyed ; but when the captains upheld his decision, he communicated his views to the King in plain language. " I was astonished when I received your Highness' orders, and when I saw the documents on which those orders were based I was still more astonished that you did not put the whole parcel into the fire." [2] To his influential friend D. Martinho de Castello Branco he wrote : " The King trusts you and takes your advice ; bid him hold on to Goa until the Day of Judgment."

To man his ships, forts and factories he encouraged the lower class Portuguese to marry Indian women. It was a practice less distasteful to them than to other peoples of Europe ; indeed they were already inured to the embraces of Guinea and Gold Coast beauties. The mother of Albuquerque's own son was a negress ; and mulatto children did not always justify the Senegalese proverb—" Allah made the coffee and Allah made the milk, but café au lait

[1] *Cartas*, p. 413. [2] *Cartas*, p. 260.

is a brew of Shaitan." Centuries of slave-owning have not kindled among the Portuguese that fierce loathing of coloured races which makes intermarriage with them appear a crime : witness Brazil, where the inhabitants of Portuguese origin live in amity with their negro and half-caste fellow-citizens, and lynch law has always been an expression of political rather than of racial enthusiasm.

If Corrêa[1] can be trusted, Albuquerque foresaw the gravest perils of his plan, and warned the King that all his Eurasian subjects between twelve and twenty-five years old ought to be educated in Europe. He began his experiment discreetly, by marrying off some transported criminals. Women of good class shunned this honour, some escaping by suicide, while others cut the throats of their children to save them from a preliminary baptism. Meanwhile the fidalgos asked, with pardonable asperity, what good thing could come of an alliance between a convict and a pariah. But time and the climate were on the side of the Governor, who soon began to provide husbands of a choicer brand. Captive Brahman and Muhammadan women were summarily baptized and wedded, and low-caste wives were discouraged, although they could not be altogether excluded. White wives were luxuries beyond reach of all but the wealthiest ; for their own sakes, also, Portuguese women were kept at home.

The married men were intended to become colonists instead of a mere garrison. They were persuaded to set up as handicraftsmen, retail traders, or farmers. Wherever the Portuguese established themselves on the shores of the Indian Ocean, special privileges were conferred on this class, which soon formed a distinct community, fiercely jealous for its rights. Minor municipal offices and other paid posts were reserved for the married men, and in 1518 all the Crown estates at Goa, consisting of arable land and palm-groves, were divided among them. The women who had been hustled into Christianity and matrimony were often little better than slaves. More than once their resentment bred conspiracies against the Portuguese, of

[1] Corrêa, vol. ii. p. 375.

which their own white husbands were not wholly innocent ; and both parties to the marriage contract were demoralized by the atmosphere of slavery. The men whom Albuquerque had induced to become armourers, cobblers, or tavern-keepers chewed betel and lounged all day in native costume, while slaves attended to their forges, their lasts, or their tuns of country liquor. Their sons and daughters went lower : the men drank the profits which their slaves acquired by robbery on land or sea ; the women dressed on the immoral earnings of their prettiest slave-girls. Had Albuquerque been followed by a succession of rulers like himself, these evils might have been stamped out before they matured ; as things were, the system of mixed marriages degraded its immediate victims and did little to staunch the terrible drain of men which was bleeding Portugal to death.

Commerce.—Albuquerque's commercial policy was outlined on a characteristically large scale. The slaves, ivory and gold which Portuguese merchants brought home from Africa were lucrative commodities, but not comparable with drugs and spices. The arrival of a consignment of camphor or cinnamon in any European port was the signal for a rush of wholesale buyers, eager to bid for these rare luxuries. Even in the Orient, spices were deemed a gift worthy to be offered by one prince to another ; in 1515 Albuquerque's envoys to Ismail Shah took pepper, ginger, cloves, cinnamon, sugar and cardamoms as presents from their master.

It should be noted that the chartered companies and associations of merchant adventurers which opened the trade-routes of the world to English commerce in the sixteenth and seventeenth centuries had few forerunners in Portugal. The sole right of sending merchant-ships to India was vested in the King, who could use the entire resources of the state to further his commercial interests. Licence to trade was only granted by way of pension and reward, or in return for a substantial fee, or else on a profit-sharing basis. The same system was applied to the natives of India wherever Albuquerque could enforce it.

He was urged by the King to boycott Musalman traders, but pointed out that, although he favoured Hindus and native Christians, the Muhammadans alone possessed sufficient capital to do business on a large scale, and almost monopolized the carrying-trade. He went on to explain that the commercial interests of every community were bound inextricably together. Hindu Rajas would not lightly forego the dues paid by Musalman merchants, and even the Hindu capitalists of Gujarat invariably entrusted their cargo-fleets to Musalman crews, though Gujarat was the one part of north-western India (*destes partes*) in which the leading ship-owners did not profess Islam.[1]

The fortified factories were designed to furnish cargo for the royal ships. Each factor was consul and shipping-agent in one ; but his responsibility for the sale and purchase of goods was shared with the captain of the fort, the commissary and the treasurer. Albuquerque wished to keep all trade between Portugal and India a monopoly of the Crown, to make Cochin the headquarters of all vessels plying to and from Europe, to make India the starting-point of ships intended to trade east of Cape Comorin, and to delegate the local carrying trade to licensed natives. He was ever anxious to discover new sources of profit— horses, opium, silk, pearls, coral, copper, mercury—and nothing irritated him more than the unenterprising ignorance of his factors. A *Bartolomeu*—a clerk from the office of Bartholomew the Florentine—would, says Albuquerque, outwit a dozen of these gentry, who had not brains enough to buy two pennyworth of bread in the bazaar. The truth was that the officials were untrained, and owed their position to family influence. Albuquerque founded classes for the instruction of Hindu clerks, and besought the King to send out schoolmasters, but he had neither time nor power to alter a system rooted in the social life of Portugal. The factors continued to owe their appointments to favouritism ; as a class, they remained inefficient ; and under weaker Governors they added corruption to inefficiency.

Foreign Policy.—Albuquerque's foreign policy was based

[1] *Cartas*, pp. 306-307.

on his desire for peace and commerce. He fished adroitly in the troubled waters of Oriental politics, taking full advantage of the differences between Raja and Samuri, Hindu and Musalman, Shia and Suni ; but he was fortunate in escaping conflict with any native power of the first magnitude—the Bahmani Sultanate of the Deccan having fallen to pieces, while the Mughals were still afar. Even more fortunate for him were the resistance of Vijayanagar to the Musalmans of the Deccan, which drew off a host of potential enemies, and the wars between Turkey and Persia.

The keystone of his foreign policy was, of course, a friendly neutrality towards Vijayanagar. Once Goa was secure he also tried to win the goodwill of his strongest Musalman neighbour, Ismail Adil Shah of Bijapur.[1] He sent commercial missions to Java and the Moluccas, in order to reach the headquarters of the spice-trade. Commercial reasons also dictated his embassies to Gujarat and Pegu. The seamen of Gujarat voyaged far and wide, conveying the silk and porcelain of Canton or the cloves of Ternate from Malacca, where they met the Portuguese, to Western India. Their home industries rivalled their commerce, and included the manufacture of delicate fabrics in cotton and muslin, ornaments and utensils wrought in ivory and metal, lacquered ware, and carved-work in black wood. Pegu was of equal importance ; every wanderer who strayed thither in the fifteenth and sixteenth centuries testified to its almost fabulous wealth and its formidable military resources. Either of these powers might have actively resented the appearance of the Portuguese as trade-rivals ; Albuquerque conciliated both, and secured a share in their prosperity. In 1511 he sent an embassy to Siam, which was hostile to Malacca and therefore likely to favour its captor. The envoys returned laden with rich presents for King Manoel, of which all save a ruby, a sword, and a gold cup, were lost at sea.

The ideas which governed Albuquerque's relations with Persia have already been outlined. He regarded Ismail

[1] Who must not be confounded with Ismail, Shah of Persia.

Shah as " a thunderbolt launched by the Almighty for the destruction of Islam " ; from the Pope he sought leave to furnish the Shah with cannon, and he besought the rulers of Christian states to aid Persia by an invasion of Ottoman territory. His first embassy to Persia was dispatched in 1510, but the envoy was poisoned at Ormuz. The second, in 1514, reached the Persian court, and presented the Shah, at his own request, with a life-sized portrait of Albuquerque. The third is of great historical interest, because Albuquerque's letter to the Shah, his instructions to the ambassador, and a contemporary account of the mission are extant.[1]

In 1514 war had broken out between Shah Ismail and the Ottoman Sultan Selim I. ; its causes seem to have been mainly religious, and in the letter which heralded his advance the Sultan charged Ismail with blasphemy, heresy, perjury and evil-doing of other kinds. The Shah replied that he saw no necessity for war, and attributed the unconventional phrasing of the Sultan's letter to the invention of some scribe not fully recovered from an overdose of opium. After this interchange of amenities the Sultan continued his march. He routed the Persian cavalry at Khoi, near the western frontier of Azerbaijan, captured Tabriz, and annexed the outlying provinces of Kurdistan and Diabekir. The power of Shah Ismail was crippled by this blow, but Albuquerque still hoped to utilize it. In the summer of 1515, he dispatched Fernão Gomes de Lemos as ambassador to the Persian court. " I believe," Albuquerque wrote to the Shah, " that with the immense assistance which the King my master will render you at sea, you will with very little trouble become lord of the Sultan's kingdom, of his city of Cairo, and of all his land an.' ·overeignty." The Shah does not seem to have shared this conviction. Although the envoys were laden with gifts, including six matchlocks and twenty quintals of sugar, they were coldly received ; for, as Galvão says, in Hakluyt's version—" This Xec or Shaugh Ismael went on hunting and fishing for trouts. And there be the fairest women in all the world.

[1] *Cartas*, pp. 387-394.

And so Alexander the Great affirmed, when he called them the women with golden eies." [1] It was not, however, these attractions, but the conduct of the Portuguese at Ormuz, which caused the mission to fail, and hastened the return of the envoys.

The fact that ambassadors from Gujarat, Pegu, Siam and Persia returned the visits paid by Albuquerque's representatives is witness to the new prestige acquired by the conquerors of Goa and Malacca. But the ambassador who most stirred the imagination of Europe was one Matheus, the first official representative of Prester John to reach Portuguese India. He was a Musalman from Cairo, who declared that he had been dispatched by the King of Abyssinia without previous notice, and had fallen among thieves on his voyage. He had contrived to retain his credentials, his wife and a chip of wood, said to be a fragment of the true Cross. The Portuguese suspected him of being an Egyptian spy, and some of them took advantage of the Governor's absence to maltreat the Abyssinian and his wife. Albuquerque proved to King Manoel that Matheus was in truth the accredited representative of the Prester, whom they had so long sought in alliance, but the mission bore no immediate fruit.

Finance.—On the eve of his death Albuquerque counselled the King to make India pay for its own administration. He could not raise revenue by taxing commerce with Europe ; such an impost would lessen the direct drain upon the royal exchequer, but it would proportionately diminish the trading-profits by which the exchequer was filled. It was necessary to find some source of income which would not infringe the commercial monopoly of the Crown, and now that the costly pioneer work of conquest and settlement might be deemed at an end, Albuquerque proposed to balance his budgets with the tribute wrung from vassal states, the fees exacted for safe-conducts and licences to trade, the proceeds of Crown property near Goa, and local taxation.

It is hard to estimate how far these receipts would have

[1] Galvão, p. 128.

sufficed if Albuquerque's successors had been skilled financiers. In his time Portuguese India was largely dependent on prizes taken at sea and other spoils of war ; it afterwards became dependent on remittances from Lisbon, but the expenses thus incurred by the King were far outweighed by the enormous profits of the spice-trade.

Administration.—The pressure of great affairs left Albuquerque no leisure to elaborate an administrative system in detail. One of his earliest endeavours to improve the machinery of government was an order for the registration of title-deeds. There had previously been no standard authority to which litigants could appeal in cases of disputed ownership. Like the British in later centuries, he deferred to native usage by uniting revenue and judicial functions in the same hands ; and he proposed to extend the term of official appointments from three years to eight. Brevity of tenure became one of the main sources of corruption, when the number of candidates for office so far exceeded the tale of vacant posts that few men could hope to be appointed twice in a lifetime. Salaries were low and perquisites many, so that every official was tempted to make the most of his three years, and to regard his appointment as a speculation rather than a career.

Albuquerque's handling of native affairs was as statesmanlike as the King permitted it to be. He set a precedent of incalculable importance by retaining intact the constitution and principal customs of the thirty village communities into which the island of Goa was divided, and from which its native name of Tisvadi was derived.[1] When Goa was first captured Timoja was nominated as *Thanadar* —or chief constable, magistrate and tax-collector in one : but his harshness towards the Muhammadans compelled the Governor to divide his authority, and afterwards to transfer it to a Hindu named Malhar Rao. In the sixteenth century this employment of natives for the management of their own affairs was an innovation as bold as it was wise.

---

[1] A register of these customs was published in 1526 : an abstract will be found in Whiteway, pp. 215-220. The original is printed in *Ar. Port. Or.*, Part v.

It is noteworthy that British statesmanship has in several respects adhered to the main lines of Albuquerque's policy. The servants of John Company followed the example he set by enlisting native soldiers, and appointing natives to subordinate official posts. They found, as he did, that sea-power and commerce led, step by step, to the annexation of territory and the control of neighbouring states. They, too, realized the truth which Albuquerque vainly strove to instil into his own countrymen, that their authority in India must be founded upon respect for Indian usages and tolerance of Indian creeds. But it was not until 1829 that they summoned up courage to emulate his one conspicuous breach of this rule, by abolishing the rite of *sati*, or widow-burning.

Those who would understand the magnitude of Albuquerque's achievement must take into account the obstacles which his own countrymen placed in his path. At first he was only one of three Governors ; not until Goa had fallen was he able to enforce his own will. Then he created a multitude of enemies by preferring public to private interests. A clique of disappointed fortune-hunters and placemen intrigued against him with surprising diligence. So notorious was their success that at last the Persian ambassador Ibrahim Beg invited Albuquerque to enter the service of Shah Ismail, where his worth would be better appreciated. The malcontents easily sowed suspicion in King Manoel's mind. Instead of thanks and support, the Governor received little from his sovereign except mistrust and opposition. His plans were countermanded and his advice neglected. Naval reinforcements were withheld until his worm-eaten vessels could hardly keep afloat ; his soldiers were equipped with lances too blunt to draw blood, and cuirasses which had made a banquet for rats. The King hinted that Goa was not worth taking and might well be abandoned. He loaded Albuquerque with absurd commissions, probably designed to conciliate certain clerical bigots in Spain and Rome. The Governor was even instructed to convert the Raja of Cochin to Christianity. He knew, of course, that success in this enterprise would stir up a mortal feud between the Raja and his Hindu subjects, but obeyed, and reported the result of his endeavours in language worthy of so expert a diplomatist. He said, in effect, that the Raja was deeply impressed with the importance of the King's proposal, and feeling that so momentous an issue deserved long and careful thought, had decided for the future to give it his most earnest consideration.[1]

Albuquerque was fifty-six when he became Governor; and most of his contemporaries had finished the active work of their lives. Until then his latent genius had lacked room to expand. " Portugal is a small country," he answered a little before his death, when his friends tried to console him for his supersession, with pictures of the honour and employment which awaited him at home. " Can Portugal offer me any task equal to one-sixth of what the Governor of India has to do ? " Placed in authority, he crowded the work of a strenuous lifetime into six years. With a small and ill-found fleet he maintained the naval supremacy of Portugal and controlled the trade-routes of the Indian Ocean. He drilled an insubordinate mob into an army, and used it to found a colonial empire. By sheer force of character he overawed those of his followers who were disaffected, and inspired the rest with his own heroic spirit of self-sacrifice. Among the early Portuguese rulers of India he alone had a real grasp of the financial and commercial side of government; he alone tried to do justice to all subject races and creeds in time of peace, however ruthless he might be in war. He was at home in the labyrinth of Oriental diplomacy, and could penetrate the veil by which the subtle processes of Oriental thought are shrouded from Western eyes. Above all he had the gift of leadership: sovereignty seemed his birthright.

It would be absurd to claim that the man who took advantage of a quibble to torture the prisoners surrendered at Goa, cut off the limbs of defenceless fishermen in the Red Sea and planned the murder of Rais Ahmad, was the type of a chivalrous hero. He belonged to a world still savage in spite of the prevalent zeal for knowledge and

[1] *Cartas*, pp. 367-369.

beauty—still pagan under the forms of Christianity. Rare spirits here and there, men of the calibre of Las Casas and Osorio, might rise to a saner and kinder humanity ; but they were unrepresentative, and such cruelties as Albuquerque committed in war-time offended against no widely-accepted code of morals. The worst that can be said of him, from a historian's point of view, is that he never shook himself free from the inhumanity of his age. This apart, there is no more illustrious name than his in all the long and splendid annals of European rule in India.

CHAPTER XV

PAINTERS and chroniclers have drawn a lifelike but hardly an attractive portrait of King Manoel, the master whom Albuquerque served so well. An inscrutable, almost sullen face, lit by greenish eyes ; dark brown hair ; tall, meagre frame with every sinew toughened by exercise ; ape-like arms so long that, when he stood upright and let them hang, his fingers extended below his knees—it is the portrait of a man whose most salient characteristic was an iron strength of mind and body.

His accession in 1495 was brought about by a series of accidents. In 1484 he witnessed the assassination of his elder brother, Ferdinand Duke of Vizeu, who was summoned to the palace on a charge of conspiracy and there stabbed to the heart by his cousin King John II. Manoel, who thus became heir-presumptive,[1] was made Duke of Beja and Grand Master of the Knights of Christ, perhaps as a reward for his acquiescence in the murder. But he was still far from the throne, which would naturally pass to Prince Affonso, only legitimate son of the reigning monarch ; and his chance of succession was diminished when, in 1490, Prince Affonso married Isabella, eldest daughter of the Catholic sovereigns, Ferdinand King of Aragon and Isabella Queen of Castile.

This match was intended not only to secure the crown of Portugal for the direct descendants of John II., but also to fuse together all the kingdoms of the Iberian Peninsula. Castile and Aragon had already been united by the marriage of the Catholic sovereigns, who were shortly to

---

[1] Failing an heir in the direct line of primogeniture, he would inherit as the grandson of King Edward (1433-1438).

bring all Spain beneath their rule by the conquest of Granada from the Moors. If an heir were born to Prince Affonso and Princess Isabella, he would inherit Portugal as well as Spain, and the union of Iberia would come to pass without wounding the pride of either nation.

The marriage was celebrated at Evora with unprecedented pomp, the wedding banquet being graced by the presence of two fat oxen with gilded horns and hooves. They had been roasted whole, but were nevertheless yoked in the most lifelike manner to a gaily decorated waggon laden with similarly cooked and gilded carcases. A high-born fidalgo posed as driver of the equipage, which was dragged round the banqueting hall on a wheeled platform, amid raptures of applause. After this " culinary idyll," as Oliveira Martins calls it, the revels were prolonged far into the night : and for years men talked of the amazing pageant in which a mimic navy was towed by some invisible mechanism over a sea of painted canvas. The flagship had sails of white and rose taffeta, rigging of silk and gold, gilded anchors, a living crew and real bombards on board : never had such splendours been witnessed in Portugal.

But the high hopes which had inspired the festival were soon disappointed, for in 1491 Affonso was killed by a fall from his horse, and Isabella was left childless and disconsolate. John II. would gladly have bequeathed the kingdom to his own natural son D. Jorge, but law and popular sentiment opposed him, and when he died in 1495 Manoel reigned in his stead.

The new King adhered to the policy of Iberian union, which soon became the master-passion of his life. He was playing for higher stakes than his predecessor, since the ruler of Spain and Portugal would also be lord over the Spanish dominions in America and the Portuguese empire in Asia and Africa. The first step towards the fulfilment of this ambition was taken when Manoel gained the consent of the Catholic sovereigns to his marriage with the widowed Princess Isabella. The match was by no means an affair of the heart. Manoel can hardly have found the Princess attractive, for he was a man of the world and a sportsman,

KING MANOEL THE FORTUNATE

FROM A SIXTEENTH CENTURY PAINTING IN THE CASA PIA, BELEM

who loved hunting and sailing, tournaments, dances, horse-races and banquets; while she, ever since the death of her husband, had led a life of conventual strictness, fasting and practising the severest forms of penance until, in Peter Martyr's phrase, she had become "drier than a withered stock"—*sicco stipite siccior*,—and had ruined her health as well as her comeliness.[1]

The fanatical Princess only agreed to the marriage on condition that Portugal should first be purged of its Jewish inhabitants. The terms were accepted and thousands of innocent victims were exiled, forcibly baptized or murdered.[2] Manoel was no bigot, though he loved the music and cere-monial of Church festivals, and was devout in his observance of fasts and holydays. He employed Jewish physicians and astrologers; he reprimanded Almeida for prohibiting the sale of the Hebrew scriptures at a large profit in Malabar; and when anti-Jewish riots took place without his authority, he gave short shrift to the leaders of the agitation, albeit they wore the habit of St Dominic. But he was willing to pay almost any price for the Crown of Spain, and it is improbable that the sufferings of the Jews ever caused him a moment's regret, save in so far as his purse was affected by the ruin of a useful class of taxpayers.

The marriage took place in 1497, and within a few months Isabella became sole heiress of the Catholic sovereigns, her younger brother, John, Prince of Castile, dying without issue. In April 1498, the King and Queen of Portugal journeyed to Toledo, to receive the homage of the realms they hoped one day to govern—Manoel as Prince-Consort, Isabella as Queen-Regnant. They were escorted under a golden umbrella to the cathedral, where they received the oaths of allegiance and swore to uphold the honour and welfare of Leon and Castile. In July they proceeded to Zaragoza, the capital of Aragon: but the national Cortes refused to acknowledge the sovereignty of a woman; and in this contention the Aragonese nobles

---

[1] *Petri Martyris Opus Epistolarum*, Amsterdam and Paris, 1570, p. 97. The first edition was published at Alcalá de Henares in 1530.

[2] The persecution is described in chap. xxi.

were supported by the representatives of Catalonia and Valencia. The deadlock lasted until the 14th of August, when Isabella gave birth to a Prince, who was christened Miguel and unanimously accepted as heir to all the thrones of Spain.

Weakened by years of asceticism, the Queen died in childbirth, and Prince Miguel survived only for nineteen months. It now seemed as though all hopes of Iberian union must be abandoned; but King Manoel's conjugal ideas were in advance of his age, and in 1500 he determined to wed one of the three surviving sisters of his deceased wife. The eldest, " Juana the Mad," was already wife to Philip the Fair of Austria; the youngest, " Catherine of Aragon," was in treaty for the hand of Arthur, Prince of Wales. Only Princess Mary was available, and Manoel promptly married her, having secured the needful dispensation from Pope Alexander VI.

She bore him nine children, but unfortunately for his ambition Juana proved an equally successful wife; and Charles, the eldest of Juana's six children, duly inherited the kingdoms of Spain, and in 1520 became Emperor, as Charles V. Meanwhile, the death of Queen Mary in 1518 left Manoel free to counter these successive blows of fortune by a further display of matrimonial activity. His choice fell upon Eleanor of Austria, niece to both his former wives, daughter of Juana the Mad, and sister of Charles V. He married her in 1519; but the match aroused little enthusiasm. Not only was the bridegroom thirty years older than the bride, but he had previously sought her hand for his own eldest son, Prince John, aged seventeen. This change of purpose he strove to excuse by the plea that Prince John was feeble-minded: Eleanor, however, was soon undeceived, and there is reason to believe that she would have preferred the son to the father.[1]

As the unity of the Church tended to influence men's minds in favour of Iberian union, Manoel was eager to conciliate the Holy See. It was also necessary for him to checkmate the Venetian diplomats who threatened

[1] See below, chap. xxxv.

Christendom with Ottoman vengeance and the destruction of the Holy Sepulchre in consequence of Portuguese interference in the East. Although it was common knowledge that the Sultan would not willingly forego the fees paid by palmers and pilgrims on their way to Jerusalem, Manoel was doubtless anxious lest a sudden outbreak of Turcophobe fanaticism in Europe might imperil his own dominions in Africa and Asia. On four occasions he sent envoys to the Vatican to treat of these weighty affairs, and he even ventured to remonstrate with Alexander VI. on the simony and irreligion prevalent in Rome. But no event of his reign, after Vasco da Gama's voyage, created so much stir as the embassy despatched to Leo X. in 1514. The chief ambassador was Tristão da Cunha, a bluff sailor, who was far more at home on his quarterdeck than in an audience-chamber. Tristão had been chosen as Viceroy of India before Almeida, but a temporary blindness compelled him to resign, and ultimately to resume a more congenial career of war, seafaring and plunder. In Madagascar his men had won some notable triumphs over an enemy armed with sticks and bones, but he also crossed swords with worthier foemen. His name, in a somewhat corrupt form, is perpetuated in that of the remote archipelago which he discovered in the South Atlantic—Tristan d'Acunha. Leo X., ever a lover of novelties, would doubtless appreciate so breezy an ambassador.

Tristão was the bearer of many gifts—gold and jewels emblematic of the riches of the Orient ; a panther, trained to hunt down game like a dog ; a Persian from Ormuz, who acted as its keeper. Strangest of all to European eyes was the Indian elephant which marched through gaping crowds to the castle of San Angelo, and there knelt before Leo X., symbolizing vividly but somewhat prematurely the homage of Asia to the Vicar of Christ. A rhinoceros from Gujarat had also been sent to Italy ; it was shipwrecked, but its body was washed ashore and stuffed. Albrecht Dürer etched its portrait, which is now preserved in the British Museum. The elephant, dying in 1516, was immortalized by Giovanni da Udine, a pupil of Raphael, and by the authors of the *Epistolae Obscurorum Virorum*, who make merry over its end.

" You have doubtless heard," they write, " how the Pope had a mighty beast which was called Elephant: and it held him in great honour, and he dearly loved it. Now therefore you should know that this animal is dead. . . . 'Tis dead, and the Pope is very sorry : and they say that he would give a thousand ducats for the Elephant, because it was a marvellous beast, having a long snout in great abundance ; and when it saw the Pope it fell on its knees before him and said with a terrible voice *Bar ! Bar ! Bar !* " [1]

The letter adds that the physicians vainly strove to avert its death by a purge costing 500 gold pieces.

Anxious though he was to associate the Church with his schemes, Manoel allowed no clerical interference with his own despotic rule. His predecessor John II. had with difficulty brought a pack of turbulent nobles to heel ; his three immediate successors were John III., a weak and immoral bigot, Sebastian, a gallant dreamer, and Henry, a dotard whose life had been spent in the service of the Inquisition. All three were puppets controlled by Jesuit or Dominican intriguers. But Manoel was such a prince as Machiavelli would have delighted to serve—a master of statecraft who permitted no scruple nor passion to thwart his policy. He was a characteristic product of the century which gave birth to Charles V., Francis I., Henry VIII., the century in which monarchs of genius borrowed the Turkish institution of a standing army, piled up huge fortunes by trade, and established personal government on a firmer basis than it had ever occupied in the Middle Ages. Fortune played into his hands, for it was in his reign that Gama reached India, Cabral discovered Brazil, Almeida secured command of the Indian Seas, Albuquerque founded an empire in Asia, and lesser men carried the flag of Portugal to the limits of the known world—from China to Greenland.[2] He used the wealth of the Indies to in-

[1] First published in 1517, p. 216 of the Leipzig edition of 1827.

[2] For some account of the Arctic voyages of Gaspar and Miguel Corte Real, see H. Harrisse, *Les Cortereals et leur Voyages*, Paris, 1888 ; Ernesto do Canto, *Os Corte Reaes*, Ponta Delgada, 1883 ; W. T. Grenfell, *Labrador*, New York, 1910.

THE TOWER OF ST. VINCENT, BELEM

crease his own prestige by a liberal patronage of art, letters and the " noble science " of heraldry. Among twenty-six monasteries and two cathedrals which he founded were some of the most exquisite examples of the style of architecture known by his name.[1] In his reign the classical period of Portuguese painting began. Humanists, historians, poets celebrated the splendours of his court ; skilled craftsmen adorned his palaces with jewelled plate and costly porcelain.

Some of his enactments were wise and useful. He gave charters to many cities and attempted to codify the customary and statute law. He imported corn in time of dearth, established a system of poor relief, built bridges, harbour-works, fortresses and reservoirs. One of the best known of these structures is the Tower of St Vincent at Belem, built to guard the landing place from which Vasco da Gama embarked for India. It is a characteristic example of the Manoeline style as applied to fortification.

Where clemency or magnanimity might serve his purpose, Manoel knew how to assume these virtues to the best effect. Nor was he often ungenerous in rewarding good service. The charge that he slighted Gama, Pacheco and Magellan has been disproved, and even in the case of Albuquerque it should be remembered that Manoel had no means of sifting the slanders annually sent home by men who should have been trustworthy.

It is easy to affirm in the light of present knowledge that Manoel was pursuing a phantom when he schemed to make Spain and Portugal one. To-day we can review the centuries of jealous ' regionalism ' from which Spain has hardly yet emerged. We know how fiercely the Catalans, Aragonese and Basques clung to their local autonomy, and we can be sure that the claims of Portugal would have strengthened the centrifugal forces which still dominate Spanish politics. But King Manoel could no more have foreseen failure than he could have commanded success. If his dream had come true, a single Iberian nation,

---

[1] The main features of the so-called Manoeline style are described below, chap. xxxiii.

loyal to itself and wielding the resources of the New World and the East, might for a time have secured the hegemony of Europe and modified the whole trend of western civilization in favour of Latin and Catholic ideas. It was only an accident, the death of Prince Miguel, which frustrated this establishment of an empire greater than Alexander's.

CHAPTER XVI

D. VASCO DA GAMA, VICEROY

THE death of Albuquerque was followed by nine years of misrule in Portuguese India. At last, in 1524, King John III. decided to send out a man strong and honest enough to re-establish discipline, and his choice fell on the veteran D. Vasco da Gama, who was accordingly nominated as Viceroy. Gama had now reached his sixty-fifth year and since 1503 had lived the life of a territorial magnate, far from the sound of the sea ; but neither his maritime skill nor his alertness of mind and vigour of will had deserted him. Taking command of 14 ships, he sailed from Lisbon on the 9th of April 1524, accompanied by two of his elder sons, D. Estevão and D. Paulo. He was not disposed to belittle his own importance as at once Count of Vidigueira, Admiral of the Indies and representative of the Crown. Corrêa gossips of the pomp with which the great discoverer chose to surround himself on board his flagship, the *St. Catherine of Mt. Sinai.*

" The said Dom Vasco brought with him great state, and was served by men bearing silver maces, by a major-domo, and two pages with gold neck-chains, many equerries, and body servants, very well clothed and cared for ; he also brought rich vessels of silver, and rich tapestry of Flanders, and for the table at which he sate brocade cloths. . . . He had a guard of two hundred men, with gilt pikes, clothed with his livery ; all the gentlemen and honourable persons ate with him." [1]

Those who may have inferred from the Viceroy's own habits that he would be lenient to his subordinates were soon undeceived. D. Vasco da Gama held that the lower classes should be taught to keep to their proper station ;

[1] Stanley's *Corrêa*, pp. 380-381.

including in the lower classes almost all persons who did not happen to be the Count of Vidigueira. Before his flotilla put to sea, he had posted at the foot of the masts an order that any woman detected on board after the ships had passed Belem would be publicly flogged. If she were married, her husband would be sent home in irons ; if a slave, she would be sold and the proceeds given to charity ; while any captain wilfully concealing such a stowaway would be cashiered. The fleet arrived at Mozambique on the 14th of August, and halted for the flagship to repair a sprung yardarm. As it lay hove-to, three women stowaways were denounced to the Viceroy, and placed under arrest.

The remainder of the voyage proved eventful. Before the coast of India was reached, three vessels had been wrecked, and the crew of a fourth had mutinied, killed their captain, and sailed away for a pirate cruise in the Straits of Bab el-Mandeb. On the evening of the 8th of September the rest of the armada lay becalmed near Dabul, when suddenly the ships began to pitch so violently that the most seasoned mariners could hardly keep their footing. Fearing to have run aground, they began to heave the lead, but found no bottom ; sails were struck and boats lowered, terrified soldiers and sailors prayed, shouted, discharged the artillery. In the midst of their panic D. Vasco bade them take courage, " for the sea trembles at us. . . . Do not be afraid," he added, " this is an earthquake."

In Goa, the Viceroy amazed everyone, as a letter from the municipality to the King affirms, by refusing to accept any gift " either from Christian or Moor." [1] Instead, he at once set about the restoration of order and justice. The Captain of the fortress had been guilty of grave irregularities ; indeed the citizens had schemed to depose him and give his office to a certain Bishop described as D. Martinho,[2] " but," says Corrêa, " the Bishop was virtuous and would not consent." D. Vasco deprived the errant Captain of his commission, and even compelled him to pay

---

[1] Stanley's *Corrêa*, p. 385 (translation) and Appendix, p. x. (text).
[2] Not Bishop of Goa, as that see was only created in 1538.

his debts. Then the dour old martinet prepared to deal with minor offenders, remarking that those who deserved mercy would doubtless receive it—in the next world.

The three unfortunate women who had been detected in his ships were sentenced to be flogged through the streets while the town-crier intoned

"The Justice of the King our Lord! It orders these women to be flogged because they had no fear of his justice, and crossed over to India despite his prohibition."

This sentence not unnaturally caused a scandal. The Brothers of Mercy,[1] the Bishop, and all the fidalgos interceded in vain ; charitable men offered to buy off the women by subscribing 3000 *pardões* for the ransom of captives— a sum large enough to have touched the heart of most Viceroys. But even when the Franciscan friars came to pray for mercy and offered to take charge of the women, Gama denounced their procession as an attempt to stir up popular feeling against himself, and refused to reconsider his verdict. He did, however, issue a general amnesty to all fugitives from justice whose offences had been committed before his own arrival in India, provided the guilty persons " returned to the service of God and the King within three months."

Candidates for any appointment were submitted to a rough and ready examination. If a man came seeking a clerkship, he was compelled then and there to furnish a specimen of his handwriting. The result was that all civil posts were given, as Corrêa says, to " very official men." From his own advantageous position the Viceroy could afford to condemn avarice. Men came to India, he said, to make their fortunes : but he would strive to make

---

[1] The *Santa Casa de Misericordia* ("Holy House of Mercy") was a lay brotherhood established in Goa about 1515. Similar associations existed in Portugal, and were afterwards founded in Ormuz and elsewhere in the East. They endeavoured to organize charity. Francis Xavier testifies to their humanity and skill in detecting impostors (letter to Gaspar Baertz, March 1549). From 1515 to 1591 the Brotherhood managed the royal hospital founded by Albuquerque in Goa, and it shared with the municipal authorities in the management of the leper hospital (founded *c.* 1530).

the King's fortune. In pursuance of this ideal, he put an end to the system by which married men were supplied with pay and free rations merely for having braved the perils of matrimony. Corrêa gives a lively account of his reforming zeal :

" The Viceroy had it proclaimed that no seafaring man should wear a cloak except on a Sunday or Saint's day on going to church, and if they did, that it should be taken away by the constables, and they should be put at the pump-break for a day in disgrace ; and that every man who drew pay as a matchlockman should wear his match fastened to his arm. . . . He ordered that the slaves they might have should be men who could assist in any labour, for they were not going to be allowed to embark pages dressed up like dolls. . . . He ordered it to be proclaimed, under pain of death and confiscation, that any person who had got any of the king's artillery should send and deliver it to the magazine, without any penalty, even though he might have stolen it anywhere, and this within the space of one month, after which they would incur the penalty. In this manner much artillery was gathered in." [1]

The Viceroy now proceeded south to Cochin, where a general stampede of the Muslim inhabitants heralded his approach : many even of the Portuguese emigrated to the Coromandel Coast. He was met by D. Luiz de Menezes, brother of the outgoing Governor. It was night when Gama's ships encountered the squadron which had put out to welcome them, but the glare of the artillery lighted up all the fleet as salutes were exchanged—a dangerous display, since every gun was fully charged. Corrêa describes the scene as wonderful ; only two lives were lost.

In Cochin Gama continued to sweep away abuses, aided first by Dr Pedro Nunes, a celebrated mathematician, who acted as Comptroller of the Treasury, afterwards by Affonso Mexia, who held the same post, and by Lopo Vaz de Sampayo, who ultimately became Governor of India. Nunes was high in favour with all who had no interest in adulteration : for he contrived to send home pepper that was never green nor mouldy nor mixed with sand and grit. Aided by these lieutenants, Gama strewed consternation through the

[1] Stanley's *Corrêa*, pp. 397-398.

RECEIPT WRITTEN AND SIGNED BY VASCO DA GAMA

FROM THE MUSEUM OF THE LISBON GEOGRAPHICAL SOCIETY

official world. He worked untiringly, dispensing with the customary siesta at noonday, and, like Albuquerque, employing no doorkeeper. Every morning and evening he betook himself to the harbour, inspected the warehouses, and hurried on the lading or discharge of cargo.

During his own voyage from Cochin, he had been harassed by the manœuvres of many fast-sailing ' pirate ' craft, which hovered round his own ponderous ships " as a light horseman hovers round a man-at-arms "—to borrow the words of Barros. Some swift native-built galleys had been ordered, but when they had been delivered, and duly admired by landsmen, the Viceroy ordered them to be burned as useless. He then summoned a Genoese boat-builder known as Master Vyne, who vowed that he could build brigantines quick enough to catch a mosquito, and proved himself a man of his word by launching two of them in three weeks. D. Vasco secured an abundance of oarsmen by the promise not only of pay and rations, but of all goods found above deck on any vessel which the rowers might overhaul. Each rower kept under his bench a steel helmet and breastplate, a lance and two powder-pots, so that on coming up with a prize he could instantly transform himself into a grenadier. Piracy was thus checked.

In November, when the retiring Governor, D. Duarte de Menezes, arrived in Cochin to make a formal surrender of the office he had misused, Gama ordered him not to disembark, but to consider himself under arrest and so to return to Lisbon on parole. D. Luiz de Menezes, whom Corrêa describes as a very discreet man, intervened on behalf of his brother, protesting that though D. Duarte might have his faults, he at least had never sold one of the King's fortresses.

To this tactful advocacy Gama made a characteristic reply : " Sir, if your brother had sold fortresses, he would not have his head where it is now, for I should have ordered it to be cut off." D. Duarte meanwhile had established himself on board his own ship the *São Jorge*, hoping to outlive the Viceroy, whose health showed signs of failing, and then to resume the governorship. " Since he chooses to take his own course, he will hear of me," said D. Vasco da Gama, and sent the Auditor-General and the Chief-Constable, escorted by two warships, to summon the erring proconsul, and if he disobeyed the summons to send his ship to the bottom. This was sufficient for D. Duarte, who shortly afterwards took his departure.

The Viceroy now felt that his own death was near. He suffered much from abscesses on the nape of his neck, which prevented him from moving his head and heightened the natural warmth of his temper. After taking counsel with his confessor, he delegated his own authority to Affonso Mexia and Lopo Vaz de Sampayo, until a new Governor should be nominated. Then he took the last sacraments and made his will, providing for the future of his servants, leaving his clothes and upholstery of silk to the church and hospital at Cochin, and bequeathing a dowry to each of the women who had been flogged by his order. Lastly, he desired that his bones should be conveyed to Portugal.

He died shortly before dawn on Christmas Eve in 1524. All day long no public notification of his death was made, and there was no sign of mourning other than the closed doors of his house until the hour of Ave Maria, when his sons and servants announced that he was dead. Then, as Corrêa says, every man showed what he felt. The prevailing emotion was probably a sense of relief; for the Viceroy was more feared than loved.

A stately white-bearded figure, he was borne to his grave robed in silk and wearing the mantle of the Knights of Christ, with a sword in his belt, gilt spurs on his riding boots and a dark biretta on his head. He had ruled over Portuguese India for three months.

None of the heroes of Portuguese history was destined to win a more enduring fame than the man who first traversed the sea-route to India, and was chosen by Camões as the central figure of *The Lusiads*. The Vasco Da Gama of Camões, however, personifies the faith and valour of Portugal, as Virgil's Aeneas personifies the faith and valour of ancient Rome; the portrait is intended to epitomize the heroism of a whole nation.

In life, Gama had the rough virtues of a pioneer and the brutal faults of an age which countenanced torture and slavery. Like Albuquerque he was iron-willed, fearless, incorruptible, born to command. Both men met danger and opposition with the same grim humour ; both understood the uses of visible splendour ; neither spared himself or others when there was hard work to be done. But Gama preferred to drive men, Albuquerque to lead them. Neither was a respecter of persons, but Gama's innate arrogance grew with the passage of time until it blinded him to the merits of any opinion which differed from his own. Both men coveted power, but Albuquerque used it solely to serve his King, while Gama exacted a full reward in wealth and dignities.

Albuquerque's was the finer personality, Gama's the greater achievement, if the greatness of an achievement may be measured by its permanent value to humanity.

CHAPTER XVII

D. JOÃO DE CASTRO [1]

DOM JOÃO DE CASTRO, called by his contemporaries "the Portuguese Cato" and "the last hero of Portugal," was the son of D. Alvaro de Castro, Civil Governor of Lisbon. A penniless cadet of the *fidalguia*, he was destined from his birth in 1500 to the one career in which poverty was no bar to preferment; and it was hoped that good brains and better fortune might one day win him a mitre, or even a cardinal's hat. But D. João himself had other ambitions.

His education was entrusted to Dr Pedro Nunes, the same scholar who afterwards aided Gama to reform the finances of India. At the age of eighteen D. João had become a brilliant mathematician and a sound Humanist; he had also formed a close friendship with his fellow-pupil Prince Luiz, a son of King Manoel. But the love of adventure was in his blood, and almost every day the tidings of great deeds done in Africa or India came to stir all generous spirits to action, as news from the Spanish Main stirred the heart of the West Country in Elizabethan England. At last the glitter of arms and the rumour of camps proved irresistible. Psalter and canon law had lost their interest, Euclid was a mass of arid subtleties, Virgil a reproach and a trumpet-call. In 1519 the student gave his guardians the slip and embarked to join the Portuguese armies at Tangier. There he learned the science and practice of war in a hard school. The tactics of the Berber tribes could only be withstood by troops of seasoned valour and discipline. Even though flight would bring certain destruction upon the Christians encumbered by their armour, it was no light matter to stand

[1] See Appendix A, Special Bibliography, " D. João de Castro."

firm against a rush of the wild desert horsemen, who charged
fearless of death and assured that all true Muslims who fell
in the Holy War would sleep that night with the damsels of
Paradise, while the Fiery Ditch yawned for their adversaries.
D. João had nine years of this experience, and then returned
to Lisbon an accomplished soldier, who had received knighthood and high praise from his commander, D. Duarte de
Menezes.

At court he found himself welcome ; and it was probably
about this period that he married D. Lenor do Coutinho,
a lady with as long a pedigree and as lean a purse as his own.
Little is known for certain of their life together, but as
eight or nine years elapsed before Castro saw active service
again, it may well have been a time of happiness. Castro
made his home near Cintra, where his two sons D. Alvaro
and D. Fernão were born. His estate, the Penha Verde
or Green Peak, is a beautiful tract of woodland and upland,
olive groves and vineyards, beside the mountain road that
leads from Cintra to Collares and the sea. After the hardships of Morocco the country quiet and leisure were doubtless welcome, especially as they were redeemed from monotony by glimpses of the court. From Penha Verde he
could almost see the Moorish chimneys of the summer
palace in Cintra, in shape like two gigantic wine-bottles,
in colour grey above red-tiled roofs, blue wood-smoke and
green foliage. Beyond rose the Pena crag, with a Moorish
castle perched on the topmost pinnacle. The castle, which
commanded a noble prospect over the Tagus estuary and
the plain of Mafra, was used as a hunting-lodge, and in the
surrounding forest of conifers and cork trees there was
royal game in plenty — boars, wolves, and warrantable
stags. Here the fidalgos would assemble to display their
skill in horsemanship or archery, attended by a host of
rangers and beaters in charge of the nets, hounds and other
accessories. In these idyllic pleasures the time passed
away, and it was not until 1535 that Castro resumed his
military career.

He accompanied his friend Prince Luiz to Tunis, which
had been seized in the previous year by the dreaded Turkish

sea-rover Khair ed-Din Barbarossa, Viceroy of all the Ottoman dominions in North Africa. A strong Spanish fleet, with Andrea Doria as admiral and the Emperor Charles V. in supreme command, sailed from Barcelona, retook Tunis, and sunk or burned many of Barbarossa's galleys. Among the incidents of the expedition was an instructive little comedy of manners, as memorable, in its way, as the episode of Raleigh and his cloak. It chanced that the Emperor and Prince Luiz had arrived together at a doorway where each stepped aside to give precedence to his companion. After a brief delay, in which the rival claims of rank and hospitality were weighed, the Emperor prevailed upon his guest to take the lead. Prince Luiz, not to be outdone in courtesy, borrowed a torch from one of the pages in attendance, and marched on in front like a linkboy, lighting the way for his betters.

Castro distinguished himself at the siege of Tunis, and enhanced his reputation by declining the rewards and honour proffered by Charles V. On his return he accepted a minor office, the commandership of São Paulo de Salvaterra, and retired to his home in Cintra. Here he devoted himself to forestry, cutting down his orchards and replacing them with timber-trees—a "novel mode of agriculture" in which his biographer Andrade finds evidence of manly fortitude. There is, however, a tradition that the orange was first brought to Europe by Castro. Citrons had been enjoyed in imperial Rome, and single trees of the sweet orange may have been imported from the Levant into Italy during the fifteenth century ; but the true China orange was first acclimatized in Portugal about the year 1548, and the tradition which ascribes its introduction to Castro may well be true.

Castro was now in the prime of manhood, and his thoughts naturally turned towards India as the only arena wide enough to give his talent and ambition free play. D. Garcia de Noronha, nephew to the great Albuquerque, was about to sail for India as Viceroy-elect, and Castro, with his elder son D. Alvaro, took the opportunity of volunteering for service. Offered the captaincy of Ormuz, he is said by the veracious Andrade to have refused it as either above or below his deserts ; but he saw no reason to decline an annuity of 1000 *cruzados* (£483) from the Treasury.

The fleet arrived at Goa in September 1538, none too soon.   Three years before, Bahadur Shah of Gujarat—son of that

> " King of Cambay, whose daily food
> Is asp, basilisk and toad,"

immortalized in *Hudibras*—had given the Portuguese licence to build a fortress in the island of Diu, off the coast of his own kingdom.   But not many months had passed ere a bitter feud arose between the Christians and the Musalman trading community, and in 1538 the fortress was for the first time besieged by the Gujaratis, aided by their formidable allies the Turks, who had sent over a fleet from Suez.   A tremendous fire was poured into the stronghold by the Turkish batteries, among which were guns capable of throwing a cast-iron ball of 100 lbs. weight. Such heavy metal outranged and silenced any cannon the defenders could mount, and only their grim tenacity kept the beleaguering force at bay.   In such a crisis the Portuguese fought as they had fought in the days of Duarte Pacheco, and many individual exploits have been recorded.   A soldier named Fonseca fought with his left hand when a bullet had disabled the right, and one unknown genius, finding his ammunition all spent, wrenched out a loose tooth and fired that.   Even the women and children displayed the same reckless valour, risking their lives to tend the wounded and scurvy-stricken garrison, to carry ammunition, or to wall up a breach—while they devoted their leisure to the pious duty of torturing the prisoners.

At last, early in November 1538, the gallantry of the defenders had its reward, for a dispute between the Turks and Gujaratis ended in the departure of the Ottoman fleet, and soon afterwards the approach of a small relieving force compelled the remainder of the beleaguering army to raise the siege.   In January 1539 the main body of the Viceroy's navy arrived at Diu, with D. João de

Castro aboard, and on the 11th of March peace was signed.

During the whole of D. Garcia de Noronha's term of office, it was only Castro's influence that kept the administrative machine in something like running order. The Viceroy openly stated that he had come to India to make money. He pocketed the salaries of all officials, who were thus encouraged to live on bribes and other " perquisites " ; he sold everything that had a market value— captaincies, trading licences, judicial verdicts. Though he was in his sixty-third year, and so racked with fever that he could not hope to live many months, he worked day and night to amass a fortune, leaving all affairs of state to take care of themselves.

On the 3rd of April 1540 he died, having spent his last hours in gloating over the execution of a man who had been condemned, without trial, for a murder of which he was known to be innocent. D. Estevão da Gama, the second son of D. Vasco, succeeded to the governorship.

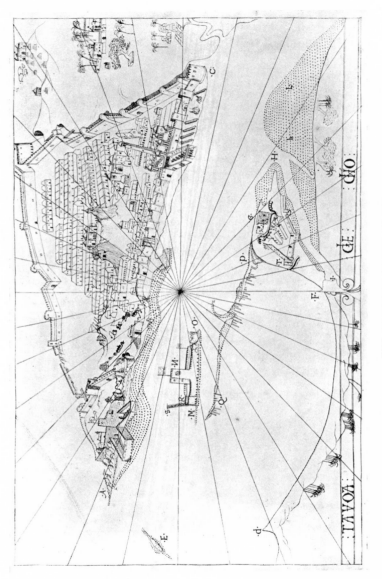

THE FORTRESS OF DIU IN 1539

FROM D. JOÃO DE CASTRO'S "ROTEIRO DE GOA À DIO"

CHAPTER XVIII

DOM ESTEVÃO had been instructed to visit Suez and to destroy the Turkish galleys stationed there ; but this expedition was delayed owing to the terrible famine which devastated the whole of India during the winter of 1539-1540. Men and women trooped down to the rivers and the sea, and drowned themselves when they could no longer endure the agony of hunger ; the natives of the Coromandel Coast were driven to cannibalism ; and in a letter to Prince Luiz, D. João de Castro estimates that two-thirds of the people of Vijayanagar perished.

At last, however, a fleet of 72 sail was collected ; on the 31st of December 1540 it received the solemn blessing of D. João de Albuquerque, Bishop of Goa ; and on the morrow it stood to sea. Castro has left a *Roteiro* (*i.e.* log-book or itinerary) of this voyage, which with the earlier itineraries of his voyages from Lisbon to Goa in 1538, and from Goa to Diu in 1538-1539, calls for more than a passing mention.[1] All three are concise and lucid ; they make no parade of learning ; and yet they are clearly the work of a scholar thoroughly at home in Greek and Latin literature—one, however, who always preferred the witness of his own eyes to authority or tradition.

The first Roteiro is the least interesting except in so far as it illustrates Castro's habit of open-minded inquiry. He notes every unusual incident from day to day, such as the presence of rare birds or animals ; he gives full details on soundings, the nature of the sea-floor, the altitude of the sun, the depth of water over a harbour bar, the position of reefs, and kindred topics. In the second Roteiro he

---

[1] See also Appendix A, Special Bibliography, " D. João de Castro."

shows himself a worthy pupil of Dr Pedro Nunes, who had already written on the subject of magnetism. In 1537, Nunes had effected several improvements in the variation-compass, invented by the German astronomer Purbach about 1460; and this instrument, which "consisted of a combination of a sun-dial with a magnetic needle," [1] was now for the first time extensively used, in a series of observations the results of which are recorded in the Roteiros. Castro not only speculates on the causes of compass-variation, but puts his theories to the test of experiment. He remarks the connexion between the movement of the tides and the phases of the moon, though at this time the phenomena of lunar attraction were almost unstudied. He was the first European to describe the cave-temples of Elephanta, now world-famous, and his measurements might almost be the work of a modern archæologist, so precise are they. He was also the first to notice the curious formation of the basalt rock-pillars near Bassein, which he likens to gigantic obelisks or organ-pipes.

The Roteiro of the Red Sea expedition is equally varied in its subject-matter, which ranges from Arabic coinage, the cause of the monsoons and the properties of a certain fleshy-leaved tree with sap like milk, to the nomenclature of Ptolemy's Island of the Satyrs, a designation which Castro seeks to explain by a reference to the spoor of wild beasts visible on the sandy soil and resembling satyrs' hoof marks.

On the 30th of April a comet was descried "in the semblance of a writhing serpent, all luminous."

"This token and similitude," says Castro, "lasted the space of half an hour, and then faded. I marked the direction of the comet by my compass, and made it north-east and a quarter of east. Throughout that night we lay at our moorings."

This passage would alone suffice to show how far Castro's scientific interests were in advance of the age; for throughout Europe a comet was regarded as an omen of impending calamity, not a natural phenomenon to be calmly studied. Superstition had been fortified by the appearance of a

[1] Ravenstein, *Roteiro*, p. 168.

comet in 1456, three years after the fall of Constantinople, when the petition " From the devil, the Turk and the comet, good Lord deliver us," was added to the Litany. The annual rise of the Nile and the colour of the Red Sea were mysteries which had long perplexed the learned. Castro attributes the overflow of the Nile to " the great and continuous rains which fall during the months of June and July in Ethiopia, or Abyssinia—which is the same." On the question of the Red Sea, most learned men of the day would have rehearsed the opinions recorded by Pliny without attempting to see beyond them. But Castro brushes aside these threadbare fables—he will have none of the legendary King Erithra, whose name was supposed to have been confused with the Greek ἐρυθρός, *red* ; he declines to be convinced either that the waters were tinged by sunbeams, or to accept the satisfying assurance that they were red " of their own nature." To the Portuguese, who had hitherto never sailed north of Massawa, yet boldly averred that the sea was coloured by clouds of desert sand, he metes out grave irony.

" I do not reprove the opinion of the Portuguese ; but I affirm that, going by this sea more often than they went, and traversing its entire extent (while they only viewed one region), I never saw in the whole what they claim to have seen in the part."

Modern philologists have sought for the origin of the name Red Sea in the ancient Edom, or Idumea, the " Red Land "—itself so called from the red sandstone range of Mount Hor. Castro lit upon a less recondite theory. The water, he ascertained, was of the common neutral tint, but seen from above it appeared as if streaks of red, white and green were mingled with it. The red predominated. This could not be due to red dust, because the shores of the Red Sea were an arid and sunburnt wilderness of grey or brown rock resembling heaps of ashes ; only thrice had hills of red stone been sighted, and in each case the formation was too hard to wear away readily into dust. Clearly the colour of the water depended on the character of the bottom, and this inference was confirmed by the divers whom Castro

sent down to explore. The " red coral-stone " which over-
spread the sea-floor " in certain trees and clusters " evidently caused the reddish tint, while growths of green weed
or ooze made the water green, and sand made it white.

The first halting-place of the fleet was Socotra, a mountainous island peopled by half-naked Nestorian Christians,
who subsisted mainly upon dates and had no weapons
except short swords of blunt iron. Castro affirms that all
the women were named Mary, but the men had the normal
choice of Biblical names. Socotra did not long detain the
fleet, and it arrived at Massawa on the 11th of February,
with the loss of one ship, which had foundered in the Arabian
Sea.

The sketch of this seaport left by Castro is a fair example
of the beautiful drawings with which he illustrated the two
latest Roteiros. As was the custom of sixteenth-century
cartographers, he generalized much of his subject. Half
a dozen houses represent a city ; a galleon stands for a
whole squadron ; the elephant pounding over the mountain
tops, the lion rampant, the strange coney with its ponderous
feet, and the other beasts in the picture are types of the
local fauna.

From Massawa the expedition proceeded northward in
a leisurely fashion, until Aden came into view, standing
out of the sea like an island in the afternoon light, and
bringing to Castro memories of the Cintra hills. He ventures
to observe that Ptolemy had assigned the wrong latitude
to Aden—a defiance of authority which would have been
regarded almost as heresy in the Coimbra lecture-rooms.

Arriving next at Suakin, the Portuguese found the city
deserted, and burned it with all the ships in the roadstead ;
there was little else for them to do, except to come to blows
over the vast quantities of loot they acquired. Castro
waxes eloquent over the natural advantages of the place.

" The water within the haven is so still, and runs so imperceptibly,
that the ebb and flow of the tides can hardly be detected. The bottom
is mud ; the anchorage nowhere in less than five or six fathoms, and
sometimes in seven. Two hundred ships and rowing-boats beyond
number can lie moored within the shelter and compass of this haven,

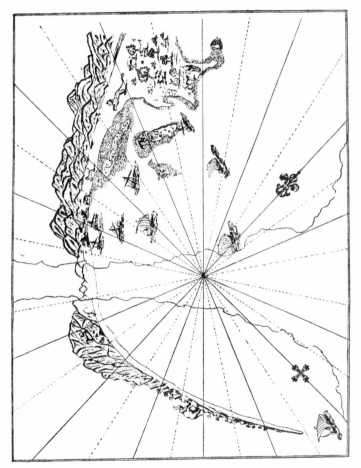

MASSAWA IN THE YEAR 1541

FROM DOM JOÃO DE CASTRO'S "ROTEIRO . . . . DE VIAGEM . . . . AO MAR ROXO "

and can load by laying a plank from the warehouses to the decks, while the galleys are made fast to the doors and stones of the houses, and rest with their bows overlapping the streets, which serve instead of gangways. There is trade with all parts of India, Arabia, Cairo and Alexandria; gold and ivory in abundance come from Abyssinia; only to Lisbon itself can such an emporium be likened."

The sack of Suakin served to advertise the voyage, and the track of two camels and some men along the sea-coast proved that information of their design had preceded the Portuguese raiders. To reach Suez at all it was needful to hasten, and only sixteen of the fastest ships were permitted to continue the voyage, while the rest were ordered, much against the desire of their crews, to return to Massawa. Kosseir was reached on the 11th of April; it was a group of wretched hovels in a desert where no green thing flourished, but it was important as the nearest harbour to the Nile valley. Here the fleet took in fresh provisions. Castro asked the inhabitants why they did not roof their huts.

" They answered me that the shelter of their mats (*histeiras*) sufficed for the sun, and by rains they were not molested; but against the wickedness of men they were forced to seek stronger defences, and therefore decided to make the walls of stone or clay and sods. I asked them who were the fierce foemen against whom they fortified themselves with bulwarks so mighty. They told me the Badois [Bedawin], a froward and a godless folk, who disquieted the place with their sudden forays, and plundered the caravans that came from the Nile with stores."

Castro avers that ' Badoil ' means in good Arabic a man who lives by cattle-rearing; he identifies the Bedawin with the Troglodytes, Ichthyophagi and Ophiotophagi of Ptolemy, Pliny, Pomponius Mela and other writers; and he declares that they inhabit the hills and the sea-coast from Malindi to Cape Guardafui, and thence up both shores of the Red Sea.

On the 21st the Portuguese arrived at the village of Tor on the Arabian coast. The inhabitants belonged to the Greek Church, and among the neighbouring foothills of Mount Sinai they had a monastery dedicated to St Catherine. This saint, as Castro was informed on the authority of

"Anthonino Archbishop of Florence," had been borne away by angels from the city of Alexandria, brought to this mountain, and buried by their hands. The monks came to their brethren of the Western Church, and, with tears in their eyes, recounted a pitiful tale. The gist of it was that the sacred relics had been exhumed for fear of the Bedawin, placed upon a gilded car and conveyed in solemn procession to Cairo. Castro, with more shrewdness than charity, suggests that the story was concocted by the monks to lull the curiosity of their visitors, who might in their turn have rectified the error made by the angels, and given St Catherine a secure resting-place upon Portuguese territory. But no attempt was made to press the matter, because the convent and village of Tor were looked upon as sacred ground. Castro had himself learned, "from a Moor of conspicuous honesty, erudition, and zeal for knowledge," that Tor was the actual spot at which Moses and the Hebrews landed after their passage of the Red Sea; while the monks of St Catherine, not to be outdone in Biblical lore by a mere Muslim, averred that any man who cared to travel a few leagues up the coast might drink at the spring unsealed by Moses when he smote the living rock with his rod, and caused the waters to flow.

These legends awoke the old crusading fervour which was ever present, though often dormant, in the most cruel and reckless of the Portuguese sea-rovers. To them the squalid hamlet of Tor was a shrine, and here, under the shadow of Sinai, where men breathed the very atmosphere of Old Testament history, some of the fidalgos sought the honour of knighthood at the hands of their commander. Among them was Castro's elder son D. Alvaro, then aged thirteen. As they knelt on the sand, waiting in awed silence for the accolade which should dedicate their lives to God and the King, it is to be presumed that no ironic reminiscence of the Jewish massacres in Lisbon intruded to break the spell of the hour and the place. Long afterwards D. Estevão caused it to be inscribed upon his tomb at Vidigueira, as the one memorable deed of his career, that he had made knights at the foot of Mount Sinai.

It was not until the 22nd of April that the Portuguese left Tor, to complete the final stage of their journey. They made Suez on the 26th, and found it almost derelict. A few thatched hovels sheltered the remnant of its people, and made a contrast with the stately ruins of its mosques, warehouses and bazaars. These had soon fallen into decay when Albuquerque won control of the converging trade routes which brought the merchandise of India and China to this inmost recess of the Red Sea. But although its commerce had vanished, Suez had gained a new importance as a base for the Ottoman navy ; and it had been rendered impregnable when the Portuguese signalled their approach by burning and sacking Suakin. Fifty Turkish galleys had been beached in a double line along a narrow bill of land which had been isolated by the construction of a canal across its landward base, and heavy guns had been mounted so as to rake any hostile ship that might venture within range. The Portuguese had little heart for a forlorn hope, and did not try to force a landing. After wasting nearly two days they hoisted sail and turned south again, glad to escape without loss. Thus the main purpose of the expedition was frustrated, largely through the dilatory tactics of D. Estevão da Gama.

At Massawa the baffled raiders rejoined their comrades in the main body of the fleet, whose numbers had been thinned by famine and the deadly climate. Their supplies were wellnigh exhausted ; and when João Bermudes, the self-styled Abyssinian patriarch, descanted on the fruitfulness of his native land beyond the mountains, and on the welcome which Prester John would give to Christian allies, the starved crews broke into open mutiny. Five deserters were hanged ; but a hundred others took arms and set forth into the barren hinterland. They made a martial show, with a flag flying and a band of music to keep them in step ; but their first bivouac followed a hot night march, through a land without water ; and when the Muslim horsemen swooped down on their camp, the Portuguese were faint with thirst, and impeded by the burden of their accoutrements. Only two, who saved their lives by counterfeiting death, ever returned to the ships.

D. Estevão found himself confronted by yet another difficulty. The Abyssinians had for years waged war with their Muhammadan neighbours of Zeila,whose matchlocks and fiery fanaticism made an irresistible combination. Couriers from the camp of Prester John were waiting at Massawa with urgent appeals for aid ; and on the 7th of July a relieving force of four hundred Portuguese was dispatched under the command of D. Christovão da Gama.[1] The fleet then left Massawa, and on the 8th of August dropped anchor before Goa. Castro soon afterwards returned to Portugal, where in 1543 he was given a fresh naval command and commissioned to suppress piracy in home waters. In 1545 he was sent back to India, as Governor in succession to Martim Affonso de Sousa.

[1] For the tragic story of this expedition, see R. S. Whiteway, *The Portuguese Expedition to Abyssinia in 1541-3*, Hakluyt Society, London, 1902. This is an annotated translation of Miguel Castanhoso's *Historia das cousas que o muy esforçado capitão D. Christovão da Gama fez nos Reynos do Preste João*, which was written by a member of the expedition, printed in 1564, and reprinted by the Academia Real, Lisbon, 1855.

CHAPTER XIX

CASTRO was forced to spend much of his time in waging unprofitable wars and in striving to raise funds for the costs of administration. But his three years' term—from September 1545 to June 1548—is memorable for the heroic defence of Diu, which forms the subject of a Portuguese epic written by Jeronymo Corte-Real.[1]

The earlier history of Portuguese enterprise in the island of Diu has already been outlined. Peace had been concluded in 1539, but its terms were so humiliating to the Sultan of Gujarat that a rupture could not long be delayed. The Portuguese warships allowed no merchantman to visit any of the ports of Gujarat unless it had first paid customs-dues at their own fortress, where their officials could buy such part of the cargo as they might covet, themselves fixing the price. Various minor grievances helped to fan the smouldering resentment of the Sultan into flame : and in March 1546 the Captain of Diu, D. João Mascarenhas, realized that war was imminent. His conviction was strengthened by the discovery that two traitors—Ruy Freire, a Portuguese, and Francisco Rodrigues, a mulatto—had nearly tunnelled an entrance into the powder-magazine, which they had been bribed to explode.

The island of Diu lies due south of the Kathiawar Peninsula, from which it is sundered by a broad fen, and by a salt-water channel navigable only for vessels of light draught. In shape like a roughly drawn diamond, it measures about two miles from north to south, and seven miles from east to west. The native city stood at its westernmost point, while

---

[1] *O segundo cêrco de Diu*, Lisbon, 1574.

the Portuguese had selected the opposite extremity as the site of their main fortress, three sides of which abutted upon the sea. The fourth or landward side was enclosed by a semicircular line of defence, consisting of three bastions linked together by curtains, and of a deep fosse filled with sea-water. Each bastion had its own name—St John, nearest the channel and the marshes, St James, in the convex centre of the fortified line, and St Thomas, nearest the sea and at the southern end of the line. The only important outwork was a fortalice built on an isolated rock in mid-channel.

The opposing forces were at first unevenly matched, for Mascarenhas could muster only 200 men-at-arms against fully 10,000 Gujaratis, Turks, Egyptians and other mercenaries, led by Sifr Aga, an Italian renegade.[1] In heavy cannon the besiegers were greatly superior, and they possessed an unlimited reserve of forced labour for the construction of roads, bridges and entrenchments.

Sifr Aga brought his siege-train into position on the night of April the 20th, and for the next four months the defenders were almost isolated. The high seas and gales of the monsoon made the dispatch of reinforcements wellnigh impossible, though one body of 200 men, under D. Fernão de Castro, contrived to reach the fortress on the 18th of May.

Meanwhile the bombardment continued day and night, until, under the ceaseless impact of flying stone and bronze, the walls began to give way. But the soldiers' wives and children came to the rescue. Organized and inspired by their elected 'captain,' Isabel Madeira, they repaired the shattered masonry and supervised the slaves and other non-combatants. Isabel Madeira was the wife of a Nestorian surgeon, one Mestre João, whose house was converted into a hospital; among the other officers of this corps of Amazons were Garcia Rodrigues, wife of the traitor Ruy Freire, and Isabel Fernandes, known as 'the old woman of Diu,' who braved the hottest fire to bring her sugar-cakes to the men

[1] Couto (*Dec.* vi. Bk. ii. chap. ii. p. 98) says that Sifr Aga's mother, a good Catholic resident in Otranto, sent him a yearly letter of good advice, addressed to " Sifr Aga, my son, at the Gates of Hell."

on duty, feeding those whose hands were occupied, and exclaiming : " Keep a good heart, my sons ; fight on, my cavaliers, for the Virgin Our Lady is with you ! "

In the last week of June, a well-aimed cannon-ball deprived the besiegers of their general, Sifr Aga, but his son and successor Rumi Khan pressed the siege with such vigour that the defence was strained almost to breaking-point. By the end of July, his artillery had breached all the bastions ; his engineers had filled in the fosse, and completed a line of semi-permanent fortifications opposite to the landward front of the fortress ; and two general assaults had been foiled only after the storming-parties had scaled the walls and fought ' beard to beard,' as Couto says, with the Portuguese.

The garrison were also menaced with starvation. For the storehouses had been riddled with shot until they were no longer weather-proof, and the only provisions left— rice and sugar—had grown mouldy in the moist, hot atmosphere. Cats and dogs had been eaten, flavoured with a stew of the weeds that flourish after tropical rain ; and any marksman fortunate enough to bring down one of the kites or carrion-crows that flocked to gorge on the dead had no difficulty in selling his game. The hospital was full and the medicine-chests empty : even the stock of gunpowder was nearly exhausted ; and only the cheerfulness and resource of Mascarenhas staved off despair. There were times when even the old campaigners of Diu lost heart, and clamoured to be led into the open, where they could die fighting like men instead of waiting for death like rats in a trap. But every emergency found Mascarenhas prepared. Even when the supply of powder-pots ran short, he was able to improvise a substitute out of two tiles, placed sandwich-fashion, with the convex surfaces outwards and the charge within.[1]

On the 10th of August D. Fernão de Castro and many of the leading fidalgos were drawn, by a series of feints, to the St John bastion. When Mascarenhas saw that no attempt was made to drive the attack home, he ordered

---

[1] *Dec.* vi. Bk. ii. chap. viii. p. 149.

the defenders to retire, warning them that the bastion was probably mined. They would have obeyed, but for the taunts of Diogo de Reynoso, D. Fernão's guardian, who shouted that only a coward would desert his post. A moment later the bastion was blown to atoms, and both Reynoso and D. Fernão lay dead. Seventy men had been killed or wounded by the explosion ; but as the dense clouds of smoke rolled away, João Coelho, the chaplain, leapt into the breach, holding up his crucifix, and the few survivors rallied round the symbol of their faith. While the fighting was still hot, a crowd of women and slaves arrived carrying beams, stones, and ammunition. Before night they had completed an inner line of retrenchment behind the bastion, which was abandoned as no longer tenable.

On the 13th of August, when all but eighty of the garrison had been disabled, a small boat came in sight, flying the flag of Portugal. She was manned by a few picked fighters, who had crossed over from Chaul in the teeth of a gale. There had been no lack of volunteers for this forlorn hope. One gigantic man-at-arms, left on shore lest his weight should overburden the boat, had swum out with his matchlock between his teeth, until the captain relented and allowed him to scramble on board. Other reinforcements followed, and on the 29th appeared a flotilla of more than forty small vessels commanded by D. Alvaro de Castro and D. Francisco de Menezes.

The new men found themselves required to stand sentry day and night over heaps of shattered masonry or flimsy barricades of timber ; to disregard the bullets and arrows singing past their ears ; not to flinch when an oath and a smothered cry told them that some invisible sniper had found his target, or when the faint clink and thud of pick-axes proved that the ground under their very feet was being mined. To such a strain their nerves were not yet equal ; and in less than three days after disembarkation they broke into mutiny, demanding that Mascarenhas should at once assume the offensive.

Their clamour prevailed. On the afternoon of September 1st, twenty score Portuguese marched boldly forth to engage twenty thousand Muhammadans entrenched behind high and massive fortifications. The mutineers advanced in three detachments, Mascarenhas leading the centre, Menezes and D. Alvaro the wings. From the time they left the fortress they were under fire. Menezes and many other fidalgos were shot down in the first rush to carry the semi-permanent works by escalade. Soon afterwards D. Alvaro ordered his own followers to retreat and set the example by taking to his heels. Mascarenhas—blackened with powder and dripping blood and sweat—strove in vain to rally the panic-stricken remnant, who crouched among the rank vegetation at the foot of the walls, refusing to budge until they felt the point of his pike. Then they broke cover and fled, having lost more than a fourth of their number in killed and wounded.

For the next five weeks the garrison stood sullenly at bay behind their inner retrenchment, which consisted of a rough breastwork forming curtains between the houses nearest to the enemy. Moonrise on the 10th of October marked the beginning of Ramadan, and for twenty-seven out of the appointed thirty days the Musalman army fasted from dawn till sunset, praying Allah to grant victory to the faithful, but making no attempt to press the siege.

At last, on the 6th of November 1546, D. João de Castro appeared off Diu in command of twelve great galleons and a host of smaller vessels. During eight months he had been collecting men and ships from every Portuguese settlement along the Malabar Coast, and waiting for the end of the monsoon. The troops had been steadily drilled and exercised in field manœuvres on the marshy plains near Goa, where a lath and plaster facsimile of Rumi Khan's fortifications had been erected, from plans supplied by Mascarenhas.

A council of war was at once held aboard the flagship, and a plan of campaign concerted. Three caravels were told off to assist the defenders of the island fortalice in bombarding Rumi Khan's left flank, and during daylight the main body of the fleet kept the enemy constantly on the move to repel any sudden landing which might threaten their right and rear. At night, however, the soldiers of the relieving army were secretly drafted into the fortress, by means of rope-ladders planted along the cliffs ; while a flotilla of small boats, with lights ablaze, trumpets sounding, and a forest of lances bristling on deck, was rowed to and fro by non-combatants, so as to distract attention from the landing-parties. This ruse succeeded so well that within three nights the whole fighting force was quartered within the Portuguese lines, though the Muhammadans were unaware that its disembarkation had begun.

A second council of war was now held to consider the next move. Castro seems to have left the matter in the hands of his captains, some of whom urged him not " to stake all India on a single cast of the dice " by risking battle against overwhelming odds. About 20,000 men garrisoned the semi-permanent fortifications which faced the Portuguese lines, and it was rumoured that the Sultan of Gujarat had another army of 50,000 in reserve. To meet this array, Castro could only place some 3500 men in the field, exclusive of a few hundred native levies. But Garcia de Sá—a veteran of fifty years' service, who after-wards succeeded Castro as Governor of India [1]—finally persuaded the assembled captains to offer battle.

The morrow was the 11th of November—celebrated by the Christians as St Martin's Day, and by the Muslims as the Lesser Feast of Bairam. At sunrise three rockets fired over the sea gave the signal for an advance, and the Portuguese ships moved out along the north-eastern shore of the island. They were preceded by the Governor's state barge, flying the royal standard ; and, as before, were chiefly manned by non-combatants, though the display of weapons and lighted matches still convinced Rumi Khan's scouts that the entire Portuguese army was on board. The object of this manœuvre was to divert a portion of Rumi Khan's troops by the threat of a descent upon their left flank, while Castro delivered a sudden frontal attack upon the positions thus weakened.

These tactics drew away Rumi Khan and some 12,000 Gujaratis to the southern bank of the channel, about a

[1] June 5th 1548 to July 6th 1549.

mile from the fortified position, which was Castro's real objective. In their absence, the Portuguese army issued suddenly from the fortress. Mascarenhas with 500 men-at-arms led the van, supported by two companies of the same strength, which were commanded by D. Alvaro and D. Manoel de Lima. These three units, together forming the first division, were followed by a second division of some 1500 men, headed by the Governor in person. Castro's troops hung back at first, but a false rumour that the enemy were in full retreat restored their courage. Meanwhile the advanced guard had charged down upon the semi-permanent works, which were held by 8000 mercenaries——the pick of the besieging army—under the Sultan's Abyssinian general Juzar Khan. There was keen rivalry for the honour of being first to scale the walls. One fidalgo, D. João Manoel, strove vainly to hoist himself over the parapet by his forearms, after both hands had been cut off : he fell back dead, and, according to Couto, the coveted distinction was shared between Cosmo de Paiva and Miguel Rodrigues Coutinho — the ' Fios Seccos ' satirized by Camões. Other storming-parties followed, and after a fierce struggle gained the whole fortified line of batteries.

Rumi Khan and his 12,000 Gujaratis now arrived upon the scene, but they had lost the advantage of fighting behind bricks and mortar, and could not cope with the mail-clad Portuguese in a hand-to-hand encounter. Even so, Castro's advance was checked by the sheer weight and mass of the opposing forces, until his Franciscan comrade, Antonio do Casal, came forward to rally the waverers, holding aloft his crucifix lashed to the end of a spear. When a stone flung by one of the Gujarati slingers shattered one arm of the cross—" Follow me," exclaimed the friar, " follow me, my children, knights of Christ ! Charge to avenge our God ! " His words revived the flagging energies of the Portuguese, who from that moment became irresistible. By the time darkness set in, Castro was master of the whole island ; Rumi Khan and 3000 of his men were killed ; 600, including Juzar Khan, were prisoners.

CHAPTER XX

THE LAST OF THE HEROES

THOUGH the war was not yet over, India had been saved. The credit belongs primarily to Mascarenhas, and after him to the council of captains whose strategy had rendered victory possible. Castro, though his fame as a commander rests principally upon the relief of Diu, had merely taken good advice and played a gallant part in the actual fighting. Mascarenhas was rewarded by an extension of his term as Captain—a duty so onerous that no other fidalgo would accept the responsibility—and throughout the winter all hands were kept hard at work in rebuilding the fortress. An epidemic, due to the number of bodies which had been buried in the ruins, cost 1500 lives, and the Governor found it hard to feed or pay the survivors. He succeeded in raising a loan of £6000 in Goa by depositing some hairs from his beard as a pledge. The historians relate that women sold their jewels, and all classes were eager to contribute ; but though the pledge was returned in a silver casket, the covering letter contains a statement of grievances and a request for early payment.[1] Fortunately the capture of a richly laden ship soon enabled Castro to discharge the debt.

In April he returned to Goa, and as a study in manners, the description of his triumphal entry into the capital is not without interest. On Sunday the 15th of April, 1547, he stepped ashore upon a specially constructed pier, gay with streamers of silk and brocade. He was wearing a suit of crimson satin and cloth of gold, with a plumed cap of black velvet ; beside him marched his son, and before him the Franciscan Antonio do Casal, carrying his broken

[1] Printed in Andrade, p. 460.

DOM JOÃO DE CASTRO
AFTER CORRÊA

crucifix. Hardly less conspicuous was Juzar Khan, walking with folded hands and eyes downcast, " for fear," as Faria y Sousa remarks, " he should see our colours flying and his own trailed through the dust." Six hundred prisoners were paraded through the streets, preceded by trophies of captured arms and armour. The water-gate had been too narrow for so much magnificence, and part of the walls had been broken down to afford an entrance worthy of the occasion. Here the procession halted to receive an address of welcome, " spoken in Latin of much elegance," and then passed on between the dense lines of spectators, whose cheers and cries of " Long live the saviour of our country ! " mingled with the din of trumpets, drums and fifes. Mortars discharged volleys of sweetmeats into the air, and from the balconies overhead the ladies of Goa showered roses and perfumes upon their hero.

By and by there was another halt : the aldermen spread a rich canopy over Castro's head, while the procurator of the city removed his cap " with much reverence and courtesy," substituting a wreath of palm and thrusting a palm-branch into his hand.[1] Small wonder that, as Couto says, the Governor proceeded on his way " cheerful and smiling." Outside the church of St Francis he was greeted by a company of friars chanting *Benedictus qui venit in nomine Domini*, and at the cathedral the Bishop and other high dignitaries of the Church were also waiting to bid him welcome, arrayed in full canonicals. Two features of the pageant which delighted the crowd were a model of the Diu fortress in wood and coloured paper, where salutes were fired from real guns and powder-pots, and an artificial forest in which living hares and birds disported themselves. In brief, as Queen Catherine remarked when she heard of the spectacle, Castro had " conquered like a Christian and triumphed like a heathen."

In 1547 the Portuguese had a last chance to annex Aden, and thus to close the main approach by which a Turkish fleet could menace India. The Arab inhabitants, weary

---

[1] Corrêa, vol. iv. p. 596. Corrêa supervised the painting of the portrait which represents Castro thus adorned.

of Osmanli rule, had revolted, expelled the Ottoman garrison, and set up an independent government under their Shaikh, Ali bin Sulaiman. Then, fearing that the Turks would return in force, they applied for aid to the Portuguese Captain of Ormuz. The opportunity was too good to be missed; and Castro's kinsman, D. Payo de Noronha, was at once sent to Aden in command of a small fleet. He found himself heartily welcome, and took up his quarters on shore while Ali bin Sulaiman sallied out to meet the Turks.

The night noises of an Oriental city troubled D. Payo's nerves. There were cries and whispers in the dark, bubbling camels and furtive pariah dogs that snarled and worried over the dust-heaps. If D. Payo peered through his lattice, he could see groups of uncanny white-robed Arabs prowling round the doorways. Heaven only knew what treason and devilry they might be plotting. The gallant commander accordingly re-embarked and slept more soundly in his own cabin. When news reached him that his allies had been routed and the Turks were at hand, he determined not to risk the precious lives of his men, but slipped away, leaving Aden to take care of itself. His memory is kept green by the anecdote of a kind-hearted citizen, who one day noticed a little girl crying on D. Payo's doorstep and stopped to comfort her. Having ascertained that D. Payo's servants had stolen her hen, he bade her dry her tears and face the inevitable. " If it were Aden," he told her, " you could have it and welcome! But a hen! No, they'll never surrender that." [1]

Tidings of Ali bin Sulaiman's appeal for help reached Castro in India long before he learned of the subsequent fiasco. As rapidly as his mutinous troops would allow, he equipped a flying squadron under the command of D. Alvaro, and dispatched it to seize the long-coveted fortress. D. Alvaro arrived to find a new Turkish garrison in possession, and did not attempt the hopeless task of an assault with his meagre force of 300 men. But he was resolved not to forego the laurels of victory, and promptly set forth

[1] Couto, *Dec.* vi. Bk. vi. chap. vi. p. 47.

to discover a sufficiently helpless foe. By skirting the Arabian shore eastward from Aden, he came presently to the town of Shakhra, which was defended by a small fort of sun-baked clay. Its garrison, consisting of 35 Arabs, inconsiderately offered to surrender, but D. Alvaro would hear of no reasonable terms. The fort was bombarded and captured, though not without heavy loss, and all the defenders were put to the sword. Fresh from this exploit, D. Alvaro returned to Goa, where he, too, indulged in a triumphal procession.

But all sense of humour was not dead, even in Goa. Couto describes a conversation between Bishop Albuquerque and a priest who was celebrated for his skill in solving riddles.

" What is it," the Bishop inquired, " that from bitter grew sweet, from large small and from small large ? "   " Bitter almonds [1] became sweet," the priest replied, " when the Governor was pelted with them on his return from Diu ; from being large, the taking of Broach became small, because the captor was D. Jorge de Menezes ; from being small, the taking of Shakhra became large, because the captor was the Governor's own son."

Couto does not quite approve of the Bishop, who " laughed heartily at this reply."

Castro was wasted with fever, when the shameful news from Aden reached him ; and it preyed upon his mind, so that he grew weaker day by day. When he was already past work, a ship from Portugal came to announce that he had been granted the title of Viceroy, with a three years' extension of his term ; soon afterwards, on the 5th of June 1548, he died in the arms of his friend and confessor, the Jesuit Francis Xavier. The cause of his death, according to the oft-quoted words of Faria y Sousa, " was a disease which to-day kills no man . . . for diseases also die. It was a keen sense of the wretched state to which India had come, and of his own inability to repair it."

Historians have extolled D. João de Castro as the type of a chivalrous soldier and gentleman. His courage was beyond cavil, his unbending honesty earned him his nick-

---

[1] Port. *maçapães*, 'marzipans,' Couto, *l.c.* p. 48.

name of ' the Portuguese Cato ' ; he was assuredly a man of higher character than any who had ruled India since the days of Albuquerque. But his biographers have, with the best intentions, caricatured his very virtues and made him appear a gasconading pedant. They delight to tell how he cut to ribbons the costly cloak ordered by his son, and bade the youth buy arms ; or how he decorated the vestibule of his audience-chamber with dummy monsters, so as to strike terror into the hearts of native ambassadors.

If we turn to his own letters and note-books, we find him a man of a different stamp ; hot-tempered, indeed, but shrewd, broad-minded, humorous and, above all, a true son of the Renaissance, combining its reverence for antiquity with its new-born interest in nature. His imitation of a Roman triumph and his discourse on the Red Sea are equally manifestations of this Renaissance spirit. In the letters there is nothing of the pedant, much that shows the writer a keen judge of men. He knew that Portuguese India was living on its reputation, that prestige was its chief asset. Hence the dummy dragons, the theatrical parade of captives, the triumphal arches. Hence also the use, in an official document, of the imposing new title " Lion of the Sea." [1] It was all a game of bluff as well as an amusing classical exercise. Castro had realized the worth of his followers : " not such that Our Lord should work a miracle for them," he explained to his royal master, after regretting that he had not so much as five loaves and two small fishes with which to fill the multitude of clamorous mouths. Knowing his men so well, he deliberately applied to them the Virgilian principle—*possunt quia posse videntur* —cheating them into a belief in their own courage which made them invincible.

But Castro himself deserves to be remembered rather as among the first of Portuguese scientists than as the last of Portuguese heroes. Not until the nineteenth century were the *Roteiros* printed and the real interest of his career

---

[1] *O lião do maar o senhor dom Johaõ de Crasto* (*sic*) : Botelho, *Tombo*, p. 39. The use of such titles was quite common in India. Bahadur Shah, for example, was styled " The Tiger of the World."

disclosed. Andrade does indeed mention his scientific tastes, but only to apologize for them as a pastime rather eccentric in so great a man. His officers probably regarded their captain with compassionate surprise when they saw him studying the footprints of a wild goat, or marking the direction of a comet, while all sane men were on their knees, praying that the omen might be averted.

He was greater than they could guess. His interest in all natural phenomena, however seemingly trivial, and his use of experiment, place him among the few men of his age who felt the spirit and essayed the methods of modern science. It was part of the tragedy of Portugal that the development of this scientific spirit was apt to be mistaken for the spread of heresy.

JUDAISM, HUMANISM AND THE CHURCH

CHAPTER XXI

WHILE new territories were being won for the Portuguese Crown in Asia and Africa, at home the monarchy was undergoing a process of gradual and painless decay. King Manoel had ruled; his successors only reigned. Their policy was directed by ecclesiastical advisers, who subordinated the welfare of their country to the interests of their Church. This change was not due merely to the ineptitude and bigotry of John III. and Sebastian, for the Church had been greatly strengthened by its victories over two formidable adversaries—Judaism and Humanism.

The history of the Jews in Portugal is one of singular and tragic interest. Their unpopularity was due to other causes than race-hatred, from which the Portuguese have ever been immune. Even in the thirteenth century Jews were eligible to high official positions; from Affonso II. (1211-1223) their courts received complete autonomy in civil and criminal cases, and the Chief Rabbi was a royal official, who bore the arms of Portugal on his seal. Though the Jews were, from the first, compelled to live in certain streets called *Juderías* or Jewries, it was not until 1325 that they were forced to wear the distinctive badge of a six-pointed yellow star in their hats or cloaks.

The Sephardic Jews of Spain and Portugal differed from the Ashkenazim of Germany and Poland in character far more than in ritual. The leading members of their communities were not retail traders but bankers or merchant princes. No Moorish emir or Castilian grandee was ever more dignified; for the Portuguese Jews saw in Israel the aristocracy of nations and in themselves the aristocracy of Israel. In culture they certainly excelled their rulers ; for to the knowledge of their own literature many of them added a profound study of Gentile art and science—the philosophy of Aristotle, mathematics, astronomy, astrology and above all medicine and surgery, of which they were the foremost exponents in Europe. Many of them attained eminence as poets or historians, and between 1487 and 1495 Hebrew printing-presses were established successively at Faro, Lisbon and Leiria.

The growth of prejudice against them was the work neither of the Crown nor of the commons, but of the two intermediate estates of the realm. The sight of a Jewish congregation going to worship in its own synagogue bitterly offended the clergy ; the furred or silken robes and gold chains of rich Hebrew merchants, their fine Barbary horses and the other symbols of their wealth filled the nobles with a sense of righteous wrath, even though the scruples of an impoverished aristocrat might, now and then, be overcome by the charms of a Jewish heiress. When a Jew was nominated receiver of customs (*almoxarife*) or medical adviser to the King, his preferment wounded the pride of Catholic subordinates and competitors. In time the influence of the clergy and the nobles helped to inflame the commons, who were taught to regard the Jews as heathen intruders who fattened on the spoils wrung from their innocent and orthodox fellow-citizens. The ghetto, and the deeper spiritual exclusiveness fostered by Judaism among its votaries produced an atmosphere of suspicion, in which fear was added to jealousy and religious prejudice. Rabbinical learning was confounded with black magic. The charges of ritual murder or of poisoning wells levelled to-day against the Jews in Russia, Rumania, or Hungary, had their counterpart in Portugal. One sinister rumour ascribed the coming of the bubonic plague to Jewish malevolence. It stands to the credit of the Portuguese Kings that they long resisted the pressure exercised by their subjects, and even by Popes and friendly sovereigns. No doubt their patronage of Judaism was not due to pure benevolence. The Juderías were models of thrift, industry, civic virtue of every kind; and without Jewish brains and capital the commerce of the country would have been paralysed. Moreover they contributed a share of the revenue not lightly to be surrendered. They paid poll-taxes, road-taxes, navy-taxes, taxes on every business transaction, however small. A Jew could not buy a basket of eggs or sell a bundle of thyme without enriching the treasury by percentage of the price. To instil into his mind a salutary consciousness of inferiority, a special poll-tax of 30 *dinheiros* was imposed, in memory of the thirty pieces of silver paid to Judas Iscariot. This somewhat grim piece of humour was borrowed from Castile. In neither kingdom did the rulers notice that, as the recipients of the money, they had cast themselves for the part of Judas.

Affonso V. (1438-81), a kindly and just monarch, permitted the Jews to reside outside the Juderías, freed them from the obligation to wear distinguishing badges, and even appointed a Jew, Isaac Abravanel, to be his minister of finance; but it was in his reign that the popular hatred came to a head. In 1449, irritated by the influence of men like Abravanel, or of Joseph ben David ibn Yahya, who entertained the King with learned discourse on theology and physics, the inhabitants of Lisbon stormed and sacked the Juderías in the city, killing several of the inhabitants. Affonso sternly repressed the rioters. But the influence of the Jews, and especially their ostentatious display of wealth provoked fresh complaints; and the Cortes four times petitioned the Crown to enforce the antisemitic provisions of the canon law. John II. (1481-95) found, like his predecessor, that Jews were useful; and when more than 90,000 Jewish refugees from Castile fled into his dominions, he promised them asylum for eight months, in return for a poll-tax of eight *cruzados* (£3, 11s. 6d.). But they were warned that after eight months they must leave the country in ships provided by the King. John hastened to collect the tax, but was less punctual in furnishing the transport. So dilatory was he that many Jews were unable to depart. Those who remained were enslaved, while their children were taken from them and shipped to the island of São Thomé, there to be devoured by wild beasts, to die of starvation, or to survive as best they might. Hardly more fortunate was the lot of those who took ship in time and found themselves at the mercy of a fanatical crew, whose ferocity was heightened by dread of the plague.

The motives which inspired King Manoel's persecution of the Jews have already been described. On the 4th of December 1496, four days after the signature of his marriage contract, he issued an ordinance commanding all Jews to leave his dominions before the end of October 1497. Those who remained would forfeit their lives and property ; any Christian who shielded a Jew after the period of grace would be deprived of all his possessions ; never again should the unbelievers be suffered to defile the Catholic land of Portugal with their presence. Meanwhile a plan was formulated by which the economic dangers of this wholesale exodus might be lessened. At the instance of a renegade, Levi ben Shem-Tob, and in spite of the protests of Bishop Fernando Coutinho and the state council over which he presided at Estremoz, Manoel determined to baptize all Jews of either sex between the ages of four and twenty-five.

The victims received two days notice of the intention to " make them Christians " (*facere Christianos*), as the process was termed by contemporary optimists. On the first day of Passover (the 19th of March), children and youths were driven in herds to the churches, joining loudly in the lamentations and protests of their elders, and declaring their undying faith in the creed of Israel. Many parents, seeing no hope of deliverance, killed their children and themselves ; some families were concealed by friendly Portuguese. When October came and the period of grace drew to an end, the King proclaimed that all Jews must assemble in Lisbon and there embark. Twenty thousand persons came, and were marshalled in a huge palace which afterwards became the headquarters of the Inquisition. They were informed that the time for sailing had elapsed and that they were now slaves of the King. Threats, promises and even the exhortations of two apostates of their own race failed to convince the Jews that the religion of their tormentors was superior to their own. So the twenty thousand " obstinate heathen " (*cafres contumasses*), as they were called, were haled by their hair or beards to the font, and forcibly baptized. The outspoken condemnation of this outrage by such men as the high-minded Bishop Coutinho, and the patronage extended to the Jews by Pope Alexander VI. led to a temporary lull in the persecution of the " New Christians " or *Maranos*, as the baptized Jews were styled. In 1498 many of them were permitted to sell their property and emigrate, but this avenue of escape was closed by a royal edict, which forbade emigration.

On the night of the 17th of April 1506 a party of New Christians were arrested for joining in the celebration of the Passover, and some of them were imprisoned for two days. Their liberation, attributed by the populace of Lisbon to bribery, aroused a storm of indignation, which broke loose on the morning of the 19th. The Christian and Marano worshippers, assembled in the church of the Dominicans to pray for a cessation of the plague which was devastating the city, were startled by the vision of a luminous reliquary and crucifix shining in one of the dimly lit side-chapels. A Jew who ventured to hint that the miracle was caused by the reflection from a sunlit window, was seized and slaughtered by a band of infuriated women, and his body was burned in the Rocio or chief square of Lisbon. A wild mob of men and women, maddened by religious zeal or the prospect of loot and bloodshed, rushed through the streets, headed by two Dominican friars, who urged them on with cries of " Heresia ! Heresia ! " Babies were strangled or flung upon the pyres where living and dead were burned together ; women who sought refuge in church were dragged from beneath the altar and slain. At least two thousand New Christians perished.

But the King, who feared the clergy as little as their victims, took summary vengeance. The lay ringleaders were hanged, beheaded, or hewn in pieces ; the two Dominicans were expelled from their order, garrotted and burned ;

all who had taken plunder were flogged and fined. So effective were these remedies that while Manoel lived none dared again attack the Jews, who from 1507 to 1521 were once more permitted to emigrate. Almost all those who were unwilling to abjure their creed now fled from the country; and after the establishment of the Inquisition in 1536, large numbers of the " New Christians " were driven by persecution to follow this example, greatly to the disadvantage of Portuguese commerce. They found one safe asylum under the Portuguese flag : this was in Brazil, where the Society of Jesus afterwards became all-powerful and successfully resisted the introduction of the Holy Office.[1]

[1] The best modern account of the Jews in Portugal is the article " Portugal " in the *Jewish Encyclopædia*. Apart from the Portuguese historians, the chief sixteenth-century description of the persecution is in Samuel Usque's masterpiece, *Consolaçam ás tribulações de Israel*.

CHAPTER XXII

WHEN John III. came to the throne of Portugal in 1521, Judaism as a separate religion had almost ceased to exist in his kingdom ; but the Church was confronted by a new and more difficult problem. To the discoveries of new continents and oceans made by Columbus and Gama, had been added an even vaster area of spiritual discovery. Manuscripts which had been hoarded for centuries in the monasteries of Greece and the Balkans, had been snatched from their dusty hiding-places at the coming of the Turks ; and now, nearly seventy years after the fall of Constantinople, the wisdom and the poetry of Greece and Rome were giving new ideals to civilization. More had published his *Utopia*, Erasmus his revised Greek Testament ; Machiavelli had composed his *Principe* ; Luther had defied the Pope.

The defenders of the old order, armed with the authority of tradition and the formidable if cumbrous weapons of scholasticism, rallied against the innovators who stood for Humanism and Reform. As yet the University of Paris, the intellectual headquarters of Europe, was open to the partisans of either side. Hither came the most promising students of all nations, among them a large contingent from Spain and Portugal, seekers for a broader culture than Salamanca or Lisbon could impart. Ste. Barbe, one of the two or three score colleges in the university, was the foundation they most frequented. John III. had commissioned its principal, Diogo de Gouvêa, to purchase the college as a training-ground for the priests and administrators intended to control his dominions overseas. Gouvêa had failed in this, but had secured a lease. One of his lecturers was the famous Scottish Humanist George Buchanan, who was destined to acquire a closer knowledge of Portugal than he could have desired.

Buchanan, born near Killearn in Stirlingshire, either in 1506 or 1507, was the son of a Highland father, possibly Irish in descent, and of a Lowland mother, Agnes Heriot by name. He graduated at St Andrews, and took his degree of Master at Paris in 1528, thus qualifying for the post of regent, or member of the teaching staff ; and this office he obtained at Ste. Barbe in the same year.

Here were educated the foremost of those thinkers and preachers who were, within a generation, to fight out in Coimbra the issues between Catholicism and the New Learning ; to organize missions throughout the Portuguese empire, to raise the authority of the Portuguese Church above that of the Crown, and finally to change the whole character and mental outlook of the Portuguese nation. It is worth while pausing to consider the environment in which these men received their early training.

University life was by no means devoid of hardship. Lectures lasted from daylight until dark, and only the teacher enjoyed the luxuries of desk and chair ; the scholars squatted round him on the floor, keeping themselves warm in winter with piles of straw. Erasmus in one of his " Colloquies," the *Ichthyophagia*, shows clearly enough how sordid was a student's lot at Montaigu, his own college. " The very walls there teach divinity," he writes, " but as for me, I brought nothing out of it but my body full of gross humours, and my clothes full of lice." '

Erasmus refers to a state of affairs which existed towards the close of the fifteenth century. The later influence of Reform, within and without the Church of Rome, tended to make the life more ascetic and discipline more harsh. In such matters the customs of Paris were no worse than those of other foundations. It was reserved for the University of Glasgow to enact, in the seventeenth century, that condign punishment should be inflicted on all students who so far forgot themselves as to play at ball, or to encounter any senior member of the staff without seeking to shun his Olympian eye ; while bathing was an offence which could only be met with flogging and expulsion.[1] Rabelais seems to be criticizing a similar perverted notion of decency in his description of the Abbey of Thélème, for which he takes care to provide not only a tilt-yard or theatre, but even " a natatory, with most admirable baths in three stages, situated one above another, well furnished with all necessary accommodations, and store of myrtle-water." [2]

In their hours of leisure the students who could afford such costly pastimes might indulge in tournaments and feats of martial skill—in hawking, hunting, gambling. Their poorer companions, when fate denied them the joys of a fight with the townsmen or with a rival " nation," could spend their time in the taverns, drinking deeply, singing, or dicing. Even such homely sports as leap-frog, bowls, and foot-racing were not neglected. Rich and poor alike might perform in Latin dramas, mysteries and moralities, or crowd round the great hall fire on winter nights to listen to the seemly jests of their regents, to readings from the Vulgate, to the wonders of the world as recorded by such famous travellers as Odoric of Pordenone. The gay, half-pagan *Carmina Burana* and other student-songs of the type of *Ergo bibamus* and *Ludo cum Cæcilia*, which have descended to us from the Middle Ages instinct with youth and the joy of life, belong to an earlier age ; but the spirit they reflect was by no means dead among the irrepressible, irresponsible scholars of Paris in the sixteenth century.

Buchanan, in one of his Latin poems, discourses upon the discomforts undergone by the shepherd of this unruly flock.

" No sooner," he writes, " has he stretched his limbs than the watchman announces that it is already the fourth hour. The din of the shrill alarm chases away dreams and reminds him that his rest is at an end. Hardly are things again quiet when five o'clock sounds, and the porter rings his bell, calling the scholars to their task. Then, in all the majesty of cap and gown forth issues the master, the terror

---

[1] *Munimenta Universitatis Glasguensis*, ed. C. Innes, Glasgow, 1854, vol. ii. p. 50.

[2] Urquhart and Motteux' *Rabelais*, Bk. i. chap. lv.

of his charge, in his right hand the scourge, in his left perchance the works of the great Virgil. He seats himself, and shouts his orders till he is red in the face. And now be brings forth the harvest of his toil. He smoothes away difficulties, he corrects, he expunges, he changes the text, he brings to light the spoils which he has won by ceaseless study. Meanwhile his scholars, some of them, are sound asleep, others thinking of everything but their Virgil. One is absent, but has bribed his neighbours to answer to his name at roll-call. Another has lost his stockings. Another cannot keep his eye off a large hole in his shoe. One shams illness, another is writing letters to his parents. Hence the rod is never idle, sobs never cease, cheeks are never dry. Then the duties of religion make their call on us, then lessons once more, and once more the rod. Hardly an hour is spared for our meal. No sooner is it over than lessons again, and then a hasty supper. Supper past, we continue our labours into the night as if the day's tasks, forsooth, had not been sufficient. Why should I speak of our thousand humiliations ? Here, for example, comes the swarm of loafers from the city, till the street echoes with the noise of their pattens. In they scramble to listen as intelligently as so many asses. They grumble that no placards announcing the scheme of lessons have been stuck on the street corners, they are indignant that the *Doctrinal* of Alexander is scornfully ignored by the master, and off they run to Montaigu or some other school more to their taste. Parents also grumble that the days pass by, that their sons learn nothing, and meanwhile the fees must be paid." [1]

At Ste. Barbe Buchanan probably came in contact with three of the most notable men of his day. One was Calvin, as yet only on the threshold of his career. Another was Francis Xavier,[2] a blue-eyed, tawny-haired Spanish Basque of twenty-two, who had forsworn the military life to which his brothers were devoted, and had chosen, like his father Juan de Jasso, to follow more peaceful pursuits. Little is known for certain about the childhood and youth of the future Apostle of the Indies. According to a practice common at this period both in Spain and Portugal, he bore the name of his mother Maria, the sole heiress of the castles

[1] The translation given here is from Prof. P. Hume Brown's *George Buchanan, Humanist and Reformer*, Edinburgh, 1890.

[2] This is the usual English form of the name ; but *Francis of Xavier* would certainly be more correct, as *Xavier* is a place-name. Torsellino, Lucena and Francis himself write *Francisco de Xavier* or its equivalent, *Franciscus Xaverius*.

and lands of Azpilqueta and Xavier, in the Spanish Basque Country.

The third was another Spaniard, a dark-skinned ascetic of thirty-seven years, whose unsurpassed powers of leadership and organization were still latent, though soon to be evoked and concentrated on the fulfilment of his dream—the formation of a missionary society which should win back the Holy Land for Christendom. Ignatius de Loyola was already famous, so that his compatriots in the Netherlands held it a privilege to supply him with funds, and thus to enable him to carry out his plans, despite his vow of poverty. Seven years had passed since his whole horizon had been changed by reading the *Lives of the Saints* and Ludolf of Saxony's *Life of Jesus*, as he lay healing of the wound which he had received in the siege of Pamplona. In his hermitage at Manresa he had drawn strength from the vision of the Montserrat, the " mountain carved in flame " which Teutonic legend identified as the resting-place of the Holy Grail; the " mountain sawn asunder," which Spanish tradition declared to have been thus cloven at the Crucifixion, when the rocks were rent. Thenceforward he renounced solitude, true to the couplet which so well differentiates the attitude of the Society of Jesus to " the world,"

> " Bernardus valles, montes Benedictus amabat,
> Oppida Franciscus, magnas Ignatius urbes."

At first the results of his freer intercourse with men and women proved not wholly successful. At Barcelona he was waylaid and left for dead by hired bravos. At Alcalá de Henares he was cast into prison because some ladies of rank, inspired by his teaching, had set forth alone and penniless on a pilgrimage. Ignatius was also imprisoned at Salamanca, where he was suspected of inculcating new and strange doctrines. But in Paris he was welcomed for his learning and reputed saintliness. Francis Xavier for a time resisted the eloquence of his fellow-countryman—Ignatius was a native of the Basque Province of Guipúzcoa—but finally accepted his guidance with a whole heart.

It is unnecessary here to describe the events of the seven years which witnessed the gradual evolution of the Society of Jesus in Paris. After Xavier and his fellow-student Peter Faber, Ignatius won over the Portuguese Simão Rodrigues, a native of Vinzella, who afterwards became the chronicler of these events and the head of the Jesuits in Portugal ; Diego Laynez, who won fame as a theologian at the Council of Trent ; Alfonso Salmerón, Hebraist and commentator on the New Testament ; Nicolás Bobadilla, who was chosen before Xavier as " Apostle of the Indies," but was prevented by illness from undertaking the task. On the Feast of the Assumption 1534, this company took the vows of chastity and poverty in the Church of Notre Dame de Montmartre. Six years later, after many difficulties, Pope Paul III. signed the Bull *Regimini militantis Ecclesiæ*, in which he announced his approval of the Society of Jesus (27th September 1540). Of all European countries Portugal was the one most affected by that decision.

CHAPTER XXIII

THE TRIAL OF GEORGE BUCHANAN [1]

WHILE the Jesuits were organizing for the defence of their Church, George Buchanan had ranged himself with its adversaries. After an honourable career at Paris, he had returned to Scotland in 1535, as tutor to the young Earl of Cassilis. He was already famous as a writer of barbed and polished Latin epigrams, and in Scotland he added to his reputation by the *Somnium*, a caustic paraphrase of Dunbar's poem 'How Dunbar was desyrit to be ane Fryer.' The *Somnium* so delighted King James V. that he appointed Buchanan tutor to his natural son, Lord James Stewart, and begged for more verse in the same strain. Buchanan's two *Palinodia* followed, but even these were not vitriolic enough, and the King asked for something which would " not merely prick the skin but probe the vitals." The *Franciscanus* fulfilled his amiable desire, and although this satire remained for many years in manuscript its contents became well enough known to provoke retaliation. A heresy-hunt was organized, and in February 1539 five Lutherans were burned in Edinburgh. The royal favour would certainly not have availed to preserve Buchanan from a like fate; but he contrived to break away from his guards and made good his escape from Scotland. After sundry adventures he was appointed professor at the newly founded Collège de Guyenne in Bordeaux, the principal of which was André de Gouvêa, a nephew of that Diogo de Gouvêa who had been head of Ste. Barbe while Buchanan was regent.

The Collège de Guyenne was designed to supersede the old type of grammar-school. Its staff included some of

[1] See Appendix A, Special Bibliography, " George Buchanan."

the most brilliant scholars of the day—erudite dreamers who hoped to create a new earth with the aid of classical literature, and had their doubts about the old heaven. In such a favourable environment Buchanan's talent could not fail to shine. Montaigne was his admiring pupil and in later life prided himself on the association with ' ce grand poète écossois.' [1] Among Buchanan's friends were Élie Vinet, the mathematician, and that most fiery and fantastic of all the Humanists, Julius Cæsar Scaliger, whose son Joseph, at this time a mere child, lived to write Buchanan's epitaph, rounding it off with the neat couplet :—

" Imperii fuerat Romani Scotia limes ;
Romani eloquii Scotia limes erit ? "

Buchanan's own pen was not allowed to rust. He translated the *Medea* and *Alcestis* into Latin, and composed the *Jephthes* and *Baptistes*, Latin dramas on the life of John the Baptist and on the story of Jephthah's daughter. These, according to Montaigne, were performed by the students " with much dignity," and all went well until Buchanan came into conflict with the monks of St Anthony, who very properly enjoyed the privilege of free trade in pigs. When the monks filled their monastery with swine, regardless of their neighbours' nostrils but much to their own profit, the local magistracy protested, and Buchanan indited a brief ode on the offence. He drew a parallel between the pigs and their owners which cannot have enhanced his popularity in ecclesiastical circles ; and he found it prudent to absent himself from Bordeaux.[2]

In 1547 he returned, having been invited to accompany André de Gouvêa, Vinet and other old friends on a journey to Portugal.

Two Portuguese friars, Jeronymo de Padilha and Jorge de Santiago, had visited the college at Bordeaux, and, on their return, seem to have described it to King John III.

[1] " Essay on Education."
[2] About 1542-1547. The dates and incidents of his life at this period are obscure.

as a model of all the academic virtues. The King determined to import its most distinguished teachers wholesale into the university of which he was himself the official protector. Coimbra University, founded in 1290, had become the educational centre of the kingdom, hardly inferior to the monarchy itself as a symbol of national unity, and thus wholly dissimilar to the great Spanish universities, Salamanca, Zaragoza, or Barcelona, each of which represented a province, not a nation.

Four times already the university had changed its seat between Lisbon and Coimbra. In 1537 it was for the last time established in the quiet city beside the Mondego, much to the displeasure of its students, whose opportunities for breaking heads and statutes were curtailed by the change. Despite a generous allowance of royal and papal patronage, the university was not illiberal.[1] Staff and students enjoyed many privileges, among them immunity from secular jurisdiction except when taken in certain grave crimes—to wit, homicide, wounding, theft, rapine, abduction of women and false coining. The last can hardly have been a common offence, even among undergraduates of the sixteenth century.

Buchanan was doubtless overjoyed at the prospect of secure and congenial employment after years of wandering in peril and poverty. He thanked King John III. in a Latin epigram which almost anticipates the phrase " an empire upon which the sun never sets " :—

> " Inque tuis Phœbus regnis, oriensque cadensque,
>   Vix longum fesso conderet axe diem ;
> Et quæcumque vago se circumvolvit Olympo
>   Affulget ratibus flamma ministra tuis." [2]

With Buchanan eight other professors had left Bordeaux for Coimbra, among them being his friends André de Gouvêa, Diogo de Teive and João da Costa. André de

---

[1] See below, chap. xxxiv.

[2]   "Within thy realms the Sun, with weary wheel,
        May rise and set, nor the long Day conceal ;
        Where'er he circles o'er the Olympian shores,
        Still on thy ships his faithful flame he pours."—H. JACOBS.

Gouvêa was appointed principal of the newly founded Royal College of Arts, in preference to his uncle Diogo, the former head of St Barbe, who bitterly and effectually resented the slight, even after André had died and João da Costa succeeded him. Diogo seems to have conspired with a certain Friar João de Pinheiro, who had been publicly flogged by Costa at Bordeaux, and therefore bore a grudge against one at least of the three friends, to swear an information which should lead to the arrest of Costa, Buchanan and Teive by the Holy Office. A preliminary inquiry, held in Paris by order of the Cardinal Prince Henry, acting as Inquisitor-General, decided that there was ground for the apprehension of the accused. The inquiry ended in December 1549, but it was not until the following August that Costa was arrested in Lisbon. Teive and Buchanan were invited to the Bishop of Coimbra's palace, and there detained while their rooms were searched.

Nothing was found more compromising than a copy of the works of Clément Marot, belonging to Costa, and some books with notes or prefaces by Melanchthon, belonging to Buchanan.

On the 15th of August, 1550, Costa and Buchanan were lodged in the prison of the Holy Office in Lisbon ; and three days later the trial began. Buchanan was accused of Judaistic and Lutheran tendencies. The first part of the indictment is easily understood ; Buchanan's piercing eyes, set widely apart, and his huge nose like the beak of a falcon, gave him an appearance extraordinarily Hebraic for one who had no Jewish blood in his veins. As for the charge of Lutheranism, it was backed by evidence to show that he had broken the law of the Church in word and act. On his own admission he had once at least " stumbled into Luther's fire " ; but his wonted attitude towards religion had hitherto been that of Erasmus, who accepted the doctrines of the Church while holding himself at liberty to criticize the clergy.

Buchanan pleaded guilty on several counts and waived his right to employ counsel. Senhor G. J. C. Henriques has suggested that he was prompted to do so by one of the Inquisitors, possibly Jeronymo de Azambuja [1] (Hieronymus Oleaster), famous as a Hebraist and notorious as an Inquisitor, and that some powerful influence was secretly at work in favour of the accused. John III. may have been anxious to save the men who had come to Coimbra at his invitation, and Azambuja may have been ordered to do his best for them. But even the King could not alter the findings of an ecclesiastical court. Buchanan knew that he was fighting for his life and that it behoved him to proceed warily : yet he showed no sign of alarm, and every now and then a gleam of his native irony lit up his answers to cross-examination. Asked what he thought of the monastic life, he replied that it was " good for those who could bear it." He denied having eaten the Passover lamb, and added that there were no Jews in Scotland. As to Lutheranism he was candour itself, admitting that " when, in England, he heard some Catholic preacher, the faith of the Church seemed to him the right one, and when later on, he heard some Lutheran, the opinions of Luther seemed to him correct."

He was urged to confess any other past iniquities he could recall, " because if he did so he would be received with much mercy." After a long interval he contrived to remember that he had eaten meat in Lent, though he excused himself for having once done so in Salamanca, on the ground that the only fish to be obtained was conger-eel —a doubtful delicacy in a city so far from the sea.

At last, after the trial had dragged on for nearly a year, Buchanan made a formal renunciation of his errors on the 29th of July 1551. He had been found guilty of heretical opinions on the teaching of Luther, on Transubstantiation, Purgatory, Confession, the validity of Canon Law, the observance of Lent ; and he had presumed to maintain " that it was better to go straight to God than to the Saints."

It was a long catalogue of deadly sins, and men had perished at the stake for less. But Buchanan was sentenced to the same punishment as his fellow-prisoners whose offences were lighter. All three were merely ordered to

---

[1] See on Azambuja, *George Buchanan : a Memorial*, pp. 77-78.

undergo a period of detention in a monastery. Buchanan performed his penance in the convent of São Bento, where he was doomed to listen to edifying Latin homilies composed by the monks. He found them, as he afterwards admitted, " not unkind but ignorant."

There is no shadow of doubt that the Cardinal Prince was justified in ordering an inquiry into the administration of the Royal College. The sworn testimony of Costa revealed a surprising state of disorder and rivalry among the staff. Langlois, a Frenchman and a dismissed regent, had libelled his chief. Manoel de Mesquita, the chaplain, " was a perfect plague in the college." Master Belchior Beliagoa possessed so keen an invention that in Paris he had been known as the ' horse-dealer ' ; the Coimbra students called him Belial Beliagoa. Jorge de Sá carried a sword under his gown and declared that it was intended for use upon the principal. Master Antonio Caiado had acquired the nickname ' Mouth of Hell.' Alvaro Lobato " who is now teaching Cato [1] to the boys " was wont to purchase the scholars' clothes, so that they might have money to gamble. He was their Father Confessor.

It is at least clear that Costa, Buchanan and Teive were no martinets, and that the discipline of the Royal College of Arts was such as to invite inquiry.

Buchanan remained in the convent of São Bento from the end of his trial until the 17th of December 1551. He was then permitted to reside in Lisbon, and on the 28th of February 1552 he received his final discharge, with permission to go whither he chose and a final caution to associate for the future with good and pious Christians.

His later career is irrelevant to the story of Portugal, and need only be sketched here in the briefest outline. In 1560, after revisiting France, he returned to his native land, and ranged himself definitely on the side of the Reformers. He was appointed tutor to Queen Mary, who read Livy with him and granted him a pension. But after the murder of Bothwell he became one of her bitterest opponents and contributed to her downfall through his

[1] See below, chap. xxxiv.

Detectio, a masterpiece of rhetorical invective, published in 1571.

He shared in the reorganization of Scottish education by the Reformers, and for eight years (1570-8) supervised the studies of the youthful Prince James Stuart, who lived to be King of England and " the wisest fool in Christendom." Though a layman, Buchanan was elected Moderator of the General Assembly ; he also held office as Director of Chancery and Keeper of the Privy Seal. But the chief labour of his later years was the composition of his *De Jure Regni apud Scotos*, in which he laid down the novel doctrine that tyrants might lawfully be deposed by their people, and of his *Rerum Scoticarum Historia*, which was intended to give the true annals of his country, purged " of sum Inglis lyis & Scottis vanite." He was always poor and often in debt. His ' singular friend ' Sir Thomas Randolph [1] urged him to take a wife, but Buchanan refused to hazard his peace among " the tempestuous stermes & naufrage of mariage," an estate which he described in terms more forcible than civil.

James Melville has left a striking account of a visit he paid to Buchanan in 1581. With him were his uncle Andrew Melville, and the great man's cousin, Thomas Buchanan :—

" When we came to his chalmer, we fand him sitting in his chaire, teatching his young man that servit in his chalmer to spell a, b, ab ; e, b, eb, etc. . . .

" ' Better this,' quoth he, ' nor stelling sheipe, or sitting ydle, qhuilk is als ill ' . . .

" We cam to Mr. George again, & fund him bedfast by [2] his custome, and asking him, whow he did, ' Even going the way of weilfare,' sayes he. Mr. Thomas, his cusing, schawes him of the hardnes of that part of his Storie, that the King wald be offendit with it, and it might stey all the wark.

" ' Tell me, man,' says he, ' giff I have tauld the treuthe ? '

" ' Yis,' sayes Mr. Thomas, ' sir, I think sa.'

---

[1] Buchanan's only surviving letters in the vernacular, two in number, are addressed to this Randolph, who was Queen Elizabeth's agent at the Scottish Court.

[2] *I.e.* ' contrary to.'

GEORGE BUCHANAN

FROM A PICTURE IN THE NATIONAL PORTRAIT GALLERY, LONDON, PAINTED IN 1581
BY AN UNKNOWN ARTIST

" ' I will byd his fead,[1] and all his Kins, then,' quoth he : ' Pray, pray to God for me, & let him direct all.' " [2]

The anecdote is characteristic not of Buchanan alone, but of the whole spirit which made the Reformation.

In September 1582 George Buchanan died.

His ' notable Portuguese expedition,' as he calls it in a letter to Vinet, was unimportant in itself. Yet it shows in sharp contrast the principles which were at issue between Humanism and the Church. Although the orthodox Catholic positions had never as yet been openly challenged in Portugal, a century of maritime exploration had given birth to the scientific spirit and taught men to inquire where the Church demanded unquestioning faith. An earnest and strictly orthodox minority had watched with dismay the spread of heretical doctrines in Northern Europe, and feared that their own countrymen might also be lured to abandon the creed of their fathers. Quite logically, they concentrated their attack on the critical movement out of which the demand for reform had arisen ; and the weapons they employed were the Inquisition and the Society of Jesus.

[1] *I.e.* abide his feud.
[2] *Mr James Melvill's Diary*, Edinburgh, 1829.

CHAPTER XXIV

AN ACT OF FAITH

BUCHANAN'S trial reveals only the best side of the Inquisition ; it is necessary to scan the reverse of the picture more closely, if one would comprehend the gradual decline of the Portuguese nation in the latter half of the sixteenth century.

The first Auto-da-Fé was held in Lisbon on the 20th of September 1540, seven years before the establishment of the Holy Office was finally sanctioned by the Pope :—

" A mournful procession formed outside the palace of the Inquisition, and marched down to the Praça da Ribeira, a wide square close to the Tagus, where the ceremony was to take place. The charcoal-burners, whose duty it was to tend the fires, led the way, armed with pikes and match-locks. Then, behind a lifted crucifix, came the Dominican friars, each carrying a black cross and wearing a white habit and scapulary. They bore the standard of the Inquisition, a silken banner upon which was embroidered the figure of St Peter, holding in one hand the sword of vengeance, in the other an olive-branch : *Justitia et Misericordia*. The friars were followed by various persons of quality, on foot, and by the familiars of the Inquisition—clad in black and white liveries, and carrying crosses of black and white thinly edged with gold. Next the prisoners, in single file ; the dead first and then the living, classified according to the sentence of the tribunal as ' confessed, negative, im-penitent, contumacious, relapsed,' or whatever else might be the precise degree of their guilt.

" From long poles resembling flagstaves dangled the fantastically robed effigies of all the condemned who were absent, including those already dead—these poles being held upright by a company of executioners so completely enveloped in their cloaks and cowls of rough black serge that only the eyes and mouth remained visible. Whenever the figure represented a corpse, it was followed by another executioner carrying a black box on which devils and flames were portrayed. This contained the bones of the dead malefactor, to be flung into the fire at the feet of his effigy.

" The living marched behind the dead, in an order of precedence determined by the gravity of their offences, the least guilty leading the way. One by one they filed onward, each with his advocate, or, if doomed to the fire, his Dominican confessor, at his elbow. The men wore long tunics striped with black and white, the women—for no distinction of sex was observed—flowing dresses of the same colour and material, and all walked barefooted, with lighted candles in their hands, and halters about their necks.

" Such as had repented or confessed were attired in the *sambenito*, a kind of white chasuble with the cross of St Andrew worked in red on the breast and sides : their heads were uncovered. Those upon whom sentence of death by fire had been passed, but remitted, were clad in the *samarra*, a grey chasuble, and the *carocha*, a tall mitre of pasteboard ; both garments were bedizened with tongues of flame—inverted, to signify the narrow escape of the wearer. No variation of garb marked the difference between prisoners doomed to perish at the stake and those condemned only to be burned after strangulation.[1] Both classes wore the *carocha* and *samarra*, on which their names and crimes were blazoned and their persons depicted in the midst of aspiring red flames stoked by sable fiends.

" The halberdiers of the Inquisition brought up the rear of this long procession, escorting the mounted officials of the supreme council—judges, qualificators,[2] reporters, and various underlings to complete the cavalcade. From every church tower sounded the ponderous tolling of bells.

" As the helpless victims filed through the streets, a surging

[1] The Holy Office never authorized bloodshed.

[2] Whose business it was to prepare causes for the tribunal and especially to examine all books before publication.

multitude assailed them with coarse insults and volleys of mud or stones ; but the Praça da Ribeira was guarded by a cordon of troops, who prevented the mob from invading the enclosure set apart for the Auto. Here, grouped by themselves on one side, stood sundry rectangular piles of wood, each with a stake planted in the midst and a chair beside the stake. The centre of the square was filled by a stage, on which two blocks of seats had been erected, those on the left being occupied by King John III., with his Queen and Court, while on the right sat his brother Prince Henry, the Cardinal and Inquisitor General, on a canopied throne flanked by the chairs reserved for other members of the Holy Tribunal.

" The altar, its front draped in black, rose in the middle of the stage. Before it, the standard of the Inquisition was set on a pedestal ; on one side stood the pulpit, on the other a table—littered with papers and pendent seals—for the use of the reporters who were to read the sentences. Below the stage stood the condemned, ranged in lines to face the pulpit, the altar, the tribunal.

" Mass was said. The Inquisitor General, robed in mitre and cope, handed a volume of the Gospels to the King, bidding him swear on them to defend the faith. King John III. and all his courtiers, standing bare-headed, took the solemn oath in all sincerity. A sermon followed ; and last of all the sentences were read, beginning with the lesser crimes.

" The adoration of images—a question treated as debate-able even by Church Councils [1]—had caused many to fall into error. Some were there for refusing to kiss the guardian saints of the money-boxes with which the friars went from door to door, seeking alms. Some for irreverence, others for misunderstanding the precepts of the canon law ; many for nothing at all ; the majority, because they had been denounced by some malignant or covetous informer. The

---

[1] One of the merits of the Society of Jesus, the great ally and rival of the Inquisition, was that in accordance with the doctine of Probabilism it dealt mercifully with such offences, absolving penitents if even one recognized authority could be cited in support of their error.

reporters read on, amid groans and cries from some of the condemned, though others exulted at the prospect of an escape from prison and torture, and secretly resolved for the future to pursue a course of the strictest hypocrisy.

" The death-sentences came last. There were three women convicted of witchcraft ; two men, New Christians, who had relapsed into Judaism ; and a third man, guilty of sorcery.

" The reporter continued his passionless recital of the sentences, in which the particulars of each crime were set forth. The New Christians had eaten unleavened bread. One of them, while sweeping his house, had blasphemed against a crucifix, made mouths at it, and scratched it whenever his broom struck the floor. These charges were wrapped up in awe-inspiring phrases and tremendous generalities, so that the courtiers, clergy and people thrilled, as they listened, with hatred of the sacrilegious miscreants.

" The charges of sorcery caused no less horror. New Christians and wizards, whose weapons were malediction and the evil eye, were well known to be the cause of plague, famine and shipwreck in the Indian Seas. On the heads of these unfortunate beings fell the curses of a stricken nation. Nobody doubted the reality of the offences, proved, as they were, by a multitude of witnesses. The devil had appeared to one of the accused and taught him to work cures by black magic. He had bled his patients in the forehead, with pins . . . one prick, and the spell was complete. ' In the name of Jesus, heal the prick and break the spell '—such had been the appeal heard by a priest of the province of Beira : and the devils had avenged themselves by breaking into the priest's house and smashing all his crockery. Here was something quite novel : and the people shuddered as they stared at the doctor, whose insanity could be read in his face.

" The witches were visited by the devil : in the semblance of a black cat, during the day, and by night ' in the human form of a little man ' ; so the sentence gravely affirmed, quoting the depositions of eye-witnesses. Witch and devil fared forth in company to a river where they were joined by others like themselves ; and after bathing indulged in a hideous orgy.[1] The sentence enumerated all the obscene and abominable details, which were at once seized by the corrupt minds of court and populace, and made a topic of conversation. At daybreak on the next Sabbath the witches became invisible, and stole into the houses of the devout and respectable families it was their delight to plague.

" The reading ended, the penitents received absolution, and the New Christians and votaries of the black art were handed over to the secular arm, to be burned. King John withdrew, accompanied by the Inquisitor General and his courtiers ; and the tolling of the bells continued, slow and funereal.

" The charcoal-burners, grasping their weapons, the hooded executioners, and the white-robed friars, crucifix in hand, drew near to the criminals they were to burn. Round the rectangular pyres the crowd packed closer, staring with eager eyes ; their heads filled with rage against the malefactors who had caused so much misery.

" All save the sorcerer died a merciful death by strangulation before they were committed to the flames. But the physician, whose guilt had been more deadly, was doomed to be burned alive. . . .

" He afforded the mob three full hours of exquisite sport." [2]

Autos-da-Fé were rare events, and the harm wrought by the Inquisition cannot be measured merely by the cruelties it authorized on such occasions. Far worse were the delation and terrorism it encouraged by paying informers out of the property of their victims ; its activity as a trading and landowning community able and ready to

---

[1] Some curious remarks on this superstition will be found in the first part of Sir Thomas Browne's *Religio Medici.*

[2] The foregoing is based on the account of the Auto given in Oliveira Martins' *Historia de Portugal,* vol. ii. pp. 35-39. I have interpolated a few explanatory words, added footnotes and omitted one or two sentences. The whole passage is well worth reading in the original Portuguese : Oliveira Martins was a master of historical impressionism, whose work necessarily loses much in a translation.

ruin any competitor ; its constitutional position as an *imperium in imperio*, practically independent of Kings and Popes ; and its use of the Censorship and Index Expurgatorius to paralyse thought.[1]

[1] Details will be found in *Historia da Origem e Estabelecimento da Inquisição em Portugal*, by A. Herculano, Lisbon, 1897 (First Edition 1854-1857) ; and *A Inquisição em Portugal* by C. J. de Menezes, Oporto, 1893. Claude Dellon's vivid *Relation de l'inquisition de Goa*, Paris, 1688 (English translation, *The History of the Inquisition at Goa*, London, 1688), though written in the seventeenth century, is largely true of the sixteenth.

CHAPTER XXV

THE CHURCH IN THE EAST

IT was widely held among the Portuguese that the civilized Indians would be a more valuable acquisition to the Church than the barbarous tribes of Africa. East of the Cape almost every enterprise of the early missionaries was directed in accordance with this view. Even the Portuguese settlements on the African seaboard were often destitute of a chaplain ; no attempt was made to convert the Hottentots or Bushmen ; and it was not until 1560 that the first mission was sent to the Bantu. This was undertaken by D. Gonçalo da Silveira, a Jesuit of noble birth and a friend of Camões, at the request of a chief named Gamba, whose son had visited Goa and become a Christian.

Silveira and his companions received an almost embarrassing welcome. Gold dust, cattle and female slaves were pressed upon them and not only Gamba but the Monomotapa or Paramount Chief himself consented to be baptized, while their subjects hailed the new religion with loyal enthusiasm. But the hospitable instincts of the Monomotapa were severely tested when he learned that baptism implied the renunciation of polygamy. Even a largesse of beads and calico could not obliterate the effect of this covert attack upon an immemorial and valued privilege ; and at last, growing weary of novelties, the Monomotapa allowed himself to be convinced by Muslim refugees that Silveira was a wizard. The missionary was ordered to depart on pain of death, and replied fearlessly, by baptizing fifty more of the Bantu. Accordingly on the 16th of March 1561, he was martyred. His surviving comrade, Father André Fernandes, was subsequently

182

recalled to Goa, and thus the first attempt to preach Christianity in East Africa ended in a not ignoble failure.

India, meanwhile, could not complain of neglect. Goa had been made an episcopal see by a Bull of Pope Paul III., issued in November 1534, and its first Bishop, D. João de Albuquerque, had arrived with D. João de Castro four years later. His vast, undefined diocese included every settlement east of the Cape in which Roman Catholics or Nestorians were to be found—an arrangement not altogether welcomed by the Nestorians.[1] Even before his arrival, priests, monks and friars had flocked to Portuguese India. While Affonso de Albuquerque lived, there was little to be feared from this concourse ; the Governor had a crisp way of dealing with clerics who sought to usurp civil power. On one occasion, when he had promoted a number of informal weddings between his veterans and some captured Indian women, the priests objected that the parties were not married in accordance with the rites of the Church. " They are married by the rites of Affonso de Albuquerque," responded the Governor, and no further challenge was issued.

But after his death a distinct ecclesiastical party arose, and as it grew in power it interfered in financial and administrative matters, and even in foreign policy. There was constant danger of an ecclesiastical dictatorship. Simão Botelho complained in 1552 to the King, that the treasury was depleted for alms, and whole towns emptied by the forced conversion of Hindus and Muslims.[2] The nature of this propaganda may be inferred from the fact that, in Goa, every " Gentile " was driven to church once a fortnight, and compelled to listen to a sermon of one hour's duration on the beauties of a Christian spirit.

Apart from the secular clergy, three fraternities, the Franciscans, Dominicans, and Jesuits were forward in sending missionaries to the East. In methods and to some

---

[1] The doctrine and liturgy of the Nestorians were finally condemned at the synod of Diamper (Udayamperur near Cochin) in 1599. The proceedings of the synod will be found in *Ar. Port. Or.*, part 4.

[2] Botelho, *Cartas*. Letter 4.

extent in aims the three societies widely differed. Each still to some extent lived up to the ideals of its originator.

The Franciscans, who came to India with Cabral, had learned from their founder to appeal directly to the poor, to bring religion into lives full of ignorance and suffering ; and to interpret it in terms of joy rather than in terms of duty. The *Canticle of the Sun*, with its delight in all created things, was still their text-book : even in the sixteenth century joy was the essence of their creed. Diego de Estella, a Franciscan whom Philip II. of Spain chose to be his intimate spiritual adviser, echoes the *Canticle of the Sun* in his *Meditaciones del Amor de Dios*, and throughout insists not upon the wickedness of the world, as most of his contemporaries would have insisted, but upon its reflected glory as the mirror of God. His book is one of many witnesses which show that representative Franciscans remained faithful to the beliefs of their founder. It would, however, be imprudent to infer that all members of the fraternity who came to India were saints and poets.

If, in general, the Franciscans brought religion as a gift to their equals, the Dominicans approached men in a different mood. They came to teach their inferiors, not to share their most precious possession with friends and brothers. It would be grossly unfair to exaggerate this aspect of their missions, or to deny that they learned willingly from their own converts. On occasion they emulated the Jesuits, who adopted the forms of Confucianism in China or Sivaism in India for the furtherance of their aims and in despite of papal condemnation. In this spirit the Dominicans countenanced the simple practice of the Guatemalan Indians, who burned two tapers before the image of St George—one for the dragon. In the same spirit they interwove Christian legends with pagan ritual, and turned the barbaric dances and sacrificial orgies of the Central American Mayas into very passable miracle-plays, in which Tamerlane, Charlemagne and St Peter figured— in wooden masks and feather mantles—along with the de- throned native deities.

A number of Dominicans came out to Goa in 1548, with

power to buy land and found a convent. They devoted themselves to the most miserable class under Portuguese rule—the slaves, who were branded like oxen, but in other respects were not so well treated as the more expensive beasts of burden. The Dominicans did their utmost to lighten the lives of these unfortunates, but were unable to accomplish very much.[1]

On many shores they proved themselves skilful leaders and rulers of unsophisticated peoples, who might need firm guidance. But their rule and creed must be unquestioned; and Portugal and India were not unsophisticated. Here from the first the Dominicans had been celebrated for their stern enforcement of orthodoxy. It was not their fault that the establishment of the Inquisition in India was delayed until 1560, though it had been authorized in 1543, after a bachelor of medicine named Jeronymo Dias had been strangled and publicly burned for heresy.[2] It was a Dominican who refused Simão Botelho absolution because that officer had reformed the custom-houses at Malacca and Bassein—under orders from the Governor, it is true, but without previously consulting the Pope, or the Dominicans.

When the Jesuits came out to India in 1542, their organization—" a sword with its hilt in Rome and its point everywhere "—had not yet been wrought and tempered to its final perfection. But their energy, their loyalty to a corporate ideal, and their genius for self-sacrifice soon became obvious. They did splendid work as medical missionaries,[3] but education was their chief secular interest and most potent weapon. They cast aside all conventual restraints which might impede their activities, and ultimately differed from the Franciscans and Dominicans as a secret society differs from a monastic order. Throughout India they were known as the " fathers of St Paul," from their headquarters, the training college of St Paul (originally the Franciscan college of Santa Fé) in Goa.

[1] Corrêa, vol. iv. p. 669 *seq.*   [2] Corrêa, vol. iv. p. 292.
[3] The royal hospital in Goa became world-famous under their management (*c.* 1591-1650) ; Fonseca, pp. 228-236.

The three fraternities did not always work together in harmony. The letters of Francis Xavier bear eloquent testimony to the bitterness of these conflicts, though they counsel peace, and warn all Jesuits to maintain an attitude of benevolent neutrality. In one case Xavier even suggests that a neophyte who had proved himself unworthy to enter the Society of Jesus would find suitable quarters among the followers of St Francis or St Dominic ; it is not known if the gift was accepted with proper gratitude.

The regular and secular clergy were quite as often at loggerheads.[1] When the Dominicans came to Goa in 1548, they brought a skull of one of the Eleven Thousand Virgins, which proved its authenticity by stopping a leak on the voyage. The sacred relic was accorded a magnificent reception, and conveyed to its shrine by a procession of monks and friars. But the secular clergy, from the Bishop downwards, scandalized the populace by holding aloof out of jealousy.

Despite the mutual antipathies of the religious, despite the evil lives led by so many of them, and despite their almost unbroken unanimity in support of " preaching by the sword," there were many brave and noble spirits among them. Such was D. Jeronymo Osorio da Fonseca, Bishop of Silves, who earned remembrance as a champion of the persecuted Jews, and as the author of a history of King Manoel's reign. Living at a time when the Holy Office was no respecter of persons, even though they wore a mitre and wielded a pastoral staff, Osorio had the courage and breadth of mind openly to condemn the whole theory of religious persecution.

In the Indies there were priests as brave, who led their flocks to battle, with uplifted crucifix, and, in the words of Faria y Sousa, " banished the fear of death with the emblem of life." Such a cleric was D. Diogo Mergulhão, who headed a storming party in Albuquerque's attack on Aden. The brave chaplain carried a cross lashed to a spear, and when he was forced to retire, wounded in six

---

[1] See the extraordinary documents reproduced on pp. 455-6 of Andrade (ed. of 1835).

places, he still bore it gallantly under an arm that was pinned to his side by two arrows. So too, in 1559, a Franciscan named Christovão de Castro refused to leave a sinking ship when all the officers had crowded into the only boat and were urging him to join them : " these two hundred souls are more precious than my poor life," he answered, and went down with the rest. A similar devotion to duty was shown forty years afterwards by a Dominican, Nicolau do Rosario, in the wreck of the *São Thomé*, off Madagascar. Yet another cleric, of whose ready wit one would gladly know more, proved by example and precept how well he could keep his head in a crisis. When a cannon-ball decapitated a soldier by his side, he began, in a loud voice, to intone the verse *Humiliate Deo capita*. But the greatest of all the ecclesiastics who laboured in India under the Portuguese flag was indisputably the Jesuit Francis Xavier, who went out to Goa in 1542.

CHAPTER XXVI

FRANCIS XAVIER IN GOA

GOA DOURADA, " Golden Goa," as it was popularly called, was already the capital of Portuguese India, the seat of the viceregal court, the military and naval headquarters, the central mart for all the produce of the East. It enjoyed the same civic rights as Lisbon itself; and as the centre from which the spiritual affairs of all the Christians scattered over the shores of the Indian Ocean were directed, it was now to become almost an Oriental Rome. A first sight of its vigorous ecclesiastical life kindled the ready enthusiasm of Francis Xavier.

" It has a college of Franciscans," he wrote, " really very numerous, a magnificent cathedral with a large number of canons, and several other churches. There is good reason for thanking God that the Christian religion flourishes so much in this distant land in the midst of heathen."

The words occur in a letter addressed to the Society of Jesus in Rome, and dated the 18th of September 1542; Francis had landed in India on the 6th of May. A closer acquaintance caused him to modify his estimate of Goanese piety.[1]

The character of the Portuguese in India had already begun to deteriorate, although society in the capital had not yet sunk to the depth it ultimately reached. Xavier

---

[1] The following account of Goa is based largely on the works of travellers who visited the city some years after Xavier — in particular Linschoten (1583), Pyrard (1608), and Mocquet (1608). But the anachronism is more apparent than real, because the conditions out of which Goanese society grew—slave-labour, the tropical climate, the influence of Oriental ideas, etc.—were precisely the same in both periods : and all the recorded evidence tends to prove that the main features of that society had already become stereotyped at least as early as 1550.

condemns several of the malpractices common among officials and merchants, such as the custom of withholding payments due from the State until its creditors were only too glad to compound for a smaller payment in cash. The " sharks of the Treasury " would then draw the whole amount due, pay over whatever the creditors would accept as a settlement in full, and pocket the balance. But the officials and traders, financiers and money-lenders, who waxed fat on these ingenious forms of enterprise were by no means the most conspicuous element in the population. That distinction belongs rather to the motley crowd of adventurers, professional soldiers and sailors, who might be encountered at any hour swaggering through the streets or lounging in the wine-shops, with nothing to do except to spend their loot and prize-money, or steal when these resources ran dry. They were a picturesque and turbulent folk—bronzed and bearded veterans with earrings in their ears and knives in their girdles—fearless and careless, steeped in a hundred vices, but full of a rough pride in their religion which would cause a man to violate half the decalogue in order to avenge a slur on his patron saint. With bravos of this type Francis Xavier loved to consort on his voyages, much to their delight and to the scandal of respectable citizens. But they and their officers were ill-fitted for civilian life. Idleness sapped their virtues and fostered their defects, until, in time of peace, it became difficult to recognize any kinship between the heroes of Diu and the indolent, dissolute crew which now made Goa a byword for its bizarre vices.

Every fortune-hunter who landed in India began by claiming the rank of *fidalgo* and prefixing *dom* to his name ; for the rich men who hired palaces and imported wives from Lisbon, and their poorer neighbours who were forced to be content with boarding-houses and local talent, were fully agreed upon the merits of long descent. It was rarely that a fidalgo would condescend to puzzle his brains with the intricacies of trade, unless all the hard work could be delegated to commoners, or better still, to slaves.

In the hothouse atmosphere of Goa an exotic taste for

display soon took root and flourished. When the sun was low each fidalgo who could afford a horse and jewelled harness hung with bells and trinkets of gold or silver, would ride forth in state, to be admired from discreetly curtained lattices. A retinue of liveried slaves would accompany the cavalier, to carry his indispensable armoury of umbrellas and inlaid weapons. So, stiff and splendid in silk, brocade and armour, he would prance through the city. The lesser nobility of the boarding-houses, unable singly to purchase this attractive outfit, would share the glory and the cost, so that each subscriber in turn could take the air in gorgeous attire, under the shade of an umbrella carried by his attendant *ad hoc*.

This ceremony had a serious rival in the gambling saloons, where determined players would sometimes take permanent quarters. Dice, cards, chess—played for money—or a main of cocks were not the only forms of sport practised here. Conjurers, musicians, dancing-girls, wrestlers, clowns and actors helped to pass the time, and besides arrack, palm-wine and other potent liquors brewed in India, the fine vintages of Portugal could be obtained at a price commensurate with the six months' voyage from Lisbon to Goa. But drunkenness was extremely rare.

The attitude of the priests towards gambling was not unduly austere. It is told of Francis Xavier that, on the voyage from Mailapur to Malacca in 1545, he stood for some time watching a card-party at which a certain soldier lost all his own money and a large sum entrusted to his care. The soldier was in despair and threatened suicide, when Xavier brought him fifty *reis* (1s. 2d.), borrowed from a friend, and bade him try afresh. The saint himself shuffled and dealt, the other players being presumably too much astonished to protest. Thus encouraged, the soldier soon recovered all he had lost, and was proceeding towards further conquests, when Xavier intervened and persuaded him to forswear gambling for ever. It is recorded that the soldier kept his vow ; but the whole anecdote is excluded from the official list of miracles.

European ladies, though rare enough to be prized beyond

A FIDALGO TAKING THE AIR IN GOA

FROM JAN HUYGHEN VAN LINSCHOTEN'S "ITINERARIO" (1595)

their deserts, were more numerous in Goa than elsewhere in the East ; for here could be found all the comforts which money could buy, and the money to buy them. But in practice the zenana life of the Hindu women threatened their Portuguese sisters. The consort of a fidalgo could not stoop to lower household duties than slave-driving. Art and literature, professional and administrative work, were reserved for her lord and master, and life tended to resolve itself into a passive endurance of the torrid climate in a magnificent but insanitary palace. Church processions or military pageants like the triumph of D. João de Castro afforded their chief amusement to the Portuguese ladies, who then as now were born sight-seers. Their lattices were glazed with thin and highly polished oyster-shells, but special peep-holes were left, through which the inquisitive beauties could see every passer-by, without being themselves exposed to the stare of the vulgar. Open windows, curtained with strings of beads, often took the place of the lattices.

The streets, with their varied and brilliant show of fashion, and the even more alluring haunts of the gamblers, were closed to decent women ; and although the dames of Goa often freed themselves from this disqualification, public and marital censure still exercised some measure of restraint. It is not wonderful that many of the fidalgas grew tired of scandal, quarrels, and the few social pleasures conceded to them, and sought variety in stolen kisses. That they did so with surprising zest and audacity is proved by the testimony of many witnesses. To gain applause from a circle of expert friends it was necessary to transcend the commonplaces of successful intrigue. No novice could win celebrity merely by losing her reputation. The heroine of a scandal must show some originality and spice it with danger—drug her husband with *datura*, for example, and entertain her cavalier under his unconscious nose.[1] The husbands repaid the compliment of infidelity with interest,

[1] " The man," says Linschoten of this drug, " sitteth with his eyes open, not doing or saying any thing, but laugh or grin, like a foole, or a man out of his wits : and when the time cometh that he reviveth out of his trance, he knoweth nothing that was done, but thinketh that he had slept." Vol. ii. p. 69.

though this did not prevent them from being inordinately jealous, and setting confidential slaves to watch their wives—a futile device, which only enabled the slaves to draw pocket-money from both master and mistress.

Many, however, and perhaps the majority, of the Portuguese merchants and officers were too poor, too prudent, or too lacking in consideration for their friends, to marry white wives. They lived instead with Hindu, Muslim, or Jewish women, whose children were frequently brought up in the faith of their mothers. The principle upon which Francis dealt with these unions is described by Torsellino in a curious passage :—

" First he went about to winne them by all courteous meanes ; then, as he met them in the streets, he would merily request them to invite a poore priest to their ordinary fare ; which they willingly accepted of. He now sitting at table, would before, or at their repast, intreat his host to cause his children to be called : whereupon the litle children comming presently at their father's cal, Francis would take them up into his armes, and hug them to his bosome, thanking God who had given the Father such children for the hope of his family, and withall would pray God to give them a good and holy life. Then would he desire that their mother might be called (a thing which in another would have bin temerity, but his Sanctity easily excused it). When she was come, he would speake sweetly unto her, and commend her beauty to his host, thereby to draw him to take her to his wife, saying that doubtlesse she was of an excellent disposition and lovely countenance, so that she might well be accounted a Portughese, that the children which he had by her were certainly worthy of a Portughese to their father. . . . But if by chance he lighted upon any one who had by some ill-favoured *Indian*-woman children like unto herselfe, then as conceiving great indignation therat, he would cry out, ' Good God ! what a monster have we here ! Do you keep a Diuel in your howse ? Can you keep company with this ugly beast ? Can you have children by her ? Follow my counsail : drive this monster, this prodigious creature, presently out of your howse, and seeke you a wife worthy of your selfe.' So in putting away his mistress, he married a wife." [1]

Francis went to and fro through the city, swinging a bell, and calling upon the people to send their children to be baptized. On Sundays and festivals he preached in

---

[1] Torsellino, pp. 107-109 of the translation of 1632.

the morning to all who would listen, in the afternoon to natives, bond or free. His charm and enthusiasm soon awakened an answering ardour in his hearers. " If I could be in ten different places at once," he wrote to the Society in Rome, " I should never lack penitents." Much of his time was given to the inmates of the prison and of the leper-hospital outside the walls, but he also contrived to keep in touch with the Bishop and the Governor, thus becoming acquainted with every class before he undertook his paramount duty—the organization of missions throughout the East.

His popularity was not likely to be diminished by the plea for certain indulgences which he addressed through Ignatius to the Pope. " Of all the nations I have seen," he wrote privately, " the Portuguese is the one which seems to me to go furthest in prizing indulgences from Rome, and to be the most drawn to the sacraments by such means."[1] One request of this nature, preferred to Francis by the Governor, was for an alteration in the season of Lent. In the spring months fish began to rot as soon as they died, and it was therefore difficult to observe the fast. The Pope was asked " to change, if it be possible, the time of Lent in these parts to the months of June and July, when the heat begins to abate, and there is much less navigation, on account of the roughness of the sea." This concession was not granted.

Xavier now took the first step towards the establishment of an organized system of conversion. A college had been founded at Goa for the instruction of native boys from every part of India, who were destined to serve as priests, catechists, or interpreters. The college was intended for the use of the Franciscan Confraternity of Santa Fé, who were the pioneers of Christian teaching among the Hindus. Its endowment was furnished by a simple and ancient device. In 1540 all the temples on the island were destroyed by order of the King, and in 1541 not only their lands but also the allotments set aside for the maintenance of the village carpenters, blacksmiths and other artisans who

---

[1] Letter of Oct. 18th 1543.

13

served the community as a whole, were appropriated by the Church. The consent of the headmen to this act of robbery was easily procured, since a refusal might have entailed some greater disaster ; and the villagers were impressively assured in an official document that they would be rewarded a hundredfold for their self-denial.[1] The funds thus procured were devoted to the upkeep of the college, which was opened with much ceremony on the 25th of January 1543, the day of the conversion of St Paul, to whom it was dedicated. Francis was not present at the opening, for in the autumn of 1542 he had set sail for a new sphere of labour. He had, however, arranged that the college should be transferred from the Franciscans to the Jesuits.

[1] Printed in *Ar. Port. Or.*, part v. (doc. no. 75).

CHAPTER XXVII

XAVIER AMONG THE PEARL FISHERS

AT the earnest desire of Miguel Vaz, Episcopal Vicar of Goa, Francis Xavier had set forth to evangelize the Paravas, low-caste Hindus who carried on the pearling industry of the " Fishery Coast," between Cape Comorin and the line of reef known as Adam's Bridge. Vaz had himself visited this region in 1532, and had converted the natives wholesale—an achievement not entirely due to his own zeal and eloquence, as the Paravas had already determined to embrace Christianity if only the white strangers would deliver them from the Muslim tyrants who devoured all the profit of the fisheries. Xavier found that they knew nothing of Christianity, except that it was their own religion. They knew even less of the Portuguese language. His companions, however, were native Christians, and with their aid he sought out the few men who could speak both Portuguese and Malayalam,[1] and so could interpret. After four months' toil he had completed a translation of the Catechism. Meanwhile he travelled from village to village, barefooted ; he subsisted on a single daily meal of rice, obtained by begging ; at night he made the earth his bed and a stone his pillow, rarely giving more than four hours to sleep, and spending the remainder of the darkness in prayer and visits to the sick. As usual he began his ministry with the baptism of all who would consent to it.

" As to the numbers who become Christians," he writes, " you may understand them from this, that it often happens to me to be hardly able to use my hands through the fatigue of baptizing : often in a single day I have baptized whole villages. Sometimes I have lost

---

[1] The principal dialect of this region, as of Malabar.

my voice and strength altogether with repeating again and again the Credo and the other forms." [1]

He enlisted a corps of children to aid in a campaign against idolatry.

" Whenever I hear of any act of idolatrous worship, I go to the place with a large band of these children, who very soon load the devil with a greater amount of insult and abuse than he has lately received of honour and worship from their parents, kinsmen and acquaintance. The children run at the idols, dash them down, break them in pieces, spit on them, trample on them, kick them about, and in short heap on them every possible outrage." [2]

It is not surprising that the children flocked to welcome a missionary who not only provided these fascinating games, but even encouraged his youthful bodyguard to preach to its parents and guardians, and to rebuke their want of enthusiasm for the new gospel. Elder converts showed, on occasion, a disconcerting desire for illumination on the problems of theology.

" They asked me how the soul of a dying man issued from the body ? ' Was it as when we seem to be conversing with friends and acquaintance in our dreams ? Was this because the soul departs from the body in sleep ? And, to crown all, was God black or white ? ' For as there is so great variety of colour among men, and the Indians are themselves black, they esteem their own colour most highly, and hold that their gods are also black. On this account the great majority of their idols are pitch-black, and moreover are generally so smeared with oil as to smell abominably and seem to be as dirty as they are ugly." [3]

Xavier could only answer through an interpreter, or in broken Malayalam eked out by signs, but in spite of all hindrances his mission made real progress, and after fifteen months he was ready to leave the Fishery Coast.

Lest his converts should relapse as they had relapsed at the departure of Miguel Vaz, he appointed native catechists in each Christian village, who were empowered to teach, to baptize newborn infants, and to celebrate marriages. It was his custom to pay part of their salary in advance. The money was provided by the viceroy out

---

[1] Coleridge, vol. i. p. 153. [2] *Id.* pp. 153-4. [3] *Id.* p. 160.

of a special fund ; according to Torsellino, it " was accustomed to be payd to Queene Catherin of Portugal, to buy her shoes, and Pantofles. Wherefore Francis wrote unto her majesty, very pleasantly and piously, that she could have no fitter shoes or Pantofles, to climb heaven than the Christian children of the Piscarian coast, and their instructions." [1]

After securing the continuance of his work in this manner, Francis revisited his headquarters in Goa ; but his stay in the capital was brief, and having entrusted the future government of the College of St Paul to a Jesuit rector, he returned to the Fishery Coast. He was accompanied by Francis Mancias, a new recruit of the Society, by two native priests and by some Portuguese laymen. Each of these assistants, it would appear, was placed in charge of a district, in which he was to act as an itinerant teacher, and to supervise the native catechists.

The letters to Mancias show that the work of the missionaries was backed by the authority of the Governor. The wives and daughters of the pearl-fishers were accustomed to expel the taste of sea-water with arrack, and a beadle was dispatched to Mancias with full power to fine drunken women, and to imprison for three days all who again offended in the same way. The village headmen were to be responsible for the enforcement of the law against arrack-drinking. In a letter dated the 24th of March 1544, Mancias is bidden to find out the truth of a complaint made by three nobles of Travancore, who asserted that a slave belonging to their Raja had been arbitrarily arrested by a Portuguese.

" If he owes the Portuguese anything, let the complaint be laid before his own prince, who is sure to decide what is just. . . . I wonder whether the Portuguese would think it good if, when one of the natives happened to have a dispute with one of themselves, he were to seize the Portuguese by main force, put him in chains, and have him deported from our territories."

The conduct of the white traders tended to frustrate the labours of the missionaries, and Xavier almost made

[1] Torsellino (1632), p. .140.

up his mind to abandon India and betake himself to the kingdom of Prester John " where there are no Europeans to pull down what we have built." Invaders from the north [1] wrought even greater havoc among the converts, who had no means of resisting, and could only take refuge in their boats while the invaders ravaged the villages on the mainland. Francis wrote a letter of protest and entreaty to the Raja of Travancore, urged the Portuguese commandant at Tuticorin to send a warship, and ordered his own assistants to post sentinels who could give timely warning of a night attack.

Part of the year 1544 was spent by Francis in the kingdom of Travancore, which he seems to have visited in the intervals of his work on the Fishery Coast. As a rule this kingdom was tributary to Vijayanagar, but at intervals the Raja of Madura succeeded in establishing a transient and incomplete suzerainty over its rulers. Its territories extended between Cochin and the Fishery Coast, and may thus be said to have lain within the Portuguese sphere of influence. Our knowledge of Xavier's work in this region is slight. It is said that he achieved a marvellous result. Multitudes gathered to hear the sermons of the barefooted mendicant, whose torn cassock and rough cloth cap were symbols of a faith that looked for no earthly reward. A tree served as pulpit ; mass was celebrated under a canopy made from the thwarts of boats. Hindus were baptized in thousands, and when the apostle departed he left behind no fewer than forty-five new-born churches. Such is the Jesuit tradition. Its value may be assessed by a reference to Xavier's own words, written at Panical on the 21st of August 1544 : " I am working in the midst of a people whose language I do not understand, and I have no interpreter." If the apostle had not been able to learn the dialects of the Fishery Coast after many months' toil, it is improbable that his eloquence in the speech of Travancore would have acquired irresistible force after a briefer study. There is,

---

[1] These *Badega*, or *Badagæ*, as Xavier calls them, were natives of Vijayanagar and spoke Telegu. The Tamil form of the name is *Vadagar*. Xavier was the first European to mention the Badega.

however, no reason to reject the story of one incident which might well have turned many hearts to the new creed. The ascetic priest was also a hidalgo of Spain, and when his converts were threatened by a hostile army from Madura, he went alone to challenge the invaders. With uplifted crucifix, he rebuked them in the name of God. The front ranks wavered and halted. Their comrades and leaders vainly pressed them to advance, but no man dared pass the black-robed figure which barred the way, and presently the whole force retreated and molested the Christians no more.

This legend was already current in the sixteenth century, and it suits the character of one whose whole missionary career was a triumph of personality.

It would be impossible to describe in detail the journeys which Xavier accomplished during the next five years in India, the Malay Peninsula and the Malay Archipelago. He continued as a general rule to apply the same methods which had proved successful on the Fishery Coast, undertaking in person the pioneer labour of founding each new church, and leaving it an organized community to be governed and enlarged by his successors. One of his lieutenants had been dispatched to evangelize the people of Manaar, a sandy island situated between the coast of Ceylon and Adam's Bridge. The success of this mission had been resented by the Raja of Jafnapatam in Ceylon, who was suzerain of the island ; many converts had been called upon to renounce their new creed, and refusal had been punished with death. Xavier hastened north, and persuaded the Governor, Martim Affonso de Sousa, to dispatch an armada against the offending potentate, but while the ships were awaiting orders to sail the whole plan was abandoned. A richly laden Portuguese merchantman, from Pegu, had run aground on the Jafnapatam littoral ; and the Government abandoned all thought of vengeance in order to redeem her crew and cargo.

A letter dated the 7th of April 1545, and addressed to Mancias, who was now head of the Travancore churches, contains the menace of yet another appeal to the secular arm. Mancias is exhorted to inquire into the conduct of the Nestorian priests on the Malabar Coast, and to visit any fault with swift severity,

"lest they not only incur eternal damnation, but draw down others also into hell . . . for if we should let the full powers we have for this purpose rest unused, like a sword in its scabbard . . . we should be arraigned of a serious crime, hardly to be expiated by much punishment."[1]

One Cosmo de Paiva, a Portuguese who had been guilty of murder, robbery and other offences on the Fishery Coast, was to be warned that, unless he mended his ways, the King, the Governor and the Holy Office would be asked to mend them for him.

Before the end of April Xavier was in Mailapur, on the Coromandel Coast. It was at this time generally believed that the apostle Thomas had preached Christianity in India, and had been martyred at Salamina, a city which in after days became Mailapur. John III. had sent an expedition to find his tomb, and it is hardly necessary to add that it was duly found—in a wooden chapel erected by the saint himself. In 1545 the relics had not yet been transferred to Goa, but the Portuguese colony at Mailapur had built them a new shrine. Xavier spent four peaceful months in the spot hallowed by memories so sacred. Then, in one of those rare moments of ecstasy to which he looked for illumination, he received what he regarded as a divine mandate. He was to go to Malacca, and thence proceed to Celebes in the Malay Archipelago.

He finished the first stage of this journey towards the end of September 1545, and remained until January working among the mariners and traders of many nationalities who were wont to forgather here on the verge of the Indian Ocean. Once more as at Goa he traversed the silent city-streets after dark, swinging his bell and calling upon the people of Malacca to pray for all sinners and souls in purgatory. The slaves and children soon learned to sing the simple verses he had written and set to music; but the

[1] Coleridge, vol. i., p. 293.

mass of the people consisted of Muhammadans, who remained obstinately deaf to the most eloquent sermons in a language they could not understand. Xavier himself was anxious to be gone. Rumour said that the people of Celebes were sun-worshippers, innocent of temples or priests and uncorrupted by contact with white men.

CHAPTER XXVIII

XAVIER IN THE MALAY ISLES

L IFE in the Malay Archipelago was less idyllic than Xavier imagined. In Java, the ruins of mighty temples bore witness to the splendour of a vanished Indian civilization, already superseded by Islam, and in the other islands every stage of social development between cannibalism and Muhammadanism was well represented. It is uncertain how far eastward the Portuguese had ventured, but the littoral of a continent resembling Australia is for the first time laid down on some French maps drawn between 1530 and 1550.[1] It has been suggested that the material for these maps was supplied by certain filibusters from Dieppe, who visited the Far East between 1527 and 1539, and employed Portuguese pilots.[2] One of their ships ran aground on the coast of Sumatra, where a member of the crew rashly boasted that he had visited the " Island of Gold " : he was an unenterprising pirate, for he protested that he could never find his way back thither, and was impaled by the local Raja for his lack of imagination.

This half-fabulous Island of Gold loomed large on the horizon of the Portuguese explorers. It was reported to lie south-east of Sumatra ; shoals and moving sandbanks enclosed it ; palms grew on its low shores ; its people were black and ferocious—so much the agent of Diogo Lopes de Sequeira learned in 1518.[3] Later rumour added that the islanders were dwarfs, but abated nothing of their truculence. It has been suggested that the Island of Gold

[1] Reproduced in *The Discovery of Australia*, by A. F. Calvert, London, 1893.

[2] R. S. Whiteway, in *The Geographical Journal*, vol. ix. pp. 80 *seq.*

[3] Sequeira was Governor of India from 1518 to 1522.

was none other than Australia, in which case the French corsairs and their Portuguese pilots must share the credit of a discovery far earlier than the first authenticated voyages to Australia, those of 1606.[1] But the story is vague and in dispute. It is, however, certain that many parts of the Archipelago were familiar to the Portuguese, who had settled in the Moluccas and established regular traffic with Farther India.

The first expedition to the Moluccas, or Spice Islands, had been dispatched by Albuquerque in 1511. The Portuguese made their headquarters in the island of Ternate, where they were at first welcomed as useful allies against the neighbouring and hostile island-state of Tidore. Among them was the famous Magellan (Fernão Magalhães), who returned to Europe, and entered the service of Spain, just as the Spanish Government was considering whether the Malay Archipelago, and even Malacca itself, did not fall within the Spanish sphere as defined by the Treaty of Tordesillas. In these circumstances, Magellan easily secured the command of a fleet under orders to find a westward passage to the Archipelago. He coasted down the Patagonian littoral as far as the " Strait of the Eleven Thousand Virgins," now known as the Strait of Magellan, and entered a calm expanse of ocean which he named the *Mar Pacifico*. In April 1521 he was killed in a skirmish with the natives of Mactan, in the Philippines, after completing a voyage of discovery which ranks with those of Dias, Gama and Columbus. After his death, his captains steered for Tidore, where they held their own until Portuguese reinforcements arrived in 1522, and compelled them to withdraw. Seven years afterwards, the rival claims of Spain and Portugal were compromised, Spain receiving the Philippines and a sum of 350,000 ducats, while all other parts of the Malay Archipelago up to an imaginary line drawn 17° E. of the Moluccas, were included in the Portuguese

[1] An expedition dispatched by Godinho de Eredia (see Appendix A) may have reached Australia in 1601. His claim, and the identity of the " Island of Gold," were discussed by R. H. Major in *Early Voyages to Terra Australis*, London, Hakluyt Society, 1859 ; and in *Archæologia*, second series, vols. xxxviii. (1860) and xliv. (1873).

sphere. But this arrangement did not prevent the recurrence of disputes and sometimes of actual fighting between representatives of the contracting powers.

Two Portuguese officials, D. Jorge de Menezes and Antonio Galvão the historian, had left their mark upon the history of the Moluccas before the coming of Francis Xavier. Menezes had visited the Malay state of Brunei, in North Borneo, and desired to win its Raja to an alliance. In 1527 he sent an embassy thither, with sundry gifts—among them a piece of tapestry on which was delineated, in life-sized figures, the wedding of Catherine of Aragon to Arthur, Prince of Wales. After due thought, the Raja concluded that these mysterious figures were bound by a magic spell, and boded him no good : they might return to life and kill him as he slept. The tapestry was accordingly removed and the envoy dismissed.

Menezes may have been soured by this disappointment, though he gained a compensating success by dislodging a Spanish force from Tidore in 1528. Whatever the reason, his rule in the Moluccas was a brutal tyranny. The native Raja of Ternate had been poisoned ; Menezes kept his successor in strict confinement ; and another member of the royal family, whom the Muslims looked upon as a saint, was also flung into prison on a charge of slaughtering a pedigree pig from China. The holy man was liberated because an angry mob threatened reprisals, but not before his face had been smeared with lard by one of his gaolers. Menezes answered all claims for redress with a bland assurance that the fellow should not escape punishment, for spoiling good bacon. His reign of terror at last provoked a rebellion, in which the people of Ternate joined their old adversaries of Tidore in a desperate endeavour to exterminate the Portuguese. Peace was not restored until, in October 1536, Antonio Galvão came to take over the government. He offered terms to the rebels ; but they mistook generosity for fear, and compelled him to continue the war, although he endeavoured to avert bloodshed by challenging the native leaders to single combat. After defeating the Raja of Ternate, who fell in battle, Galvão completely broke up the league of malcontents and left them no alternative but surrender. He then set himself to win the goodwill of the islanders by his just and enlightened rule ; and so well did he succeed that when a Spanish fleet arrived off Ternate they risked their lives to prevent the strangers from landing without permission. They urged Galvão to become their Raja, and under his influence many of them even became Christians. He demolished their mosques and temples, built churches, founded a school for "infidel children"—and was still beloved. But his term of office came to an end in 1540, and he went home to claim his reward ; for he had spent his own fortune in the service of the crown. No reward was forthcoming, but Galvão found a home in the Lisbon hospital, where he remained until his death in 1557. Six years after his departure from the Moluccas, his missionary work was taken up by Francis Xavier, who sailed from Malacca on New Year's Day 1546, and landed in Amboyna six weeks later. A Spanish fleet was temporarily stationed there, but Xavier's first thought was for the natives, and he hastened inland to visit the Christian villages and to baptize every newborn infant. He found the islanders a less gentle folk than the sun-worshippers of whom he had been told.

" Send me assistants," he wrote to the rector of the Jesuit college in Goa, " and if they be not priests, let them at all events be men who have been roughly handled by the world, the flesh, and the devil. They must bring the sacred vessels and vestments . . . but the chalices must be of tin ; they will be safer than silver." [1]

The scurvy-ridden Spanish fleet kept him busy for two months among the penitent and dying. In his rare leisure he mused upon a rumour, current in Malacca, that St Thomas had preached in China, and founded a church there. Might not his own endeavours evoke a readier response in the land of sages than here, among the barbarous islanders and their lawless rulers ? The local customs were certainly not attractive :—

---

[1] Coleridge, vol. i. p. 370.

" If we are to believe what is reported of them," Xavier writes, " they are so extreme in their savagery that when a man is preparing a specially choice banquet, he asks his neighbour to give him his aged father, and . . . promises to do the same . . . if that other should desire to give a like entertainment. . . . Should any of their own people die by disease, they do not touch the rest of the body, but cut off the hands and feet, which they regard as great delicacies." Nevertheless he believes " that they are willing to be converted from all their detestable wickedness to Christian piety." [1]

His mission in the Malay Archipelago lasted a year and a half. It is difficult to identify all the islands to which the letters refer ; from his headquarters at Amboyna and Ternate he made numerous journeys by sea, visiting, it would appear, every spot where a Christian community had been established, and winning new converts everywhere. The Archipelago, he wrote in one of his moods of exaltation, " should be called the Islands of Divine Hope . . . in a few years one might lose one's eyesight from weeping tears of joy." [2] The Malay dialect of Malacca was a *lingua franca* in which, through his interpreters, he could preach and catechize with the certitude of being understood ; once more he taught through music, so that

" the native boys in the streets, the young maids and women in their huts, the labourers afield, and the fishermen on the sea, were ever singing the elements of the Christian faith, instead of their own lewd and blasphemous ditties."

The idyl was not, however, perfect. Europeans were untrustworthy, Muslim and pagan enemies harried the converts, and there were times when even the earth and sea appeared actively hostile. The letters are full of the earthquakes which made the captains of passing ships believe they had struck a shoal, and of the volcanic fires which " broke forth with a crash louder than the largest brass gun makes when firing a full charge." Xavier's comment may be quoted :—

" They asked me what it all meant. I told them this place was the abode of hell, into which all idolaters would be cast. How severe

---

[1] Coleridge, vol. i. p. 381.   [2] *Id.* p. 387.

the earthquakes are, you may judge from this—when I was saying mass on the feast of the Archangel St Michael, the earth was so violently shaken that I was in great fear the altar itself would be upset. Perhaps St Michael, by his heavenly power, was driving into the depths of hell all the wicked spirits of the country who were opposing the worship of the true God." [1]

For himself Xavier had no fear, though the worshippers fled panic-stricken. It was not unnatural that after this the islanders should listen reverently to one who seemed unmoved by the forces of earthquake and storm. Even those who were unconvinced by his teaching must have regarded him as a wizard more potent than any native magician.

But by this time he had prepared the soil for other missionaries to cultivate. It was necessary for him to return and attend to the larger affairs of India ; and about the middle of July 1548, he once more landed in Malacca. Here a sudden crisis evoked his genius for command. An armada of sixty ships and 5000 men from Sumatra had stolen under cover of night into the harbour of Malacca, where much of the shipping had been burned, though the landing-parties had failed to rush the defences of the city. It was a skilfully planned surprise, carried out under the leadership of the Raja of Pedir. As the triumphant raiders stood to sea again, they fell in with some fishermen, cut off their noses, ears and heels, and sent the captives home with a letter written in their own blood, in which Simão de Mello, Captain of Malacca, was formally challenged to battle. Mello affected to see a joke in this unconventional cartel ; his sense of humour may have been abnormal, but it is more likely that he dared not accept the challenge, inasmuch as his whole force consisted of eight unseaworthy ships, which had been beached for repairs. Xavier, however, refused to countenance delay. His eloquence and fiery enthusiasm put fresh courage into the garrison ; the crazy ships were patched up, and the crews dispatched with a blessing and an assurance of victory. The flagship foundered in sight of the shore, but Xavier promised a

[1] *Id., l.c.*

reinforcement of two ships, and towards nightfall their sails showed in the offing. They were the galleys of one Diego Suarez de Melo, a Galician merchant who had fled to sea under sentence of death, and had taken to piracy until, meeting the new Governor, Martim Affonso de Sousa, he had won pardon by a timely invective against the previous holder of that office, D. Estevão da Gama. Francis rowed out to the galleys, and enrolled this unorthodox recruit in the " armada of Jesus," as the fleet was called.

The armada put off without further mishap, and for some weeks no tidings of its fortune arrived. Torsellino has preserved the legend that Xavier proclaimed the precise hour of its triumph and predicted the time of its return, so accurately that, on the day foretold, the armada sailed into Malacca harbour, with twenty-five captive vessels and three hundred cannon. Four-fifths of the enemy had perished, and the remainder of their ships had been burned or shot to pieces.[1] In the solemn procession of thanksgiving Xavier took precedence of the captain and magistrates, while salutes were fired in his honour from the forts and ships. Never had his fame stood so high.

Already men came from afar to be cured by him of their spiritual maladies. One such pilgrim now reached Malacca, a man of that race which, according to Xavier, " surpasses all others in its desire for knowledge," a native of " some large islands which have lately been discovered." His name is given as Anger, Angero, or Anjiro, a corruption of Yajiro. He had left his home at Kagoshima, in the south of Japan, hoping by travel both to disburden himself of remorse for his many crimes and to escape the vengeance of his enemies. Portuguese friends had bidden him entrust his soul to the great seer and healer who alone could give him absolution and a quiet mind. Yajiro found what he sought in Malacca, and became the first of Japanese Christians. His influence upon his teacher was marked ; thenceforward Xavier saw in Japan the promised land which he had dreamed of finding in Ethiopia or China. No preachers

---

[1] The reader may believe as much of this story as he thinks fit. It is based almost entirely on the Jesuit histories.

of Islam could have forestalled him there, and no evil-living Europeans would be at hand to corrupt and maltreat converts.

The mission to Japan was postponed for nearly a year owing to the pressure of administrative work which recalled Xavier to Cochin and Goa ; but in May 1549 he returned to Malacca, and late in June he departed " in the junk of a Chinese corsair named Necoda," accompanied by two Castilian Jesuits, Juan Fernandez and Cosmo Torres, and by Yajiro—who " thanked God that no other European but these entered Japan along with Francis."

It was not the first time that Yajiro had proved his intellectual subtlety. When required to explain the direction of Japanese writing down the page, he had answered, " The head of a man is at the top and his feet at the bottom ; and so it is proper that when men write it should be straight down."

CHAPTER XXIX

A PIOUS PIRATE

THE most detailed account of the mission to Japan occurs in the " Peregrination " of Fernão Mendes Pinto, whose quaint record of adventure deserves notice. " 'Tis as diverting a book of the kind as ever I read "—so Mistress Dorothy Osborne wrote to Sir William Temple ; but the prevailing view is expressed by a character in Congreve's *Love for Love* : " F. M. Pinto was but a type of thee, thou liar of the first magnitude," and in the hideous pun of a Portuguese sceptic—" *Fernão, mentes ?* " " *Minto* : " " Do you lie, Fernão ? " " I do." These critics had reason. Pinto underwent the liveliest changes of fortune, but his memory was as apt to create as to preserve. His first translator, one Henry Cogan, gentleman, believed in him, and, in 1653, produced a version of his *Peregrinaçam* which is a classic in its way, though incomplete.[1] Editors have since avoided a text so littered with unknown names, improbable spellings, and irreconcilable dates.

According to his own account, Fernão Mendes Pinto embarked for India in March 1537, " meanly accommodated " but resolute to mend his fortunes in a land which afforded lackeys or private soldiers, such as he, the chance of acquiring wealth and a long line of ancestors. He arrived at Diu, and forthwith departed to the Red Sea with a scouting expedition sent to watch the movements

---

[1] All the passages quoted in this chapter are taken, after verification, from Cogan's version. The chief modern books on Pinto are *Fernão Mendes Pinto : subsidios para a sua biographia*, by Christovão de Magalhães Sepulveda, Lisbon, 1904 ; *Farnão Mendes Pinto e o Japão, id.*, Lisbon, 1906 ; *Subsidios para . . . a biographia de Fernão Mendes Pinto*, by Jordão A. de Freitas, Coimbra, 1905 ; and *Fernão Mendes Pinto : sua ultima viagem á China*, 1554-1555, etc., *id.*, Lisbon, 1905.

of the Turkish fleet, which was mobilizing for a raid on India. From Massawa he was dispatched with letters to the Abyssinian court, but after a journey through the dominions of Prester John he was shipwrecked near Aden, fell among Arabs, and was sold as a slave. This chapter of his adventures ended happily; the purchaser was a Jew, who resold him at a profit in Ormuz.

After making his way to Goa and thence to Malacca, Pinto was employed as a political agent in Sumatra and in Keda, a small state on the west coast of the Malay Peninsula, tributary to Siam.[1] But he could never have become the ideal ambassador defined by Sir Henry Wotton; however well he might perform the duty of lying abroad, the good of his country would always have been an afterthought. He therefore sought a career better suited to his talents.

The China Seas were much frequented by certain craft of the kind which subsequently made history in the Caribbean. In port they were peaceful tramps though they carried ordnance, pots of " wildfire," and a large store of unslaked lime to be flung at opponents " after the Chinese manner," besides stones, javelins, arrows, half-pikes, axes and grappling-irons. It was aboard these vessels that Mendes Pinto, who had something of Gil Blas and something of Captain Silver about his character, found messmates and a calling after his own heart. He roamed the Eastern seas, and helped a crew of criminals, pressed men and other light-hearted vagabonds to take toll of the native shipping. When he wrote his book he was posing as a penitent sinner, but there is a kind of suppressed relish in the passages which describe how he and his comrades tortured old men and children, " made their brains fly out of their heads with a cord," or looked on while the victims died raving " like mad dogs." Nothing pleased him better than to surprise some defenceless junk and fling powder-pots among the sleeping crew; it was exquisite sport to see the wretches dive and drown. The captain of one such junk was " a notorious Pyrat," and Pinto complacently draws the moral—" Thus you see how it pleased God out

[1] Since 1909 a British protectorate.

of his Divine justice to make the arrogant confidence of this cursed Dog a means to chastise him for his cruelties."

Every Portuguese buccaneer was of course a pillar of orthodoxy. Even Antonio de Faria, by no means the most humane of Pinto's captains, had his religious scruples, and would doubtless have excused his own career as a kind of maritime crusade. Antonio had vowed to make an end of one Kwaja Husain, a Muhammadan corsair from Gujarat, and had passed through many adventures on the China Seas, capturing pirate crews, dashing out their brains, and amassing amber, gold and pearls after the most approved manner of his class. Off Hainan he struck such terror into the local buccaneers that they proclaimed him their king, and arranged to pay him tribute if he would grant them licence to trade. His vessel was cast ashore on a desert island; but Faria and his crew discovered a deer which had been considerately left uneaten by a tiger, and supplied themselves with fish by shouting to scare the gulls that flew overhead, and so compelling the astonished birds to "let fall their prey." As a final stroke of good fortune they found a Chinese junk whose crew had gone ashore and left her in charge of an old man and a child. Faria sailed off in this vessel, amid the lamentations of its rightful owners, and after fitting out a new expedition, resumed the quest of his Muslim foe. On a Sunday morning in the year 1542 he arrived off Ningpo (Liampo), his ambition fulfilled and his holds crammed with booty. The inhabitants turned out to give him a royal welcome which both his subordinate, Mendes Pinto, and his " kinsman," Faria y Sousa, have described with picturesque minuteness. But Antonio positively blushed when a sermon was preached in his honour, so ill-placed were the words and so far did the preacher stray from his text. "Whereupon some of his friends pluckt him three or four times by the surplice, for to make him give over."

The jolly life of the freebooters had its ups and downs. Pinto once visited a small Malay state in company with a Muslim factor, who was asked to dine with a fellow

Muhammadan and rashly spoke evil of the Raja. That potentate got wind of the slander, for which host and guest alike were made to suffer by having their feet, hands and heads sawn off in succession. Pinto showed himself no hero, but fear sharpened his wits. He claimed to be the nephew of D. Pedro de Faria, an influential fidalgo, whose kinsmen the Raja would be loath to injure ; adding that the factor was an employee of his distinguished uncle, had embezzled the great man's money and fully deserved death. This tale, Pinto adds, was extemporized " not knowing well what I said."

Shipwreck interrupted his career as a corsair. He was captured, enslaved and carried first to Peking and afterwards to " Quinsay," a city of North China. On the way he was compelled to assist in repairing the Great Wall. The need for this outwork was never more keenly felt than in the middle years of the sixteenth century, when China was hard pressed by the Mongols of Central Asia. Although the mediæval empire of Kublai Khan and Jenghiz Khan had split and crumbled away, the descendants of these warriors had built up a number of smaller states out of the ruins. None was more formidable to China than the principality ruled by Altan Khan, whose tribe, the Tumeds, dwelt near the Yellow River, south-east of the Gobi Desert and east of Lake Kuku Nor. In 1544, if Pinto's memory served him aright, Altan Khan swept down upon Quinsay with a host of horsemen and footmen, and with forty thousand " rhinocerots "—camels, it may be—which drew the baggage-carts. The Mongols battered down the city-gates with iron rams, and sacked and slew without mercy. They then marched on Peking, whither Pinto was conveyed to be confronted with Altan Khan. The conqueror

" was set on his Throne under a rich cloth of state, and had about him twelve young boys kneeling on their knees, with little Maces ol Gold like Sceptres, which they carried on their shoulders ; close behinde was a young Lady extremely beautiful, and wonderfully richly attired, with a Ventiloe in her hand, wherewith she ever and anon fanned him. . . . The King was about forty years of age, full stature, somewhat lean, and of a good aspect ; his beard was very short, his mustaches after the Turkish manner, his eyes like to the *Chineses*, and his countenance severe and majestical ; As for his vesture it was violet-colour, in fashion like to a *Turkish* Robe, imbroidered with Pearl, upon his feet he had green Sandals wrought all over with gold-purl, and great Pearls among it, and on his head a Sattin cap of the colour of his habit, with a rich band of Diamonds and Rubies intermingled together."

When the siege of Peking was raised, Pinto accompanied the Mongol army on its retreat to the Tumed territory. He found favour with his captors, and was permitted to join an embassy to the court of Cochin China. Striking south-west from the region of Lake Kuku-Nor, he passed through Tibet, then turned south-east down one of the great rivers which rise in the Tibetan highlands, traversed Yunnan, and reached the sea by following the river Songkoi through Tongking. His exact route cannot be traced, but it was assuredly the longest and most arduous overland journey which any European traveller of the sixteenth century accomplished in the Far East. Some of its incidents are curious. At one of the first halting-places, which Pinto calls " Puxanguim," he noticed some cannon made with iron breeches and wooden muzzles ; these, he was told, had been fashioned by certain men called Almains who came out of Muscovy and had been banished by the King of Denmark. At " Quanginau " in Tibet he encountered the " Talapicor of Lechuna," who preached in the pagoda of a Lamaist monastery, " delivering a world of extrava- gancies and fooleries." The Talapicor was " the Pope of those parts," and may have been a sixteenth-century *avatar* of the Grand Lama. Lechuna, which the travellers reached a fortnight afterwards, proved " the chiefest city of the religion of those Gentiles " ; it contained sumptuous temples, and the tombs of seventeen Tatar kings. Unless Lechuna is to be interpreted as a transliteration of the Tibetan *Lha-kiang*,[1] a temple, this may well have been Lhasa. The Talapicor urged his congregation not to suffer the priests to starve—

---

[1] As Mr S. Wheeler suggests : see below.

" which would be as great a sin before God, as if you should cut the throat of a little white heifer when she is sucking of her dam, by the death of whom a thousand souls would die, which are buried in her as in a golden Tomb, in expectation of the day which is to accomplish the promise that was made unto them, wherein they shall be transformed into white Pearls for to dance in Heaven, like unto Moats which are in the beams of the Sun."

From Cochin China Pinto resumed his wanderings, and visited Burma, Macao, Japan and other outlandish regions. He claimed to have been one of the castaways who discovered Japan in 1542; but by some oversight, contemporary annalists have neglected to mention his share in that exploit. Galvão gives the names of the discoverers as Antonio da Mota, Francisco Zeimoto and Antonio Pexoto. These three were carried by a typhoon to the island of Tanegashima, off Kiushiu, the southernmost of the main islands of Japan. Here they were hospitably treated; and though conversation was impossible in the absence of any interpreter, they contrived to make themselves understood with the aid of a Chinese seaman, whose ideograms, roughly traced on the sand, were intelligible to the Japanese. Three matchlocks—the first firearms introduced into Japan —were presented to the local feudatory and afterwards copied by native armourers.[1]

It was on his third voyage to Japan that Pinto came in contact with Xavier.

In 1558, so the legend runs, he returned to Lisbon, after twenty-one years of adventure in which he was five times shipwrecked, and seventeen times sold as a slave.[2] He asserts that he went home a reformed sinner, after devoting the whole of a vast fortune to the endowment of a Jesuit seminary in Goa; and he laments the indifference with which the Portuguese authorities received one who had dared and suffered so much for his country! Whatever else may be disputable in the *Peregrinaçam*, its author certainly possessed a sense of humour. In the end he

---

[1] Until modern times the Japanese name for firearms was *Tanegashima*.
[2] I borrow these statistics from the *Encyclopædia Britannica*, ninth edition, s.v. PINTO.

was taken at his own valuation, for in January 1583 he was granted a pension by Philip II. of Spain. He died on the 8th of July, in the same year. His trustworthiness is a matter which must be carefully weighed by all who may be interested in the biography of Francis Xavier. Some of his statements are demonstrably false, even when he does not contradict himself, but elsewhere he shows an intimate personal knowledge of the Far East. His account of Tibetan hydrography and his use of Tibetan place-names have been shown, by Mr S. Wheeler,[1] to contain a large element of truth ; his mention of the French cannon found in Sumatra is a fragment of genuine observation ; and he gives some examples of Japanese folk-lore which can be paralleled from the pages of Lafcadio Hearn. Much evidence for and against his veracity could be adduced, but until a critical edition of the *Peregrinaçam* is published by the Academia Real, the Hakluyt Society, or some equally competent body, it will remain impossible to characterize the book as on the whole true or false. Travellers and historians so authoritative as Sir Henry Yule, Dr Arminius Vambéry, Sir R. K. Douglas and Mr E. C. Danvers have testified to its value either explicitly or by reproducing its assertions. Mr R. S. Whiteway, who knows as much as any Englishman about the history of the Portuguese in the East, stigmatizes the *Peregrinaçam* as " a romance with some traditions embedded in it," and thinks that the Jesuits may have had a hand in its composition. Mr Donald Ferguson concurs in this view.

The *Peregrinaçam* was published in 1614, twenty-one years after its author's death and fifty-six years after his return to Europe. During this interval it may well have been edited, partly, like Couto's Sixth Decade, to meet the requirements of the censorship, partly to enable the Jesuits to complete the biography of Francis Xavier. As Pinto bequeathed his manuscript to the Casa Pia, a home for women in Lisbon, which was under clerical control, there were ample opportunities for such revision. It seems to me probable that the original document on which the ecclesiastical editors

[1] *Geographical Journal*, vol. i. p. 139 (1893).

may have worked was not a mere romance, but a record of actual travel, embellished to make it more amusing; such a record as Ludovico di Varthema composed. To hold this view is not to deny that the *Peregrinaçam* has a definite historical value. The adventures of Antonio de Faria, whom no other sixteenth-century historian mentions, may be fact or fable : nothing can be inferred from the silence of these writers The latitude and longitude of such places as " Quanginau " and " Puxanguim " may rest for ever undetermined. But the *Peregrinaçam* was written for a public acquainted with the broad features of life in the Far East. It may not describe what happened ; it probably does describe the kind of event that happened. In this lies its worth. If moreover the chapters on Francis Xavier were compiled or edited under Jesuit influence, they doubtless embody all the information which his missionary heirs could have secured, either from oral or written records.

CHAPTER XXX

THE FIRST MISSION TO JAPAN

XAVIER'S voyage from Malacca to Japan lasted seven weeks, being delayed by heavy gales which the Chinese crew strove to calm by burning candles and sticks of aloe-wood before their joss. They also cast lots or, as Xavier expresses it, "consulted the devil," to ascertain their destiny, learning that their junk would arrive safely in Japan but would never return to Malacca. The alarm caused by this oracle was heightened when the captain's daughter fell overboard and was drowned, so that the Chinese made for Canton, intending to abandon the venture. But the threats and entreaties of the passengers prevailed upon them to continue, and they steered for Changchau,[1] hoping to winter there, as it was already late in the season for a run to Japan. As, however, Changchau was found to be beset by robber junks, the voyage was hastily resumed.

Japan, and especially the main island of Nippon, had for nearly two centuries been rent by dynastic wars. From Kioto, which was then the capital, the Mikado, or titular sovereign, and the Shogun, who ruled as his deputy, still exercised a nominal authority over the entire empire; but the actual authority had been usurped by the Daimios, or feudal chiefs, who had taken advantage of the incessant civil strife to make themselves independent, each in his own fief. Bands of brigands infested the highroads, while the inmates of the Buddhist monasteries, through being

---

[1] The *Chincheo* of Portuguese historians, and the *Chinchew* of old English writers, situated on the Amoy inlet, province of Fukien. It is not to be confused with *Chwanchau* (farther north in the same province), to which the name of *Chinchew* was afterwards transferred.

compelled to bear arms for their own defence, had acquired a taste for fighting and plunder which added to the general chaos.

Kagoshima, Mendes Pinto's " Canquexumaa "—where Xavier and his three companions landed on the 15th of August 1549, stands on the western shore of a deep inlet which indents the southern coast of Kiushiu. Here they were made welcome by the friends and kinsfolk of Yajiro, who acted as interpreter. The Daimio of Satsuma, in whose territories Kagoshima was included, at first permitted them to preach freely, an act of tolerance which was probably dictated by hopes of commercial advantage : for since the first landfall of the Portuguese at Tanegashima, other Portuguese merchants had found their way to the harbours of Kiushiu, and no Daimio could afford to neglect any chance of filling by increased trade the coffers which had been emptied by endless campaigns. The Buddhist hierarchy in Kagoshima was equally ready to welcome the new-comers, and listened with tolerant courtesy to the creed expounded by Yajiro.

Xavier's first letters from Kagoshima show how deeply he was impressed by the character of the Japanese. He notes their love of honour, their reverence for long descent rather than riches, their elaborate code of etiquette, their hatred of gambling and theft. Almost all men, he says, are able to read, and all are trained from childhood to the use of arms. " The finest of uncivilized nations " is his verdict, delivered with the unconscious arrogance of the West.[1] Though the " bonzes "—Buddhist monks and priests—provoked his wrath by smiling when he denounced their evil lives, Xavier soon made a friend of one of them, a priest nearly ninety years old, whose name was interpreted to mean " Heart of Truth." The two venerable teachers sat for hours together, debating as best they might —with no common language except signs and Xavier's broken Japanese—the tremendous questions of immortality and the nature of God. But mission-work made slow progress when Yajiro was not at hand to interpret.

[1] Letter to the Society of Jesus at Goa, dated November 11th, 1549.

" At present," Xavier writes after six weeks' experience, " we are like so many dumb statues in the midst of the people. They talk about us and discuss us a good deal among themselves, and we are able to say nothing all the time, not knowing their language. We are making ourselves children over again in learning the elements of it." [1]

The Satsuma Daimio granted an audience to Yajiro; his mother was so delighted with a painting of the Madonna and Child, brought from Goa, that she asked for a copy and for a written statement of the chief doctrines of Christianity. Curiously enough, no artist could be found sufficiently skilled to reproduce the picture.

A change came in September 1550. Xavier had condemned Buddhism root and branch. In his zeal he had repaid courtesy with invective, and at last his strictures on the cenobites who disregarded their own rule of celibacy had goaded his victims to retaliate. They pointed out to the Daimio that these alien firebrands were preaching in a tone which must sooner or later provoke violence. Meanwhile some Portuguese traders were discharging a rich cargo at Hirado, an islet off the north-west coast of Kiushiu, in the territories of a rival potentate. The remonstrance of the Buddhists and his own disappointment moved the Daimio to issue an edict forbidding any of his vassals to embrace Christianity, on pain of death. His mandate was obeyed; but the converts who had already been won, to the number of about 150, were left unmolested. Seeing that they could accomplish no more in Kagoshima, the three Europeans took ship for Hirado, leaving Yajiro in charge of the neophytes.

Xavier had already learned that his chances of success in Japan were dependent on the goodwill of the local rulers which could only be secured by the bribe of trade with Portuguese India. " We must catch every soul with its proper bait," he writes, unfolding a scheme for the mutual benefit of Christianity and the King's revenue :—

" It would be easy to obtain permission for a house in the maritime city of Osaka, the chief emporium of all Japan, to be publicly assigned

---

[1] Coleridge, vol. ii. pp. 251-252.

to the officials of the King of Portugal, as well as store-houses for European goods. These could be exchanged at a high profit for silver and gold of the best quality, large quantities of which are brought to Osaka from the mines of the country, which are very productive ; a factory and exchange would be set up, all to the great benefit of the royal revenue of Portugal." [1]

He proceeds, with his usual businesslike attention to the details of any project, to enclose a catalogue of the goods best suited to the Japanese market, adding a few notes on the right season for a voyage, on freights, provisions, and the danger of touching at Chinese ports on the outward passage.

The Portuguese traders at Hirado greeted Xavier and his companions with a salute from their artillery, and escorted them to the presence of the Daimio, by whom they were allowed to preach and baptize without hindrance. Eager listeners flocked to hear the sermons of Juan Fernandez, who was now beginning to make himself understood in Japanese ; but unless the traders could provide an interpreter, Xavier and Torres had to content themselves with reading aloud from a manual of Christian doctrine which Yajiro had composed in his native tongue and transcribed into Latin characters.   In little more than a week the new religion had gained a hundred adherents.   Xavier rightly attributed this success to the friendliness of the Daimio, and argued that if the favour of one local chief could be turned to such splendid account, the goodwill of the Emperor himself might influence thousands to turn to the Catholic faith.   Upon this theory he at once acted, by setting out overland for the capital.   Cosmo Torres remained to carry on the work in Hirado.

After crossing the Strait of Shimonose'‥ Xavier and Fernandez continued their journey to Yamaguchi, a great inland city, which was the capital of the Choshu fief and had been the headquarters of Japanese trade with China. Halting here, they found the Daimio friendly, but unimpressed by the two travel-stained wayfarers who came without gifts, promise of trade, or credentials.   In the

[1] Coleridge, vol. ii. pp. 270-271.

streets they were mobbed by a jeering rabble of boys, who assailed them with stones and with shouts of " There go the men who declare that it is wicked to have more than one wife ! "

Thus encouraged, Xavier decided to push on towards Kioto without delay, although the season was midwinter (1550-1551) and the cold would be doubly keen to men who had spent years under a tropical sun. The road lay over frozen highlands and through flooded watercourses ; at times the two missionaries were forced to run barefooted beside the stirrup of some grandee, in order to secure the protection of his bodyguard against the brigands who watched by pass and ferry. But after many hardships they at last found themselves safe in a huge city—larger than Lisbon itself, though devastated by long wars. Here dwelt the Mikado and the Shogun, in a seclusion which no stranger might violate. For two unknown vagabonds to demand an audience was merely to invite ridicule. Street-preaching had no effect on a populace which took its cue from the local ruler, and listened with good-humoured apathy or not at all. Father Coleridge rightly remarks that Xavier " laid the foundation of the future Church of Meaco [Kioto] by his sufferings rather than by his successes." [1]

It was necessary to return to Yamaguchi, but Xavier had now mastered the art of conciliating a Japanese feudatory. He summoned Cosmo Torres, ordering him to bring from Hirado the letters and presents which had originally been sent for the Mikado by the Governor of India, the Bishop of Goa, and the Captain of Malacca. Among these gifts were a clavichord (*manicordio*) and a clock. At the sight of such treasures, the Daimio [2] realized that he was dealing with an ambassador instead of a crazy tramp. His courtesy became cordiality, and he pressed his visitors to accept a return gift of gold and silver, which they declined. Notices

[1] Vol. ii. p. 293.

[2] The Jesuit historians give his name as *Oxindono* : from Japanese sources we know that it was *Uchi*, pronounced similarly to the Portuguese *Oxin*. The second half of the name is an honorific suffix. The whole affords a good example of the difficulty of identifying Eastern names in their Portuguese dress.

were posted in the most frequented streets to announce that Christianity might be taught and believed, and a vacant monastery was assigned to the missionaries, who preached twice daily to crowded congregations and held public debate with the bonzes.

About the end of August 1551, Xavier learned that a Portuguese ship had arrived at Hiji, a seaport in the fief of Bungo, which comprised the north-eastern part of Kiushiu.[1] The captain, Duarte da Gama,[2] was the bearer of letters for the missionaries, and Mendes Pinto claims to have been on board. As Xavier was now anxious to return to India, in order to prepare for a voyage to China, he re-crossed the Strait of Shimonoseki early in September, and joined the ship. The salvos of artillery with which he was received seem to have astonished the Japanese, and a messenger was sent by Otomo, the feudal chief of Bungo, to inquire if the Portuguese had been engaged with a squadron of corsairs, whose approach had been signalled.

Xavier had now finally adopted the policy which experience in Hirado and Yamaguchi had shown to be most advantageous. Finding that poverty and asceticism were ignored, he came forward as the accredited envoy of Portugal, taking care that his rank and power should be attested by the homage of the merchant adventurers. He desired to figure before the Daimio as a magnate whose favour it would be worth while to gain. The merchants gladly accepted the part assigned them—Xavier was ever popular with seafaring men—and arranged for an audience at the court of Bungo. When the day came, they donned their gold chains and full gala costume, and rowed ashore with flags flying and with trumpets and hautboys playing in antiphon, much to the excitement of the townsfolk, who trooped down to the harbour as soon as they heard this novel music. According to Pinto, the " Quamsyandono, captain of Canafama," had been sent by the Daimio to escort his guests to the palace.

---

[1] Pinto's narrative of Xavier's stay in Japan begins with the visit to Hiji (Pinto's *Fingeo*).

[2] Not in any way connected with the family of Vasco da Gama.

" As for the Father," says Pinto, " he wore a full cassock of black camlet, a surplice over it, and a stole of green velvet edged with brocade. Behind him walked our captain, holding a major-domo's bâton as though he were a chamberlain, and in his retinue four or five of the most honourable and richest merchants, who, after the manner of servitors, ceremoniously carried certain articles in their hands. One, for example, carried a book in a white satin cover, another some slippers of black velvet which we chanced to have by us, another a Bengal cane inlaid with gold, another a figure of Our Lady, swathed in a scarf of violet damask, and another a small parasol." [1]

Pinto goes on to describe the audience at length. Xavier passed through the Daimio's bodyguard, whose uniforms were of silk and damask, and their sabres plated with gold. He was received by a child of some six or seven years, who bade him welcome in a speech beginning—

" May thy coming to this house of my sovereign lord the king be as grateful to him and to thee as the rain which God sends from heaven to the rice-fields, when they have need of it." [2]

The Portuguese were then conducted into the presence-chamber, where the Daimio saluted Xavier by bowing thrice until his forehead touched the ground, while Xavier repaid the compliment by kneeling to kiss his host's sabre. After a further exchange of courtesies, varied by the expulsion of a too critical bonze, the audience terminated.

Xavier had achieved his purpose, and was free to carry on his work in Bungo until it was time to set sail. Through the goodwill of the feudal government, he was able to ensure the safety of Torres and Fernandez in Yamaguchi, when " Oxindono " committed *hari-kari* as the result of a successful revolution, and was succeeded by a brother of Otomo. It is noteworthy that during the troubles in Yamaguchi the missionaries were given shelter by two of their rivals, the bonzes.

Pinto describes with his usual graphic minuteness sundry debates in which Xavier routed the theological champions of Bungo, but it is to be feared that the details of these encounters originated in the chronicler's own teeming

[1] Pinto, chap. ccix.   [2] Pinto, chap. ccx.

brain.[1] We learn how "Fucarandono, the Superior of Miay Gimaa," claimed to have bested his adversary over the purchase of some silk, just fifteen centuries before. The exploit had been performed in an earlier incarnation ; and the Fucarandono proceeded to edify his hearers with a dissertation upon metempsychosis. This, says Pinto—

" the Father refuted thrice over, with words so clear, reasons so evident, and comparisons so apt and true to nature, that the bonze remained utterly bewildered : of the which reasons I will not now speak, inasmuch as I would not lapse into prolixity, and even more because I avow that they pass the comprehension of my own wit." [2]

From Xavier's own correspondence, it is clear that the problems set by the Japanese were subtle enough to tax all the resources of his dialectic. It is for this reason that he urges Ignatius de Loyola to recommend no missionaries for duty in Japan except those of high mental attainments as well as of robust physique.[3] His own vigour had withstood the strain of the winter journey to Kioto, though hair and beard were grown white ; and he was already preparing for new and more arduous labour elsewhere. In Japan he had found that the Chinese classics were what Aristotle and the Scriptures had been to mediæval Europe. They outweighed logic, and constituted a supreme tribunal to which the Japanese controversialists could safely resort if ever they were at a loss for argument. Xavier cites an instance of this triumphant appeal to authority :—

" If there existed a single First Cause of everything, surely, they said, the Chinese, from whom they derive their religion, must have known it." [4]

It followed, for them, that no First Cause could exist : for their antagonist, that the conquest of China must precede the final subjugation of Japan. When Xavier

[1] Pinto makes Otomo suggest that Xavier should say *Beate Petre*, for *Sancte Petre*, on the ground that *Sancte* was an obscene word in Japanese. An acquaintance with Latin cannot have been common among Daimios in 1551.

[2] Chap. ccxi.

[3] Letter to Ignatius, dated from Cochin on January 29th, 1552.

[4] Coleridge, vol. ii. p. 337.

15

set sail from Hiji, on the 20th of November 1551, he took with him a copy of his Japanese manual transcribed into Chinese ideograms. He had spent two years and three months in Japan, and the Church which he left to the care of Torres, Fernandez and Yajiro had already a membership of some 800 souls.

CHAPTER XXXI

THE PORTUGUESE IN CHINA

IT was in the harbour of Malacca that the Portuguese first saw the great Canton junks, with their mat-sails, painted eyes staring from the bows, coops of live ducks, and vegetables flourishing on deck. They had heard of the inscrutable beings who manned these floating markets ; and in 1508 Diogo Lopes de Sequeira was instructed to inquire about them—were they Christians and what were their resources ? Sequeira failed to solve these problems, though he encountered three or four junks at Malacca, whither they came to load spices and sell their " musk, rhubarb, pearls, tin, porcelain, silk and wrought stuffs of all kinds, such as damask, satins and brocades of extraordinary richness " : the list is taken from a letter which Andrea Corsali, an eye-witness, sent in January 1515 to Duke Giuliano de' Medici.[1]

Jorge de Albuquerque, Captain of Malacca, was the first to send an expedition to China, in 1514, but little is known of its fortunes. In the next year Rafael Perestrello, a member of the Madeiran family into which Columbus had married, accomplished the voyage in safety, and announced that the Chinese desired friendship with the Portuguese.

An effort to grant this laudable desire was made in June 1517, when Fernão Pires de Andrade set sail from Malacca, conveying as ambassador to the court of Peking an apothecary named Thomé Pires. The flotilla of eight Portuguese vessels dropped anchor off the island of Tamão or Tamou, known also as the Ilha de Veniaga ;[2] two ships went forward

---

[1] Reproduced in vol. ii. of Sir H. Yule's *Cathay and the Way Thither*, London, Hakluyt Society, 1866.

[2] This island, one of those at the mouth of the Canton River, has not

to Canton itself. They signalized their arrival by firing a salute from their cannon and dressing the masts with flags, thereby committing a breach of Chinese etiquette. This was explained by the local officials, and Fernão apologized. A native treatise on the Art of War, published in 1621, declares that as the strangers knew nothing of etiquette the Viceroy ordered that they should be instructed for three days in the proper ceremonies. The same authority adds that the commander of the Firingis was named Ka-pi-tan, and that his men " manifested much fondness for the study of the Buddhist Scriptures." [1]

Giovanni de Empoli,[2] an Italian, was chosen to expound the motives which had brought the embassy to Canton. His march through the city was a pageant, in which trumpeters led the way and a glittering suite escorted the envoy. The Chinese interpreters stated that " they were come from the King of the Firingis, to beg for a seal from the Lord of the World, the Son of Heaven, in order to yield obedience to him " ; this was the correct formula, though hardly the mode of address a Portuguese ambassador would have chosen. Charmed by so much courtesy, the officials promised to communicate with the Emperor, allotted a house to Thomé Pires, and licensed Fernão and his men to trade. The ships put to sea again with a rich cargo.

Fernão had conciliated his hosts by his tact and prudence. His brother Simão, who arrived in August 1519, shocked them by building a fort and setting up gallows, on which he was indiscreet enough to hang one of his crew. Not content with this violation of Celestial sovereignty, he kidnapped the children of some Chinese traders—boys and girls who had been placed on board as security for debt. Simão managed to escape, but in September 1521 the

---

been identified. It is certainly an error to confuse it with Shangchwan, or St John's, where Xavier died. *Veniaga* (Malay, *barniyaga*) means trade. The name and situation of the island are discussed by Ferguson (see Appendix A) in his introduction.

[1] Ferguson, p. 41.

[2] His narrative is printed in Ramusio, vol. i.

next Portuguese fleet was blockaded at Tamão. Tidings had come that the Emperor was dead, and all foreigners were commanded to advertise their regret by leaving the country. The Portuguese, seeing their holds half-empty, refused to comply. In the end they were glad to escape with the loss of many killed and prisoners.

Thenceforward it was enacted that any ship entering a Chinese port with a foreign devil aboard should be confiscated. Fr. Gaspar de Santa Cruz, whose *Tractado . . . de China*, etc., was published at Evora in 1569, declares that the Chinese " through hatred and abhorrence now called the Portuguese *fâcui*, or men of the devil." This appears to to be the first notice of the term *fan kwei*, " foreign devil," as applied to a European. Couto asserts that an imperial ordinance, forbidding " the men with the beards and the large eyes " to enter Chinese territory, was inscribed in golden letters on the gates of Canton.

Meanwhile Thomé Pires and his retinue remained behind. They reached " Piquim " only to find themselves mistrusted as possible spies, and no nearer to the imperial presence. Thomé was even denied the consolation accorded to other envoys, who were graciously permitted, on the fifteenth day of the moon, to prostrate themselves before the palace wall which hid the Son of Heaven from profane eyes. In 1524 he died in captivity. The same fate befell most of his retinue and their companions in misery, the prisoners taken in 1521. Two of these unfortunates wrote home in 1534 and 1536 ; by some happy chance the letters reached Lisbon, where they were read by the historian Barros, and five centuries later they reappeared in the Bibliothèque Nationale in Paris.

The two letters are full of interest and pathos. It says much for the spirit of the writers, Vasco Calvo and Christovão Vieyra, who had seen their comrades tortured and mutilated, that they could send King Manoel a detailed scheme for the conquest of China. " Another India would be won," they write ; " there is not a Malabari that could not fight with forty of these men and kill them all, because they are just like women : they have no stomach ; simply outcries." The two writers grow enthusiastic over their scheme. In Canton, they allege, the Indian fleets could be built; wood abounds, "carpenters are as plentiful as vermin . . . not a Portuguese need put his hand to stone or wood." They fight their battles over again, and the letters live. One can imagine the thrill with which a patriotic Portuguese would hear these voices from the grave telling how "Father Mergulhão died fighting" in the affray of 1521.[1]

The Chinese reciprocated the scorn which animated their prisoners. They maintained that the Portuguese could not fight on land, but were "like fishes, which when you take them out of the water or the sea straightway die." Their resentment was fanned by envoys who came from the Raja of Bintang, son of the exiled Sultan of Malacca, to complain to their suzerain, the Emperor of China. There was also a mandarin, who stated that the Portuguese in Tamão had knocked off his cap and beaten him. The Portuguese were even accused of stealing dogs and eating them roasted, which does not seem the most atrocious of crimes.

The fate of Thomé Pires and other explorers proved no deterrent to traders hungry for the profits of a China voyage, and such adventurers as Fernão Mendes Pinto—sanctimonious ruffians with a taste for piracy and sermons—found full scope for their talent in enterprises of this class. Avoiding the dangerous vicinity of Canton, they would bring-to their ocean tramps off the Fukien littoral, farther north, and there carry on a brisk contraband trade with the native smugglers. In time the policy of exclusion was relaxed. The Portuguese may have conceded commercial advantages to secure this end; for in 1543, when Simão Botelho was sent to reorganize the Malacca customs service, he was instructed to levy duties in kind at the rate of ten per cent. *ad valorem* on all merchandise imported from China in Portuguese bottoms, while only six per cent. was to be imposed on cargo brought by the Chinese themselves.

[1] This was the Mergulhão whose gallantry at the siege of Aden has already been mentioned, p. 186.

Governments do not grant such preference out of sheer altruism, and the Portuguese settlers who had already established themselves on the outer fringe of the Chinese Empire no doubt reaped some benefit.

Many vessels of both nations resorted to the islands near the mouth of the Canton river. It is generally believed, however, that Ningpo, or Liampo as it appears in the chroniclers, was the chief centre of intercourse. Here, according to Mendes Pinto, more than three thousand Christians had settled, and had prospered until their own folly brought ruin.

They do not seem to have understood their own peril, and treated the Chinese, citizens of the mightiest empire on earth, as though they were the subjects of some petty Indian prince, to be bullied and plundered by a factor and his handful of men-at-arms. A Portuguese magistrate who had the worst of a bargain sought to recover his money by violence, and brought down upon the settlement an army of sixty thousand Chinese, commanded by the provincial governor. Four hours later Liampo had ceased to exist.

A philosophic Chinaman pronounced its epitaph with appropriate brevity. " Let them go on," he remarked, " for whatever they gain as brave soldiers they will lose as avaricious traders. They now conquer Asia. Asia will soon conquer them." [1] In 1547 the Portuguese obtained leave to settle in Changchau, where the tragedy of Liampo is said to have been re-enacted ; and it was not until 1557 that they were permitted to colonize the island city of Macao, one of the few relics of their eastern empire which still remain in their possession. Meanwhile the foreign devils were more than ever unwelcome on the mainland, though still able to trade off the estuary of the Canton River and off the Fukien littoral. All the omens were unfavourable to the Jesuit mission.

[1] The epigram is reminiscent of many passages in the writings of Faria y Sousa, who tells the story ; and the whole history of the Liampo affair is open to grave suspicion.

CHAPTER XXXII

FRANCIS XAVIER sailed from Goa on the 25th of April 1552, bound for China. It had been arranged that he should go in the train of Diogo Pereira, a wealthy merchant, who was to be accredited as envoy from the King of Portugal to the Emperor of China. Pereira and his ship the *Santa Cruz* met the Jesuits at Malacca, where Francis was detained by an outbreak of plague. D. Pedro da Silva, a son of D. Vasco da Gama, had vacated the captaincy of the port, and his younger brother, D. Alvaro de Athayde, had succeeded him—helped to this office by Xavier himself, if Couto and the ecclesiastical writers may be trusted, which is by no means certain. D. Alvaro had accompanied Xavier out to India in 1542, and had been deprived of the ship and kept for months under arrest by the Admiral and Governor-designate of India, Martim Affonso de Sousa, a friend of the great missionary. The charge against him was that he had intended to warn his brother, D. Estevão da Gama, the actual Governor, that a successor was at hand.

It seems unlikely that D. Alvaro and Francis Xavier can have been on terms of friendship, if the Captain inherited anything of the proud and resentful temper of his father, D. Vasco da Gama. Whatever the cause may have been, a very pretty quarrel arose. Athayde claimed, probably with justice, the right to appoint the commander of the ship which would take Xavier to China ; Xavier was bound to Pereira by many ties of gratitude ; Pereira would certainly have made a profit on the voyage, and was determined to go. Athayde then caused the rudder of the *Santa Cruz* to be unshipped and set up, a visible symbol of triumph, in front of his own house.   In reply to all protests he declared that Pereira was a low-born knave, unfit to represent the Crown ; if Xavier wished to convert the heathen he would find an adequate supply in Brazil or Monomotapa.

Pereira then offered to pay 30,000 ducats for the privileges at stake ; but D. Alvaro had estimated the profits of the venture at 100,000, and when some highly placed officials laid the offer before him, he vowed they should have thirty thousand blows from his halberd-staff.   So saying, he ran to take the weapon down from its peg, " which," says Mendes Pinto, " made them get to the door very fast." It is not to be supposed that Xavier softened the Captain's heart by offering public prayers and masses for his con-version.   When all else failed, he produced the papal briefs investing him with the office of Nuncio Apostolic, which he had brought from Europe, and announced that the Captain was then and there excommunicated, as were all who wilfully impeded the representative of the Pope. D. Alvaro, however, stood his ground, and it was the Nuncio Apostolic who gave way at last.   He was suffered to proceed in the *Santa Cruz*, without Pereira.   Thus the mission be-came a private enterprise instead of an embassy, and its chance of entering China was correspondingly diminished.

After touching at Singapore and possibly Changchau, the *Santa Cruz* reached Shangchwan, or St John's Island, during the last week of August.   The island was overgrown with brushwood, and overrun by tigers ; its trading-station was a cluster of wooden shanties, gambling-hells and grog-shops, where the gentlemen-adventurers from Europe foregathered to while away the intervals between voyages.   They welcomed Francis as became dutiful sons of the Church, but held out no extravagant hopes of his success.   He had been abed with fever, but landed in buoyant spirits, the difficulties before him awakening all his zest for combat.   Canton was only 120 miles away, and the prospect of martyrdom no farther.   For twenty piculs of pepper, a Chinese merchant had undertaken to convey him to Canton.   The journey promised to be most attractively perilous, and though the first trader repudiated his bargain, another consented to take his place for 200 gold pieces.

" It is possible," Xavier writes complacently, " that the Chinese merchant after receiving the gold may throw us into the sea, or leave us on a desert island to conceal his crime ; and again, if we reach Canton, the Viceroy may put us to all kinds of unheard of tortures, or make slaves of us for life. It is a capital crime for a foreigner to enter any part of China without a passport." [1]

But the start was always delayed : the authorities at Canton cut off food-supplies and reduced the settlement almost to famine ; a Chinese interpreter whom Xavier had brought from the College of St Paul inconsiderately forgot his native language.

Xavier himself had no difficulty in tracing these hostile influences to their source. " I cannot express to you," he says, " how enraged the devil is that the Society should invade China . . . it makes him rage with impotent fury, and lash himself up, and boil over with passion." [2]

On clear days Xavier could almost discern the dim outline of China rising beyond the strait which sunders Shangchwan from the mainland ; but weeks passed and brought him no nearer. On Sunday the 20th of November, after he had celebrated the early morning mass, he was again stricken by fever. At first he was conveyed on board the *Santa Cruz*, but he was unable to bear the rocking of the ship. Then Jorge Alvares, the master of a Portuguese barque, gave him shelter in his hut, and persuaded him to let himself be bled ; but Xavier fainted under the operation, which only intensified his fever. He lay in the hut all day long, gazing at the sky through the aperture which served as a window and talking to a small crucifix which he held. His mental powers began to ebb ; in his delirium he spoke aloud of China, the Land of Promise which he was never to enter and conquer. All his speech was in Latin. After a time he regained consciousness ,and ordered that his vestments and the consecrated vessels for mass should be

[1] Coleridge, vol. ii. p. 550.   [2] *Id.* p. 565.

transferred to the *Santa Cruz*; but this transient recovery was soon followed by a relapse, and on Friday the 2nd of December, about two o'clock in the afternoon, Francis Xavier died.

On the next Sunday he was buried on the summit of a knoll overlooking the sea. Two half-castes bore the coffin, and only the Chinese interpreter and the pilot of the *Santa Cruz* followed it to the grave. A wooden cross, and a mound of stones, over his head and feet, marked where the Apostle of the Indies lay. But in the ensuing spring the body was exhumed, and conveyed to Goa, where it was reinterred with magnificent ceremony in the Jesuits' church.

It will not perhaps be superfluous to attempt some estimate of Xavier's work and character; for these topics have been discussed in too partisan a spirit by all his modern English biographers save one—Sir James Stephen, whose brilliant and sympathetic essay entitled *The Founders of Jesuitism* was first published in its final form some sixty years ago.[1]

Xavier's opinion of the Eastern religions which he encountered was unswervingly hostile, and he made no attempt to emulate his famous fellow-countryman, Ramon de Lull, who had preluded his mission to the Moors by an endeavour to gain some insight into their own creed. The Apostle of the Indies chose to wrestle blindfold against unknown adversaries. It is fair to ask what such a critic as he would have replied if confronted with those chapters in the Koran which soar to a height hardly surpassed by the most sublime pages of Isaiah and Ezekiel. In the later literature of Islam, how would he have regarded the *Mathnawi* of Jalal ud-Din, with their mystical and rarefied philosophy? The *Mathnawi* tell of the Beloved whose door remained shut fast until, in answer to the challenge *Who is there?* the Lover could truthfully answer not, *It is I*, but *It is Thou*. Ramon de Lull would have understood such a passage, for it is conceived in the spirit of his own book of the "Friend and the Beloved," being allegorical of the soul

---

[1] In his *Essays in Ecclesiastical Biography*, London, 1849. It originally appeared in the *Edinburgh Review*.

on its pilgrimage towards God, and of a unity embracing all that is divine within and beyond humanity. Luís de León and St Theresa might also have understood. But it would have been incomprehensible to almost any other theologian trained in the schools of the West. Yet it contains the key to the mystical doctrine which is expressed in the very name of Islam, " Resignation "—a doctrine common to all the higher creeds, for it means self-surrender to the divine will.

In Portuguese India there was none who took the trouble to understand the Oriental religions, among many who were zealous to supersede them. Men looked at every Oriental idea from without, never lifting aside the embroideries of sensuous imagery with which the East loves to veil its thought and faith from profane eyes. When the Persian poets wrote mystically of life and fate, untaught Western ears could only catch the praises of wine drunk in cool rose-gardens. That the Portuguese lacked insight into the spirit of Islam is less astonishing when their ignorance even of its law and custom is remembered. Couto asserts that the Muslims at the second siege of Diu bore into battle a flag with the portrait of Muhammad painted upon it.[1] Andrade credits D. João de Castro with having sprinkled the blood of cows over certain mosques, because the Muhammadans venerated cattle as the depositaries of their own souls. From the very first it was the same with Hinduism. Vasco da Gama and his men cheerfully worshipped in a Hindu temple, under the impression that it was a sort of Christian church ; and when the error was detected, Europeans came to regard Hinduism and even Buddhism, the most humane and not the least intellectual of religions, as mere grossness and idolatry.

Xavier bluntly declares that " the gods of the heathen are all devils, and their prayers an abomination in the sight of God." In Japan he judged Buddhism by the immorality of the Buddhist monks and nuns : an Oriental visitor to Europe, judging the doctrine of Christ by the customs of

---

[1] Even Corrêa makes this error, after a lifetime spent in the East. See Stanley's *Corrêa*, p. 372.

the laxer convents, might have reached an equally valuable conclusion. In his opinion of the Chinese Xavier inclined to leniency ; in Japan he had heard much of their learning and piety, and some fragments of condensed wisdom may have come within his ken, such as the Taoist maxim, " He is the great man who has preserved the heart of his childhood," or the Confucian version of the " golden rule "— " Do not unto others what thou wouldst abhor if done to thyself." The homely lore of the Chinese sages was less alien from his mind than the more speculative beliefs of Buddhism and Islam. But on the whole his attitude towards every creed outside the pale of his own Church was that of a Hellene to " barbarians " or of a Musalman to " kafirs "—a mental attitude varying from sincere but ignorant pity to fierce hatred.

In consequence, it was upon the externals and not upon the spirit of Oriental creeds that Xavier was compelled to concentrate his attack. His most destructive arguments were aimed against customs and ceremonies, or the distorted versions of doctrine which were supplied by untaught natives and prejudiced Europeans ; for there is no evidence to show that he had any frequent intercourse with educated Muslims or Hindus.

It was not for this reason only that his Indian converts belonged almost exclusively to the lower castes. The caste-system has ever been the ally, up to a certain point, of imported creeds. Men and women bound for life to a calling which their countrymen viewed with loathing, were naturally glad to embrace Christianity and the hope of a career. In Portuguese India, moreover, the state stood ready to reward the pious convert and to punish the recalcitrant.

His lack of sympathetic insight into alien minds, his reliance upon force, and his attempt to subordinate secular to ecclesiastical interests do seriously detract from the fame of the Apostle of the Indies. Nevertheless, if the mere magnitude of his labours be considered, Francis Xavier has had no rival in modern times. Jesuit annalists credit him with the salvation of 700,000 souls in some ten years. While statistics are absurd, the number of his converts must have been enormous, though allowance should be made for the reckoning of babies in arms—*facere Christianos* is the optimistic synonym for infant baptism used by Xavier himself. The area over which he toiled and the perils and hindrances he surmounted are surely unsurpassed in the history of missions. Only to travel from Rome to Lisbon, and thence by the Cape to Goa, Malacca, Amboyna and Japan took more than two years, if the winds blew fair, and no mishap delayed the voyage. Yet while Xavier journeyed from city to city at the end of the world, preaching, catechizing, baptizing, tending the sick and leaving behind him in each place the rudiments of a Christian community, he found time to direct the large interests entrusted to him as representative of the Pope and Superior of the Society of Jesus in India, and still to keep in touch with Rome and Lisbon.

His energy was always at white heat. In most of his letters there is a note of disappointment at the slow progress achieved, an impatience for some sphere—in Ethiopia, Japan, or China—where his activities might have free play. His ability hardly fell short of his energy, but it was not these qualities alone that gave him ascendancy over the minds of men and women. He held them by the spell of personal charm. The blue-eyed, white-haired priest, with his drawn, ascetic face, his diminutive stature [1] and his known desire for martyrdom, was not as other men. In some of the slums of our western cities a special reverence is paid to celibate clergy as to beings who have risen above the passions and frailties of their fellows. Francis Xavier, with his air of otherworldliness, inspired a like respect. His worn cassock hardly covered a frame etiolated and refined by suffering and the workings of an inward fire. He had proved himself fearless of death when he quelled

[1] In its present shrunken state the body of St Francis is $4\frac{1}{2}$ feet long; the length of the coffin is $5\frac{1}{10}$ feet. In 1859 the body was examined by a committee of medical men in Goa; a drawing of it was made subsequently and is lithographed in Fonseca (p. 296). I have compared this drawing with the portrait in Torsellino's *Vida* (1596), and find so strong a resemblance, despite the lapse of centuries, that the portrait must be authentic.

Satis
eft Domi
ne, satis
eſt.

ℙ. Franciscus Xauerius; qui primus ex Societate
Ieſu fidem in Indiam inuexit. Obijt anᵗ 1552. Decemb. 2.
Hieronymus Wierx fecit et exc.

FRANCIS XAVIER
FROM THE "VIDA" OF ORAZIO TORSELLINO, S.J. (1596)

the Maduran army with a glance, or calmly ministered at the altar shaken by earthquake. Like any mediæval saint, he had conquered the dread of pain by constant fasting, and scourging himself, and rejecting the pleasant things of life.

For all his crystal sincerity, he was touched by the emotional mysticism common among those who practise austerities of the same kind. He had his hours of rapt vision, when, like Moses upon Sinai, he seemed to hear the very voice of God. It is impossible to read many of his letters without being convinced that here was a man to whom the unseen world was as vivid and actual as the seen.

The rumour of his miracles was probably current in his lifetime. When the Processes for his canonization were formed, all the evidence bearing upon this topic was collected from the surviving eye-witnesses, and sifted by the Auditors of the Rota, who drew up a list of authentic miracles. The gift of tongues is attributed to St Francis in the office of his festival, though his letters prove him no great linguist. The other recorded miracles are sometimes of the most tremendous character, sometimes merely grotesque. The *Relatio super sanctitate et miraculis F. Xaverii*,[1] compiled by the Auditors, credits Xavier with powers of prophecy, with restoring the dead to life and staying epidemics. It also tells, with no sense of bathos, how a crab emerged from the sea to greet him, holding in its claws a golden crucifix which the saint had lost at sea. From another source comes the anecdote of a praying-mantis, which alighted on Xavier's finger. The discerning insect at once began to intone a canticle.

Xavier himself nowhere lays claim to miraculous power, except in a few cases where he succeeded in curing disease ; these are of a kind easily explained as faith-healing. But devout friends may have made him a wonder-worker against his will, and the fame thus acquired probably deepened the awe which his personality inspired.

---

[1] Frequently quoted by Coleridge, who states that he examined the original MS. in the Vatican Library. Similar miracles are described by Lucena and the other Jesuit historians.

The figure of Francis Xavier, as it appears in the Jesuit histories, is larger than human. But the true secret of his mastery over men seems to have lain less in his prestige and ability than in a certain sweetness of temperament, as impossible to recapture and dissect as the vanished scent of a flower, though its shadow may be traced in the letters to Ignatius. It was this charm which made him more than a great Churchman and a saint—which won him the hearts of children, lepers and pirates.

ART AND LITERATURE

CHAPTER XXXIII

THE ART AND LITERATURE OF DISCOVERY

EVEN a casual tourist who enters the Cathedral of St Mark in Venice can hardly fail at once to be reminded of the East and of Africa. St Mark's was a shrine for the precious and fantastic treasures which Venetian traders brought home and consecrated as votive gifts. In the glittering marvels of its interior the whole maritime history of the republic is reflected. In like manner many of the older products of Venetian artificers, their metal-work and pottery and embroideries, are in a sense historical documents, eloquent of past intimacy with Egypt, the Levant and the remoter Orient.

What the shores of the Eastern Mediterranean were, as a source of inspiration, to Venetian art, the shores of the South Atlantic and the Indian Ocean were to Portuguese art in the sixteenth century. When the wonderland of the tropics was suddenly opened to European eyes, men shook off the *tædium vitæ* of the Middle Ages, and awoke to the interest of the world about them. The botanical experiments of Garcia de Orta[1] and the researches of D. João de Castro in the Red Sea were signs that the Portuguese had begun to study nature, and so to lay the foundations of modern science. This, indeed, is one of their chief services to the Europe of the Renaissance. Every forecastle hand who prized and brought home a branch of Indian coral, a handful of quartz from the Gold Coast, or a green parrot from the Amazon, contributed his humble share towards the same movement of ideas.

As a race of seafarers, trained to note every mood of the

[1] See below, chap. xxxvi.

sky and ocean on which their lives depended, and glad to give their attention to any novel accident which might break the long monotony of their voyages, the Portuguese learned to see with a keener, more direct, more intimate vision than landsmen are wont to acquire.

In art the results were twofold—the introduction of new forms and ideas, and their representation in a realistic manner. Both tendencies are patent in the architecture, the goldsmith's work and pottery, the painting and the literature of the time.

The architect and sculptor Andrea Contucci of Monte San Savino, resided in Portugal, as Vasari says, from 1485 to 1494 ; but in spite of this Italian influence, it was long before the new Renaissance architecture displaced the older Gothic. Meanwhile, there arose an intermediate style, transitional between these two orders, which was named Manoeline or Manueline, after the reigning monarch. Its groundwork is flamboyant Gothic, but the round Roman arch appears side by side with the ogival, while Italian decorative forms are freely borrowed. Prince Lichnowsky, who visited Portugal in 1842, was further able to detect the presence not only of Moorish but even of Byzantine and Norman motives.

So hybrid a style may not be one of the most sublime forms of architecture. Its elements are not always harmoniously blended, and thus it may lack unity of purpose and design. Nor has it power to express that sense of awe and brooding mystery which the artists of Northern Europe knew how to build into their shadowy cathedrals. But it has individuality, originality, an exquisite and fantastic character of its own. This distinction it owes in large measure to the richness and audacity of its superficial ornament, the carved stonework in which the wonders of the newly discovered coasts and islands were displayed.

The characteristics of Manoeline may best be studied in the Church of the Order of Christ at Thomar, in the so-called Imperfect Chapels of Batalha Abbey, and, above all, in the Convento dos Jeronymos, a magnificent monastery and church facing the Tagus at Belem.

Batalha Abbey was built to commemorate the victory of Aljubarrota, which liberated Portugal from the dread of Castilian supremacy. King Manoel founded the Jeronymos as a symbol of national thanksgiving for a still greater triumph.

Near the foreshore, on the north bank of the Tagus, stood a little chapel and a hostel for mariners, built by Prince Henry the Navigator. Here Vasco da Gama had spent the night before he embarked for India, and here King Manoel had vowed to dedicate a convent to Our Lady of the Sea, if she would bring the explorers safe home. Within a few months of their return the foundation-stone had been laid, and the slow trains of ox-waggons were discharging their load of white limestone quarried from the Alcantara valley. The whole fabric was constructed of this rare material, which retains its whiteness under the clear skies of Portugal. Though the plans were chiefly furnished by a less famous architect named Boutaca, their execution was finally entrusted to João de Castilho, supreme master of the Manoeline style and creator of the Church of Christ at Thomar. To Castilho alone is due the design of the exquisite cloisters—shaped like a square with blunted corners and encircled by an arcade in two tiers—which constitute the prime glory of the Jeronymos.

In the church, and especially in the cloisters, the bizarre and delicate forms of Manoeline decoration may be studied in their most perfect development. Every accessible surface is so minutely sculptured that at a distance it appears like a web of lace, while near at hand it is seen to have the finish and sharp definition of carved ivory.

The cloisters have been called " a tropical jungle in stone " ; their contrasts of relief and shadow simulate the effect of sunshine among leaves ; their arches recall the boughs of an equatorial forest, as surely as the pillared aisles of a Cistercian abbey bring to mind the dark woodlands in which the monks first fixed their hermitages. Exotic fruits and flowers run wild over the graceful window-shafts ; parrots and lories swing overhead ; here is an elephant, there an Indian cane-brake. Interwoven with these are the cross of the Order of Christ, the armillary sphere chosen by King Manoel as his own device, and the more conventional traceries of Gothic and Renaissance art. The medallions which occur at intervals show the figures of men from the shoulders or waist upwards—lifelike figures which seem, like sailor sentinels, to watch the horizon. Among them is a head of Vasco da Gama; and Prince Henry the Navigator keeps guard over the main entance. The realism shown in these figures is as apparent as the influence of African, American and Asiatic themes. *Estoy esperando que me habla,* " I am waiting for it to speak to me," said Philip II. of Spain, no mean judge of sculpture, when he first saw the statue of St Jerome in one of the chapels. The beasts and birds are modelled with equal truth to nature ; and it is significant, as illustrating the effects of maritime discovery upon architecture, that the other great seafaring race of the Peninsula, the Catalans, reproduced their observation of living forms in almost the same way.

Even the goldsmith's work of the time stood in a certain symbolic relation to the progress of discovery and conquest. Outside Portugal the plate and jewellery of the Manoeline period are little known ; the more familiar chains, hearts, and crosses in gold or silver filigree, which tourists buy, are copies from Moorish designs, though their origin has by some been wrongly traced to India. It is especially in ancient church plate that the influence of the Farther East is to be sought. The treasure of gold brought home by Vasco da Gama from Kilwa was wrought into a service of sacred vessels ; Dr Braga has written of the exquisite *Custodia* which " synthetized the faith of the explorers with their heroism." Among the gifts presented to Leo X. in 1514 was a pontifical in heavy brocade, ornamented with pure gold and with flowers formed of emeralds, rubies, pearls, diamonds and amethysts ; with this went a mitre and pastoral staff, rings, crosses, chalices, and censers, all of beaten gold set with gems, and all emblematic of the Orient, laying its untold riches at the feet of the Vicar of Christ.

CLOISTER OF THE CONVENTO DOS JERONYMOS

The influence of the East on ceramics was more direct ; as in architecture, it resulted in the adoption of new decorative designs, such as the antelope-and-star pattern common in Persian pottery. But the best porcelain and faience produced in Portugal were of later date ; in their case it was only the creative impulse, and not the realization, which synchronized with the reign of Manoel.

The painting of the Manoeline epoch was intensely national, despite its Flemish origin. During the first forty years of the sixteenth century the school of painters commonly associated with the name of Grão Vasco [1] was producing its finest work. Though Flanders itself had surrendered to the spell of the Italian masters, Portuguese artists still consciously adhered to the old manner. The spirit which informed their work was not Italian ; itself an outcome of the curiosity learned by men " for ever roaming with a hungry heart," its result was such realism as the skill of the artists allowed. Its themes are still such as the Flemings might have chosen ; accessories are finished with the loving patience and conscientiousness which early Flemish painting has in common with mediæval illumination. But the figures, flat, stiff and crude though they may be, are not merely conventional types ; they are portraits of Portuguese men and women—women especially, " set," as Dr Braga says, " against a background of Portuguese landscape, in the opaline lights of the Portuguese atmosphere."

Quite apart from any intrinsic interest which the school of Grão Vasco may possess, it has in all likelihood a further title to attention. Just as the nascent scientific ideas tentatively seized by Castro and Orta were left to be fulfilled and transcended by the thinkers of other nations—Bacon, Descartes, Galileo—so the naturalism nascent in Portuguese painting was left to be perfected by Velazquez. May not the realism of Velazquez, so, foreign to his Spanish

[1] Volumes have been written about Grão Vasco, who is usually identified with Vasco Fernandes of Vizeu, a painter who was probably the best representative, though not the creator, of a school. A list of the chief authorities is given in *Ar. Hist. Port.* I. iii. 66 *seq.* (1903).

contemporaries, be more or less a national trait inherited through his father, Rodrigues da Silva of Oporto ? This claim will seem the less unreasonable if it be remembered that Velazquez came nearer to Portugal than to Spain on another side of his character.

The Spanish painters, as a class, never " saw life steadily and saw it whole." They fixed their eyes with a passionate intentness upon a single aspect of life. Their art was the handmaid of the Church ; beauty of colour and form were subordinated to the beauty of holiness. Their pictures were signposts, marking the divergence of the broad and narrow ways. Except in a society of saints an art of this devotional type could hardly refrain from over-emphasizing the contrast between the actual world and the ideal world, by too much insistence upon the evil and horror of life.

Nothing illustrates the spirit in which the Spanish painters worked better than the picture of Death by Juan de Valdes Leal. Death, hugging a coffin under one arm, is about to extinguish a taper which glimmers over a table littered with diadems and precious stones. On the floor lies another coffin, open, and discovering the shadowed outline of a corpse ; and round the candle-flame appears the legend *in ictu oculi*, " in the twinkling of an eye." Murillo, who said that the spectator of this picture should cover his nostrils, represents in his own work, delightful and restful though it is, an opposite weakness which resulted from the same narrowness of vision and intention. With him, sublime and sacred things became pretty, as, so often, the majesty of southern churches is obscured by gilt and tinsel.

Between these two extremes, a painter here and there —Zurbarán or Murillo at their best—might achieve the faultless expression of his subject-matter by some happy chance. There was only one artist who habitually pre-served a perfect balance, never lapsing into understatement or overstatement. The pre-eminence of Velazquez among Spanish painters is not so much due to any technical supe-riority—sleight of brushwork, science in composition or modelling—as to his unfailing sense of proportion. It was a matter of temperament rather than of dexterity. Critics have sought its origin in his Portuguese blood.

The same sense of proportion, the same restraint, characterize the best Portuguese art of the sixteenth century. It was this subduing influence which prevented the richness of Manoeline sculpture from degenerating into a mere orgy of ornament, a precursor of that Churrigueresque architecture which exemplifies the Spanish zest for extravagance at its worst. The writer of the best known, and best, English book on Portugal,[1] has chosen the lines—

> " Climas passé, mudé constellaciones,
> Golfos innavegables navegando . . . "

with their "heroic hyperbole," as typical of the Spanish spirit. Camões and Bernardim Ribeiro would have known better than to provoke their countrymen to laughter by such an outburst. From their poets, far more than from their statesmen, the Portuguese required clear thinking and logic. They also required faultlessly correct expression. To this extent they anticipated the canons of the Augustan Age in England and France ; and that is one reason why *The Lusiads* was so popular in those countries while the ideals of the eighteenth century remained in vogue.

The literature of the sixteenth century, in so far as it was an indigenous growth, and not a mere exotic transplanted from the soil of Italy or Castile, was marked by the same naturalism which has left its imprint on the other arts.

The Eclogues of Bernardim Ribeiro exemplify this naturalism in the sincerity with which they reproduce Portuguese character and peasant life. Englishmen are apt to find fault with the best pastoral poetry of the South as artificial and imitative. The resemblance to Vergilian and Theocritean archetypes may, in the present case, be conceded, but does not involve any departure from truth. For the Portuguese countryman is by nature conservative, and still carves on his ex-yoke the same design with which the silversmiths of the twelfth century

---

[1] *Portugal, Old and New*, by Oswald Crawfurd, London, 1880.

adorned the christening-cup of Affonso Henriques, first ruler of independent Portugal; in the remoter regions still unsubdued by bagman from Ipswich, or drummer from Chicago, his plough is fashioned after the manner of his ancestors, the Roman provincials; his wine is matured according to the rules expounded by Columella in the first century after Christ; the refrain he sings to his sheep, as they tread the threshing-floor firm and level, is probably even older. And he still has a genuine gift for poetry, and for such amœbæan songs as Daphnis and Amyntas sang; he can improvise exquisite trifles in that language which still echoes so closely the speech of imperial Rome. To put lines like

> " Os teus olhos, o menina,
> São gentios da Guiné,
> Da Guiné, por serem pretos,
> Gentios, por não terem fé," [1]

into the mouth of a Wessex yokel would invite derision. But wherever the Latin survives, on the banks of the Rhone, the Tagus, or the Dîmbovitza, he has preserved his ancient grace of thought and expression; and the lines just quoted are unedited rustic verse of Portugal. In the sixteenth century there were, no doubt, purely artificial pastorals, written, like those of Sá de Miranda, under the influence of classical Italian models; but the best work of Bernardim Ribeiro exhibits all the naturalism and sharp-sightedness of the age of discovery.

Still more clearly is this true of the *autos* (dramatic pieces) of Gil Vicente, who lived from 1470 to 1540, and delighted the courts of Manoel and John III. with his talents as playwright and actor. Vicente is one of the great figures of the age. It is strange that he, who took so prominent a part in the development of European drama, should have been so neglected by its chroniclers; perhaps the omission is due to the fact that his topical allusiveness

---

[1] " Maiden, your eyes are heathen of Guinea; of Guinea, for their blackness—heathen, because they keep no faith." The original is quoted by Oswald Craufurd in *The Nineteenth Century and After*, vol. lxiii. p. 73.

and the form of his *redondilha* verse make him unusually difficult to translate. Forty-four of his *autos* have survived, eleven written in Castilian, fourteen in Portuguese, the rest in both languages. Despite this concession to the mode of the day, the *autos* are in a real sense national, although some of the earlier ones betray the influence of the Spaniard Juan de Encina, while others were evidently inspired by Dante. Even the sacred pieces, such as the " Auto of the Wise Kings," which were written to be performed on Church festivals—Christmas, Twelfth-Night, Corpus Christi—and were akin to the moralities and mysteries of the Middle Ages—even these are full of unforeseen flashes of satire or humour, which bring them into touch with the daily life of the nation. Life is, indeed, the keynote of Vicente's work, whether sacred drama, comedy, or farce. For sheer vivid vitality, as for irony, for mordant wit, for Rabelaisian laughter, no European playwright of the time produced anything to compare with his sketches of the amorous, needy squire and his ragged retinue, of the lax clergy and their mistresses, the magistrates who knew no law, the charlatan doctors, the pilots who flung away ships and human lives on the voyage to India, the poor Jewish tailor,[1] the gipsies. Bishop Bale's *Kynge Johan*, half morality, half historical drama, was the most famous contemporary play of English authorship ; set beside the meanest of the *autos* it seems insufferably tame and wooden.[2]

It is only in a secondary sense that the art of Ribeiro and Vicente illustrates the change of mental outlook wrought in their countrymen by a hundred years of discovery and conquest. With Luiz de Camões it is otherwise. His *Lusiads* fills in Portuguese literature the same place that belongs to the Convento dos Jeronymos in Portuguese architecture. It is a direct outcome and expression of the spirit of maritime adventure.[2]

[1] Twice, in 1506 and 1531, Gil Vicente denounced the persecution of the Jews with the most outspoken courage.

[2] Even the " interludes " of John Heywood, though they approach more nearly to the spirit of Vicente's work, are far inferior in dramatic power.

CHAPTER XXXIV

CAMÕES AT COIMBRA

THE ancestral home of the house of Camões stood not far from the Galician promontory of Finisterre, in a land of sea-mist and rain, and salt, north-westerly gales. It was a fit cradle for the race that was destined to produce the greatest poet of the sea since Homer.

Poetry, patriotism and maritime adventure were in the blood of Luiz. The founder of his family, Vasco Pires de Camões, was a warrior fidalgo and a troubadour, who emigrated in 1370 from his native Galicia to Portugal. His lyrics, national in spirit and form, helped the singers of his own and his adopted country to repulse the influence of the Breton *lais* and the Dantesque allegories in rhyme which were then in vogue. João Gonçalves Zarco, the Portuguese discoverer of Madeira, was also an ancestor of Luiz de Camões, though not in the direct line ; while the poet's grandfather, Antão Vaz de Camões, served under Albuquerque in the Arabian Sea. He wedded D. Guiomar da Gama, a kinswoman to Vasco da Gama, and through this marriage the discoverer of the sea-route to India and the author of *The Lusiads* were related.

Two sons, Simão Vaz and Bento, were born to D. Antão and D. Guiomar. Bento, a younger son with no fortune, sought a career in the Augustinian priory of Santa Cruz in Coimbra, a rich foundation at which many cadets of the *fidalguia* were professed, and many of their elder brothers grounded in *letras e virtudes*. Simão served his King at sea, and at the sales of merchandise from Guinea and India. He married Anna de Sá e Macedo, a lady of Santarem ; and his only child, Luiz Vaz de Camões, was born in Lisbon, in 1524.

Three years afterwards, when the plague broke out in

the capital, John III. and his court fled north to Coimbra, accompanied by Simão Vaz, with his wife and infant son.

Legend, song and history had already invested the " Portuguese Athens " with an atmosphere of romance. Here Affonso Henriques held his court and defied the Moors ; here, in the Quinta das Lagrimas and beside the Fonte dos Amores, Ignez de Castro, the beautiful mistress of the Crown Prince Pedro, had been done to death by order of King Affonso IV. The city stands on a chalk ridge, whose southern base is washed by the lucid waters of the Mondego, " River of the Muses." Its houses and convents are faced with the white or pale-tinted plaster which accords so well with the delicate half-tones of a Portuguese landscape ; its gardens bear comparison with those of Cintra, in which sub-tropical fruits and flowers—orange and loquat, aloe, tree-fern and bougainvillea—thrive at all seasons in the open, side by side with the pines and birches of Northern Europe. As a cathedral city and a focus of monastic learning, Coimbra had a further charm of its own, an air of serene and studious dignity. Picturesque and stately figures climbed its steep and stony by-ways—white-robed Augustinians of Santa Cruz shepherding their pupils in black gowns, canons secular and other magnates of the cathedral chapter, lordly bedels, grasping their maces and wearing the insignia of their office with conscious pride.

In after life Camões loved to dwell upon the remembrance of his childhood, passed in this *florida terra*, as he calls it, to which the advent of the court imparted a touch of pageantry. From his father he no doubt acquired much lore of the sea, of ships and of strange isles beyond the sunset. After his seventh birthday, at latest, he would be promoted from the ranks of the *abecedarios*, and would join the more advanced seekers after truth, who imbibed morality and a taste for Latin verse from " Gaton," or " Cato "—the *Disticha Catonis* or *Cato pro Pueris*, which successive generations of children had for centuries striven to write out from memory and repeat without a fault.[1]

---

[1] An edition annotated by Erasmus was printed by Wynkyn de Worde in 1513.

It is to be hoped that he had a tutor less vivacious than Belial Beliagoa.

While the youthful Luiz was thus preoccupied with slate and copybooks, his pastors and masters were undergoing the painful process of reformation. In 1527 John III. had thoughtfully decided to relieve the monks of Santa Cruz of worldly cares, by instituting a stricter conventual rule and confiscating no small part of their estates. At the same time the King saw that plague threatened to become endemic in Lisbon, and that a seaport had certain attractions of its own, potent to lure students away from the lectures of even the most erudite professors. He therefore decided to remove the university to Coimbra, to incorporate the schools of Santa Cruz into it, and to set aside for its endowment the manors and villages of which the monks would have no further need.

For a decade (1527-1537), the Manoeline architects were kept busy in preparing for the transference. In 1530 the College of All Saints was founded for " honourable poor students " who might aspire to the mysteries of theology and arts ; St Michael, for theologians and canonists, was begun in the same year ; St John Baptist and St Augustine were added for the accommodation of the Lisbon scholars.

In 1537, at the ripe age of thirteen, Luiz de Camões matriculated at All Saints as an *estudante honrado pobre* ; it is probable that he was aided by the royal bounty, in the shape of a bursary or scholarship. In 1539, his uncle D. Bento was elected Prior-General of all the Augustinian communities in Portugal, and during the same year was nominated Chancellor of the University, an office which he retained until 1542. It is obvious that so distinguished a patron could render many services to his nephew.

Luiz spent two years over the courses of grammar and rhetoric, and three more over arts, logic and natural philosophy. Coimbra had welcomed, as apostles of a new spirit, the forerunners of Gouvêa, Buchanan and Vinet, who had come over from France. The old names, such as grammar and rhetoric, were retained in a system of reformed education, which no longer consisted merely of exercises in memory or verbal ingenuity, but had an organic connexion with life. Even for one who, like Luiz, did not attend the lectures on medicine, law and music, the range of instruction was encyclopædic. Most of the poems written later in his life were composed far from libraries, in an age when books were luxuries; yet he shows an intimate knowledge of classical literature and mythology, of history, geography, astronomy and of the literatures of Portugal, Spain and Italy. His familiarity with at least nineteen Greek and Latin authors has been demonstrated, and some of them must have been read in the original, as they had never been translated. This learning must have been acquired at Coimbra; it is a testimonial not only to his diligence and power of memory, but equally to the thoroughness with which Coimbra had realized the ideals of Humanism.

It would, however, be a mistake to suppose that all his time was devoted to sober study. Coimbra, like other universities, had its dramatic performances, often based on the improving comedies of Terence and Plautus. One such play, the *Auto dos Enfatriões*, written by Luiz himself, has escaped the moths and worms. It treats of the condescension which Jupiter displayed towards the lovely Alcmena, after assuming the outward shape of her lawful husband, Amphitryon. Significantly enough, its form is that of the national *autos* composed by Gil Vicente.

The diversions of the students can be inferred from a series of repressive edicts issued by John III., who forbade undergraduates to draw their swords, even in full daylight, and denounced their propensity for carrying " daggers and poniards " beneath their gowns. Epiphany was celebrated by the election of a King of Fools or " Lord of Misrule," whose subjects were bound to justify the title. Music, such as the composition of *jusquinas* in the style of Josquin des Près, and verse-making after native models, were by no means discountenanced; did not the good monk D. Heliodoro de Paiva give lessons in counterpoint and in the playing of organ, harp, viol and other instruments ? *En musica gasté mi tiempo todo*, " I wasted all my time in music," wrote Jorge de Montemôr,[1] with whom Luiz formed, on the banks of the Mondego, a friendship destined to endure. The two men were of kindred nature. Montemôr, a brother poet, though he wrote in the fashionable Castilian, became one of the court musicians after he went down from Coimbra, and in 1543 followed in the train of Princess Mary, daughter of John III., when she married Prince Philip (afterwards Philip II.) of Spain. Thence, after the death of his patroness, he probably accompanied Philip to the English court, wandering back into the Low Countries, to Portugal again, and last of all to Italy. An ardent traveller, with the same zest for adventure that animated his friend, he burned incense at many wayside altars, loving not wisely but far too often, until, in 1561, death overtook him in a duel fought for the sake of some Piedmontese enchantress.

The Muses were still considered respectable in those liberal days ; but dire penalties awaited the student who dared affix his *vejamen, invectiva,* or other defamatory lampoon, to the door-posts, or, worse still, the inner walls of the schools. The King also frowned upon *musicas nocturnas* ; it might well be thought unseemly that students should go serenading under the balconies of the Rua dos Grillos, which winds uphill between the sacred precincts of Santa Cruz and the Old Cathedral.

Luiz of course took his share in these delights. His final departure from the city, in 1542, was probably hastened by the rudiments of a love-affair. No doubt the youthful troubadour, with his broad brow and chest, his curling hair as yellow as saffron, and his eyes of the blue-grey tint admired in all the classic heroines of all the Spains, from the Lady Dulcinea del Toboso downwards, made an attractive enough figure, even in academic dress. In Coimbra, the students still retain part of their mediæval costume—a black coat buttoned to the throat and a black gown—though they have discarded the bag-like cap in which, if the tradition be sound, they were wont to collect alms for their fees and battels. Such attire would suit

---

[1] Better known by the Spanish form of his surname—Montemayor.

Luiz, as black suits a fair woman. There is no record of the conquests he achieved before taking his degree as Bachelor of Arts, and setting out for the wide world of Lisbon ; but doubtless he left some Maria or Esperança temporarily inconsolable.

CHAPTER XXXV

CAMÕES AT COURT

THE exchange from the academic groves of Coimbra to Lisbon, with its clamant vitality, reacted for a while upon the character of Luiz. His ardent and ambitious temperament found, for the moment, no career worthy of pursuit. Alone in the capital,[1] he fell in with a set of boon-companions whose ringleader was the poet, playwright and wit, Antonio Ribeiro " Chiado," an unfrocked friar. " Chiado," or the " mocking-bird," was so called for his gifts of satire and mimicry. He claimed to be " a Golias of a toper "—*em beber sou um Golias*, the allusion being not to any Philistine feats of his own, but to a certain band of joyous clerks known as the Goliards, who had shocked northern Europe in the thirteenth century, and honoured as their pious founder a legendary Pope Golias. They sang, as an ancient Provençal ballad avers, of *Dieus et amors*, and the medley was profane. In what esteem their minstrelsy was held may be learned from the description of the Miller, in the *Canterbury Tales*—

> " He was a janglere and a goliardeys,
> And that was moost of synne and harlotries."

Luiz, who received from Chiado the title of *Trinca-fortes*, or " the swashbuckler," refused to take his new comrades too seriously, though he joined their revels, frequented their taverns and other pandemian resorts, and boasted that he had seen the soles of many feet while no man had seen his. With a fine inconsistency, he beguiled his leisure by

---

[1] This episode is placed by some authorities later in his life, *i.e.* after his return from Africa in 1549. I have followed the version approved by Dr Braga, which seems more in accordance with the evidence.

addressing a panegyric of country pleasures to a friend who was bored by them. Much better, he affirmed, to doze in the shadow of a tree, with the sonnets of Petrarch, the *Arcadia* of Sannazaro or the Eclogues of Virgil in one's hand ; to listen, in a half-dream, to the lilt of running water or the complaint of some lovelorn shepherd. At the same time he showed no desire to act on these original sentiments.

For a year he gave himself to the ribald joys of town. Then, on an April day in the year 1544, came the sudden emotional crisis that shaped his destiny. Its cause was a fugitive vision of green eyes, under dark eyebrows and a wave of gold hair. Luiz had caught a glimpse of Catherina de Athayde at her devotions in one of the chapels-royal.

Catherina, whose name appears henceforth in a host of lyrics, under the anagram of Nathercia, was a maid of honour to the Queen, though still *muito môça*—little more than a child. She was certainly not much more than thirteen. Dr Braga [1] submits her mind to the test of a profound *criterio psychologico* devised by himself, and after citing the precedents of Beatrice and Juliet, concludes, sagely enough, that she was already conscious of her own charms.

The image of this *rara e angelica figura* filled Luiz with a new anxiety to enter the Court, which a few months previously had seemed an appropriate foil for his eulogy of rural delights. His gift of song and epigram furnished him with a passport ; by birth he was a fidalgo with influential kinsmen ; and the friendships he had made at Coimbra would pave the way to advancement. Before the year ended, he was free to enter the royal palaces, to see Nathercia, and to win her regard.

He came to Court when the issue of the Portuguese *Kulturkampf* was still doubtful and social life was full of contradiction. One coterie was deep in Loyola's *Exercitia Spiritualia* while another was joyfully absorbed in a treatise on the art of gallantry. Queen Catherine owned a good library and patronized the Muses. Princess Mary had surrounded herself with a circle of brilliant women, some of

---

[1] Braga, pp. 346-351.

whom were scholars, wits, or poets. Bullfights at Almada, tournaments at Almeirim, hunting at Cintra helped to kill time pleasantly ; there were pageants and ceremonies borrowed from the Provençal Courts of Love and from the ritual of mediæval chivalry. Lords and ladies would assemble in the evenings to hear a Castilian folk-song from the lutanist Paula Vicente, or to dance a stately measure to some French ballad sung by Angela Sigêa, while the moon shone overhead or the brave flambeaux made points of light on swordhilts and jewelled hair. Sometimes the entertainment would be a game of " questions and answers "—a battleroyal of wits, in which every player strove to give the aptest reply to some such question as " What is Hope ? "—" What is Sorrow ? "—" What is Honour ? " The *Cortegiano* of Baldassare Castiglione and the opening chapters of the *Compleat Angler* are well-known examples of this kind of disputation, of which Luisa Sigêa, Angela's sister, was a famous exponent. Luisa was an accomplished damsel, and could express herself in Latin, Greek, Hebrew, Arabic, Syriac. On one occasion she was moved to write to the Pope in all these languages at once.

Versification was perhaps the most favoured pastime of all. Every lady and lover, in a society where love was the first duty of a soldier and a gentleman, exchanged rhymes, metrical anagrams, innumerable conceits in verse. And here Camões came to the fore. The brilliant and beautiful D. Francisca de Aragão, a star whose adoring satellites were innumerable, deigned once to ask him for a poem, instead of waiting for the customary tribute to be offered ; and thenceforward his reputation was made. He became " the Swan of the Tagus," " the Siren of the Palace " ; and great was the envy felt by the Court poet, Pedro de Andrade de Caminha, and by other aspiring rhymesters.

But in the midst of these gaieties an austerer philosophy of life was gaining ground. Prince Luiz, a poet himself, had set the fashion by choosing a Jesuit for his Father Confessor, and the *Exercitia* were at least as well thumbed as the *Cancioneiro*. Francis Xavier had reason when he likened the Court of John III. to a well-disciplined monastery.

It was high praise from him, but there were others who watched the lengthening shadows with distrust. The King and Queen were degenerates, with the taint of murder and madness in their blood. John, a weak bigot, had already half repented of his Humanism and was soon to demand that the Coimbra scholars should show more zeal for Catholicism and less for Latinity. Catherine had inherited the mental instability of her mother, Juana the Mad, and the fanaticism as well as the culture of her grandmother, Isabella the Catholic. Foreign monks and friars swarmed in the royal palaces. Conspicuous among them were the Jesuits or " Apostles," who were already planning to win control of all education. Castilian was the language of the Court, and many of the religious came also from Castile as agents of Charles V., seeking to subordinate Portugal to Spain, and to make her a pawn in the great game of the Counter-Reformation.

Piety became the mode. Camões wrote to his friend in the country that the high-born dames around him were behaving as though they were all honest widows or wives who had seen their husbands sail away for Cape Verde. " They never miss Wednesday at St Barbara's, Friday at Our Lady of Calvary, Saturday at Our Lady of Grace, Sunday at the Church of the Holy Ghost." If they were praying for a second marriage or the return of a sailor husband, could they do more ?

In his opinion these religious ecstasies were more often inspired by the preacher than by the sermon. He hints, like any Lutheran scandal-monger, that the confessional [1] was a screen for quite uncanonical avowals, and that some of the reverend clerks would have been thoroughly at home with Chiado and his merry men. The official *Instructions concerning the Affairs of Portugal* given to the Papal Nuncio, Aloysio Lippomano, confirm the charge which Camões only suggests, adding that the excessive trust which the King placed in friars and Jesuits had estranged the goodwill

---

[1] The *Instrucções* quoted in the next sentence bring this charge quite definitely against the King's Confessor, Brother João Soares, " a friar of little learning "—*faz negocios de toda a casta, sob pretexto da confissão.*

of his people, and that Portugal no longer counted among the great powers. As for the Queen, the Nuncio is advised in dealing with her " ever to make mention of conscience, of the other world and of the danger of heresy ; of the censures of the Church—in fine, of everything which instils terror into devout ladies."

Rulers who had learned to cringe before a monk were no fit inheritors of the dominions which had been won by men like Gama and Albuquerque. Already the control of education was passing into the hands of the Jesuits, whose new system of teaching was cosmopolitan instead of national, and substituted the fear of heresy for the love of honour.[1] The world had changed indeed since that night when the laureate Garcia de Resende had charmed King John II. with the lyrics of Jorge de Manrique ; and the King had vowed that it was as clear a duty to remember such poems as to have the *Pater Noster* itself by heart.

In time the power wielded by the Inquisition and the Jesuits rotted the moral fibre of Portuguese society, which, as Dr Braga says, it not only denationalized but actually dehumanized. But this calamity was still in the future. In the Court of John III. there were as yet many who strove to make life gracious and humane, and among them Camões spent two years in the sunshine of Nathercia's presence.

Meanwhile he made enemies. There were some who looked askance at the former associate of the Chiado ; others, rival poets, who envied the vogue of this upstart. He may also have been too little Platonic in his wooing. The parents and guardians of a high-born damsel would require a better match than this youth who had only genius to recommend him, nor would their anxiety be lessened by a recent drama in which a too enterprising gallant and a too kind maid of honour had played the leading parts, to the scandal of the Court. Thus arose the *damnadas vontades*, the " cursed spite " to which Camões attributed his exile in 1546. His own judgment had also to be blamed, for in the previous year he had composed the *Auto del Rei Seleuco*,

---

[1] It is only fair to add that it also substituted order and discipline for the chaos revealed in Buchanan's trial.

which was founded on the story of King Antiochus of Syria, one of the Seleucids. Antiochus had taken the unusual course of marrying his own stepmother, Stratonice ; and the Lisbon busybodies were not long in detecting an allusion to King John III., whose union with Eleanor of Austria, his own still youthful stepmother, was said to have been prevented only by the interference of the Emperor Charles V., in 1523.

There was a custom that no young fidalgo should be received at Court until he had proved his manhood in the desultory fighting which was always in progress between the Moors and the Portuguese garrisons in Morocco. This rule was enforced against Camões, who had no alternative but to acquiesce ; and in 1547 he set sail for Africa.

For a century, from the capture of Ceuta in 1415 to the capture of Azamor in 1515, the history of Portuguese arms in Morocco had been an almost unvarying record of victories. Latterly some ground had been lost and a new enemy had entered the lists. Ever since the taking of Cyprus in 1538, by Khair ed-Din Barbarossa, the Ottoman empire had been the strongest maritime power in the Mediterranean, and Turkish corsairs threatened every Christian stronghold along the North African seaboard. It is probable that Camões went to the wars in the spirit of a crusader, eager to strike a blow at those historic enemies of his creed and country, the Muhammadans. The memory of Nathercia went with him, and inspired him with a longing to achieve renown. That desire took definite shape in Africa.

" Um novo pensamento Amor me cria,"

he wrote to a comrade ; and that new thought, which love had first awakened in him in 1544, was the germ of his *Lusiads*.

Two years, the compulsory period of service for all who would hold any office of profit under the Crown, passed in the routine of garrison duty, varied perhaps by an occasional lion-hunt and by skirmishes with the Moors. In one such affray he lost his right eye. He returned to Lisbon in 1549, disillusioned of his crusading hopes ; for John III. had wisely refused to squander his resources in an enterprise from which nothing more marketable than glory was to be gained, and had withdrawn the Portuguese garrisons from every fortress in Morocco except Ceuta, Tangier and Tetuan.

On his return, Camões was not readmitted to the palace, and although he probably contrived to see Nathercia and found her loyal, other ladies were less kind. They mocked at his honourable disfigurement, dubbing him "Eyeless Head" (*Cara sem olhos*) and "Devil without lights" (*Diabo sem luzes*) ; but the satire was too dull to wound, and Camões retorted with good humour : "You, lady, are the lovely Galatea," he sang, "and I the wretched Polyphemus."

In 1550 he enlisted for India, but did not embark. There were many things to detain him—Nathercia, and the hope of a revived interest in his poetry. But hostile influences remained in the ascendant ; it was the year of Buchanan's trial. If friends at Court interceded for the poet, their efforts ended in failure ; and soon he was in desperate straits, almost penniless and with no prospect of a career. Worst of all was his own indiscretion ; for on the 16th of June 1552 he was so unwise as to intervene in a street affray and so unfortunate as to wound an official in the royal household, Gonçalo Borges by name. The occasion heightened his offence ; it was the festival of Corpus Christi, when multitudes of pious holiday-makers flocked to Lisbon for a sight of the great religious pageant in which the King himself took part, walking in solemn procession with his nobles and officers, the clergy and the merchant gilds. Camões was lodged in goal for eight months, and only released after he had apologized to Borges and volunteered once more for service in India. He received the King's pardon on the 7th of March, bade a last farewell to Catherina de Athayde, and took up his quarters on the *São Bento*, the flagship of a squadron of four vessels commanded by Fernão Alvares Cabral. On Palm Sunday, the 24th of March 1553, he sailed for the East.

LUIZ DE CAMÕES
FROM A BUST IN THE MUSEU NACIONAL DAS BELLAS ARTES, LISBON

CHAPTER XXXVI

CAMÕES IN THE EAST

A S the *São Bento* crossed the bar of the Tagus and
stood south-westward in fair weather, a group of
disconsolate watchers lingered on her deck until
nightfall, straining their eyes for a farewell glimpse of the
Cintra hills. Among them stood Camões, who, as he
scanned the receding shore, murmured to himself the words
of Scipio Africanus, " *Ingrata patria, non possidebis ossa
mea.*"

Many incidents and emotions of the next few months—
the first sight of the Southern Cross, the apparition of St
Elmo's fire hovering among the yards—are recalled in that
wonderful Fifth Canto of *The Lusiads*, which chronicles
the outward voyage of Vasco da Gama in verse full of the
sense of lonely spaces between sky and ocean, and of the
sound of moving waters. The poet syncretized his own
experience with the adventures of his hero. Throughout
the voyage his mind was busy acquiring a store of new
impressions, material for his epic. The drifting islands
of sea-fog passed by the *São Bento* may have suggested to
him the character of Adamastor, the bearded and gigantic
wraith who personifies the wild sea south of the Cape.
Here, like Vasco da Gama before him, Camões encountered
heavy weather ; and the *São Bento* parted from her consorts,
arriving alone at Goa in September.

He was not left long in the state of unemployment which
turned so many of his former messmates into footpads,
or drove them to enlist in the armies of native states. Towards the end of November 1553, a punitive armada was
sent to the Malabar Coast, to break up a league of petty
principalities which had interfered with the pepper trade.

Camões took part in the expedition, which achieved its object and returned to headquarters in February 1554. Being bound to complete five years of service before he could return to Portugal, he enlisted in the Armada of the North, a squadron which cruised in Arabian waters, hunting for pirates and prizes. Between two voyages—to the Persian Gulf in 1554 and to the Red Sea in 1555—he wintered in India. Always adept in the art of making enemies, he seems to have added to the number by too breezy a condemnation of the diversions for which Goa had already become infamous. "You may say of the country," he declared, in a letter written in January 1555, "that she is a mother to the vilest rogues, and a stepmother to men of honour."

From September 1555 to April 1556 Camões was again in Goa. A new Governor, Francisco Barreto by name, had been installed during his absence, but the festivities customary on such an occasion had been postponed in consequence of a terrible fire, which had broken out during the celebration of St John's Eve, and had destroyed much of the shipping in the harbour. The Governor had worked gallantly to extinguish the flames, even stripping himself of his jewels to reward brave rescuers. So, after a decent interval of four months, his friends determined to celebrate his accession, his courage, and the baptism of a Sinhalese potentate for whom he acted as godfather, in one splendid pageant. When Camões landed, triumphal arches were being erected, tournaments and processions organized. The one thing lacking was a suitable play. Fortunately Camões had brought to India the manuscript of his own *Filodemo*, which had already been acted at the court of John III.; and so the gap was bridged. But whatever popularity Camões may thus have earned was speedily obscured. One item in the programme was a *jogo de cannas*, a kind of mimic tournament in which fidalgos of the bluest blood displayed their mettle, using bamboo canes for lances. It would seem that some of the noble sportsmen had drunk their Governor's health too fervently ; and Camões was moved to write his *Satira do Torneio*, a mild burlesque of the performance, which " delighted all who failed to recognize their own portraits." This was followed by another satire, the *Disparates da India* ; and the poet found himself heartily detested.

About this time, he passed under the yoke of a new enchantress, the captive Barbora. She was certainly one of the Indian slave-girls described by Pyrard and Linschoten,[1] dusky or tawny beauties who had been trained in every branch of their vocation. They could compound the most delicate of sweetmeats ; they had been schooled in each sinuous attitude and significant gesture of their native dances ; and they could play on barbaric instruments, while they crooned the melodies of their own folk to charm uncomprehending lovers from over the sea. Camões sang of Barbora and her exotic spell in some of his most impassioned lyrics ; for he, in his turn, had been enslaved by her strangeness and submissiveness—as of some graceful, dark-eyed creature from the jungle, " still," says Dr Braga, who, as an anthropologist, speaks authoritatively in such matters, " reminiscent of her life among wild things, though tamed and glad to surrender at the first caress."

It is permissible to ask if Nathercia had been forgotten ; but Camões would have held himself guiltless of inconstancy, and in the sixteenth century all masters of the *ars amandi* would have concurred. Nathercia, his *princesse lointaine*, had already grown more and less than human ; she had been transmuted into such an ideal as Beatrice became in the eyes of Dante. There was room in the lives of both poets for a woman to be kissed, as well as a goddess to be worshipped. Nor does the parallel end thus ; Nathercia inspired *The Lusiads*, as Beatrice the *Divine Comedy*.

The pleasant idyll ended in April 1556, when Camões sailed away in the Armada of the South, leaving Barbora to find the usual consolations. He had still three years of service to fulfil, and the Armada of the South promised him a sight of Malacca, the Spice Islands and even the mysterious land of the " Chins." There is a legend that he was driven to enlist by the malevolence of the Governor,

---

[1] Linschoten, vol. i. p. 186 ; Pyrard, vol. ii. p. 135.

but two intimate friends of the poet have given Francisco Barreto a certificate of good character. " Never was man so loved and desired by the populace," D. Alvaro da Silveira writes in a letter to King John III., while Couto calls the Governor " liberal, a loyal comrade, and ever quick to forgive an offence." It seems certain that, instead of persecuting Camões, Barreto granted him the coveted privilege of dealing in China merchandise, the most lucrative commerce of the time. Before he sailed, the poet sowed the seeds of future trouble by borrowing money from a rich gentleman adventurer, Miguel Rodrigues Coutinho, more commonly known by his nickname of *Fios Seccos*, " the Skinflint." [1]

The Armada of the South touched at Malacca, and continued its eastward voyage through the *infinitas ilhas* of the Malay Archipelago. Camões visited Tidore, Banda and Amboyna—islands of troubled history, where Galvão had conquered like a hero of romance and ruled like a saint, where Xavier had wrought miracles and Menezes had left a name at which all men shuddered. Camões saw the crater of Ternate hurling forth sheets of flame, and learned the legend of the golden birds, which were fabled to live out their halcyon lives in mid-air, unseen until they died and fell to earth. After helping to repress a mutiny, which had broken out among the Ternate garrison, he returned to Malacca in 1557, with a little hoard of savings, and a rich store of memories. His unresting spirit led him east and north again in the following year, and, after an engagement with a flotilla of Chinese pirates, he landed at Macao, which had been newly ceded to his countrymen as a tradingstation. Here the grotto in which he is said to have laboured at his beloved epic may still be viewed. His five years of service had expired, and he could live in comfort by selling or exercising his commercial privilege. Tradition has invested him with a curious office, that of " trustee for the defunct and absent," but it is doubtful if he ever assumed any such charge. Certainly he made no long stay in the island, for he was arrested and ordered to return forthwith

[1] Literally " Dry Threads."

to Malacca. The nature of his alleged offence has never been ascertained, nor did the poet ever undergo a trial. The vessel in which he sailed was struck by a typhoon off the Cambodian littoral, and foundered in the estuary of the river Mekong ; but Camões swam ashore, contriving to keep his treasured manuscript above water. This befell him in 1559 ; it was not until the autumn or winter of 1560 that he again set foot in Malacca. He had probably worked his passage thither in some cargo-boat, either as a soldier or before the mast.

Gaspar Corrêa had married and settled down in Malacca, where Camões may have examined his *Lendas da India* for light upon the deeds of Vasco da Gama. The poet had arrived at Malacca penniless, having lost all but life and *The Lusiads* under the waves of the Mekong ; but in an evil hour he succeeded in borrowing money from one Pedro Barreto Rolim.

With this provision for the needs of the moment, he took ship for Goa, arriving early in June 1561. He was at once flung into prison, probably on the same charge which had caused his arrest in Macao. His friend Francisco Barreto was no longer in power, and even a laudatory poem failed to move his successor, D. Constantino de Bragança, who believed in letting the law take its course. Camões was now almost at the nadir of his fortunes. Many travellers have seen the dark and noisome lock-up in Cintra, and have pitied the crowd of dirty and half-starved prisoners who stretch imploring hands between the bars, or fish for alms with a basket tied to a piece of string. Such on a larger plan was the common gaol in Goa, where felons, slaves and innocent men awaiting trial were herded together, between plaster walls which mouldered and grew verminous as the rainy season' advanced.[1]

No poet had ever more thoroughly " learned in suffering what he taught in song." Cloister and tavern, court and camp, were familiar to him when first he left the Tagus, southward and eastward bound. Since that afternoon he

[1] Compare Claude Dellon's description of the archiepiscopal dungeon in Goa, *Relation de l'inquisition de Goa*, Paris, 1688, p. 47.

had seen and endured as much as any hero of saga or romance. He had wandered over half the seas of the world, undergoing exile, imprisonment, wounds, hunger, shipwreck ; and through it all he had remained a singer like the Angel Israfel, whose heartstrings were a lute. The thought of Nathercia and *The Lusiads* had been his unfailing moral refuge through years of adversity.

Now, in his prison, he was told that Nathercia was dead. The tidings wrung from him the famous sonnet, beginning—

"Alma minha gentil, que te partiste,"

which, for sincerity and sheer lyrical beauty, has rarely been equalled.

Catherina de Athayde had died unmarried in 1556, the year of Camões' departure in the Armada of the South. The cause of her death is unknown, though Dr Braga [1] confidently attributes it to grief at the loss of her lover, basing his judgment on such scraps of her handwriting as are extant. These have, it is true, an agitated appearance, but no reader whose imagination is clogged by a sense of humour will accept the learned critic's inference from such slender evidence.

A new Viceroy, D. Francisco Coutinho, Count of Redondo, disembarked at Goa in September, and at once liberated Camões, whom he had known as a favourite of the Lisbon Court. Unfortunately the Viceroy's namesake,[2] " Fios Seccos," reappeared about the same time, and demanded repayment of the capital which he had lent Camões in 1556. Once more the poet found himself under arrest and without the means to purchase liberty. He accordingly addressed the Viceroy in a rhyming petition, which begins with the inquiry, " What devil is so doubly damned but feels the edge of Fios Seccos' sword ? "—and closes with an execrable pun. Some of his friends in Goa either backed the appeal or paid the debt, with the result that " Fios Seccos "

[1] Braga, p. 645.

[2] Camões' creditors, Miguel Rodrigues Coutinho and Pedro Barreto Rolim, must be distinguished from the Viceroy of India, D. Francisco Coutinho and the Governor, Francisco Barreto.

released his prey. Camões proved his gratitude by inviting his friends to the famous *Convite das Trovas*, a banquet at which every invited guest found, on lifting his cover, a neat epigram in verse served as the first course. This feast of reason took place early in December 1562. The death of Nathercia had, in all likelihood, robbed Camões of his eagerness to return home, the Viceroy gave him employment, and the companionship of a brilliant circle of friends helped to make life in Goa less arid than of old.

Of his associates at this period, the most remarkable was Garcia de Orta, a botanist and physician, who holds a permanent place in the annals of medical science. Born in 1490, about the same time as Paracelsus and Copernicus, he belonged to a generation which had begun to breathe the air of intellectual freedom. After studying his profession at the Spanish Universities of Alcalá de Henares and Salamanca, he was licensed to practise in Portugal, and lectured at Lisbon University from 1532 to 1534. At this period the medical world was rent by a great controversy. The groundwork of fifteenth-century practice had been laid in the mediæval Arabian schools, where Avicenna and Abu Bakr had interpreted and enlarged the teaching of Aristotle and his forerunners. But with the Revival of Learning and the discovery of many unknown treatises on medical science, notably those of Celsus, there arose a demand for the uncorrupted lore of the ancients. The works of Hippocrates and Galen were re-edited, explained, translated into Latin ; a stream of original texts issued from the Aldine Press ; Servetus and the Hellenists delivered a furious onslaught on the Arabists, who retaliated with delightful venom. Only Paracelsus stood scornfully aloof, absorbed in his own dogmatic theories, and vowing that his shoe-buckles—the shoe-buckles of Philippus Aureolus Paracelsus Theophrastus Bombastus von Hohenheim—contained more medical knowledge than all the treatises of Galen and Avicenna put together.

Garcia de Orta distrusted the new school ; it seemed to him to have gone back to the rudiments from which Arabian science had started. But he was more than a mere partisan ;

and in 1534 he sailed to India to make an exhaustive practical test of his beliefs, in lands " where," as Diogo de Couto said, " there was no Inquisition " to ferret out the skeleton from every doctor's cupboard.

Orta roamed from city to city, noting the properties of plants, experimenting with new drugs and systems of treatment. He established a botanical garden where Bombay now stands. In an age in which every idea tainted with novelty was subjected to a rigorous quarantine, his scientific habit of thought was so rare that even Luther could claim to have demolished the revolutionary doctrine that the earth moves round the sun, by simply quoting one text of Holy Writ : " The sun stood still in the valley of Ajalon." The Scriptures would evidently have declared that the earth stood still, if this new-fangled theory of the planets were correct.

Orta forsook authority for nature, and his patients recovered with a speed hardly respectful to the wisdom of the past. Convalescent Rajas and Amirs rewarded him with huge fees, and at last, after nearly thirty years, he returned to Goa with a fortune and a manuscript which embodied the results of his research. His " Colloquies of the Drugs and Simples of India " introduced *Nux vomica* to the pharmacopœia, and contained the first exact account of the symptoms of Asiatic cholera ; completed about 1561, they exemplify that method of observation and experiment which Francis Bacon, born in the same year, was the first to formulate. The book is written as a dialogue, so as to represent the views of both Arabists and Hellenists. Its range is far wider than the title suggests, for although he was a specialist, Garcia de Orta was also a true son of the Renaissance, with all its catholicity of interest ; and his *Colloquies* are rich in notices of Indian creeds, manners, races and history.

Through his own intimacy with the Viceroy, Camões was able to serve the rich and famous doctor, who had come to Goa to secure the publication of the *Colloquies*, with three years' copyright and a licence from the Holy Office. The grant of copyright was obtained on the 5th of November

1562, and the book emerged unscathed from the censor's office on the 10th of April 1563. Dr Braga declares [1] that the *Colloquies* and *The Lusiads* must be classed together as the two supreme expressions of the Portuguese genius, in science and in literature respectively. The friendship between the two authors is commemorated in an ode of classical frigidity, which avers that Orta, inspired by the " Gangetic Muses," had outstripped Chiron himself in the art of healing.

In 1564 Camões made the acquaintance of Diogo de Couto, that brilliant young writer who afterwards became celebrated as the author of the later *Decadas da Asia*, and of the *Soldado Practico*.[2] Friendship soon sprang up between the pair ; Couto read *The Lusiads* and undertook to write a commentary on it, even completing this task as far as the Fifth Canto, though every fragment of his work subsequently perished.

In March of the same year, D. Antão de Noronha, who had been Camões' companion in arms at Ceuta and aboard the Armada of the North, came to Goa as Viceroy. He demanded a set of verses, received an ode, and paid for it cheaply by offering his old friend the post of factor at Chaul, so soon as it should fall vacant. This honour Camões might have accepted for his heirs. To himself it was useless, for there was already an interminable list of candidates for the vacancy ; each of these had a prior claim to the spoils of office, and each in turn must enjoy them for three long years before the poet could fatten on what was left.

So, after fourteen years in the East, Camões at last turned homeward in 1567. He could see no promise of a career in India ; many of his friends were dead or back in Lisbon ; and he too may well have desired to revisit his native country once more and there to publish his epic.

But on the homeward voyage he was detained at Mozambique ; for since 1560 he had owed a sum of 200 *cruzados* (£53, 6s. 8d.) to Pedro Barreto Rolim, who was now Governor of Mozambique. More than a year later D. Antão de Noronha found Camões still there, so poor that he was

[1] Braga, p. 676.　　　　　　　　　　[2] See Appendix A, 1.

dependent on the charity of his friends, even for food. The poet was then working hard at *The Lusiads* and at his *Parnaso,* a collection of lyrical pieces.[1] He was taken aboard the flagship and made a member of the Governor's mess. This was in November 1569, and in the following April Camões landed at the little seaport of Cascaes, just outside the Tagus estuary on the north, and proceeded to Lisbon.

[1] Any detailed criticism of his sonnets and lyrics would be out of place here ; it is enough to say that even if he had never written *The Lusiads,* Camões would still justly be considered the greatest of Portuguese poets.

CHAPTER XXXVII

CAMÕES : LAST YEARS

H E found Lisbon in mourning, for the bubonic plague had revisited Portugal in 1569.

The conditions of life in any crowded city were such, at this period, as to invite disease. Leprosy, small-pox, and ophthalmia raged at all seasons in the noisome alleys where the poor herded together and the rudiments of hygiene were unknown.[1] Little children played naked beside the open gutters into which household refuse was flung from the windows, to breed flies in the sunshine or to be devoured by dogs, rats, and carrion-crows. When the plague appeared, the wisest physicians were impotent ; rich and poor became equal. Men and women ran shrieking to the churches, or loitered aimlessly about the streets— waiting and furtively watching one another ; each fearing at any moment to read his own death-sentence in his neigh-bour's eyes. Sudden panics arose from time to time ; it was whispered that wells had been poisoned by the converted Jews ; a mad friar announced that the end of the world was at hand, and thousands believed him.

The mortality increased as the spring days grew longer and the heat more sultry. A contemporary witness esti-mated it at 500 deaths daily throughout July, August and September.[2] The churchyards were soon overcrowded,

[1] The learned were not much wiser. In the *Oriente Conquistado* of Francisco de Sousa (vol. i. p. 22 ; vol. ii. pp. 53 *seq.*), a temporary improve-ment in the health of Goa after 1510 is attributed to the introduction of Christianity. The author explains the subsequent outbreak of plague as due to the cooling of religious ardour, though he admits that the danger of infection may have been increased by the corpse of an elephant, which was left to putrefy in a pool near one of the churches.

[2] In a MS. of 1569, published by Dr R. Guimarães in *Summario da varia historia*, vol. xi. p. 160, and quoted by Braga, pp. 702-706.

and it became necessary to consecrate olive-groves and vineyards, to which the dead were carted away by convicts from the galleys. Some were buried where they had fallen, in streets or cellars ; and although the clergy displayed a noble self-sacrifice in ministering to sufferers, little could be done to stay the plague, which only began to abate with the advent of winter.

It was followed by a famine, caused by the neglect of all industries and aggravated by debasement of the coinage. If the current rumour was true, quantities of inferior copper coins had been struck in England and smuggled into Portugal in bales of wool and sacks of meal, to be exchanged for silver and gold pieces.[1] To remedy this evil, King Sebastian had been advised to lower the standard value of all Portuguese issues in copper, and thus a pennyworth of bread cost nearly twopence, while trade was stagnant and wages were low.

In this tragic environment, where disaster and fanaticism had clouded the mind of a whole nation, Camões prepared to publish his epic of the Golden Age of Portugal.

On the 24th of September 1571 he received the royal licence to publish *The Lusiads*, with copyright for ten years in Portugal and India. Fortunately for him, he was now on friendly terms with the Dominicans in Lisbon, whom he probably consulted before parting with his manuscript. The censor's verdict ran as follows :—

" I have seen, by order of the Holy and General Inquisition, these ten Cantos of the *Lusiadas* of Luiz de Camões, concerning the valiant feats of arms done by the Portuguese in Asia and Europe ; and I have found in them nothing scandalous, nor contrary to Faith and good manners ; only it seemed to me necessary to warn readers that the author, to magnify the difficulty of the navigation of the Portuguese in India, makes use of a fiction of the Gods of the Heathen. And inasmuch as St Augustine admits, among his *Confessions*, that in the books which he composed *De Ordine*, he invoked the Muses, being Goddesses, therefore, as this is Poesy and invention, and the author as a Poet claims only to adorn his poetic style, we hold this fable of the Gods in his work not to be unseemly, it being recognized as fabulous,

---

[1] Braga, p. 706.

and saving the truth of our holy faith, that all the Gods of the Heathen are devils.[1] Wherefore it seems to me that the book is worthy to be printed, and the author shows in it much talent, and much erudition in the humane sciences." [2]

Despite these monkish pedantries Camões was fortunate in his censor, Bartholomeu Ferreira. In that era of fanaticism no liberal mind was safe. In 1564 all the works of Clément Marot, and some of those of Boccaccio, Dante, Pulci and Sannazaro were placed on the Index ; in 1571 Damião de Goes, the greatest of Portuguese Humanists, was imprisoned by the Inquisition, on a charge of heresy brought secretly by the Jesuit Simão Rodrigues, twenty-six years before. But Ferreira was a man of culture and a bibliophile, though he wore the habit of St Dominic ; in that same year of 1571 he passed Bishop Osorio's outspoken chronicle *De Rebus Emanuelis* for the press.

The Lusiads was printed in 1572.

Camões was rewarded by King Sebastian with an annuity of fifteen milreis (£10), to be paid for three years. It was not a princely sum : [3] far less, indeed, than the pension bestowed for life on the messenger who brought to Lisbon the glad tidings of St Bartholomew's Night. But it placed Camões beyond the reach of immediate want, and the grant was renewed for a second term of three years in August 1575 and again in June 1578. Camões probably lodged with his mother, occasionally seeing the friends he had known at court or in India. For one period of some eighteen months his annuity was left unpaid, and the numerous anecdotes of his poverty may be referred to this time.[4] A fidalgo named Ruy Dias da Camara asked him for a translation of the penitential Psalms, and received the answer :—

---

[1] Some English readers may also hesitate at this " fiction of the Gods of the Heathen," forgetting that Camões wrote for an age in which educated people quite commonly thought in Latin. Venus and Jupiter were still on speaking terms with mortals, and Bacchus could appear on board a ship dedicated to the Archangel Gabriel without provoking a single impertinent inquiry.

[2] The document is undated, but may reasonably be assigned to the winter of 1571-1572.

[3] See Appendix B.

[4] January 1575 to the 22nd of June 1576.

" Sir, when I wrote my poems I was young ; I had the love of ladies and all that is necessary for life. And now I have neither spirit nor quietness of mind for anything, because I have lost all that I had ; and am in such misery that here is my Javanese come to ask of me a penny for fuel, and I have none to give him."

According to another tradition, Camões—

" lived in such poverty that he could not have kept alive, had he not possessed a Javanese, called Antonio, whom he had brought from India, and who went by night to beg alms for his aid and sustenance ; as is clearly seen from the fact that when the Javanese died his master did not survive him for many months."

Couto mentions no such attendant in his narrative of the voyage from India to Lisbon, and Java was not a happy hunting-ground for slave-raiders. Its people were, as Linschoten says, very stiff-necked, *hart neckish en opstinaet* ; Couto calls them " so determined that they run amok (*se fazem amoucos*) at the slightest offence " ; and Galvão declares that " their favourite pastime is bloodshed." It is, however, quite possible that a stray Javanese may have been brought to Lisbon, and there purchased by Camões ; a servant liable to run amok might well be cheap enough even for a poet's purse.

The peril of starvation had passed, but Camões still suffered from the fever which had assailed him in India, and from a profound depression. Lisbon society reflected the sombre and fantastic mind of King Sebastian ; the light-hearted cavaliers ever ready for a song or an adventure, whom the poet had known in his youth, were being replaced by a generation of fanatics, and Portugal was sinking back into the Middle Ages.

The leaders of the nation, whose first duty in such a season of pestilence and famine was " to bury the dead and feed the living," were knightly mystics plunged in dreams of ascetic chivalry. The outcome of their visions was the last and most futile of the Crusades, which ended in the defeat and death of King Sebastian at El-Kasr el-Kebir, in 1578. This was followed by the accession of the Cardinal King Henry, a dyspeptic bigot who subsisted on human milk, and schemed for a union with Spain in the interests of the Church. In 1579 the plague broke out afresh, and on the last day of January 1580 the King died. There was no legitimate heir, and although a provisional Government was established, its members were pledged to support Philip II. of Spain, who moved towards the frontier at the head of his army. Those Portuguese of rank and influence who might still care to strike a blow for national independence were ordered to assume command of various provincial fortresses, where their eccentricity of patriotism could do no harm.

Camões, to whom the heroic past was more real and vivid than the present, saw his own countrymen preparing to welcome an alien ruler to the throne of Affonso Henriques. In his eyes it was a supreme act of betrayal and apostasy. Towards the end of March he wrote what may well have been his last letter, to D. Francisco de Almeida, one of the nationalists who had been relegated to provincial commands. A few fragments are extant.

" Who ever heard that Fortune should care to represent so great a tragedy on so mean a bed ? And I, as if such did not suffice, range myself on her side, since to try to withstand her would seem, as it were, effrontery. And so I shall finish my life ; and all will see that I so loved my country that I was content to die not only in, but with her."

A few days after these words were written, Camões was removed to one of the temporary hospitals which received all sufferers from the plague. He lingered for some ten weeks, in complete seclusion from the outer world, and died on the 10th of June 1580.

There is extant a copy of *The Lusiads* once owned by Fray José Indio, a Barefooted Carmelite from Guadalajara, in Castile. On the fly-leaf are written. the following words :—

" How piteous a thing to behold so great a mind so meanly housed. I saw him die in a hospital in Lisbon, without a sheet to cover him, after having triumphed in Oriental India and sailed over 5,500 leagues of sea ; what warning so great to those who by night and by day weary themselves in studying without profit, as the spider spins her webs to catch flies ! "

Camões has been by general consent accorded a place among the four or five great epic poets of the Western world. The verdict of his own contemporaries was passed by a courtier in the train òf Philip II., who declared that *The Lusiads* had but one fault : it was neither short enough to learn by heart nor long enough to have no end.

It is the last great epic of maritime daring. There are lines in it which, as Matthew Arnold said of the *Odyssey*, seem to " sum up the spirit of all adventure." There are passages in which even a landsman can almost hear the wind among the sails, almost feel the exultation of steering through seas never before whitened by the track of a ship.

Apart from its value as literature, few poems can have had so deep and permanent an effect upon the life of a nation. During the sixty years of the " Spanish Captivity," *The Lusiads* was a voice crying in the wilderness, reminding the Portuguese people of its lost greatness and its ancient love of liberty. It was Camões, more than any living statesman or soldier, who led his countrymen in the rising of 1640, when they began the reconquest of their independence. It was the statue of Camões that was draped in black during the crisis of 1891, when Lisbon was threatened with a bombardment by the British fleet. For over three hundred years the influence of *The Lusiads* upon Portuguese character and ideals has been comparable with the influence of the Bible in England.

The subject of the poem is simply the first voyage to India, preceded by a sketch of Portuguese history from the beginning of national life under Affonso Henriques, and accompanied by a forecast of the deeds of Albuquerque, Castro, and other great men of the sixteenth century. Every heroic or dramatic incident in the annals of Portugal is interwoven into the poem, without detriment to its unity of interest. The whole is a portrait gallery of heroes, grouped round a transfigured Vasco da Gama, who stands for that chivalrous valour which was the ideal of every noble-hearted Portuguese.

LUIZ DE CAMÕES

FROM A STATUE BY VICTOR BASTOS, IN THE LARGO DE CAMÕES, LISBON

THE DECLINE OF PORTUGAL, 1548-1580

CHAPTER XXXVIII

THE LAST CRUSADE

THE personality of King Sebastian helped to bring about the last tragedy of Portugal. He was the posthumous son of Prince John, a boy of sixteen, whose eight brothers and sisters had all died in infancy or early youth ; for the rulers of Castile and Portugal had paid for their policy of intermarriage in the epilepsy, madness, or premature decay of their children.

In 1557, on the death of his grandfather John III., Sebastian became King. He was a child of three, flaxen-haired, blue-eyed and large of limb, but disfigured by the drooping Habsburg lip which he had inherited from his grandmother, Queen Catherine. During his minority, the government was nominally vested in Catherine and her brother-in-law the Cardinal Prince Henry, who were themselves dominated by their Jesuit Confessors ; while another Jesuit, Luiz Gonçalves da Camara, undertook the education of Sebastian. The House of Aviz had crushed the feudal nobility and made the monarchy almost absolute : now, however, the monarchy was itself controlled by the Society of Jesus.

In 1568, the Cortes declared Sebastian of age. He was then a grave and introspective boy of fourteen, living less in the present than in a dream-world of his own, where ascetic knights still rode forth to seek the Holy Grail, or died to redeem Jerusalem. He longed for the day when he, too, might win fame or martyrdom in such an enterprise.

Luiz Gonçalves, his tutor, was one of the many nobles who had renounced all worldly aims in order to consecrate their lives to the Society of Jesus. He was ugly and elderly,

boorish in manner, blind in one eye, and further handi-
capped by an impediment in his speech ; but his worst
enemies could find no flaw in the stern austerity of his life
or the subtlety of his dialectic, and he dominated the Court
by sheer force of intellect.

His associate in the task of rendering Sebastian unfit to
rule was D. Aleixo de Menezes, a veteran who had fought
under Albuquerque. Menezes taught his pupil to excel
in all feats of arms, and helped to inspire his passion for
military renown.

Under these influences, Sebastian grew up resolved to
order his conduct after the rule of those military knights
who had been vowed to poverty, chastity and a life of
service against the Moors ; and thus, when Portugal most
needed strength and sanity in her ruler, the supreme
authority passed into the hands of a child and a mystic.
An heir to the throne [1] was urgently required to save the
nation from a Spanish dynasty, and the King was implored
to marry ; but he contrived to elude even the most eligible
brides.

He delegated the business of administration to the Jesuits
and their partisans, who tampered with the coinage and
issued various strange sumptuary edicts. They forbade
any man to eat of more than three dishes at dinner, and
solemnly banned the use of " sweetmeats such as blanc-
mange (*manjar branco*), buns (*bolos de rodilha*), or the
like." As plague and famine had placed these deleterious
dainties beyond reach of all but the nobles, who could
not be compelled to forgo them, the law soon became a
dead letter.

Meanwhile the King retired for weeks together to his
forests, and spent his time in spearing wild boars and shoot-
ing wolves ; sport he regarded as a kind of ascetic discipline
which might serve to keep the body in due subjection.
For the same reason he courted peril and hardship, risking
his neck and the independence of his country by attempting
th most hazardous feats of the bull-ring. On one occasion,

---

[1] Sebastian's great-uncle, the Cardinal Henry, was the only direct heir
in the male line of Aviz.

having ordered the Belem garrison to fire on any vessels which failed to give an account of themselves when challenged, he made sure that his commands were obeyed by rowing past in an open boat, and as he escaped recognition, he was able to enjoy his baptism of fire.   He fasted, scourged himself, and spent whole days in ecstasies of religious meditation.   He visited Coimbra to muse on the sword with which Affonso Henriques had carved out a kingdom ; there also he chose the place for his own sepulchre.   The royal vaults in the convent of Alcobaça were opened so that he might meet his ancestors face to face ; and as he stood in the presence of the dead, Sebastian began a loud oration, praising the martial exploits of Affonso III., and rebuking the withered corpse of Pedro I., who had forgotten the joys of conquest in the arms of Ignez de Castro. At Batalha Abbey a similar scene was enacted : Sebastian bowed low before the body of John II., whom he venerated as the conqueror of Arzila, the monarch who had done his duty best of all.

The King's extravagances did not add to his popularity. Pope Pius V. and D. Jeronymo Osorio, Bishop of Silves, urged him to provide an heir to the throne ; confirmed courtiers openly regretted that the ladies did not please Sebastian so well as Sebastian pleased the ladies.   The city fathers of Lisbon also ventured on a gentle remonstrance, and even hinted that no harm would follow if the Cortes were occasionally summoned ;   " for," said the worthy aldermen, " it is written in the Books of Joshua and Samuel that such assemblies were common when Israel was ruled by the Almighty."

All protests proved ineffectual.   Even when D. João Mascarenhas, the hero of Diu, urged Sebastian to forgo his plans for a crusade, the youthful monarch merely ordered a committee of doctors to investigate the problem, " Do advancing years diminish courage ? " He asked Mascarenhas his age, and received the curt reply, " I have twenty-five years of your service—and eighty for advising you not to invade Africa."

In 1574 Sebastian paid a brief visit to Tangier, where he

was entertained with a little hunting and fighting. On the homeward voyage he was driven by stress of weather to Madeira, and returned to find the capital in mourning for his supposed death. But this escapade only augmented his zeal for an African adventure. In 1576 the opportunity arrived, when Mulai Ahmad, a claimant to the throne of Morocco, promised to become a faithful vassal of the Portuguese Crown if Sebastian would enable him to dispossess the reigning Sultan.

Sebastian dreamed of nothing less than the capture of Fez and the conquest of all Morocco, forgetting that his own kingdom was nearly bankrupt of men and money, and that his armies were in Asia. He buckled on the historic sword of Affonso Henriques and provided himself with a consecrated banner upon which the royal arms were for the first time surmounted by an imperial crown. Thus equipped, he felt secure of victory, and prophesied that the coming campaign would be but " a brief absence." His cavaliers shared his enthusiasm : a valiant carpet-knight registered a vow that he would fry the infidel Sultan's ears and eat them with oil and vinegar ; a courtly priest composed the sermon which was to celebrate Sebastian's triumphal entry into Fez. But Philip II. of Spain took a cynical view of the whole affair : " If Sebastian should win," he remarked, " we shall have a good son-in-law ; if he should lose, a good kingdom."

Funds for the expedition were screwed out of the unfortunate " New Christians," and on the 24th of June 1578, the King set sail from Lisbon with a force of about 18,000 men, fully half of whom were untrained lads or worn-out veterans, while the other half consisted of foreign free-lances. Instead of attempting a sudden raid, Sebastian halted at Lagos and Cadiz, where he wasted precious time in banquets and tournaments ; and on his arrival at Tangier he once more surrendered himself to the delights of hunting. His next step was to transport his troops to Arzila.

Meanwhile the reigning Sultan Mulai Abd el-Malik had been able to muster a force numerically superior to the Portuguese in every arm, even in artillery, and far better able to endure the hardships of a midsummer campaign among the mountains and deserts of Africa. Knowing that Sebastian's immediate objective was the seaport of El-Araish, on the Atlantic littoral, he offered to cede that city to Portugal if the King would withdraw his forces and conclude peace. This offer, which may have been intended merely to gain time, was contemptuously rejected ; nor would Sebastian heed the advice of Mulai Ahmad, who warned him not to risk an engagement far from his base and ships. Instead of proceeding by sea, Sebastian determined to march across the arid hill-country which rises between Arzila and El-Araish. After a five days' march rendered intolerable by heat, thirst and swarms of Muhammadan skirmishers, he encamped in a valley near the hamlet of El-Kasr el-Kebir, and ordered his parched and weary troops to spend the night in prayer and fasting. His position was strategically absurd. Behind his camp flowed the El-Kus, a river eighty yards wide ; both flanks could easily be turned, and the level ground favoured the Moorish cavalry.[1]

At dawn, on the 4th of August 1578, the battle began. Neither side knew that the Sultan had died at the same moment ; for Mulai Abd el-Malik, who had long suffered from a mortal disease, had given orders that the news of his death should be concealed from his followers. The Portuguese charged impetuously, vainly hoping to cut through the Moorish squadrons which had advanced in crescent formation and threatened to surround the camp. They and their allies fought with desperate courage, but were unable either to break through the enveloping force or to stem the onrush of the Muslim cavalry. Mulai Ahmad was drowned in the Wady M^chassan, an affluent of the El-Kus ; Sebastian, who had long before chosen for his motto the Petrarchan sentiment—

" Un bel morir tutta la vita onora,"

probably fell fighting, though the accounts of his death

[1] On the topography of the battle, see notes in Burton's *Camoens*, vol. i. p. 358.

vary in almost every detail; and of the entire Christian army not more than fifty survivors won back to the ships.

Eighteen months afterwards, both King Manoel's dream of Iberian union and King Philip's prophecy that he would gain " a good kingdom " had come true. But meanwhile a curious legend had arisen. Men refused to believe that Sebastian was really dead, and declared that he would come again to deliver Portugal, as he had returned in 1574. Like King Arthur in Avalon, the *Rei Encuberto*, or " Hidden King," was only biding his time somewhere across the sea ; it might be for generations or even for centuries, but he would surely return.[1]

From time to time pretenders appeared—among them a Calabrian peasant who knew no word of Portuguese—each claiming to be the rightful heir to the throne of Aviz.[2] These unfortunates were duly captured and executed ; but " Sebastianism " became a religion, and its votaries were prominent not only when the " Spanish Captivity " was ended by the rising of 1640, but long afterwards, whenever the independence of Portugal was endangered.[3]

The rapid spread of such Messianic ideas after 1578 illustrates clearly the psychological change which had been effected by years of calamity, culminating in the rout of El-Kasr. As a nation, the Portuguese had lost the splendid self-reliance which had distinguished them in the days of discovery and conquest ; and those who still dared to hope at all could see no salvation for their country except through a miracle.

[1] The death of Sebastian is well attested by contemporary documents. See, for example, J. Teixeira's *De Bello Africano*, Nuremberg, 1580, cap. xiii. p. 110—" *Cadaver regis Lusitani . . . inventum est per duos ipsius servos, captivos, quos novus rex* [Ahmad ibn Muhammad, who had sucded Mulai Abd el-Malik] *ea de causa miserat circa diluculum illud*," etc. The body was buried at El-Kasr, reinterred at Ceuta, and in 1582 removed by Philip II. to the Convento dos Jeronymos.

[2] For the details, which are very curious, see M. Miguel d'Antas, *Les faux Don Sébastien*, Paris, 1866.

[3] Burton claims to have spoken with *Sebastianistas* in Brazil ! *Camoens*, vol. i. p. 363.

KING SEBASTIAN

FROM A SIXTEENTH CENTURY PAINTING IN THE CASA PIA, BELEM

CHAPTER XXXIX

THE DECADENCE AND ITS CAUSES

IT is customary to write of the downfall of the Portuguese empire as though it were almost a single catastrophe, sudden, dramatic and complete. The idea thus conveyed is a misleading one. At the close of the Napoleonic wars, Portugal still ranked third, after Great Britain and Spain, among the colonial powers of Europe. What she lost in the first quarter of the seventeenth century was not her empire, but her maritime and commercial ascendancy. The loss was inevitable after the disaster of El-Kasr, the " Spanish Captivity," and the growth of English and Dutch sea-power. It is, however, worth while to trace some of the main causes which rendered it impossible for the Portuguese to make a prolonged stand against their rivals.

Stress is always laid on the moral decadence of the nation ; and there can be no escape from the conclusion that the society which Couto, Osorio, Corrêa, Xavier, Camões, Linschoten and other contemporary witnesses have criticized from so many points of view was one in which the seeds of decay had readily germinated. But the admitted defects in the character of the nation were not the sole cause, perhaps not even the main cause, of its overthrow. The numerical strength of the Portuguese was inadequate ; the movement of European commerce was against them ; their administrative and fiscal systems were hopelessly bad ; their policy towards the natives was worse. Each of these four points deserves some consideration.

(1) *Shortage of men.*—Portugal had never made good the losses incurred in a thousand battles with the Moors. Slaves were imported from the West Coast to till the wasted fields of Estremadura and Alemtejo, and to breed a degenerate

race of half-castes in the heart of the empire, while freemen of the old stock were daily growing fewer. All the white inhabitants which the kingdom then possessed could easily be housed in South London ; and it was hard for so small a nation to garrison a line of colonies extending from Brazil to Amboyna, and to guard every trade-route in the South Atlantic and Indian Ocean. War and the accidents of the sea thinned the ranks fast ; wounded men were treated by an untrained barber, with a razor for surgical outfit and a smear of pitch for antiseptic dressing. When the fleet lay becalmed and the deck-seams bubbled under an equatorial sun, scurvy waited on the hands who gathered in the shadow of the idle sails to eat their dinner of salted stockfish and weevil-riddled biscuit. In the hot, breathless nights, the glimmer of an oil lamp showed crew and soldiers cooped together in a stifling and filthy forecastle, which probably leaked where the dry timber had warped and cracked. Wine turned sour ; fish rotted as soon as it was caught ; the *escrivão* waged a never-ending conflict with cockcroaches, rats and other vermin. In low latitudes cholera, malaria and dysentery killed more than the arrows and bullets of the enemy, despite the bleeding and dosing with decoctions of herbs which made up the art of tropical medicine.

Even before 1525 it was impossible to furnish a full complement for the fleets without raising it from a lower class than the peasants. Recruiting-agents visited the gaols ; sentences of death were commuted to perpetual banishment ; convicts were allowed to work out their term in the Indian forces ; amnesties were granted to all criminals who would enlist, except those guilty of high treason and canonical offences. The most singular case was that of Manoel de Mendonça, who was allowed to share his term of nine years' transportation with his two brothers, each serving three years in India.

Under this system, convicts and half-grown lads were called on to do the work of honest men and veterans, throughout the oversea empire of Portugal ; while at home the sources of free labour were drained dry, slaves became a necessity instead of a luxury, and intermarriage with Africans of a low type permanently injured the national character and physique.

(2) *Commercial.*—Because she was isolated from the rest of Europe, and compelled to seek her fortune across the Atlantic, Portugal had been the pioneer of commerce in Africa and India ; for the same reasons she was impotent to keep that commerce within her grasp.   Lisbon was the natural home-port of all the treasure ships which returned from the Indies.   Some years after the Dutch had broken the monopoly of their rivals, Cervantes could still truthfully describe Lisbon as " the greatest city in Europe . . . where the riches of the Orient are discharged for distribution to all the world." [1]   But it was only in a limited sense that the Tagus estuary could claim to be a great centre of distribution.   To sell the bulk of their cargoes, shipmasters were forced, after unloading such portion as the local merchants could handle, to steer for some more central market.

The profits of the voyage returned to Portugal in bullion, a result approved by the economists of the time, who confused wealth with heaps of gold and silver, and sought commercial prosperity, not in the exchange of commodities, but solely in the exchange of goods for money.   Among the effects of this bullionist policy may be noted, first, a vast influx of capital, which was engrossed in a few hands and squandered on war, luxury, the Church, instead of being employed in remunerative enterprise ; and, second, the growth of arts, manufactures and shipping in those countries which purchased the tissues, foodstuffs, dyes, metals, and other raw materials brought by the Portuguese from the East and America.

But no amount of foresight or economic science could have altered the situation of Portugal.   The more convenient markets of central Europe were difficult of access, if not inaccessible, without the aid of middlemen.

The main volume of the Indian trade was thus diverted elsewhere, and especially to the great world-mart of Antwerp,

---

[1] *Persiles y Sigismunda*, Bk. iii. chap. i.

which not only possessed a fine harbour, close to the markets of central Europe by way of the Scheldt and Rhine, but was now the headquarters of European finance. No seaport was so well equipped for the distribution of imports ; none had gained more advantage from the immigration of the exiled Portuguese Jews. For the yearly fairs of St Badon and Pentecost, merchants of all nations came to Antwerp, certain to find the wares or the customers they needed. Among them came the Portuguese, bringing all the rare and costly products of the Orient. Guicciardini [1] gives a long catalogue of these commodities : he mentions " perfect oriental pearls " and gems, gold ore and refined gold, ivory, amber, spices, drugs, musk, civet, aloes, incense, rhubarb, China-root and indigo—all these from both Asia and Africa ; raw sugar from São Thomé, Guinea and Morocco ; wine from Madeira ; leather, gums, skins and feathers from North-West Africa ; salt, wine, oil, sumach and fruits from Portugal itself.

John Wheeler, secretary to the Society of Merchant Adventurers, comments shrewdly on the disadvantages of the Antwerp trade to Portugal :—

" First for the *Portingall*, we knowe, that like a good simple mã, he sailed euerie year full hungerlie (God wotte) about three partes of the Earthe almoste for spyces, and when he had brought them home, the great ryche purses of the *Antwerpians*, subiecks of the King of Spain, engrossed them all into their owne handes, yea oftentimes gave money for them beforehandes, making thereof a plain Monopolie ; whereby they onely gaigned, and other Nations lost." [2]

When the intermediaries whom the Portuguese were forced to employ were traders so apt as those of the Netherlands or England, it was unlikely that they would long remain mere agents. In due time they would fit out their own vessels, import and sell on their own behalf. By undertaking the whole venture of Indian traffic they could reduce expenses and double profits.

[1] Ludovico Guicciardini, *Descrittione* . . . *di tutti Paesi Bassi*, etc., Antwerp, 1567, p. 124.

[2] J. Wheeler, *A Treatise of Commerce, Wherein are Shewed the Commodies arising by a wel ordered and ruled Trade*, etc., Middelburg, 1601, p. 47.

Their appearance in the Indian Ocean was long deferred, not through dread of the Portuguese navies, but by distress at home.   The spread of Calvinism drew down the wrath of Spain upon the Low Countries, which were visited with fire and sword by the Duke of Alva and his veteran persecutors.   Antwerp itself was stormed in 1576 and delivered for three days to the " Spanish Fury " ; and it was long before the Netherlands could so far retrieve their position as to be ready for new ventures overseas.   But in 1595 the first Dutch fleet rounded the Cape ; in 1602 the Dutch East India Company was incorporated ; in 1625 a Dutch settlement was made on the shores of Table Bay, and Portugal had lost its monopoly of the Far Eastern carrying trade.

(3) *Administrative and Fiscal.*—Two vital defects were the power wielded by ecclesiastics and the system by which officials were chosen and paid.   The first, which did not become acute while King Manoel was alive, has already been illustrated, but one more example may be quoted. In 1560 the famous *dalada* or tooth of Buddha was captured in Ceylon, and brought to Goa by the Viceroy, D. Constantino de Bragança.   The Raja of Pegu, who had every year sent envoys to pay homage at its shrine, now offered to buy it for 300,000 or 400,000 *cruzados* (£80,000 to £105,000), and promised to keep the Malacca garrison permanently supplied with provisions if his offer were accepted.   India was bankrupt, as usual, and the fidalgos were eager to complete the bargain.   But the ecclesiastics forbade.   In the presence of an immense crowd, and with the Viceroy's approval, the Archbishop of Goa solemnly pounded the tooth to fragments in a mortar, burned the fragments in a brazier, and flung the residue of ashes into the river Mandavi. D. Constantino then ordered a commemorative escutcheon to be designed, on which the whole inspiring scene was figured—flaming brazier and Buddhists offering untold sums for the sacred tooth.   The motto selected for this work of art was the cryptic legend C.C.C.C.C.; but for the benefit of the uninitiated a key was furnished, consisting of the words, *Constantinus cupidine cœli crumenas cremavit—*

19

" Constantine, eager for heaven, burned the treasure." The whole affair was a piece of extravagance so monstrous that it was condemned even in Lisbon. It was also a failure from the missionary point of view, for the ingenious Sinhalese at once proclaimed that the *dalada* destroyed in Goa was a mere copy, and fabricated a new tooth which they passed off as the genuine one. This is still preserved in Kandy, where it has been venerated by generations of Buddhist pilgrims.[1]

The other vital defect showed itself even in Albuquerque's time. When a Viceroy or Governor died, the patents or sealed documents containing the name of his successor were opened, and another nominee of the Crown assumed office. There was little to secure continuity even of misgovernment. The incoming despot usually began by making as clean a sweep as possible of his predecessor's friends and administrative system. This would have been an excellent base for reform, but as a rule the vacancies were filled with placemen as hungry as any they dispossessed, while the system underwent no very startling improvement. Tenure of office usually lasted for three years, and the grantees were expected to make the most of their opportunity. It might be long delayed. Couto mentions the case of a man who received the reversion of an appointment to which thirty other claimants enjoyed a prior right. Such reversions could be sold, given, or gambled away ; in some cases they formed the dowries of unmarried women. Military posts and licences to make trading-voyages were treated with an equal regard to the public interest. Such property had a market value, and anyone might buy or sell it ; a hospital might be endowed with the privilege of slave-raiding in Monomotapa, or a community of monks might purchase the command of a fortress. When D. Garcia de Noronha became Viceroy in 1538, he declared that he intended to gather the fruits of fifty years' service. He began to recoup himself by selling every vacant office, civil and military, to the highest bidder, and though he

---

[1] A detailed account of the episode of the *dalada*, with a translation of the chief authorities, will be found in *Ceylon*, vol. ii. pp. 197-219.

paid no salaries except to himself, he found no difficulty in disposing of his wares.

The reason of this is to be sought in the system by which men were remunerated. The titular nobility and fidalgos received *soldo*, or payment based on their rank. *Mantimento* was an allowance given for expenses such as board and lodging. *Ordenado* was the salary attached to an office. *Percalços* were the perquisites which enabled a smart man of business to make a fortune in his three years' term. Even judges were expected to live on their *percalços*, in the shape of bribes. Early in the seventeenth century the Captain of Malacca received a salary amounting to rather less than £300 yearly ; his annual profits were officially valued at £20,000.

While the Governors and their friends grew rich, the common soldiers starved. Before the middle of the century it had become a regular custom to defer payment until the troops landed in India. Even then the arrears were often withheld for months. Meanwhile the men were left to fend for themselves ; some became professional thieves and hooligans, some subsisted on charity, some entered the service of native states, or joined the nearest gang of pirates. A large number lived on the rich fidalgos who kept open house for all comers ; these men were bound to serve their patron as the members of a clan serve their hereditary chief. In 1539 D. João de Castro wrote to the King that out of 16,000 men who figured in the pay-lists only 2000, apart from the garrisons of the fortresses, were to be found. The remainder were convenient fictions, designed to provide sundry officials with an enlarged income.

The systematic debasement of the coinage, which also began before the middle of the century, was felt by all classes. A few sentences may be quoted to illustrate some of the more flagrant abuses which were rife.

" There were three classes of coinage in circulation : (1) Good— which was current at its face value ; (2) Poor—current at the rate of the good metal the coin contained ; (3) Bad—which was not current at all. No prudent person received money until it had been tested by a shroff or money-changer. Every petty governor all over India coined at least his own copper, and travellers found that small change received in the morning was useless at the evening's halt." [1]

(4) *Native Policy*.—The attitude of the Government to the natives provoked disaster and ultimately furnished the Dutch with many willing helpers. In Ceylon, for example, the way for an alliance between the Dutch and the Kandyans was smoothed by the deeds of Jeronymo Azevedo in 1594. It was this humorous general who, punning on the Portuguese word for cocks, *gallos*, and its resemblance to the name of his native victims, the Gallas, " caused his soldiers to take up children on the points of their spears, and bade them hark how the young cocks crow." [2]

Peace was essential if Portuguese commerce were to be fostered and the scanty resources of the kingdom conserved ; instead, the Government was always embroiled with some Hindu or Muslim power, and could only pay the expenses of one campaign by the plunder got in another.[3] The ever-growing demands of the missionaries turned friends into enemies ; thus the Raja of Vijayanagar, whose empire was a breakwater, shielding the Portuguese colonies from the Muslims of the North, could hardly feel enthusiasm for the men who persecuted, robbed and burned his fellow-believers. But the Portuguese went beyond this. If there was a chance of making any profit by raiding the territories of an ally, they took it.

The Conjeveram temples in Vijayanagar were rumoured to contain a fabulous treasure, and no Indian city, not even Benares itself, was more sacred. A fair held yearly in August, at the full moon, drew pilgrims in tens of thousands to its shrines ; every worshipper, according to Corrêa, had his head shaved, and so vast was the number that the

---

[1] Whiteway, pp. 67-68.   [2] "Ceylon," vol. ii. p. 23.
[3] The history of Malacca affords a good instance of the continuous character of these small but costly wars. Crawfurd (vol. ii. pp. 404-405) estimates that during the 130 years of Portuguese rule Malacca was besieged six times by the Malays of Bintang, seven times by the Achinese, thrice by the Javanese and twice by the Dutch.

barbers were positively hidden by the masses of cut hair, while the heap of cash paid by the devout was as high as ten piled-up measures of wheat. Martim Affonso de Sousa, Governor of India from 1542 to 1545, thought that it would be a pious deed to spoil the heathen of these ill-gotten gains ; but when the Portuguese ships entered the Gulf of Manaar on their way up the Coromandel Coast, they were met by such a display of force that they dared go no further. Instead, they made for a temple near Khulam (Quilon) which promised to yield a store of gold. Its guardians could offer no effectual resistance ; Martim Affonso and his suite entered, barred the gates, and spent the night in torturing the priests and digging for treasure. One gold vessel was their ostensible reward ; but a couple of empty powder casks had been taken inside the temple, and sixteen slaves in relays were required to carry them away. This evoked some comment.

The sack of temples in an allied state and by the representative of the Portuguese Crown was not, of course, an everyday affair. It was, however, typical of the spirit in which many Portuguese viewed their engagements to native princes. Antonio Corrêa, who arranged a treaty of commerce and friendship with the Raja of Pegu, kissed an old song-book as he swore to keep faith. It was a handsome volume, the best in his library ; moreover, the contracting parties did not intend to observe the treaty should it prove irksome. Officials of higher rank were not so scrupulous as the good Antonio. They would not have troubled to pick out a song-book when they wished to forswear themselves. Gaspar Corrêa relates how the wealthy and powerful Sultan Bahadur of Gujarat, whose existence was inconvenient to the Portuguese, once came to visit their fort at Diu, very drunk, and accompanied by a mere handful of guards. The weakness of the captain, in suffering him to depart unmolested, was deplored by the garrison, and Corrêa's own regret found vent in a phrase which is, to say the least, memorable—" For our sins we were not allowed to seize such a chance."

Had Portuguese rule been from the first an unbroken and

constant tyranny, it might have been less hated. Eastern races have often welcomed a stern and strong despotism such as Albuquerque established. Almost all the later Viceroys were liable to be swayed by fear, favour, bribery, or mere caprice. When Lopo Soares, Albuquerque's successor, visited a small town in which twenty-four Portuguese sailors had recently been killed in a riot, the head-men sent him three broken-down old men as the culprits. It was a fairly deliberate challenge, but the Governor kindly returned the old men and took no punitive measures. A massacre would hardly have injured Portuguese prestige to the same extent.

The results of all this folly and crime were none the less disastrous for being often difficult to trace in their underground action; for the resentment of the natives never flamed forth into such a conflagration as the Mutiny; it was a slow fire, which ate away the fabric of Portuguese supremacy, and left a mere shell untenable against the Dutch and English.

CHAPTER XL

THE age was one of violent ethical contrasts. The same men who despoiled the Hindus in Goa established the Brotherhood of Mercy. The Dominicans, for ever associated with the Inquisition at its worst, strove hard to lighten the sufferings of the Goanese slaves. In Brazil, the Jesuits successfully withstood the advocates of religious persecution. Francis Xavier, the friend of children and of all the oppressed, favoured conversion by force. Many an inquisitor must have entered the torture-chamber as calmly as a surgeon goes to the operating-table, and with as high a sense of duty towards the patient.

But these antinomies were not peculiar to Portugal. They occurred in every European state, almost in every individual mind, where the ideas of the Renaissance and the ideas of the Middle Ages strove together for mastery. Even so strong a champion of the new spirit as Francis Bacon affirmed that torture resembled experiment as a means of eliciting truth. There is no figure more characteristic of Renaissance feeling, none who more aptly illustrates the contrasts in its morality than Benvenuto Cellini, who devoted such leisure as he could spare from sacred art to debauchery and murder, yet believed that he went guarded by the special favour of God, and that his own saintly person was at certain times encircled by an aureole of celestial brightness.

These instances, which could easily be multiplied, throw light on one of the most curious psychological phenomena of the time. They show that certain humanitarian sympathies which are now common to every civilized man and woman were, as a rule, either absent from the best minds of the sixteenth century, or merely latent in them ; and where such as Xavier and Bacon went astray, simple traders and soldiers might well err.

In this way it is fair to explain the atrocities for which Portugal and the rest of Europe were culpable, without wishing to minimize or justify them. It may well be that, four centuries hence, some Tibetan or Hottentot student will try to solve certain kindred problems of our own society and politics on similar lines. He will have to explain the contrast between our half-grown humanitarianism and such institutions as the white slave traffic and sweating, or quite recent events in Macedonia and the Congo. The ethical difference between these graces of civilization and sundry incidents in the history of the Portuguese conquests is merely one of degree.

There is an old story that a certain lady, after watching a performance of *Antony and Cleopatra* with rapt interest, was heard to murmur regretfully, " How different from the home life of our beloved Queen Victoria." Historical criticism on those lines is not unknown ; but it is perhaps fairer to judge men according to their lights, and not by the standards of a later and possibly a more humane epoch.

There is, however, no need to apologize overmuch. When all criticisms have been weighed and all defects discounted, Portugal has a past which any nation might envy. The annalists of the sixteenth century realized the magnitude of their theme. There are moments when even Barros, for all his stilted rhetoric, and Faria y Sousa, for all his bombast and sententiousness, catch fire and write with the march and rhythm of an epic. The story which begins at the siege of Ceuta and ends in the disaster of El-Kasr is, indeed, an epic of war and seafaring, of great men and great adventures. Courage and a serene magnanimity are the fundamental virtues it extols. It tells us little of the rank and file, less of the women whose destiny was to reward victory or console in defeat. Its interest is focussed upon the leaders—courtier, crusader, militant priest and rough sea-captain. Its hero, under many names, is the fidalgo, the complete gentleman, dauntless, accomplished and gay, by birth the equal of princes, by conviction the most dutiful servant of Church and Crown. Such a one could steer by the stars, use a sword with deadly science, govern a province, converse in half a dozen languages, compose a sonnet and play a sound game of chess. It has been said that the Renaissance came late into Portugal and went early ; but the finest bloom of the Renaissance spirit, its ideal of many-sided activity, remained and grew. Rarely has there been a society so versatile and brilliant as that of the fidalgos. Life has often run in a broader and deeper channel, not often with a more sparkling current. Men " warmed both hands at the fire of life " ; they knew how to fight and love, laugh and die. By husbanding their energies, and steadily devoting them to the pursuit of one end, they might, perhaps, have achieved a larger and more durable result. Critics have suggested a similar charge against the Elizabethans. In each case the reply is of the same character. Even if a career is to be judged like a mine or factory, merely by output, it is enough to point to Bacon and Raleigh, Albuquerque and Camões. When the modern cult of specialism can produce men more " efficient," its advocates will be justified of their censure.

Even then there will always be a few too wary or too young to have been caught in the machine of civilization and clipped to any standard type. For these there is good company in the pages of the old Portuguese histories, where one may navigate the uncharted seas with Vasco da Gama, improvise an empire with Albuquerque, or, with Camões, turn the din of battle and shipwreck into song.

APPENDIX A

AUTHORITIES

A comprehensive bibliography of Portuguese history between 1460 and 1580 would fill many volumes. I have confined the following list to works accessible in the chief public libraries— *e.g.* at the British Museum and the Bodleian—and of real value to any reader who may wish to make a study of the period.

1. General Bibliography

a. *Periodicals and Collections of Documents*

Archivo Historico Portuguez.—Lisbon, monthly from 1903. How cited Deals with art and literature as well as history and geography, *Ar. Hist. Port.* and is now the principal medium for the reproduction of newly discovered MSS.

Boletim da Sociedade de Geographia de Lisboa.—A monthly *Boletim* gazette (from 1877), containing many reprints of documents and articles by the foremost Portuguese geographers and historians. Some of the most important numbers have been reissued in pamphlet form.

Archivo Portuguez Oriental.—State papers from the Goa *Ar. Port. Or.* archives, dating from 1515. In six parts, arranged as follows :—

No. 1 (1 vol.), Letters from the King to the city of Goa, 2nd ed., 1877.

No. 2 (1 vol.), Privileges of the city and petitions to the Crown, 1857.

No. 3 (2 vols.), Letters, etc., from the King to Viceroys and Governors, 1861.

No. 4 (1 vol.), Ecclesiastical Councils of Goa and Synod of Diamper, 1862.

No. 5 (3 vols.), Miscellaneous papers, 1863.

No. 6 (1 vol.), Seventeenth-century documents.

Subsidios para a historia da India Portugueza, ed. R. J. de *Subsidios* Lima Felner, and forming vol. v. of the *Collecção dos Monumentos ineditos para a historia das Conquistas dos Portuguezes em Africa, etc.*, Lisbon, Academia Real das Sciencias, 1868, contains (1) *Livro dos pesos, medidas e moedas*, by Antonio Nunes, written in

How CITED 1554 (see Appendix B) ; (2) Four letters and the *Tombo* of Simão Botelho (see below, *s.v.* Botelho) ; (3) An anonymous register of state property dated 1525, and entitled *Lembrança das cousas da India.*

Alguns docu- *Alguns documentos do archivo nacional da Torre do Tombo*
mentos *ácerca das navegações e conquistas Portuguezas*, ed. José Ramos Coelho, Lisbon, 1892. The documents date from 1416 to 1554 and are of the highest importance.

Memorias do Ultramar. Viagens, explorações e conquistas dos Portuguezes. A collection of documents, ed. Luciano Cordeiro, Lisbon, 1881.

Annaes maritimos e coloniaes, 6 vols., Lisbon 1840-46. Some important documents are reproduced, but the editing and arrangment are unsatisfactory.

Ramusio Giovanni Battista Ramusio, *Viaggi e Navigationi*, 3 vols., Venice, 1663. In this edition only the alternate pages are numbered. The collection, made in the last quarter of the sixteenth entury, contains numerous documents of which no other copies exist.

b. Early Chronicles, Books of Travel, etc.

The four principal chronicles are those of Barros (to 1526), Castanheda (to 1538), Corrêa (1512-1550), and Couto (1526-1580).

Barros (i-iii.) João de Barros and Diogo de (or do) Couto, *Décadas*, 24 vols.,
& Couto (iv. Lisbon, 1778-88. Sub-title, *Dos feitos que os Portuguezes fizeram*
et seq.) *na conquista, e descubrimento das terras, e mares do Oriente.* Barros, as factor of the " House of India, Mina and Ceuta " in Lisbon, had access to many state papers, and his writings are of exceptional value. But he never visited India and his knowledge of Eastern affairs was slender. As a historiographer-royal, he was liable to strict censorship, and his choice or presentment of facts was designed to place his own countrymen in the most favourable light. Only three Decades, ending with the death of D. Henrique de Menezes (Feb. 2nd, 1526), were written by him, and published during his lifetime, from 1552 to 1563. The fourth Decade is inferior : it is said to have been compiled from notes by Barros, and was published in 1615.

Couto also was an official historian, but from 1556 until his death in 1616 he lived almost entirely in India or Malacca ; and where it has not been edited, his work is trustworthy. He began where Barros ended. The fourth, fifth, sixth, and seventh Decades were published during his life, but the original copy of the sixth was destroyed before publication, in order to conciliate

certain persons who disliked its too truthful record of their own
exploits, and a bowdlerized version was produced by Adeodato
da Trinidade, Couto's brother-in-law and literary executor.
The eighth and ninth Decades were stolen in MS., but the author
compiled an abstract of the contents, half of which was printed
in 1673, half in 1736. The tenth Decade, though the first composed, was never published in full before 1788. The eleventh
is missing, and only five books of the twelfth, first published in
1645, are extant.

Gaspar Corrêa, *Lendas da India*, ed. R. J. de Lima Felner,
and forming the first four vols. of the *Coll. dos Mon. ined.*, Lisbon,
Ac. Real, 1858-64. Corrêa or Correia was an eyewitness of much
that he describes ; his book, which deals with the period 1497-
1550, is graphic and animated. He first visited India in 1512
and was still writing in 1566. The date of his death is uncertain.
As no part of the *Lendas* appeared while he lived, he could write
without fear. He served as secretary to Albuquerque, and his
last three vols., which begin with Albuquerque's term of office,
may be trusted. Vol. i. is largely imaginative. See· below,
Special Bibliographies, *s.v.* Vasco da Gama.

Fernão Lopes de Castanheda, *Historia do Descobrimento e*
Conquista da India, Lisbon, 1833. Castanheda visited India in
1528 and remained there ten years. He collected his facts with
diligence and good judgment. According to Couto (*Dec. iv.*,
Bk. v., ch. i.) the last two books of the ten originally included
in the *Historia* were suppressed by order of John III. The
first six books were published 1552-54 ; the last two in 1561.

Duarte Pacheco Pereira, *Esmeraldo de situ Orbis*, ed. with notes,
illustrations and many important documents, by R. E. de Azevedo
Bastos, Lisbon, 1892. Pacheco, famous for his defence of Cochin
in 1504, was born in Lisbon in 1450, went to India under Cabral
in 1500 and served under Albuquerque in 1503. For some account
of his career, see ch. xi. King Manoel commissioned him to
write a survey of the coasts of Africa, at which he worked between
1505 and 1520. The original MS. being lost, the printed edition
of 1892 is made from a late sixteenth century copy. The
Esmeraldo, though unfinished, is among the most important
authorities for the history of Portuguese exploration.

A. Galvano, *Discoveries of the World*. Portuguese text and
translation, London, Hakluyt Society, 1862. The translation
is inaccurate ; originally made for Richard Hakluyt, it was reprinted without correction, but has much literary charm.

How CITED   Galvão, of whom a brief account will be found in ch. xxviii., is trustworthy and well-informed. The first edition of his book was published posthumously in Lisbon, in 1563, the 2nd in 1731.

Barbosa   Duarte Barbosa, *A Description of the Coasts of East Africa and Malabar in the beginning of the Sixteenth Century . . . translated from an early Spanish MS. in the Barcelona Library, with notes and a preface by the Hon. H. E. J. Stanley*, London, Hak. Soc., 1866. Barbosa went to India in 1500 and his book was written before 1516.

Varthema   Ludovico di Varthema, *The Travels of L. di Varthema in Egypt, Syria, Arabia Deserta, Arabia Felix, in Persia, India, and Ethiopia, A.D. 1503-1508.* Translated from the original edition of 1510, with a preface, by John Winter Jones; and edited, with notes and an introduction, by G. P. Badger, London, Hak. Soc., 1863. A very valuable book, although the author's account of his own adventures cannot be accepted without reserve, and the editorial matter needs revision.

Eredia   Manoel Godinho de Eredia, *Malaca, l'Inde Méridionale et le Cathay*, Brussels, 1882. A facsimile of Eredia's MS. (discovered 1861, in the Royal Library, Brussels), ed. and trans. by Léon Janssen, with preface by C. Ruelens, maps and illustrations. Eredia, an ardent and intelligent explorer, was born in Goa in 1563. See p. 203 note.

Linschoten   Jan Huyghen van Linschoten, *Voyage to the East Indies, The First Book, containing his Description of the East*, 2 vols., London, Hak. Soc., 1885. A reprint of part of the English version of 1598, ed. A. C. Burnell (vol. i.) and P. A. Tiele (vol. ii.). The original Dutch edition of 1595-96 contains interesting copperplates. Linschoten, who was in Goa 1583-88, gives an invaluable account of manners and customs in Portuguese India.

Mocquet   Jean Mocquet, *Voyage en Afrique*, etc., Rouen, 1645, reprinted 1830. Mocquet travelled much in the East, visiting Goa in 1608. He describes life in the Indo-Portuguese settlements, giving much curious detail.

Pyrard   François Pyrard de Laval, *Voyages*, etc., Paris, 1679. Pyrard was in India at the same period as Mocquet, and his book is similar in character.

Botelho, *Tombo*, and Botelho, *Cartas*   Simão Botelho, *O Tombo do Estado da India*, published in *Subsidios*, Lisbon, Ac. Real, 1868. In the same volume are four of Botelho's letters (*Cartas*), written 1547-52. Botelho came to India in 1532, and held the posts of Comptroller of Revenue and Captain of Malacca. He was an able and honest official, whose writings throw much light on Portuguese finance and administration.

Diogo de Couto, *Observações sobre as principaes causas da* HOW CITED
Decadencia dos Portuguezes na Asia, escritas em forma de dialogo *Soldado*
com o titulo de Soldado Practico, publicadas por A. Caetano do
Amaral, Lisbon, 1790.   By the author of the later *Décadas.*

Garcia de Orta, *Colloquios dos simples e drogas e cousas medi-* Orta
cinaes da India, Lisbon, 1872, 1st ed., 1573.   See ch. xxxvi.

Fernão Mendes Pinto, *Peregrinaçam*, Lisbon, 1614.   See Pinto
ch. xxix.

Firishta or Ferishtah (Muhammad Kasim ibn Hindu Shah), Firishta
History of the Rise of the Mahomedan Power in India, till the year
1612.   Trans. from the Persian by J. Briggs, 4 vols., London,
1829.   Firishta lived *c.* 1550–*c.* 1612.   In 1585 he was commissioned by Ibrahim Adil Shah of Bijapur to write a history
of the Muhammadans in India.   Though he rarely quotes an
authority, his work serves as a useful corrective to the European
chronicles of his time.   The translation mentioned above is
generally considered the best available, though based on incomplete texts and containing some matter not in the original.

Zain al Din, *Tohfat ul Mujahideen*, trans. by M. J. Rowlandson, *Tahafut*
Oriental Translation Fund, 1833.   Describes the relations between Portuguese and Muhammadans from 1498 to 1583.

Damião de Goes, *Commentarius Rerum gestarum in India citra*
Gangem a Lusitanis, Louvain, 1539 ; *Chronica del Rei D. João II.*,
Lisbon, 1567.   Goes (1501-73) was one of the most distinguished
of Portuguese humanists and an intimate friend of Erasmus.
John III. (1521-57) entrusted him with diplomatic missions in
Flanders, Poland, and Scandinavia, afterwards appointing him
keeper of the royal archives.   An enlightened thinker and erudite
historian, he was deprived of his office and imprisoned by the
Inquisition in 1571.   For his most important chronicle see below,
p. 307.

Manoel de Faria y Sousa, *Asia Portugueza*, 3 vols., Lisbon, Faria y Sousa
1666-75 ;   trans. by Capt. J. Stevens, London, 1695.   Faria y
Sousa (1590-1649) was an industrious but somewhat uncritical
compiler, who borrowed impartially from all his predecessors,
and added details invented by himself.   He wrote in Spanish
and had a remarkable gift of epigram.   Other works include
Europa Portugueza, 3 vols., Lisbon, 1667 ; *Africa Portugueza*,
Lisbon, 1681 ; and *Epitome de las Historias Portuguezas*, Madrid,
1628, of which there is an English version by Stevens, London,
1698.

Ruy de Pina, *Chronica do Princepe D. João II.*, 2nd ed., in Pina
Collecção de livros ineditos da Historia Portugueza, vol. ii., Lisbon,

How CITED 1792. Pina was royal librarian and chronicler from 1497 until his death in 1521.

Resende Garcia de Resende, *Chronica del Rei D. João II.*, 1st ed., Lisbon, 1545 ; numerous later editions. Resende (1470-1536) borrows freely from Pina, but relates many of his own experiences at Court.

c. Secondary Authorities

J. P. Oliveira Martins, *Historia da civilisação iberica*, Lisbon, 1879 ; *Historia de Portugal*, 2nd. ed., 2 vols., Lisbon, 1901. Impressionist studies, often of great brilliancy, though inaccurate in detail. The author, who rarely quotes any authority except his own voluminous writings, was a student of national psychology, at his best when writing of ideas rather than events.

J. P. Sousa Viterbo, *Trabalhos nauticos dos Portuguezes, nos seculos xvi e xvii*, etc., 2 vols., Lisbon, 1898 and 1900. Contains much information on the less familiar voyagers.

Whiteway R. S. Whiteway, *The Rise of the Portuguese Power in India, 1497-1550*, London, 1899. The author's acquaintance with Indian life and thought, and his profound knowledge of the original Portuguese authorities, give this book a special value. It contains chapters on arms and methods of warfare, navigation, religion and coinage.

A. C. Burnell, *A Tentative List of Books and some Manuscripts relating to the History of the Portuguese in India Proper*, Mangalore, 1880.

Fonseca J. Nicolau da Fonseca, *An Historical and Archæological Sketch of Goa*, Bombay, 1878. Originally compiled in connexion with the 1st ed. of the " Imperial Gazetteer of India " ; out of print and rare. A vast number of documents were collated by the author, whose work will not soon be superseded.

Ferguson Donald William Ferguson, *Letters from Portuguese Captives in Canton. Written in 1534 and 1536*, Bombay, 1902. The text of two letters written jointly by Christovão Vieyra and Vasco Calvo (see ch. xxxi.), with translation and introductory account of Portuguese intercourse with China up to 1550. The letters are important and the introduction summarizes almost all that is known on this obscure subject.

Crawfurd John Crawfurd, *History of the Indian Archipelago*, 3 vols., London, 1820. The Portuguese period is dealt with in vol. ii.

Ceylon J. Emerson Tennent, *Ceylon*, 2 vols., 5th ed., London, 1860. Vol. ii. gives the history of the Portuguese in Ceylon, quoting largely from native as well as European sources.

Donald William Ferguson, *The History of Ceylon from the*

Earliest Times to 1600 A.D., as related by João de Barros and Diogo How cited
do Couto, trans. and ed. D. Ferguson, in *Journal of the Ceylon Branch of the Royal Asiatic Society*, No. 60 (1909).

II. Special Bibliographies

These supplement, but do not as a rule supersede, the authorities quoted above under 1 *a* and 1 *b*.

Prince Henry the Navigator

Gomes Eannes de Azurara, *The Chronicle of the Discovery* Azurara
and Conquest of Guinea, trans. and ed. by C. R. Beazley and E. Prestage, 2 vols., London, Hak. Soc., 1896-1899. Azurara (d. 1474) was appointed keeper of the archives and historiographer-royal in 1454. His chronicle is the principal authority for the explorations undertaken during Prince Henry's lifetime. It is a lively and well-informed narrative. The introductions to the two vols. of this edition are of great value. The original text (G. E. de Zurara, *Chronica do Descobrimento e Conquista de Guiné*) was ed. by the Visconde de Santarem, Paris, 1841.

The *Voyages* of Alvise da Ca' da Mosto, one of Prince Henry's captains, were first printed in *Paesi novamenti retrovati et novo mondo de Alberico Vesputio Florentino intitulato*, Vicenza, 1507 ; there are numerous discrepancies in later reprints, but a useful text will be found in vol. i. of Ramusio ; see also C. Schefer, *Relation des voyages de Ca' da Mosto*, Paris, 1895.

The best biography is *Prince Henry the Navigator*, by C. R. Beazley (" History of the Nations Series "), London, 1895. Other books which should be consulted are J. P. Oliveira Martins, *Os filhos de D. João I.*, 2nd ed., 2 vols., Lisbon, 1901 ; R. H. Major, *Life of Prince Henry of Portugal*—a classic—London, 1868 ; H. E. Wauvermans, *Henri le Navigateur et l'académie portugaise de Sagres*, Brussels, 1890.

Vasco da Gama

A Journal of the First Voyage of Vasco da Gama, 1497-1499, Roteiro
trans. and ed. with introduction, appendices, and many illustrations and maps, by E. G. Ravenstein, London, Hak. Soc., 1898. This *Roteiro* (log-book, itinerary) was written by an unknown sailor aboard Gama's fleet. The critical and explanatory matter in Dr Ravenstein's edition is of the highest value and interest : the appendices include translations of two letters written by King Manoel in July and August, 1499 ; of three letters written from Lisbon by Girolamo Sernigi about the same time, and of three

HOW CITED   Portuguese narratives of Gama's first voyage to India, dated 1608, 1612 and 1646. There are two Portuguese editions of the *Roteiro* —ed. Diogo Kopke and A. da Costa Paiva, Oporto, 1838; and ed. A. Herculano and Baron do Castello de Paiva, Lisbon, 1861.

The chief authorities for Gama's first voyage may be classified as follows, in order of merit—*Roteiro*, Castanheda, Barros, Goes, Osorio, Corrêa.

Lopes   Two descriptions of the second voyage by seamen who took part in it have been preserved. The first, by Thomé Lopes, is entitled *Navigatione verso l'Indie orientali scritta per Thomé Lopez Portoghese*, and was first printed in Ramusio (vol. i. p. 133 *seq.* of the ed. of 1663). Lopes, who was *escrivão* aboard one of Gama's ships, shows much literary talent and appears to be

Calcoen   thoroughly trustworthy. The second narrative, which is brief and sometimes demonstrably inaccurate was written by an anonymous Flemish pilot, and is usually known as *Calcoen* (*i.e.* Calicut). Internal evidence tends to prove that its author was a man of little education, who had not previously visited the tropics. *Calcoen* was first printed in Antwerp, in 1504, without a title. The edition to which I have referred is the English version entitled *Calcoen, a Dutch narrative of the second voyage of Vasco da Gama to Calicut*, ed. and trans. J. P. Berjeau, London, 1874 (unpaged). There are also French and German versions—Paris, 1881, and Brunswick, 1887.

For Gama's viceroyalty and third voyage the chief authority is Gaspar Corrêa, who was then in India. There is a volume

Stanley's *Corrêa*   of extracts from the *Lendas* entitled *The Three Voyages of Vasco da Gama and his Viceroyalty*, ed. and trans. Lord Stanley of Alderley, London, Hak. Soc., 1869. Readers should beware of regarding Corrêa as a trustworthy historian of the first two voyages, and should use the editorial matter in the above-named volume with caution.

The other documents relating to Gama's life will be found scattered up and down various books and periodicals—notably *Vasco da Gama e a Vidigueira*, by A. Teixeira de Aragão, 3rd ed. (containing material not elsewhere printed), Lisbon, 1898 ; *O premio da descoberta*, by Luciano Cordeiro, Lisbon, 1897 ; *Os primeiros Gamas, id.*, Lisbon, 1898 ; *De come e quando foi feito Conde Vasco da Gama, id.*, in the *Boletim* for 1892, pp. 257-303, and as separate pamphlet, Lisbon, 1892 ; *Vasco da Gama em Evora*, by A. F. Barata, Lisbon, 1898 ; and *Alguns documentos*. The principal biographies are *Vasco da Gama*, by J. M. Latino Coelho, Lisbon, 1882—largely out of date—and *Le Comte-Amiral D. Vasco da Gama*, by D. Maria Telles da Gama, Paris, 1902—a fantastic book dedicated to the Emperor Menelik.

Affonso de Albuquerque

Of the principal chroniclers, Corrêa, who was an eyewitness of much that he describes, is to be preferred to Barros, Castanheda and Goes. But the chief authority is Albuquerque's own letters —*Cartas*, ed. R. A. de Bulhão Pato, 1 vol., Lisbon, Ac. Real, 1884. A second volume of elucidatory documents was promised but not published. The *Commentaries of the Great Afonso Dalboquerque*, trans. and ed. W. de Gray Birch, 4 vols., London, Hak. Soc., 1875-84, is an excellent translation of an indispensable book. The original was written by Braz (afterwards D. Affonso) de Albuquerque, half-caste natural son to the great governor. It is laudatory in tone, but fairly trustworthy (see p. 100) ; and it has great literary merit. Portuguese text : *Commentarios do grande A. Dalboquerque*, 4 vols., Lisbon, 1774 (1st ed. 1557). The best English account of Albuquerque will be found in Whiteway. There is also a biography by Prof. H. Morse Stephens, in the " Rulers of India " series—*Albuquerque*, London, 1892.

How cited

Cartas

Commentaries

King Manoel

Damião de Goes, *Chronica do felicissimo Rei D. Emmanuel*, Lisbon, 1566-1567. This is the most important of Goes' books on Portuguese history, For some account of its author, see above, *General Bibliography*.

Goes

Jeronymo Osorio da Fonseca, Bishop of Silves, *De rebus Emanuelis*, Lisbon, 1571. Confessedly based on Goes, this chronicle has some independent merits, and is singularly outspoken. There is an English translation by James Gibbs, *The History of the Portuguese during the Reign of Emmanuel*, 2 vols., London, 1752. See also *Ordenações do S. R. D. Manoel*, Coimbra, 1757, and *El Rei D. Manoel*, by M. B. Branco, Lisbon, 1888. The last-named is a useful biography.

Osorio

D. João de Castro

Jacinto Freire de Andrade, *Vida de Dom João de Castro*, ed. D. Fr. Francisco de São Luiz, Assistant Bishop of Coimbra, Lisbon, 1835. This is the best of many editions, including the later ones (Paris, 1861 and 1869) attributed to the same editor. It contains valuable critical matter, and transcripts of many letters to Castro from the King and Queen of Portugal, besides other original documents. The *Vida*, first published in 1651, has been called " the type of perfect biography." A more accurate characterization is that of Mr R. S. Whiteway—

Andrade

fit only " to relate the history of that Portuguese ship's captain who, hearing one of his sailors ask the cook for an onion, roared at him ' Onion ! What the devil do you mean ? Our only luxuries here are powder and shot.' " [1] The book is as untrustworthy as it is pompous. There is an English translation by Sir P. Wyche, London, 1664.

Castro's letters have never been collected, but specimens will be found in the two volumes of *O Instituto*, Coimbra, 1854 ; in vol. xvi. of the *Investigador Portuguez*, Lisbon, 1811 ; and in vol. i. of the *Revista Universal*, 2nd series, Lisbon, 1849.

Three *roteiros* written by Castro are extant (see chap. xviii.), and were first published in the nineteenth century under the following titles :—

(i) *Roteiro de Lisboa à Goa, 1538*, ed. J. de Andrade Corvo, Lisbon, 1882,

(ii) *Roteiro de Goa à Dio (1538-39)*, anonymously edited but produced by Diogo Kopke, with facsimiles of the MS. and a separate volume of the original illustrations, Oporto, 1843.

(iii) *Roteiro de Dom Joam de Castro de viagem que fizeram os Portuguezes ao Mar Roxo no anno de 1541*, etc., ed. A. Nunes de Carvalho, Paris, 1833. A Latin version of the disquisition on the Red Sea (*Itinerarium Maris Rubri*) is included, and there is a separate volume of the original illustrations. A very incomplete English translation, entitled the *Rutter of Don John of Castro*, was first printed in 1625, in *Purchas his Pilgrimes*. Some of Castro's observations on compass-variation and kindred topics are reprinted separately in G. Hellmann's *Neudrucke von Schriften und Karten über Meteorologie und Erdmagnetismus* (No. 10, *Rara Magnetica*), Berlin, 1898.

GEORGE BUCHANAN

George Buchanan : Glasgow Quatercentenary Studies, Glasgow, 1906, and *George Buchanan : a Memorial*, ed. D. A. Millar, St Andrews and London, 1906, are collections of essays and translations of Buchanan's writings, published to celebrate the fourth centenary of his birth. The standard biography is *George Buchanan : Humanist and Reformer*, by Professor P. Hume Brown, Edinburgh, 1890. The records of Buchanan's trial were discovered in 1890 by Senhor G. J. C. Henriques, and published with an English translation and notes under the title *George Buchanan in the Lisbon Inquisition*, Lisbon, 1906. Senhor Henriques also contributed a chapter on " Buchanan in Portugal " to *George Buchanan : a Memorial*. His researches have entirely superseded the traditional account of the trial, which was still

[1] Whiteway, p. 301.

current up to 1906, although the true facts had been com- How CITED
municated by Senhor Henriques to Professor Hume Brown.
and published by him in the *Scottish Review* for April 1893.

FRANCIS XAVIER

Xavier's own correspondence, supplemented by a few other
sixteenth-century documents, affords the only sound foundation
upon which to reconstruct his biography.   A critical text, preceded by a life of Xavier in Spanish, and containing a bibliography and notes, will be found in *Monumenta Xaveriana ex
Autographis vel ex Antiquioribus Exemplis Collecta*, vol. i., Madrid,
1899-1900, included in *Monumenta historica Societatis Jesu*.   The
letters are translated in *The Life and Letters of St Francis Xavier*,
by H. Coleridge, S.J., 2 vols., London, 1872.   The translator Coleridge
claims to have consulted certain manuscript sources, but the
historical and biographical parts of his *Life* appear to be based
on late and doubtful evidence.   There are numerous older
biographies by members of the Society ; all are frankly uncritical,
but together they probably embody a mass of oral and written
information, partly genuine though impossible to verify.   To
this information I have referred under the general name of
" tradition."   The best of the early Jesuit biographies are those
of Torsellino (Tursellinus) and Lucena ; viz. *De vita Francisci
Xaverii . . . libri sex*, by Orazio Torsellino, Antwerp, 1596 ; Torsellino
English translation, *The Admirable Life of St Francis Xavier*,
translated by T. F., Paris, 1632 ; and *Historia da Vida do Padre
Francisco de Xavier*, etc., by João Lucena, Lisbon, 1600.   The Lucena
later works of Bartoli, Maffei, Poussines, Menchacha, Léon
Pagès and other Jesuits borrow freely from Torsellino and
Lucena.   The essay by Sir James Stephens is mentioned on
p. 238 (note).   *The Missionary Life of St Francis Xavier*, by the
Rev. H. Venn, Prebendary of St Paul's Cathedral, London, 1862,
contains an interesting map, but is mainly an Anglican polemic.
The *Resumo historico da maravilhosa vida . . . de S. Francisco
Xavier*, by F. N. Xavier, S.J., Nova Goa, 1861, and *St François
de Xavier, sa vie et ses lettres*, by J. M. Cros, S.J., 2 vols., Toulouse,
1900, contain the results of original research, though they carry
on the Jesuit tradition.   On Fernão Mendes Pinto as an
authority for the life of Xavier, see ch. xxix. ; see also *A History
of Christianity in Japan*, by Otis Cary, 2 vols., London, 1910.

LUIZ DE CAMÕES

The best biography is Dr Theophilo Braga's *Camões, epoca e* Braga
vida, Oporto, 1907.   Dr Braga is the first among modern Portu-

guese critics, and his book is as brilliant as it is learned. But allowance should be made for the anti-clerical bias of the author, whose dogmatic Positivism occasionally colours his interpretation of historical fact. *Camões e o sentimento nacional*, also by Dr Braga, Oporto, 1891, and *Camões, os Lusiadas, e a Renascença em Portugal*, by J. P. Oliveira Martins, Lisbon, 1891, are useful and suggestive. Dr Wilhelm Storck's *Luis de Camões' Leben*, Paderborn, 1890, is usually considered the best biography not of
Camoens Portuguese authorship. *Camoens, His Life and his Lusiads : A Commentary*, by Sir R. F. Burton, 2 vols., London, 1881, includes an exhaustive bibliography of the books previously written on the same subject, besides invaluable notes on Oriental customs and history. But as a biography it has been superseded.

A complete edition of the works of Camões was compiled by the Visconde de Juromenha in 9 vols., Lisbon, 1860-1869. Some pieces of doubtful authorship are included. Among many English translations of *The Lusiads*, the best is that of J. J. Aubertin, 2nd. ed. (with Portuguese text), 2 vols., London, 1884. Text and translation of 70 of Camões' sonnets, by the same author, London, 1881. Burton is said to have translated all the works of Camões : but only his versions of *The Lusiads* (2 vols., London, 1880) and Lyrics (2 vols., London, 1884) have been published.

BIBLIOGRAPHICAL NOTES

Brief bibliographical notes on special subjects are appended to pp. 10 (alleged Portuguese discovery of America), 17 (determination of longitude), 26 (Kongo), 27 (Cão and Dias), 46 (Muhammadanism in E. Africa), 46 and 87 (Ophir), 65 (the Mithkal), 72 (Almeida), 74 (Vijayanagar), 120 (the Corte-Reaes), 142 (Christovão da Gama in Abyssinia), 161 (the Jews in Portugal), 181 (the Inquisition), 203 (early voyages to Australia), 210 (Pinto) and 245 (" Grão Vasco ").

APPENDIX B

COINAGE

It is impossible to secure more than approximate accuracy in converting Indo-Portuguese coinage of the sixteenth century into its modern equivalent in sterling. The unit of value, then as now, was the *real* (plur. *reis*), worth about one farthing in 1500 and less than one-fifth of a farthing at the present day. Sir H. Yule (in *Hobson-Jobson, a Glossary of Anglo-Indian Words and Phrases, s.v.* Pardão) worked out the value of the *real* at different periods, making it approximately ·268d. in 1513 and ·16d. in 1600. Somewhat similar results were obtained by Mr G. M'C. Theal, who based his estimates on the actual weight of fine gold in certain sixteenth-century coins (*History and Ethnography of Africa South of the Zambesi*, vol. i., London, 1907, pp. 259-260, note).

The value of the *real* fluctuated enormously in the sixteenth century (see Whiteway, pp. 67-72), largely owing to the frequent debasement of the coinage ; but for purposes of conversion it is necessary to adopt some fixed standard, and I have taken the *real* at ·268d. up to 1560 and thenceforward at ·16d. ; the *cruzado* at 390-420 *reis* ; the gold *pardão* at 360 *reis* ; the *xerafim* and *pardão de tanga* at 300 *reis*. The equivalence thus obtained is, of course, never more than approximately correct, owing partly to the fluctuation of the *real*, partly to changes in the purchasing power of money. It may be stated as a general rule, admitting of many exceptions, that any sum of money nominally the same in the sixteenth century and the twentieth would have a higher power of purchasing necessaries in the earlier period, and a higher power of purchasing luxuries in the later. A fowl could be bought for 2d. in 1500 ; but an ounce of spice now worth 4d. would then have cost something much nearer to its own weight in silver. This difference in purchasing power should be borne in mind in estimating, *e.g.*, the pensions received by Gama, Magellan, or Camões. An income which would mean starvation to-day may have been a " living wage " to its recipients.

The chief sixteenth-century book on the subject is that of Antonio Nunes, mentioned above (Appendix A, *s.v. Subsidios*). Modern authorities, in addition to those already cited, are J. M.

do Carmo Nazareth, *Numismatica da India Portugueza*, Lisbon, 1890 ; and J. Gerson da Cunha, *Contributions to the Study of Indo-Portuguese Numismatics*, Bombay, 1880. The comparative values given in the last-named are illusory, so far as the sixteenth century is concerned, as the basis of the author's calculations is the *real* taken at its modern *par* value.

INDEX

ABD UR-RAZZAK, 54, 94, 96.
Abravanel, Isaac, 158.
Abu Bakr, 269.
Abyssinia, 36, 141-142, 211. See also " Prester John."
Achinese, 292 (note).
Adam's Bridge, 195, 199.
Adamastor, 263.
Aden, strategic importance of, 80-81 ; attacked by Albuquerque, 91-93, 186-187 ; Castro on, 138 ; fiasco of 1547, 151-153.
Affonso I., King of Portugal. See Affonso Henriques.
Affonso II., King of Portugal, 156.
Affonso III.,   ,,   ,,   281.
Affonso IV.,   ,,   ,,   251.
Affonso V.,   ,,   ,,   5, 24, 78-79, 158.
Affonso, Prince, son of John II., 115-116.
Affonso, Martim, 43.
Affonso Henriques, 248, 251, 277, 281, 282.
Africa, exploration of, 10, 13-14, 24-28, 40-51.
Agulhas current, 43, 45.
Ahmad ibn Muhammad, 248 (note).
Ailly, Pierre d', 29, 31 (note).
Albuquerque, Affonso de : name and ancestry, 78 ; career before 1509, 78-79 ; first attack on Ormuz and dispute with Almeida, 76-77 ; becomes Governor of India, 77, 79 ; his governorship, 79-114 ; defeat at Calicut, 79-80 ; capture of Goa, 81-82 ; expulsion and blockade by Adil Shah, 80-83 ; commandeers a fleet, 84 ; retakes Goa, 84-85 ; treatment of Diogo Mendes de Vasconcellos, 85 ; conquers Malacca, 86-88 ; returns to India, 88 ; relieves garrison of Goa, 88-90 ; expedition to Red Sea, 91-93 ; attacks Aden, ib. ; builds fort in Calicut, 93 (note) ; occupies Ormuz, 93-96 ; illness and supersession ; 96-97 ; return to Goa and death, 96-98 ; last letter to King Manoel, 97 ; personal appearance, 99 ; character, 99-100, 113-114, 183, compared with Gama, 129 ; business habits, 100 ; mastery of detail, 101-102 ; cruelty, 85, 89-90, 93 ; statesmanship, 80-81, 101-114 ; colonial and marriage policy, 102-106 ; commercial policy, 106-107 ; foreign policy 107-110 ; finance, 110-111 ; administrative system, 111-112 ; summary of his work, 113-114 ; bibliography, 307.
Albuquerque, Braz de (afterwards D. Affonso de), son of A. de Albuquerque, 97 (note), 99-100, 307.
Albuquerque, D. Gonçalo de, father of A. de Albuquerque, 79.
Albuquerque, D. João de, Bishop of Goa, 183, 151, 153.
Albuquerque, Jorge de, 227.
Albuquerque, Pedro de, 95.
Albuquerque, town, Spain, 78.
Alcalá de Henares, town, Spain, 166, 269.
Alcmena, 253.
Alcochete, town, Portugal, 49.
Alemquer, Pedro de, 35, 41.
Alexander VI., Pope, 5, 31-32, 62, 118, 160.
Alexandria, 101, 139, 140.
Algarve, 3.
Algoa Bay, Africa, 27.
Alhandra, town, Portugal, 78.
Ali bin Sulaiman, Shaikh of Aden, 152.
Aljubarrota, 3, 243.
All Saints, college, Coimbra, 252.
Almada, town, Portugal, 258.
Almeida, D. Francisco de, first Viceroy of India, 72, 119 ; his policy 73-74, 102 ; defeats Egyptian navy, 74-76 ; quarrels with Albuquerque, 76-77 ; killed by Hottentots, 77.
Almeida, D. Francisco de, friend of Camões, 277.
Almeida, D. Lourenço de, 74.
Almeirim, town, Portugal, 258.

313

Altan Khan, 213-214.
Alva, Duke of, 289.
Alvares, Jorge, 234.
Amboyna, island, Malay Archipelago, 205, 206, 266.
Amoy River, China, 218 (note).
Amphitryon, 253.
Andrade, Fernão Pires de, 227-228.
Andrade, Jacinto Freire de, 307-308, 236.
Andrade, Simão Pires de, 228-229.
Anger, Anjiro. See Yajiro.
Anjadiva, island, India, 84.
Anthonino, Archbishop of Florence, 140.
Antiochus, King of Syria, 261.
Antwerp, 60, 287-289.
Arabists, in medicine, 269, 270.
Arabs, 7, 45-46.
Aragão, D. Francisca de, 258.
Aragon, 117-118, 121.
Araujo, Ruy de, 86, 87, 88.
Arfet, Anna d', 9.
Aristotle, 7, 19, 157, 225, 269.
" Armada of Jesus," 208.
Armada of the North, 264.
Armada of the South, 265-266.
Art, Portuguese, in sixteenth century, 241-249.
Arthur, King, 284.
Arthur, Prince of Wales, 118, 204.
Artillery, 48, 126, 133; types of, 75; in Tibet, 214; in Japan, 223, in Morocco, 282.
Arzila (Asila), seaport, Morocco, 282-283.
Ascension, island, Atlantic, 64.
Ashkenazim, 156.
Athayde, Alexandre de, 95, 232-233.
Athayde, D. Alvaro de, sixth son of Vasco da Gama, 69.
Athayde, D. Alvaro Gonçalves de, grandfather of A. de Albuquerque, 79.
Athayde, Catherina de, wife of Vasco da Gama, 67.
Athayde, Catherina de (Nathercia) 257, 260, 265, 268, 269.
Atlantic Ocean, in mediæval legend, 7-9; exploration of, 7, 9-10, 13-14, 24-28.
Atlantis, 7.
Auditors of the Rota, 239.
Aurea Chersonesus, 87.
Australia, 202-203.
Auto, meaning of, 248-249.
Auto-da-Fé, described, 176-180.
Auto del Rei Seleuco, 260-261.
Auto dos Enfatriões, 253.

Avalon, 7-8, 284.
Avicenna, 269.
Aviz, town, Portugal, 4.
Aviz, dynasty, xviii., 3, 279, 280 (note).
Aviz, Order of, 4-6.
Azambuja, Diogo d', 24.
Azambuja, Jeronymo d', 172.
Azamor, town, Morocco, 261.
Azerbaijan, 109.
Azevedo, Jeronymo, 292.
Azores, 58.
Azurara, Gomes Eannes de, 305.

BAB EL-MANDEB, STRAIT OF, 91, 124.
Bacon, Francis, 245, 270, 295.
Badega, 198 (note).
Bahadur Shah, 133, 154 (note), 293.
Bahia da Roca. See Algoa Bay.
Bahia dos Vaqueiros. See Mossel Bay.
Bahmani Sultanate, 108.
Bale, Bishop, 249.
Balthasar the German, 15.
Banda, island, Malay Archipelago, 266.
Bantu, 43-45, 182-183.
Barbary Corsairs, 60.
Barbora, 265.
Barbosa, Duarte, 302.
Barcelona, 166, 170.
Barreto, Francisco, 264, 265-6, 267, 268 (note).
Barreto Rolim, Pedro, 267, 268 (note), 271.
Barros, João de, 300.
Bartholomew the Florentine, 107.
Basques, 121.
Basra (Bussorah), 74.
Bassein, seaport, India, 136.
Batalha Abbey, 243.
Bazaruta Islands, E. Africa, 46.
Bedawin, 139.
Behaim, Martin, 30.
Belem, port and suburb of Lisbon, 37, 59, 124, 121, 243.
Beliagoa, Belchior, 173, 252.
Benares, 292.
Benasterim, 89.
Berbers, 130.
Bermudes, João, 141.
Béthencourt, Jean de, 9.
Bijapur, 81, 103, 108.
Bimini, legendary island, 8.
Bintang, island, Malay Archipelago, 230, 292 (note).
Blaise, St., 76.

Boa Gente, Terra da. See Limpopo.
Bobadilla, Nicolás, 167.
Boccaccio, 275.
Bons Signaes, Rio dos. See Kiliman River.
Bonzes, 219, 220, 224-225.
Bordeaux, 168-169.
Borges, Gonçalo, 262.
Borneo, 204.
Botelho, Simão, 183, 185, 230, 299, 302.
Boutaca, 243.
Braga, Dr Theophilo, 309-310.
Bragança, D. Constantino de, 267, 289-290.
Bragança, Duke of, 70.
Brahmans, 53, 55.
Brazil, legendary island, 8.
Brazil, supposed discovery in 1447-1448, 10 (note) ; discovery by Cabral, 63 ; Jesuits in, 161.
Brendan, St., legendary island of, 8.
Bristol, 60.
Broach, town, India, 153.
Brown, John, 66 (note).
Browne, Sir Thomas, 180 (note).
Brunei, Borneo, 204.
Buchanan, George, early life, 163 ; in Paris, 163-165 ; in Scotland, 168 ; at Bordeaux, 168-169 ; at Coimbra, 169-171 ; trial and imprisonment 171-173 ; subsequent career, 173-175 ; writings, 168, 169, 170, 174 ; bibliography, 308-309.
Buchanan, Thomas, 174.
Buddhists, in Japan, 219-220, 223-225 ; in China, 228 ; Portuguese opinion of, 236 ; dalada incident, 289-290.
Bungo, fief, Japan, 223-226.
Burma, 215.
Bushmen, 45.

CABO DA BOA ESPERANÇA. See Cape of Good Hope.
Cabo Tormentoso. See Cape of Good Hope.
Cabral, Fernão Alvares, 262.
Cabral, Pedro Alvares, 62-64.
Ca' da Mosto or Cadamosto, Alvise da, 15, 305.
Cadiz, 60, 282.
Caiado, Antonio, 173.
Cairo, 109, 139, 140.
Calcoen, 306, 64 (note), 65, 66.
Calicut, trade of, 53, 57-58 ; government, 53-54 ; Gama at (1498), 52-58 ; Cabral at, 63 ; attacked

by Gama (1502), 65-66 ; Portuguese defeated at, 79-80, 100 ; Portuguese fort built, 93 (note).
Calvin, 165.
Calvinism, 289.
Calvo, Vasco, 229-230.
Camara, Luiz Gonçalves da, 279-280.
Camara, Ruy Dias da, 275.
Cambodia, 267.
Caminha, Pedro de Andrade de, 258.
Camões, Antão Vaz de, grandfather of L. de Camões, 250.
Camões, D. Bento de, uncle of L. de Camões, 250, 252.
Camões, Luiz Vaz de : life, 250-278 ; family and early education, 250-252 ; at Coimbra University, 252-255 ; relations with " Chiado," 256 ; meeting with Nathercia, 257 ; at Court 257-261 ; in Morocco, 261-262 ; return to Lisbon (1549-1553), 262 ; voyage to India, 262-263 ; service in Arabian Sea, Red Sea, Persian Gulf, 263-264 ; in Goa (1555-1556), 264-265 ; in Malacca and Malay Archipelago, 265-266 ; at Macao, 266-267 ; shipwreck and return to Malacca (1560), 267 ; life in Goa (1561-1567), 267-271 ; in Mozambique, 271-272 ; return to Lisbon (1570), 272 ; last years in Lisbon (1570-1580), 272-278 ; pension, 275 ; death, 277 ; minor works, 253, 260-261, 264-265, 267, 268, 270, 272 (and note) ; bibliography, 309-310. See also Lusiads.
Camões, Simão Vaz de, father of L. de Camões, 250-251.
Camões, Vasco Pires de, 250.
Cana, 51.
Cananor, 63, 66.
Canary Islands, 8, 9.
Canerio, Nicholas de, 53.
Canquexumaa. See Kagoshima.
Canterbury Tales, quoted, 257.
Canton, 221-230, 218, 233.
Cão, Diogo, 25-27.
Cape of Good Hope, 27-28, 41-42, 263, 289.
Cape Verde Islands, 15, 37-39, 259.
Carocha, 177.
Carthage, 60.
Casa Pia, 216.
Casal, Antonio do, 149, 150.
Cascaes, seaport, Portugal, 272.
Cassilis, Earl of, 168.
Castanheda, Fernão Lopes de, 301.

Caste, 237.
Castello Branco, D. Martinho de, 104
Castiglione, Baldassare, 258.
Castile, 2-3, 243, 158.
Castilho, João de, xiii., 243.
Castro, D. Alvaro de, father of D. J. de Castro, 130.
Castro, D. Alvaro de, elder son of D. J. de Castro, 131, 132; knighted, 140; at Diu, 146-147, 149; in Arabia, 152-153.
Castro, Christovão de, Franciscan, 187.
Castro, D. Fernão de, younger son of D. J. de Castro, 131, 145-146.
Castro, D. Guiomar de, grandmother of A. de Albuquerque, 78.
Castro, Ignez de, 251, 281.
Castro, D. João de: life, 130-155; early career (to 1538), 130-132; first experience of India, 132-134; Red Sea expedition, 135-142; return to Portugal, 142; Governor of India, 142-155; defeats Gujaratis at Diu, 147-149; "triumph" at Goa, 150-151; fiasco at Aden, 151-153; death, 153; character, 153-155; as scientist, 130, 135-139, 154-155, 241, 245; his Roteiros, 135-139; his letters, 154; as soldier, 131, 150; as administrator, 134, 154, 291; bibliography, 307-308.
Catalans, 9, 17, 118, 121, 244.
Catherine of Aragon, 118, 204.
Catherine, Queen-consort of John III., 151, 197, 257, 259, 279.
Catherine, St., convent and tomb of, 139-140.
"Catholic sovereigns," 115.
Cato, Disticha Catonis, Cato pro Pueris, Gaton, 173, 251 (note).
Celebes, island, Malay Archipelago, 200, 201.
Cellini, Benvenuto, 61, 295.
Celsus, 269.
Censorship, 181, 270-271, 274-275.
Cervantes, 287.
Ceuta, 10, 261, 262, 271.
Ceylon, 86, 199, 289, 290, 292, 304-305.
Changchau, 218, 231, 233.
Charles V., Emperor, 118, 120, 132, 259, 261.
Chaul, seaport, India, 74, 146, 271.
"Chiado" (Antonio Ribeiro), 256, 259, 260.
China, 86, 87, 94, 211; Pinto in, 213-215; Japanese opinion of, 225; early intercourse with

Portugal, 227-231, 226. See also Xavier.
Chinchew, 218 (note).
Chittagong, 86.
Choshu, fief, Japan, 221.
Christ, Order of, 4-6, 34, 37.
Church, Portuguese, relations with Monarchy, 3, 118-120, 258-260, 279-280; conflict with Judaism, 156; with Humanism, 162, 175; in the East, 182-187, 235-237, 289-290. See also under Censorship, Crusades, Dominicans, Franciscans, Index, Inquisition, Jesuits, Military Orders, Missions, Xavier.
Chwanchau, 218 (note).
Cintra, 131, 132, 138, 258, 263.
Cipangu, 8, 29, 31.
Clement V., Pope, 4, 5.
Cobre, Rio do. See Limpopo.
Cochin, 63, 66, 71, 104, 107, 112-113, 126-128.
Cochin China, 214, 215.
Coelho, João, 146.
Coelho, Nicolau, 35, 58.
Cogan, Henry, 210.
Coimbra, 251, 281.
Coimbra University, early history, 170; colleges, 252; curriculum, 252-253; student customs, 253-254; Buchanan at, 170-171; disorder at (1550), 172-173.
Coinage, Indo-Portuguese, values, 311-312; debasement, 274, 280, 291-292.
Collares, town, Portugal, 131.
Columbus, Bartholomew, 29.
Columbus, Christopher, 8, 24, 28-31, 40.
Columbus, Diego, 31.
Columella, 248.
Comet, observed by D. J. de Castro, 136-137.
Commerce, Portuguese, 2, 287-289. See also Albuquerque and Spice-trade.
Comorin, Cape, 195.
Confucius, 237.
Congo, river, 25-27.
Congreve, Richard, 210.
Conjeveram, town, India, 292.
Consolat del Mar, 17-19.
Constantinople, 137.
Contucci, Andrea, 242.
Copernicus, 269.
Coromandel Coast, 126, 135, 293.
Corrêa, Antonio, 293.
Corrêa, Gaspar, 301, 306, 95-96, 236 (note), 293.

Corrêa, Pedro, 30.
Correntes, Cape, 43, 44.
Corsali, Andrea, 227.
Cortex-Real, Gaspar, 120 (note).
Corte-Real, Jeronymo, 143.
Corte-Real, Miguel, 120 (note).
Cortes, 3, 158.
Corunna, 60.
Costa, João da, 170-173.
Coutinho, Bishop Fernando, 159.
Coutinho, D. Fernando, Marshal of Portugal, 77, 79-80.
Coutinho, D. Francisco, Count of Redondo, 268 (and note).
Coutinho, D. Lenor de, wife of D. J. de Castro, 131.
Coutinho, Miguel Rodrigues (Fios Seccos), 149, 266, 268-269.
Couto, Diogo de (or do), 300-301, 271.
Covilhã, Pedro de, 36.
Crato, Order of, 4.
Crusades and Crusaders, 3-6, 11-13, 33, 101, 140, 261, 276, 279-284.
Cruzado, 311.
Cunha, Tristão da, 119.
Cyprus, 261.

Dabul, 124.
Daimio, 218; of Satsuma, 219-220; of Hirado, 221; of Yamaguchi, 221-223; of Bungo, 223-225.
Dalada, the, 289-290.
Dalai Lama, 214.
Dante, 249, 250, 265, 275.
Deccan, 108.
Dely, Mount, 52.
Descartes, 245.
Diarbekir, 109.
Dias, Diniz, 13.
Dias, Diogo, 35.
Dias, Jeronymo, 57.
Dias, Ruy, 83.
Diasde Novaes, Bartholomeu, at São Jorge da Mina, 24; voyage round the Cape, 27-28, 33; association with Gama, 35-38; last voyage, 62-63.
Dieppe, 9, 60, 202.
Diniz, King of Portugal, 4-5, 15, 78.
Disparates da India, 265.
Diu, seaport, India: naval action off, 74-76; Portuguese settlement and first siege, 133-134; second siege, 143-150.
Dominicans, attack Jews, 160; connexion with Inquisition, 176,

177, 180, 274-275; as missionaries, 183-185.
Doria, Andrea, 132.
Dunbar, 168.
Dürer Albrecht, 119.
Dutch East India Company, 289.

Edinburgh, 168.
Edom or Idumea, 137.
Edrisi, 7.
Education, Portuguese, in sixteenth century, 162-165, 251-253, 259, 296-297.
Egypt, 74-77, 101, 103 (note), 138-139.
El-Araish, town, Morocco, 283.
El-Kasr el-Kebir, town, Morocco, 276, 283-284, 285.
El-Kus, river, Morocco, 283.
Eleanor of Austria, 118, 261.
Elephanta, 136.
Elephants, 88, 119-120.
Empoli, Giovanni de, 228.
Encina, Juan de, 249.
England, 2-3, 20, 285, 288.
Epistolæ Obscurorum Virorum, quoted, 102.
Erasmus, 162, 163, 171, 251, 303.
Eredia, Manoel Godinho de, 302, 203 (note).
Erithra, King, 137.
Escrivão, 19.
Estella, Diego de, 184.
Estremoz, town, Portugal, 33, 159.
Eugenius IV., Pope, 5.
Evora, town, Portugal, 69, 116.

Faber, Peter, 167.
Factory-system, in colonization, 102, 107.
Famine, in the East, 135; in Portugal, 179, 274.
Faria, Antonio de, 212, 217.
Faria, D. Pedro de, 213.
Faria y Sousa, Manoel de, 303.
Faro, town, Portugal, 157.
Ferdinand, Duke of Vizeu, 115.
Ferdinand, King of Aragon, 62, 115-116.
Fernandes, André, 182.
Fernandes, Isabel, 144-145.
Fernandez, Juan, 209, 221-226.
Ferreira, Bartholomeu, 275.
Fidalgo, 296-297.
Fidalgo, João, 92.
Filodemo, 264.
"Fingeo." See Hiji.
Finisterre, Cape, 250.
"Fios Seccos." See Coutinho, Miguel Rodrigues.

Firishta, 303.
Fishery Coast, 195-199.
Flanders, 2, 287-289.
Florence, 61.
Fortunate Isles, 8.
France, affected by Portuguese discoveries, 61.
Francis I., King of France, 120.
Franciscans, missions of, 183-184, 188, 193-194.
Francis, St. 184.
Franciscanus, 168.
Freire, Ruy, 143, 144.
Fucarandono, 225.
Fukien, province, China, 218 (note), 230, 231.
Fulad Khan, 88-89.

GALEN, 269.
Galileo, 245.
Gallas, 292.
Galle, seaport, Ceylon, 87 (note).
Galvão, Antonio, 204-205, 266, 301-302.
Gama, Ayres da, brother of V. da Gama, 68.
Gama, D. Christovão da, 4th son of V. da Gama, 69, 142.
Gama, Duarte da, 223.
Gama, Estevão da, cousin of V. da Gama, 64 (note).
Gama, Estevão da, father of V. da Gama, 49.
Gama, D. Estevão da, 2nd son of V. da Gama, 69, 123, 134, 135, 140-142.
Gama, D. Francisco da, eldest son of V. da Gama, 69.
Gama, D. Guiomar da, grandmother of D. J. de Castro, 250.
Gama, Paulo da, eldest brother of V. da Gama, 34, 35, 41, 47, 49, 58.
Gama, D. Paulo da, 3rd son of V. da Gama, 69, 123.
Gama, João da, uncle of V. da Gama, 69.
Gama, Tareyja da, sister of V. da Gama, 68.
Gama, Vasco da (after 1499 D. Vasco, after 1519 Count of Vidigueira) : early life 33-34 ; preparations for voyage to India, 34-36, 18, 243 ; the outward voyage, 37-52 ; at Calicut, 52-58 ; return voyage, 58-59 ; results, 60-61 ; second voyage to India, 64-66 ; retirement and rewards, 67-70 ; Viceroy of India,

123-129 ; death 128 ; character, v., 34, 65-66, 68, 123-124, 125, 128-129 ; bibliography, 305-306.
Gamba, Bantu chief, 182.
Genoa, 20, 33, 61.
Glastonbury Tor, 9.
Goa, 68 ; described, 80-81 ; first capture by Albuquerque, 81-82 ; recapture by Adil Shah, 82-83 ; recapture by Albuquerque, 84-85 ; besieged by Fulad Khan, 88 ; relieved by Albuquerque, 89-90 ; value to Portugal, 80, 103-104, 112 ; village communities in, 111 ; bishopric, 124, 183 ; Gama in, 124-126 ; Castro's triumph in, 150-151 ; social life, 188-193 ; monastic orders, 183, 185, 188, 193-194 ; hospitals, 125 (note), 185 (and note) ; prisons, 267 (and note), bibliography, 299, 304. See also Albuquerque.
Gobi Desert, 213.
Goes, Damião de, 303, 307, 275.
Gold, Island of. See Australia.
Goldsmith's work, Portuguese, in sixteenth century, 244.
Goliards, 256.
Gomes, Fernão, 24.
Gouvêa, André de, 168-171.
Gouvêa, Diogo de, 162, 168, 171.
Great Fish River, S. Africa, 27, 43.
" Green Sea of Darkness," 7.
Greenland, 120 (note).
Guanahani, island, W. Indies, 40.
Guanchis, 9, 20.
Guicciardini, Lodovico, 288.
Guinea, 9, 24, 288.
Guipúzcoa, province, Spain, 166.
Gujarat, 75, 103 ; trade of, 107, 108, 143 ; wars with Portuguese, 133, 143-150.
Guyenne, Collège de, 168-170.

" HEART OF TRUTH," 219.
" Hellenists," in medicine, 269, 270.
Henry, Cardinal Prince, afterwards King of Portugal, 120 ; Inquisitor 171, 178, 180 ; Regent, 279, 280 (note) ; King, 276-277.
Henry of Burgundy, Count, 1.
Henry the Navigator, Prince ; life and work 5, 7-14, 62 ; death, 24 ; bibliography, 305.
Henry VIII., King of England, 120.
Heriot, Agnes, 163.
Heywood, John, 249 (note).
Hierro or Ferro, island, Canaries, 17.

Hiji, seaport, Japan, 223-226.
Hindus : mistaken for Christians, 47, 49 (note), 50, 53, 58, 62 ; error detected, 63 ; opinion of Portuguese, 54, 103 ; relations with Muhammadans, 73, 107 ; with Almeida, 73-74 ; with Albuquerque, 98, 107, 112-113 ; with later Portuguese rulers, 183, 193-194, 236-237, 292-294.
Hippocrates, 269.
Hirado, seaport, Japan, 220-221, 222, 223.
Holland, 61, 285, 287-289, 292, 294.
Homem, João, 72.
Honawar, state, India, 73, 82, 84.
Hong-Kong, 104.
Hor, Mount, 137.
Hospitallers, Order of, 4.
Hottentots, 40-42, 77.
Hudibras, quoted, 133.
Humanism, 162, 168-169, 175, 253, 259.
Hunyadi János, 81.

IBN BATUTA, 7.
Ibrahim, Emir of Kilwa, 64.
Ibrahim Beg, 94, 112.
Ichthyophagi, 139.
Idumea or Edom, 137.
Ignatius de Loyola, 166-167, 225, 240, 257.
Index Expurgatorius, 181. See also Censorship.
India : sea-route to, 11, 33, 60-62, see also Gama ; Admiralty of, 68 ; Portuguese rule in, 72-74, 102-114, 183-187, 197-198, 236, 289-294.
Indio, Fray José, 277.
Infante, Rio de (or do). See Great Fish River.
" Infant's Town," Portugal, 10.
Inhambane, town, E. Africa, 46.
Inquisition, 159, 161, 171-173, 175-181 (note), 185, 260, 270, 275, 295.
Isabella, Princess of Castile, afterwards Queen-consort of Portugal, 115-118.
Isabella, Queen of Castile, 62, 115-117, 259.
Ismail Adil Shah of Bijapur, 84, 88, 108.
Ismail Shah of Persia, 94, 101, 108-110.
Isuf, Shaikh of Sofala, 64.
Italy, affected by Portuguese discoveries, 61.

JAFNAPATAM, TOWN, CEYLON, 199.
Jalal ud-Din, 235.
James II. King of England, 174.
James V., King of Scotland, 168.
Janeo, 55.
Japan, discovery of, 215 ; political condition in 1550, 218-219 ; first mission to, 219-226.
Jasso, Juan de, 165.
Java, Javanese, 86-88, 108, 202, 276, 292 (note).
Jenghiz Khan, 213.
Jeronymos, Convento dos, 242-244, 249, 284 (note).
Jerun, island, Persian Gulf, 93.
Jerusalem, 13, 101, 279.
Jesuits : formation of Society, 166-167 ; missions, 183, 185, see also Xavier ; power in Portugal, 175, 257-260 ; in Brazil, 161, 295 ; doctrine of Probabilism, 178 (note).
Jews, Portuguese, 156-161, 249 (note). See also New Christians.
Jidda, seaport, Arabia, 93, 101.
João, Master, 144.
John II., King of Portugal : African policy, 24, 281 ; relations with Columbus, 30-31 ; crushes feudal nobility, 115, 120 ; treatment of Jews, 158-159.
John III. King of Portugal : relations with stepmother, 118, 261 ; character, 120, 259-260 ; African policy, 261 ; educational reforms, 162, 169-170, 251, 252, 253.
John, Prince, son of John III., 279.
John, Prince of Castile, 117.
" John Company," 112.
Jorge, D., natural son of John II., 116.
Juana " the Mad," Princess of Castile and Queen of Spain, 118.
Juari, river, Goa, 81.
Juderías, 156.
Julius II., Pope 32.
Juzar Khan, 149, 151.

KAGOSHIMA, SEAPORT, JAPAN, 219-220.
Kamaran Island, Red Sea, 93.
Kandy, Ceylon, 290, 292.
Kathiawar Peninsula, Gujarat, 75, 143.
Keda, state, Malay Peninsula, 211.
Keda, state, Malay Peninsula, 211.
Kiliman (Quilimane) River, S.E. Africa, 46-47.
Khair ed-Din Barbarossa, 131-132.

Khoi, town, Persia, 109.
Khulam (Quilon), seaport, S. India, 293.
Killearn, town, Scotland, 163.
Kilwa, city and state, E. Africa, 46, 48, 64, 244.
Kioto, 218, 222.
Kistna, river, India, 73.
Kiushiu, island, Japan, 219, 223.
Kongo, kingdom of, 26.
Koran, 235.
Kosseir, seaport, Egypt, 139.
Kublai Khan, 213.
Kuku-Nor, Lake, 214.
Kurdistan, 109.
Kwaja Husain, 212.

"LA MINE," 9.
La Salle, Gadifer de, 9.
Laccadive Islands, 52.
Lacerda, Manoel de, 100.
Lagos, town, Portugal, 21-22, 282.
Lançarote, 13-14.
Langlois, 173.
Las Casas, Bartolomé de, 20, 114.
Laynez, Diego, 167.
"Lechuna," See Lhasa.
Leiria, town, Portugal, 3, 157.
Lemos, Duarte de, 79, 80.
Lemos, Fernão Gomes de, 109-110.
Leo X., Pope, 61, 119, 244.
Leon, kingdom of, 1, 2.
León, Luís de, 236.
Lhasa, 214.
Liampo. See Ningpo.
Libelle of English Polycye, quoted, 2.
Lichnowsky, Prince, 242.
Lima, D. Manoel de, 149.
Limpopo, river, Africa, 43-44.
Linschoten, Jan Huyghen van, 302.
Lippomano, Aloysio, 259.
Lisbon, captured from Moors, 3; as commercial centre, 28, 60, 287; Jews in, 157-160.
Literature, Portuguese, in sixteenth century, 247-249. See also *Lusiads*.
Lobato, Alvaro, 173.
Lopes, Thomé, 306, 64 (note).
Luiz, Prince, son of King Manoel, 21, 130, 131-132, 135, 258.
Lull, Ramon de, 235.
Lusiads, The, 128, 247, 249, 261, 263, 265, 266, 267, 268, 271, 272; publication, 274-275, 277; plot, etc., 278.
Luther, 162, 168, 171, 270.

MACAO, SEAPORT, CHINA, 231, 266.
Machiavelli, 120, 162.

Machin or Macham, Robert, 9.
Mactan, island, Philippines, 203.
Madagascar, 119.
Madeira, 9, 10, 29-30, 250, 282, 288.
Madeira, Isabel, 144-145.
Madura, state, India, 198.
Mafra, town, Portugal, 131.
Magalhães, Fernão. See Magellan.
Magellan (Fernão Magalhães), 70, 80, 121, 203.
Mailapur, seaport, India, 200-201.
Malabar, 52, 93, 195 (note), 200, 263-264.
Malacca, 68; Sequeira at, 80; conquest by Albuquerque, 80-81, 85-88, 108, 110; later sieges, 207-208, 292 (note); captains of, 69, 291. See also Xavier.
Malayalam, 194, 195.
Malay Archipelago, Portuguese in, 202-207, 266-267.
Malays in Malacca, 80, 86, 88.
Malhar Rao, 111.
Malik Aiyaz, 75, 100.
Malindi, town, E. Africa, 49-51, 58, 139.
Malocello, Lancelot, 9.
Manaar, island, Ceylon, 199, 293.
Mancias, Francis, 197, 199-200.
Mandavi, river, Goa, 81, 82-83, 97.
Manoel I., King of Portugal: life and reign, 115-122; persecutes Jews, 159-161; relations with Gama, 33-34, 67-70; with Pacheco, 71; with Albuquerque, 96-98, 101-102, 104, 111-113; Oriental policy, 62, 72-73; 284; bibliography, 307.
Manoel, D. João, 149.
Manoeline architecture, 121, 242-244, 247.
Manresa, town, Spain, 166.
Manrique, Jorge de, 261.
Mantimento, 291.
Maranos, 160.
Marcos, Lucas, 36.
Marot, Clément, 171, 275.
Married men: status in Portuguese India, 105-106, 126.
Martellus Germanus, Henricus, 27, 36.
Martinho, D., Bishop in Goa, 124.
Martins, D. Theresa, 78.
Martins, Fernão, 47.
Mary, Princess of Castile, Queen-consort of Portugal, 118.
Mary, Princess, daughter of John III., 254, 257-258.
Mary, Queen of Scots, 173.
Mascarenhas, D. João, 143-150, 281.

Massawa, 101, 137-139, 141-142, 211.
Masser, Leonardo, 67-68.
Matheus, 110.
Mathnawi, 235-236.
Meaco. See Kioto.
Mecca, 7, 65, 101.
Medici, Guiliano de', 227.
Mediterranean, commerce in, 60-62.
Mekong, river, Cambodia, 267.
Mela, Pomponius, 139.
Melanchthon, 171.
Mello, Simão de, 207.
Melo, Diego Suarez de, 208.
Melville, Andrew, 174.
Melville, James, 174.
Mendonça, Manoel de, 286.
Menezes, D. Aleixo de, 280.
Menezes, D. Duarte de, 127-128, 131.
Menezes, D. Francisco de, 146, 147.
Menezes, D. Jorge de, 153, 204, 266.
Menezes, D. Lenor de, 79.
Menezes, D. Luiz de, 127.
Menezes, D. Pedro de, 30.
Mercy, Brotherhood of, 125.
Mergulhão, D. Diogo, 186-187, 230.
Meri, Muhammadan pilgrim-ship, 65.
Mesquita, Manoel de, 173.
Mexia, Affonso, 126. 128.
Michael Angelo, 61.
Miguel, Prince of Portugal and Spain, 118.
Mikado, 218, 222.
Military Orders, in Portugal, 3-6, 279.
Mir Amrjan, 91.
Mir Hussain, 74-76.
Missions, 182-185. See also Xavier.
Mithkal, 64 (and note).
Mocquet, Jean, 302.
Molay, Jacques de, 5.
Moluceas, 108, 203-207.
Mombasa, 48-49.
Monarchy, Portuguese: relations with Cortes, 3, 281 ; under John II., and Manoel 120 ; relations with Church, 157, 259, 279-280.
Monçaide, 52-53.
Mondego, river, Portugal, 1, 251.
Mongols, 213-214.
Monomotapa: (1) Bantu chief, 182 ; (2) name applied to his territories, 233, 290.
Montaigne, 169.
Montaigu, college, Paris, 163, 165.
Montemôr (Montemayor), Jorge de, 254.
Montemôr-o-Novo, town, Portugal, 34.

Montserrat, mountain, Spain, 166.
Moors : (1) Arab and Berber invaders of Peninsula, 1, 3, 116, 285 ; (2) inhabitants of Morocco ; see Morocco ; (3) generic term for Muhammadans ; see Muhammadans.
Moplas, 53, 54.
Morales, Pedro, 9.
More, Thomas, 163.
Morocco, 130-131, 261-262, 281-284.
Moses, 140.
Moses, Jewish mathematician, 30.
Mossel Bay, S. Africa, 27, 42.
Mota, Antonio da, 215.
Mozambique, 47-48, 124, 271-272.
Mozambique current, 45.
Mughals, 108.
Muhammad Ankoni, 64.
Muhammadans : in E. Africa, 45-51 ; Gama's view of, 66 ; King Manoel's, 62 ; Almeida's, 73 ; Xavier's, 232-237 ; attitude towards Portuguese 52-53, 57, 103 ; relations with Albuquerque, 98, 99, 107, 111, 113.
Mukdishu, seaport, E. Africa, 58.
Mulai Abd el-Malik, 282, 283.
Mulai Ahmad, 282, 283, 284 (note).
Murad II., Sultan of Turks, 81.
Murillo, 246.

Nairs, 53, 57, 76, 79.
Natal, 43.
" Nathercia." See Athayde, Catherina de.
Necoda, 209.
Nestorians, 183 (note), 138, 200.
New Christians, 160-161, 179, 282.
Nikitin, Athanasius, 94.
Nile, river, 12-14, 101, 137-138.
" Nile of the Negroes." See " Western Nile."
Ninachetty, 86, 88.
Ningpo, 212, 231.
Noronha, D. Antão de, 271-272.
Noronha, D. Garcia de, 92, 132-134, 290-291.
Noronha, D. Payo de, 152.
Nova, João de, 64, 77, 99.
Nunes, Gonçalo, 35.
Nunes, João, 52-53.
Nunes (Nonius), Pedro, 126, 130, 136.
Nur ud-Din, Rais, 94-95.

Odoric of Pordenone, 164.
Ophiotophagi, 139.
Ophir, 46 (note), 87 (note).
Opium, 102.

Oran, 52.
Oranges, 132.
Ordenado, 291.
Ormuz, 68 ; strategic and commercial importance, 80-81 ; Albuquerque at (1508-09), 76-77, 79 ; annexation by Albuquerque, 93-96, 100, 109.
Orta, Garcia de, 241, 245, 269-271, 303.
Osaka, town, Japan, 221.
Osborne, Dorothy, 210.
Osorio da Fonseca, Jeronymo, Bishop of Silves, 114, 186, 275, 281, 307.
Otomo, Daimio of Bungo, 223-225.
Otranto, 144 (note).
" Oxindono," Daimio of Yamaguchi, 222 (note), 224.

PACHECO PEREIRA, DUARTE, 71, 63 (note) 301.
Padilha, Jeronymo de, 169-170.
Padrão (plur. *padrões*), 25 (and note), 26.
Painting, Portuguese, in sixteenth century, 245-247.
Paiva, Cosmo de, 149, 200.
Paiva, D. Heliodoro de, 253.
Pamplona, 166.
Pandarani Kollam, seaport, India, 54-58.
Panical, town, S. India, 198.
Paracelsus, 269.
Paravas, 195-198.
Pardão, 311.
Parnaso, 272.
Pasai, seaport, Sumatra, 86.
Paul III., Pope, 167, 183.
Pedir, seaport, Sumatra, 86.
Pedro I., King of Portugal, 281.
Pegu, 108, 86, 94, 289.
Peking, 213-214, 227, 229.
Pena Castle, 131.
Penha Verde, 131.
Percalços, 291.
Pereira, Diogo, 232-233.
Perestrello, Bartolommeo, 29-30.
Perestrello, Felippa Moniz, 29-31.
Perestrello, Isabella Moniz, 30.
Perestrello, Rafael, 227.
Persia, 94, 101, 108-110.
Persian Gulf, 74, 81, 264.
Pessagna. See Pezagna.
Peter Martyr, 117.
" Petit Dieppe," 9.
" Petit Paris," 9.
Petrarch, 257.
Pexoto, Antonio, 215.

Pezagna or Pessanha, Emmanuele, 15.
Philip (the Fair) I., King of Spain, 118.
Philip II., King of Spain, 118, 216, 244, 254, 277, 278, 282, 284 (note).
Philip IV., King of France, 4-5.
Philippine Islands, 203.
Pina, Ruy de, 303-304.
Pinheiro, João de, 171.
Pinto, Fernão Mendes : life, 210-217 ; with Xavier, 223-226 ; his *Peregrinaçam*, 303.
Piracy, 127, 202, 211-213.
Pires, Thomé, 227-229.
Pius V., Pope, 281.
Plague, in Portugal, 157, 159, 179, 250, 273-274, 277.
Plautus, 253.
Pliny, 137, 139.
Polo, Marco, 7, 29, 36.
Porto Santo, island, Madeiras, 29-30.
Portucalia, Terra Portucalensis, 1.
Portugal, early history, 1-6.
Portuguese, characteristics of, 2-3, 5-6, 22, 247-248, 284, 285.
Portuguese, empire 285-297. See also Albuquerque, Almeida, Brazil, China, India, Malay Archipelago.
Portus Cale, 1.
Pottery, Portuguese, in sixteenth century, 245.
Powder-pots, 145.
Près, Josquin des, 253.
" Prester John," 12-13, 33, 47, 62, 101, 110. See also Abyssinia.
Printing, 157.
Probabilism, 178 (note).
Promontorium Sacrum. See Sagres.
Ptolemy, 36, 136, 138, 139.
Pulci, 275.
Purbach, 136.
" Puxanguim " 214, 217.
Pyrard, François, 302.

" QUAMSYANDONO," 223.
" Quanginau," 214, 217.
" Quinsay," 213.

RABELAIS, 164.
Ragusa, 33.
Rais Ahmad, 94-95, 113.
Ramadan, 147.
Ramusio, Giovanni Battista, 300.
Randolph, Sir Thomas, 174 (and note).
Ras ul-Khan, 88-89.
Real (plur. *reis*), 311.
Red Eric, 7.

Red Sea, Egyptian supremacy in, 74 ; Albuquerque's expedition to, 80-81, 91-93 ; expedition of 1541, 135-142 ; Castro's disquisition on, 137-138 ; Camões in, 264.
Relatio super sanctitate, 239.
Renaissance, 154, 163, 241-242, 252-253, 295-297.
Resende, Garcia de, 260, 304.
Reynoso, Diogo de, 146.
Rhine, 288.
Ribeira, Praça da, 178.
Ribeiro, Antonio. See Chiado.
Ribeiro, Bernardim, 247-248, 249.
Riu Kiu Islands, Japan, 86.
Rocio, the, 160.
Rodrigo, Jewish physician, 30.
Rodrigues, Francisco, 143.
Rodrigues, Garcia, 144.
Rodrigues, Simão, 167, 275.
Rome, 61.
Rosario, Nicolau do, 187.
Rouen, 9.
Rubrouck, William of, 7.
Rumi Khan, 145, 147-149.

SÁ GARCIA DE, 148.
Sá, João de, 53.
Sá, Jorge de, 173.
Sá de Miranda, Francisco de, 248.
Sá e Macedo, Anne de, 250, 275.
Sagres, promontory, 11.
Saif ud-Din, King of Ormuz, 94.
St Andrews, 163.
St Anthony, convent of, Bordeaux, 169.
St Augustine, college, Coimbra, 252.
St Helena Bay ; S. Africa, 40-41.
St Helena Island, 64.
St John Baptist, college, Coimbra, 252.
St John's Island. See Shangchwan.
St Mark's, Venice, 241.
St Michael, college, Coimbra, 252.
St Michael's, island, Azores, 8.
St Paul, Jesuit college, Goa, 193-194, 197.
Ste. Barbe, college, Paris, 162-165.
Sal, island, Cape Verdes, 38.
Salamanca, 166, 170, 172, 269.
Salamina (Mailapur), 200.
Salmerón, Alfonso, 167.
Samarra, 177.
Sambenito, 177.
Sampayo, Lopo Vaz de, 126, 128.
Samuri of Calicut, 53-54 ; relations with Gama (1498), 54-58 ; with Cabral, 63 ; with Gama (1502),

65-66 ; attacks Cochin, 71 ; relations with Almeida, 75 ; with Albuquerque, 79-80, 93 (note).
Sanches, D. Affonso, 78.
Sancho III., King of Castile, 78.
Sannazaro, 257, 275.
Santa Cruz, convent and college, Coimbra, 250-252.
Santa Cruz, Gaspar de, 220.
Santa Cruz, Terra da (Brazil), 63.
Santa Fé, college, Goa. See St Paul, college of.
Santiago, Jorge de, 169.
Santiago (São Thiago) Order of, 4-5, 68, 97.
São Bento, convent, Lisbon, 173.
São Bento, ship, 262, 263.
São Braz, Angra de. See Mossel Bay.
São Jorge, island near Mozambique, 48.
São Jorge da Mina, town and fort, Guinea, 24-25, 37, 67.
São Paulo da Salvaterra, town, Portugal, 132.
São Thiago, island, Cape Verdes, 37-38.
São Thiago de Caçem, town, Portugal, 67.
São Thomé, island, Atlantic, 159, 288.
Sati (Suttee), 112.
Satira do Torneio, 264-265.
Satsuma, fief, Japan, 219-220.
Satyrs, Isle of, Red Sea, 136.
Scaliger, Joseph, 169.
Scaliger, Julius Cæsar, 169.
Scanderbeg, 81.
Scandinavian explorers, 7.
Scheldt, river, 288.
Scipio Africanus, 263.
Seamanship and seamen, in fifteenth and sixteenth centuries, 15-19, 35-36, 40 (and note), 48, 75-76, 286.
Sebastian, King of Portugal, 120, 274, 276 ; biography, 279-284.
Sebastianism, 284.
Seleucids, Kings of Syria, 261.
Selim I., Ottoman Sultan, 74 (note), 109.
Senegal, river, Africa. See "Western Nile."
Sephardim, 156.
Sequeira, Diogo Lopes de, 79-80.
Serra Mendro, Portugal, 70.
Serrão, João, 84.
Servetus, 269.
Seven Cities, legendary island of, 8.
Shakhra, seaport, Arabia, 153.

Shangchwan Island, China, 227-228 (note), 233-235.
Shem-Tob, Levi ben, 159.
Shia Muhammadanism, 94, 101, 108.
Shimonoseki, Strait of, 221.
Ships and Shipbuilding, 127; caravel, 15-16; dhow, 15, 46; the *São Raphael* and *São Gabriel*, 34-35; almadia, 49; foist, 73; junk, 227.
Shogun, 218, 222.
Siam, 94, 108, 110, 211.
Sifr Aga, 144-145.
Sigêa, Angela, 258.
Sigêa, Luisa, 258.
Silva, Pedro da, 69, 232.
Silva, Rodrigues da, 246.
Silveira, D. Alvaro da, 266.
Silveira, D. Gonçalo da, 182-183.
Sinai, Mount, 101, 139-140.
Sines, seaport, Portugal, 34, 67-69.
Singapore, 233.
Slaves and Slavery, 19-23, 104-106, 185, 265, 285-287.
Soares, João, 259 (note).
Soares de Albergaria, Lopo, 96, 294.
Socotra, island, Arabian Sea, 138.
Sodré, Vicente, 66.
Sofala, town, S.E. Africa, 46, 64.
Soldo, 291.
Songkoi, river, Indo-China, 214.
Sousa, D. Aldonsa, de, 78.
Sousa, Garcia de, 92.
Sousa, Martim Affonso de, 142, 199, 208, 233, 293.
" Spanish Captivity," 278, 284, 285.
Spice-trade, 33, 53, 57, 58, 60, 106, 109, 288.
Stewart, Lord James, 168.
Stratonice, 261.
Stuart, Prince James, 174.
Suakin, 138-139, 141.
Suez, 101, 133, 135, 139, 141.
Sumatra, 86, 202, 207.
Suni Muhammadanism, 108.

Tabriz, 109.
Tagus, river, 287.
Tahafut ul-Mujahidin, 303.
" Talapicor of Lechuna," 214.
Tamão, island, China, 227-229.
Tanegashima, island, Japan, 215, 219.
Tangier, 36, 139, 262, 281.
Taoism, 237.
Tarshish, 46 (and note), 87 (note).
Teive, Diogo de, 170-173.
Templars, Order of, 4-5.
Temple, Sir William, 210.

Terceira, island, Azores, 58.
Terence, 253.
Ternate, island, Malay Archipelago, 203-206, 266.
Tetuan, 262.
Teutonic Knights, 4.
Thanadar, 111.
Theresa, St., 236.
Thomar, city, Portugal, 242.
Thomas, St., 200, 205.
Tibet, 214-215.
Tidore, island, Malay Archipelago, 203-206, 266.
Timoja, 73, 82, 84, 111.
Tisvadi (Ilha de Goa), 81, 111.
Toar, Sancho de, 64, 66.
Toledo, 117.
Tongking, 214.
Tor, town, Arabia, 139-141.
Tordesillas, treaty of, 32, 203.
Torres, Cosmo, 209, 218-226.
Toscanelli, 8.
Travancore, 197-199.
Trimumpate, Raja of Cochin, 71.
Trinidade, Adeodato da, 301.
Tristan d'Acunha, archipelago, S. Atlantic, 119.
Troglodytes, 139.
Tumeds, 213-214.
Tungabhadra, river, India, 73.
Tunis, 131-132.
Turan Shah of Ormuz, 94-96.
Turks : invade Europe, 12, 13, 162 ; effect of Portuguese discoveries on, 119 ; sea-power of, in Europe, 60-62, 131-132, 261 ; in Asia, 74, 103, 133, 135, 141, 211 ; conquer Egypt, 74 (note) ; invade Persia, 109 ; at Aden, 151-152.
Tyre, 102.

Udine, Giovanni da, 119.
Uso di Mare, Antonio, 15.
Utemuta, Raja 87-88.

Valdes Leal, Juan de, 246.
Vallarte the Dane, 15.
Varthema, Ludovico di, 302.
Vasco, "Grão," 245.
Vasconcellos, Diogo Mendes de, 84, 85, 96-97.
Vaz, Miguel, 195, 196.
Vecinho, Joseph, Rabbi, 30.
Velazquez, 246-247.
Velloso, Fernão, 41.
Veniaga. See Tamão.
Venice, 33, 61, 102, 118-119, 241.
Vicente, Gil, 248-249, 253.
Vicente, Martim, 30.

Vicente, Paula, 258.
Viceroys and Governors of India, xix., 72 (and note).
Vidigueira, 70, 140.
Vienna, 62.
Vieyra, Christovão, 229-230.
Vijayanagar, Hindu empire, 73-74, 103, 108, 135, 198, 292-293.
Vilhegas, D. Diogo Ortiz de, Bishop of Ceuta and Tangier, 30, 36.
Villa de Frades, town, Portugal, 70.
Villa Nova de Milfontes, town, Portugal, 67.
Villafranca de Xira, town, Portugal, 69.
Vinet, Élie, 169, 175.
Vinzella, town, Portugal, 167.
Visigoths, 3.
Vyne, Master, 127.

Wady M'hassan, Morocco, 283.
Western Ghats, India, 52, 84, 97.
" Western Nile," 12-14.
Wheeler, John, 288.
" Wineland," 7.
Women, in Portuguese India, 104-106, 124-125, 128, 133, 144-145, 146, 190-192.
Wotton, Sir Henry, 211.

Xavier Francis, 153 ; early career, 165-167 ; in Goa (1542), 187-194 ; in South India, 195-200 ; at Mailapur, 200 ; in Malacca (1546), 200-201 ; id. (1548), 207-208 ; id. (1549), 209 ; id (1552), 232-233 ; in Malay Archipelago, 205-207, 266 ; mission to Japan, 208-209, 218-226 ; to China, 225-226, 232-234 ; death 234-235 ; work and character, 235-240 ; miracles, 239 ; bibliography, 309.
Xavier y Azpilqueta, Maria de, 166-167.
Xerafim, 311.

Yahya, Joseph ben David ibn, 158.
Yajiro, 208-209, 218-221, 226.
Yamaguchi, town, Japan, 221-224.
Yusuf Adil Shah of Bijapur, 81-84.

Zacuto ben Samuel, Abraham, 30, 36.
Zamorin. See Samuri.
Zaragoza (Saragossa), 117, 170.
Zarco, João Gonçalves, 9, 250.
Zeila, town, N.E. Africa, 141.
Zeimoto, Francisco, 215.
Zimbabwe, Great, S. Africa, 46.
Zurbarán, 246.